T
5

D0323349

THE
NEW TESTAMENT ERA

THE
NEW TESTAMENT ERA

THE WORLD OF THE BIBLE
FROM 500 B.C. TO A.D. 100

By

BO REICKE

Translated by David E. Green

FORTRESS PRESS   PHILADELPHIA

This book is a translation of *Neutestamentliche
Zeitgeschichte* by Bo Reicke, published by
Alfred Töpelmann, Berlin
© 1964 by Verlag Alfred Töpelmann, Berlin

TRANSLATOR'S NOTE

For the present translation the author has
provided a number of corrections of the German
text plus some additions to the bibliography. In
addition, he has gone over the translation,
revising and rewording in order to make it best
express his intentions. This will explain apparent
departures from the German original. The footnotes generally follow those in the German
edition, with further bibliographical data being
omitted, in accord with the wishes of the author.

Copyright © 1968 by Fortress Press

Library of Congress Catalog Card No. 68-15864

ISBN 0-8006-1080-6

First Paperback Edition 1974

Second Printing 1975

5464K75   Printed in U.S.A.   1-1080

CONTENTS

ABBREVIATIONS

Billerbeck
H. L. Strack and Paul Billerbeck, *Kommentar zum Neuen Testament aus Talmud und Midrasch*
(7 vols.; Munich: C. H. Beck, 1922–1961).

Dead Sea Scrolls
1QS   Manual of Discipline (or Community Rule)
1QM   The War Scroll
CD   Cairo Damascus Document

Eusebius, *Chron.*   *Chronicon*
     Hist.   *Historia Ecclesiastica*
     Praep.   *Praeparatio Evangelica*

Josephus, *Ant.*   *Antiquitates Judaicae*
     Ap.   *Contra Apionem*
     Bell.   *Bellum Judaicum*
     Vit.   *Vita*

LXX   Septuagint

Pap. Cowley   *Aramaic Papyri of the Fifth Century* B.C.
A. Cowley, editor and translator
(Oxford, Clarendon Press, 1923).

PRE   *Paulys Realencyclopädie der classischen Altertumswissenschaft.* Ser. I (A–Q), 48 vols.; Ser. II (R–Z), 18 vols.; 10 Suppls. (Stuttgart: Metzler, later A. Druckenmüller, 1894–   ).

Schürer   E. Schürer, *Geschichte des jüdischen Volkes im Zeitalter Jesu Christi*
(3 vols. plus index vol.; 3d and 4th ed.; Leipzig: Hinrichs, 1901–11).

Other abbreviations, such as those for biblical and rabbinical books, are standard.

INTRODUCTION

> . . . from the deportation to
> Babylon to the Messiah, there
> were fourteen generations.
>
> Matthew 1:17

THE secular history constituting the background and environment of the Gospel and the primitive church is the subject matter of the discipline called history of New Testament times [*Neutestamentliche Zeitgeschichte*]. Here theological questions are deliberately avoided; a historical stance is taken, with no attempt being made to illuminate any heavenly reality or to explain the unique significance of the biblical message. Only the earthly circumstances are analyzed, using the methods of inductive and causal historical scholarship. But there is also theological justification for this undertaking, if one bears in mind the basic theme of Christology: the Word became flesh, when the time had been fulfilled (John 1:14; Gal. 4:4).

Christ and the church were to bring the fulfillment of Jewish history. *De facto*, they were related in different ways to Judaism, and indirectly also to Hellenism and the Roman Empire. In order to elucidate these factors in the background and environment of the New Testament, it is necessary to survey several centuries, during which their characteristics and significance developed. Since the development of Judaism began shortly before 500 B.C., and since the period covered by the New Testament lasted until around A.D. 100, these dates will be the termini of our study. Furthermore, since Jesus and his disciples were particularly confronted with political, social, and religious factors in Judaism, Hellenism, and the Roman Empire, we shall devote most of our attention to such matters.[1]

By *Judaism* we mean the Jewish community, culture, and religion from the Babylonian exile until the end of the New Testament period. Chapters 1–5 are devoted to the development of Judaism in this era. The crucial importance, both cultural and religious, of the restoration of Judaism after the Babylonian captivity (586–539 B.C.) justifies taking the Persian hegemony and the return of the Jews from the exile as our point of departure (539–332 B.C.). Even at this early date, phenomena and institutions came into being that were characteristic of Jewish society in the time of primitive Christianity. Next we must touch on the period of the Hellenistic rulers (332–142 B.C.), giving attention to the intense cultural struggle of Judaism with *Hellenism*. We must also discuss the political glory of the Hasmonean kingdom (142–63 B.C.), which the New Testament period still indirectly reflects. More important, however, is the Roman period, down to the beginning of the political collapse of Judaism (63 B.C.—A.D. 66), because we are dealing here with the period immediately preceding Christianity and the time of Jesus and the Apostles. Even in the apostolic age (A.D. 33–66) our description takes Judaism as its point of departure; for despite the internal detachment of the Gospel from Judaism and despite the mission to the Gentiles, the apostolic church remained in part associated with Judaism, and was also regarded by others as a form of Judaism. The church was convinced that it was the bearer of the promises of the Old Testament. Jerusalem was therefore considered the focal point of the church until the Jewish revolt in the year 66; the Apostles preferred to establish relationships with the colonies of Jews throughout the Roman Empire; and their preaching—consciously or unconsciously—was often

[1] The prototype of modern presentations of the history of New Testament times concentrated quite properly on political and social history: E. Schürer, *Geschichte des jüdischen Volkes im Zeitalter Jesu Christi*, Vols. 1–3 (3d and 4th eds., 1901–11). The second edition was translated into English by J. Macpherson, S. Taylor, and P. Christie, *A History of the Jewish People in the Time of Jesus Christ* (5 vols.; Edinburgh: Clark, 1897–98). Other general presentations are mentioned in our bibliography (below, pp. 319–30). Studies and texts are cited in the footnotes only when such reference appears particularly desirable.

modeled on the oral and written traditions of the missionary propaganda of Hellenistic Judaism (the correspondence between Wisd. of Sol. 13:1–10 and Rom. 1:18–23 is typical). In addition, the Roman administration thought of Christianity as an offspring of Judaism until the Neronian persecution (A.D. 65), and to some extent also during the Domitian persecution in the years 93–95.

Chapters 6–7 deal with the position of the church in the *Roman Empire*. For the apostolic period, we must also take cognizance of the empire and its provinces, in which Jesus and the Apostles were active. The subsequent examination of the subapostolic age (A.D. 66–100) is concerned with the relationship between church and state. During this period, Judaism no longer constituted the external framework of Christianity; instead, the church found itself directly confronting the imperial government, whose attitude was frequently hostile, as witness the persecutions under Nero and Domitian. Because the last fifth of the New Testament canon (the Pastoral Epistles, the Epistle to the Hebrews, the Catholic Epistles, and Revelation) reflects the circumstances of this period, we must go beyond the limits of the traditional handbooks and devote some attention to the period of the Apostles' followers.

The primary sources for the history of this entire period come from the Old Testament and Judaism:

(1) Some books of the Old Testament which in the Hebrew canon have been placed at the end of the sections containing the Prophets and the Hagiographa (or Writings). In the Prophets, these books are Haggai, Zechariah, and Malachi; in the Hagiographa, they are Ecclesiastes, Esther, Daniel, and particularly the work of the Chronicler: Ezra, Nehemiah, I and II Chronicles. The late dating of other books is disputed or doubtful.

(2) The so-called Apocrypha and Pseudepigrapha of the Old Testament,[2] as well as the Qumran documents.[3]

[2] R. H. Charles (ed.), *The Apocrypha and Pseudepigrapha of the Old Testament*, Vols. 1–2 (1913; reprinted 1963); P. Riessler, *Altjüdisches Schrifttum ausserhalb der Bibel* (1928).

[3] J. Maier, *Die Texte vom Toten Meer*, Vols. 1–2 (1960); T. H. Gaster, *The Dead Sea Scriptures in English Translation* (rev. ed., 1964); E. Lohse, *Die Texte aus Qumran* (1964).

(3) The historical works of Josephus (A.D. 37–*ca.* 95) : *De Bello Judaico, Antiquitates Judaicae, Vita Josephi,* and *Contra Apionem.*[4]

(4) The earlier rabbinic texts, especially those of the Mishna (*ca.* A.D. 200) .[5]

Greek and Latin writers will be considered insofar as they shed light on the situation of postexilic Judaism and primitive Christianity. This is especially true of Polybius (*ca.* 200–120 B.C.) , Diodorus (*ca.* 90–30 B.C.) , Statius (*ca.* A.D. 40–96) , Tacitus (A.D. 55–*ca.* 120) , Pliny the Younger (A.D. 61–115) , Suetonius (*ca.* A.D. 75–150) , and Dio Cassius (A.D. 155–235) .

The writings of the New Testament itself also contain details that illuminate their historical situation. It must be understood, though, that our rather frequent references to New Testament passages are intended only partially as documentation. Their main purpose is to invite comparison with the New Testament, which is not the basis of our presentation, but its goal.[6]

[4] *Flavii Iosephi opera edidit et apparatu critico instruxit* B. Niese and J. V. Destinoa, Vols. 1–7 (reprinted, 1955) ; *Oeuvres complètes de Flavius Josèphe traduits sous la direction de Th. Reinach* Vols. 1–6 (1900–32) ; *Josephus,* trans. H. St. John Thackeray, R. Marcus, L. H. Feldman, Vols. 1–9 (1926–65) ; Flavius Josephus, *De bello judaico* (Greek and German) , herausgegeben von O. Michel and O. Bauernfeind, Vols. 1–2 (1959–63) ; Flavius Josèphe, *Autobiographie. Texte établi et traduit par A. Pelletier* (1959) .

[5] H. Danby, *The Mishna* (6th ed., 1956) .

[6] Schürer (cited above, n. 1) and others have included a history of Jewish literature in their histories of New Testament times. Such a procedure seemed inappropriate for this book, in part because new discoveries have multiplied the available material. For the literary history of both Judaism and primitive Christianity, the reader should consult the standard introductions to the Old and New Testaments.

I

JUDAH UNDER PERSIAN RULE

539–332 B.C.

> In the first year of King Cyrus,
> he commanded me to be strong
> and of good courage.
> Daniel 11:1 (LXX)

As early as the Book of Daniel the crucial epoch of history preceding the coming of the Son of man is said to have begun with the Persian Empire (539–332 B.C.). In Daniel 11:1–45, an angel predicts the future history of the Jews, which is to culminate in the time of salvation (Dan. 12:1), and he begins his prediction with the Persian period (see the chronological tables below, pp. 8 and 26). First of all, Daniel 11:1 (following the LXX text, since the Masoretic text of this verse is ambiguous) mentions the founder of the Persian world empire, Kores or Cyrus.[1] This refers to the fact that, after taking Babylon in 539 B.C., Cyrus freed the Jews from the so-called Babylonian captivity, thereby making possible a reorganization of Judaism that was to make its effects felt until the political catastrophe of A.D. 70. Daniel 11:2a mentions three more kings without naming them; they can be taken to be Darius I, Xerxes, and Artaxerxes I. Finally, in Daniel 11:2b, the angel speaks of a king of Persia who, despite his great power, will struggle in vain against Greece; this refers to Darius III, whose empire Alexander conquered in 333–331 B.C. Thus the angel, speaking in prophetical style,

---

[1] The Masoretic text of Daniel 11:1 mentions "Darius the Mede"; but this figure cannot be squared with known facts, and the name may be a scribal error. The LXX text of the verse, however, offers no difficulties of historical interpretation.

describes the two hundred and seven years of Persian hegemony as a period of revival for the people of God, preceding the final affliction and salvation.

What are the historical circumstances of this epoch, a period so important for Judaism?

1. THE IRANIAN SPHERE OF INFLUENCE

Geographically and historically, the Persian Empire centered in Iran, the vast mountainous region between Assyria and India, extending from Transcaspia to the Persian Gulf. Iran comprises modern Iran together with Afghanistan and Beluchistan; its area is roughly five times that of France. Mountain ranges traverse it from northwest to southeast. Before and during the period of the Israelite and Judahite monarchies, groups of cossack-like tribes led by families of nobility penetrated into the plains and valleys between these ranges from the northeast. The invaders spoke Indo-European languages and called themselves Aryans. They gave their name to the Iranian Plateau: the land of the Aryans (Old Persian *Aryānam*).

Three of these tribal groups were to achieve historical significance and play an important role for the Jews.

(1) First, the Medes proceeded westward along the Elburz Mountains, settling near Assyria. About 700–550 B.C., they established a mighty empire in northwest Iran, which was accordingly named Media (Jer. 25:25). Their major cities lay along their path of advance from the east: Rages (Tob. 1:14; etc.), near the modern Iranian capital Teheran; and Ecbatana (Jth. 1:1; etc.), corresponding to the modern Hamadan.

(2) The Persians' course took them to southwest Iran. They settled in the southern region of the Zagros Mountains, which separate Iran from Assyria, to the east of the inner Persian Gulf. Because of them the Greeks called this mountainous region Persis; it is the modern province of Fars. From here and from Elam, the adjacent alluvial plain east of the lower Tigris, which they occupied after the fall of Assyria in 612, the Persian kings of the Achaemenid dynasty dominated international politics from about 550 to 331 B.C. After

525, their power extended in the west to the Hellespont and Syrtis Major (the Gulf of Sidra), and in the east to the Indus Valley. The Persian capitals were Persepolis (II Macc. 9:2), newly established in the mountains of Persis, and Susa (Neh. 1:1; etc.), the ancient royal capital of Elam (Gen. 14:1) north of the Persian Gulf, on the boundary between the plain and the Zagros Mountains. After the collapse of the Persian Empire, Iran and the Near East were ruled and hellenized by Alexander the Great and then primarily by the Seleucids.

(3) About 250 B.C., the Parthians, coming from Transcaspia, began to threaten the Seleucid Empire. They conquered Hyrcania and Parthia, the modern province of Khurasan southeast of the Caspian Sea, and fortified the caravansary of Hecatompylos. From their base in northern Iran, the Parthian kings and horsemen undertook surprise raids toward the east and along the Median highway to the southwest. Under Mithradates I, about 150 B.C., they conquered Mesopotamia. After this, the kings of the Parthian dynasty of the Arsacids were able to control the trade routes between the Roman and Chinese empires throughout the pre-Christian and early Christian periods. They remained the most dangerous enemies of the Romans until a Persian vassal ousted them in A.D. 224. Ecbatana, in Media, and Seleucia, on the west bank of the Tigris, were the royal capitals of the Parthians. The latter was a stronghold of Hellenism; in A.D. 42, in connection with a renaissance of Orientalism, it was displaced by the Parthian Ctesiphon.

(4) After the collapse of the Parthian Arsacids in A.D. 224, the Persians ruled once more, now as the Sassanid dynasty. These Zoroastrian kings contended with the Roman Empire for world dominion until the Arabs conquered Mesopotamia in 636. Ctesiphon remained the capital of the Neo-Persian Empire and of Orientalism.

This survey of the ancient Iranian empires shows that the Iranians, and particularly the Persians, greatly extended the cultural realm to which Palestine and the Jews belonged. Israel and Judah had previously been under the influence of either Egypt or Mesopotamia. Cyrus and the Persians made the Jews free members of a cosmopolitan empire comprising not only these venerable countries, but also Iran, with its great natural resources, and Asia Minor, with its highly developed territories. This was a civilization which included both Semites and eastern peoples like the Aryans, along with western elements like the Greek colonists. This cosmopolitan character of the first Persian Empire aided the expansion of Judaism and also provided a basis for the rapid growth of Hellenism, both very important factors for the missionary activity of the primitive church. Later on, the second Persian Empire constituted the framework that was to be filled out by Islam.

2. THE EARLY ACHAEMENIDS 539–425 B.C.

In order to illustrate the chronological framework of the rise of the Persian Empire and the restoration of Judah, we present here a list of the earlier Achaemenids, together with some of the figures mentioned by the Chronicler.

Kings:	Provincial Officials:	Jewish Authorities:	High Priests (Neh. 12:10):
Cyrus, 539–529		Shesh-bazzar (Ezra 1:8)	
Cambyses, 529–522			
Darius I, 522–486	Tattenai, Satrap in Syria; Shethar-bozenai, Pasha in Samaria (Ezra 5:3)	Zerubbabel (Ezra 2:2)	Jeshua
Xerxes, 486–465			Joiakim
Artaxerxes I, 465–425	Sanballat I, Pasha in Samaria; Tobiah, in Ammon; Geshem, in Edom (Neh. 2:19); Nehemiah, in Judah, 446–434 (Neh. 5:14)	Ezra, 459 (Ezra 7:7)	Eliashib Joiada

With reference to all dates given here and elsewhere, it should be noted that ancient time reckoning included both the initial year and the concluding year. If, for example, Artaxerxes seized power in 465, "in the twentieth year" of his reign (Neh. 1:1) means not 445, but 446 B.C.

A. CYRUS, DARIUS I, XERXES, AND ARTAXERXES I

In 559 B.C., Cyrus, the first great Persian king, became a Median vassal ruling over the territory of Anshan, which had formerly belonged to Elam. With the aid of the Neo-Babylonian king and the Median nobles, he overthrew the Median monarchy in Ecbatana. In 546, he conquered Croesus, the wealthy king of Lydia, and took possession of Asia Minor. Having secured his empire through victories in Phoenicia and central Iran, in 539 he entered Mesopotamia and the gates of Babylon were opened to him by the priests of Marduk. Thus he became the ruler of a commonwealth whose area far surpassed all previous empires and over which he retained control until his death in 529 (the important dates in his life define three intervals of about ten years). His domestic policies also marked a new departure in the history of the Middle East: Cyrus made his governors and viceroys rule the subject nations leniently. Unlike the Babylonians and Assyrians, he did not seek to suppress foreign nationalities, languages, and cults; he expressly supported their recognition and, where necessary, their restoration.[2] Even Greek tradition pictures Cyrus as the model of a humane prince (Xenophon *Cyropaedia*).

For the Jews of the Diaspora and in Palestine, the policies of Cyrus, hailed by Deutero-Isaiah (Isa. 44:28; 45:1), were of crucial importance.

(1) The end of the Babylonian captivity itself contributed to the preservation of the Jewish nationality. It is true that the Babylonians had deported only the leading men of Judah; but because the aristocrats were considered symbols of the nation as a whole, the possibility of their return meant that a dissolution of the Jewish identity could be averted. According to an account in the Chronicler, which may deserve credence even though the latter idealizes, a few patricians and priests returned as early as the time of Cyrus (Ezra 1:5), under the leadership of a certain Shesh-bazzar, who is called privy councillor for Jewish affairs (1:8, 11; 5:15 f.). This event is said to have provided the groundwork for the later return under Zerubbabel (2:1–70; 5:13—6:12). In any case, Cyrus' policy of toleration made possible the postexilic return and repristination of Judaism.

2 M. Noth, *The History of Israel* (2d ed., 1960), pp. 300–308.

9

(2) Cyrus and his successors also recognized the most important languages of the countries they ruled and issued their edicts in the languages of those countries (Esther 1:22), a practice attested by the trilingual cuneiform inscriptions of the Persian kings. Toward the end of the Judahite monarchy, Aramaic had already become the generally accepted language of commerce and politics in Syria and Palestine (II Kings 18:26), largely because of the importance of the kingdom of Damascus and the other Syrian states. In addition, the Assyrians and Babylonians had settled Aramaic-speaking peoples in Israel and Judah. During the exile, the Israelite and Judahite nobility adopted Aramaic because it was the international language, and brought it with them when they returned to their former homeland. Because the Achaemenids accepted the dominance of Aramaic, they made it the official language of Syria and Palestine (Ezra 4:7), thus permitting a special Imperial Aramaic to develop. Hebrew remained the language of the Jewish cult, but Aramaic gradually became the generally spoken language of Palestine. It remained the language of Jews and Christians in Palestine until late antiquity. This linguistic factor, to which Cyrus and the Achaemenids contributed, was essential to the intellectual and spiritual unity of Judaism.

(3) In contrast to earlier rulers, Cyrus neither demolished nor desecrated the religions and cultic sites of the nations he conquered. He did not have them subordinated to the official high god of the Empire. Instead, he authorized their revival; the Cyrus Cylinder in the British Museum, containing instructions for the restoration of the Babylonian cults, provides explicit proof of this.[3] As the representative of the God of heaven, Cyrus is also said to have commanded the rebuilding of the Temple in Jerusalem. This account constitutes the culmination of the Chronicler's entire history (II Chron. 36:22 f.; Ezra 1:1–4); he finds evidence for it in a later official document of Darius (Ezra 6:3–12). However, after his success at Babylon, Cyrus had to contend with unrest in the east and was killed in 529 during a campaign in

---

[3] F. H. Weissbach, *Die Keilinschriften der Achämeniden* (1911), pp. xi, 2–8.

Iran; it appears doubtful, therefore, that he really took such an interest in Judah, a small country far to the west. The idealized portait of Cyrus given by Deutero-Isaiah may have contributed to the development of this tradition. This much is clear, however: as early as the time of Cyrus, the Jewish patricians, priests, and prophets seized the opportunity to begin work on the Temple, but soon gave up their common work because of difficulties and private conflicts (Hag. 1:1–11).

After the death of Cyrus in 529 B.C., the reign passed to his choleric son Cambyses (529–522), who is never mentioned in the Bible. In 525, Cambyses conquered Egypt and Libya.

Then, after severe struggles, Darius I (522–486) took control of the enormous Persian Empire and organized it magnificently. He divided it into twenty satrapies, with a viceroy called satrap in charge of each. These were in turn subdivided into districts, each under a pasha (Heb. and Aram. *pehâ*). Syria and Palestine constituted the fifth satrapy, Transeuphrates or Beyond the River (Ezra 5:3) ; the satrap probably resided in Damascus and Phoenicia. This satrapy created a new cultural region that was to retain considerable individuality for a long period. Syria or Transeuphrates was frequently administered as though it were an independent kingdom; the rank of satrap seemed almost hereditary. The territory was divided politically during the years when the Ptolemies controlled Palestine (320–200 B.C.), but it achieved a relative unity again under the Seleucids and once more under the Romans. Despite the efforts of the Jews to maintain their purity, the territory preserved its cultural individuality even longer, thanks to the unifying effect of commerce and language (Aramaic and, later, Syriac and Arabic). Palestine was a district within the Persian satrapy of Transeuphrates. Its governor or pasha resided in Samaria (Ezra 4:17; Neh. 4:2 [Hebrew, 3:34]), which had not been laid waste like Jerusalem, but was filled with numerous immigrants of various origin (Ezra 4:9 f.).

Cultural exchange within the Persian Empire was also furthered by the military highways and postal service organized by Darius. As an example of the communications system, we may mention the magnificent royal highway from Susa to Ephesus; the postal service is illustrated by the official correspondence embedded in Ezra-Nehemiah. These two innovations of the Persians, as further developed by the Greeks and Romans, were later important for the missionary activity of the Apostles. Around 520 B.C., Darius could send forth his couriers like the horsemen of Zechariah's first vision throughout great portions of the earth and find everything in reasonably good order (Zech. 1:8–11).

These favorable circumstances stirred up in the Jewish patricians, priests, and prophets a powerful yearning for the restoration of Zion, after the attempt made under Sheshbazzar had failed. As a result, in 520 a large group of Zionists from the Diaspora, under the leadership of a patrician, Zerubbabel, and a priest, Jeshua, traveled to Jerusalem (Ezra 2:1–10). Zerubbabel, a descendant of the Davidic kings (I Chron. 3:17 in combination with Ezra 3:2; etc.), was able to appear in Jerusalem as the president of the Jewish community (Hag. 1:1: "governor [pasha] of Judah"). He was surrounded by patricians called "elders" (Ezra 5:5; etc.), an assembly of noblemen still found in the High Council or Sanhedrin of the New Testament period. Jeshua, a descendant of the Zadokite priesthood (I Chron. 5:4, in combination with Ezra 3:2; etc.), was looked upon in Jerusalem as a new high priest (Hag. 1:1). Prophets like Haggai and Zechariah supported the policies of the returning settlers (Ezra 5:1 f.; 6:14; Hag. 1:2–11; Zech. 1:12—2:5). The reconstruction of the Temple was once more undertaken courageously. On account of interference by the native population (Ezra 4:1–5) and the satrap of Syria (Ezra 5:3–17), the Jews sought to base their undertaking upon a decree of Cyrus. They succeeded in winning the support of Darius (6:1–13). And so the Second Temple, the work of Zerubbabel, could be dedicated in 515 B.C. The high priest, the priests, and the Levites began their service in the form that was to be characteristic of the postexilic period (Ezra 6:15–18), even after the rebuilding of the Temple by Herod, until the fall of Jerusalem in A.D. 70 (see below, pp. 163–68).

Politically, it was Darius' desire for good relations with Jerusalem and Judah in order to protect the land route to Egypt that made possible the establishment of the Jewish assembly of patricians just mentioned as well as the restoration of the Jerusalem cult. Therefore the Jerusalem priesthood was not only expected to offer sacrifice to the God of heaven, who was understood to be the god of all nations and peoples, but also to pray for the king and his dynasty (Ezra 6:10). In other words, the restoration of Judaism under Zerubbabel was the result of a favorable situation in the Persian Empire.

Darius' son is known from Greek history as Xerxes (486–465) and from the Bible as Ahasuerus (Ezra 4:6). He "reigned from India to Ethiopia over one hundred and twenty-seven provinces" (Esther 1:1), and during his reign the house of Darius remained wealthy, as the colossal buildings of Xerxes in Persepolis and Ecbatana show. Of course the famous victories of the Greeks at Salamis and Plataea set a limit to Persian expansion westward, which led to some unrest in Babylon. For the Jews, however, Xerxes' reign brought no important changes.

His son and successor, Artaxerxes I (465–425), the *Artaḥšaśtā'* of the Hebrew Bible, had to fight for the hegemony during the first half of his reign; afterward he exercised it brilliantly. From 463 on he was engaged in a violent struggle with Athens for control of Egypt, until in 449, at the peace of Callias, the Greeks renounced all claim to the rich land of the Pharaohs, so that Artaxerxes controlled the entire Empire. It was the Egyptian question and its resolution under Artaxerxes I that influenced the events in Jerusalem connected with the appearance of Ezra in 459 and of Nehemiah in 446. The following section will give the chronological and political details.

B. Ezra and Nehemiah in Jerusalem

The Chronicler's history tells how, during the reign of Xerxes and Artaxerxes, powerful opponents of the Zionist movement put in their appearance (Ezra 4:6, 7–23). It describes in detail how Ezra nevertheless restored the cult and

13

the law in the time of Artaxerxes (Ezra 7:1—10:44) and how Nehemiah then fortified Jerusalem as capital (Neh. 2:1—7:4). For the Chronicler, Ezra, who came from the temple city of Babylon, is the priestly counterpart of Nehemiah, the political leader, who came from the royal capital of Susa, just as previously Jeshua and Zerubbabel made up a sacral-secular pair. The Chronicler's stylized interpretation obscures somewhat the historical relationship between Ezra and Nehemiah; he has not arranged the traditions quite in systematic order. Nevertheless, this much is certain: Ezra is occasionally assumed to precede Nehemiah (Neh. 8:1–6, 9, 13; 12:26), but never the reverse (Ezra 2:2 refers to a different Nehemiah). Even in details that have neither been reported tendentiously nor added by the redactor, Ezra appears as a reformer arriving *before* Nehemiah, just as the explicitly chronological passages suggest.

Ezra, who is called a "scribe," i.e., a notary, and an expert on Jewish religious law, is said to have come to Jerusalem with some supporters "in the seventh year of Artaxerxes" (Ezra 7:6–9). Since the Chronicler dates him definitely before Nehemiah, and since Nehemiah can only be dated within the reign of Artaxerxes I (465–425) [see p. 18 f.], the seventh year of Artaxerxes according to the Chronicler must be the year 459 by our reckoning.

The stylized presentation makes it impossible to determine whether Ezra's expedition took place exactly as described. The view that it belongs to a completely different period, however, is an hypothesis based on dubious considerations.

(1) Many scholars prefer to view Ezra as a later contemporary of Nehemiah and assign him to the last years of Artaxerxes I. They do this in order to explain Nehemiah's failure to refer as explicitly as one might wish to Ezra's restoration. Ezra's arrival is placed either between the two visits of Nehemiah to Jerusalem (Neh. 13:6) or after the second.[4] Both datings are open to the following objections: (a) To disregard the explicit and repeated statement about

---

[4] W. Rudolph, *Esra und Nehemia samt 3. Esra* (1949), pp. 70 f., 168; *et al.*

the seventh year of Artaxerxes (Ezra 7:7 f.) is an arbitrary judgment, because it is impossible to derive this chronological datum from any imposed literary structure. (*b*) The text describes Ezra consistently (though not tendentiously) as a somewhat earlier contemporary of Nehemiah, while there is no trace of the opposite view (see above). The proposed redating therefore undermines a basic structure of the sources, a structure that shows no sign of being a later addition. Another fatal argument against redating is the fact that it is Nehemiah who knows of the existence of Ezra; for experts are generally convinced that Nehemiah's account, based on memoirs, is the more reliable historically. It is of course noteworthy that Nehemiah mentions Ezra only rarely, but we must seek an historical explanation of this fact (see below pp. 16 ff.). To use the small number of references to Ezra as a reason to undertake a redating that makes these references absurd is methodologically unsatisfactory. (*c*) According to his memoirs, Nehemiah carried on his work in Jerusalem from the twentieth to the thirty-second year of Artaxerxes I (i.e., 446–434) and then once more at a later date (Neh. 5:14; 13:6 f.); he obviously succeeded quite well. His success, however, would certainly have made Ezra's activity superfluous during the few remaining years of Artaxerxes (434–425), whether before or after Nehemiah's second visit.

(2) Others have sought to date Ezra's activity in the seventh year of Artaxerxes II (404–358 B.C.).[5] This dating was formerly based on a merely instinctive late dating of the "law" brought by Ezra (Neh. 8:1).[6] Actually there is no objective reason for this violent redating: (*a*) We recall once more that the Chronicler both consciously and unconsciously considers Ezra an earlier contemporary of Nehemiah (see above p. 14). In addition, Nehemiah made his appearance during the reign of Artaxerxes I (i.e., 465–425) [see pp. 18 f.]. It

[5] Among others, K. Galling, *Die Bücher der Chronik, Esra, Nehemia* (1954), pp. 13 f.
[6] A. Alt, "Zur Geschichte der Grenze zwischen Judäa und Samaria," *Palästina-Jahrbuch*, Vol. 31 (1935), pp. 107 f., reprinted in *Kleine Schriften*, Vol. 2 (1953), pp. 357 f. The argument runs that Ezra must be assigned a late date because the Pentateuch only came into being quite a while after the time of Nehemiah. Such an argument is a *petitio principii*.

is hard to see how the Chronicler, who is well informed about much earlier events and is working with archival material, could for no apparent reason ascribe a date sixty-one years too early to a man who, if the suggested relationship with Artaxerxes II were correct, would have belonged to the Chronicler's own immediate past. (*b*) Josephus tells us that, during the reign of Artaxerxes II, Bagoas, the Persian pasha of Judah, imposed a penalty tax upon the Jerusalem Temple for seven years (*Ant.* xi. 297–301). Three papyri from Elephantine (see below, p. 25) show that this Bagoas was an official in Judah at least in the years 411 and 409 B.C. (*Pap. Cowley* xxx–xxxii); there is no reason not to assume that he occupied the same position under Artaxerxes II in the years after 404. This Temple crisis under Bagoas can simply not be squared with Ezra's mission to restore the Temple, supported juridically and monetarily by the Persian throne (Ezra 7:6, 11–28). In addition, the feud in 401 between Artaxerxes II and his brother Cyrus the Younger (recorded in Xenophon's *Anabasis*) makes it very improbable that Jerusalem would have been allowed to take this step toward independence in the period immediately following.

In short, then, these two attempts to date Ezra later than the seventh year of Artaxerxes I involve considerable difficulties. This is not to deny that the Chronicler's history contains inaccuracies; but to reverse the dating of Ezra and Nehemiah or to date Ezra late only involves us in greater difficulties.

The traditional chronology of Ezra fits in with what we know of the period of Artaxerxes I. Furthermore, the situation we shall describe in a moment explains why Nehemiah mentions Ezra so very circumspectly.

In the seventh year of Artaxerxes, as stated, Ezra journeyed from Babylon to Jerusalem, with a letter of introduction from the Persian king (Ezra 7:11–26). The Chronicler has probably idealized and clericalized his quotation from this letter. With reference to the political situation of 459 B.C., however, it appears natural that at this time the Persian government was backing a plan to strengthen Jerusalem.

Ever since 463, Egypt, supported by Athens, had been in revolt against Persia. After large-scale mobilization and ma-
neuvers in Phoenicia, in 460 the troops of Artaxerxes
marched along the coast through Palestine to Egypt, where
they put down the rebellion (Diodorus Siculus xi. 71.3–6;
74.1–75.4; 77.1–5). In the course of this campaign, the
officials must have become aware of the psychological importance of Jerusalem for the borderland. It is therefore
easy to understand how the Syrian satrap Megabyzus, who
was generalissimo of the Persian armies, and the King himself could be persuaded in 459 to support the plan of a cultic
reinforcement of the city by Ezra.

One gains the impression that some of those in Ezra's
company later intended to fortify the city. Ezra himself may
have suggested it (Ezra 9:9). In particular, the Chronicler
cites a letter according to which supporters of the King depicted a planned rebuilding of the walls as an attempted
revolt, so that Artaxerxes forbade any such undertaking
until further notice (Ezra 4:7–23). Although this section
does not mention Ezra by name, the settlers mentioned in the
document (4:12) were clearly part of his company. This
incident can only be dated within the first half of Artaxerxes'
forty-year reign, for Nehemiah's officially authorized rebuilding of the wall precludes such a prohibition in the latter half
(Neh. 1:1), and in the time of Artaxerxes II the Temple
crisis under Bagoas would have made Ezra's mission completely impossible (see above, p. 16). During the first twenty
years of Artaxerxes I, it is scarcely possible to think of any
other group of returnees than that led by Ezra, even if it is
not certain that all returned at the same time. The political
situation of this period shows at once how such tension could
arise between members of Ezra's company and representatives of the regime. Zealous correspondents warned the King
in the letter mentioned above that the whole satrapy of Syria
was about to revolt (Ezra 4:16). Such a revolution actually
took place under Megabyzus in 455, five years after the sub-
jugation of Egypt (Ctesias *Persica* 36). Artaxerxes and Megabyzus were reconciled only after a violent struggle (*ibid.*,

37–39). It is easy to see that Megabyzus, pursuing his own policies as satrap, supported a fortification of Jerusalem prior to or during this revolt, and that this was prevented by the King. If members of Ezra's company took part in these plans, they may well have been politically suspect later on. This explains why Ezra described his mission as being purely cultic and completely nonpolitical, emphasizing his refusal of military protection (Ezra 8:22), while Nehemiah, as a loyal servant of the King, mentioned Ezra's followers only with great caution (in particular, there is apparently no trace of them in the account of the building of the wall, Neh. 3:1–32[7]).

In any event, Ezra became for Nehemiah and above all for posterity the restorer of the Jewish cult and law. He was depicted as a new Moses (Exod. 24:1, 9 provides the model for Neh. 8:4), and Judaism considered him the greatest of the scribes (e.g., II [IV] Esd. 14:37–47 reports Ezra's restoration of the canonical and apocryphal Scriptures).[8]

Politically, however, Nehemiah played a more important role. The special circumstances during the reign of Artaxerxes I made his success possible; it would not have been so under any later Artaxerxes. For the social restoration and later development of Judaism, Nehemiah's initiative was ultimately decisive.

Nehemiah was royal cupbearer in Susa. In the twentieth year of Artaxerxes, i.e., 446 B.C. (Neh. 1:1; 2:1), he was granted authority to restore Jerusalem and even fortify it (2:5–8). When he arrived, Nehemiah met resistance from the pashas of Ammon and Samaria and their people (2:10, 19; 4:1–23), who with good reason feared competition from Jerusalem, the latter all the more because he was directly responsible for the administration of Judah. Nevertheless, with the help of the local population, Nehemiah was able to rebuild the walls of Jerusalem (3:1–32; 6:15) and even fortify the citadel of the Temple (2:8; 7:2). This construction went on for twelve years, until 434 (5:14). On a later

---

[7] Rudolph, (cited above, p. 14, n. 4), p. 69.
[8] For a discussion of the person of Ezra cf. *ibid.*, pp. 167–71.

occasion, Nehemiah returned to Jerusalem in order to effect some Levitical reforms (13:6 f.) . For the first period of twelve years at least Nehemiah was obviously able to function as Persian pasha or prefect of Judah (5:14–19; 7:2; 8:9; 10:2) .[9] He dared to stand up to Sanballat I, the pasha of Samaria, as well as some Jews who were conspiring with the magistrates of Transjordan (6:1–19) .

How did this political and military emancipation in the years after 446 become possible, even though a few years previously the King had forbidden a projected rebuilding of the wall? The answer is connected with the altered world situation. Artaxerxes I had overcome the difficulties with Egypt and Megabyzus, who had become loyal to the King once more and, in 449, had arranged the advantageous peace of Callias with Athens. It was now possible to consolidate the Persian Empire. Together with Lachish, where at roughly the same time a Persian fortress was built,[10] Jerusalem was an important strong point on the military route to Egypt. At this time it was also more reliable than Samaria, which was associated more closely with the formerly rebellious satrap. Artaxerxes could therefore afford to make Judah a separate prefecture; it retained this status until roughly 400 B.C., as Josephus and the Elephantine papyri show (see above p. 16) , and quite probably even longer.

Jerusalem, as fortified by Nehemiah, contained a population that was further augmented by synoecism (Neh. 7:4; 11:1–19) . But the city probably comprised only the Temple area together with the Ophel, a tongue of land stretching toward the south, and a portion of the plateau to the west of the Temple. It did not include the large hill to the southwest, where the first evidence of urban settlement dates from the Hellenistic period. The land belonging to this polis consisted solely of Benjamin and the northern portion of Judah. The other parts of Palestine were under foreign rule (Neh.

---

[9] A. Alt, "Die Rolle Samarias bei der Entstehung des Judentums," in *Festschrift O. Procksch* (1934) , pp. 21–28, reprinted in *Kleine Schriften*, Vol. 2 (1953) , pp. 330–37.
[10] W. F. Albright, *The Archaeology of Palestine* (rev. ed., 1960) , p. 144, fig. 47.

2:19; Obad. 19). Galilee and Samaria were populated primarily by Arameans; the coast was ruled by the Phoenicians; Arabic Idumeans and Nabateans had penetrated into the Philistine plain, southern Judah, Edom, Moab, and Ammon or Transjordan. Samaria, Tyre, and Gaza, the most important cities of these regions, were wealthier and more powerful than Jerusalem. But Nehemiah transformed the holy city once more into a center of considerable political and military power, which increased greatly in the following period.

Nehemiah's work, which the Persian king made possible and for which Ezra prepared the way, had threefold significance for Jerusalem and Judaism, significance that extended into the New Testament period and lasted until the catastrophe of A.D. 70.

(1) The tiny colony of patricians and priests in Jerusalem, hitherto dependent on the Babylonian Diaspora, achieved relatively independent political status. So the Zionist movement, founded by Zerubbabel in 520, gradually led to the possession of a political homeland by the Jews, like that which they have had since the founding of the state of Israel in 1948. Of course the kings continued to exercise hegemony from Susa and Persepolis. But for the preservation of Jewishness in antiquity, it came to be considered essential that every Jew be able to look toward a geographical center, as Daniel is said to have done at prayer (Dan. 6:10), even though there could be nothing like political control over the Diaspora by the priests and elders in Jerusalem.

(2) The central position occupied by Jerusalem was actually sacral, because the city stood out as the precinct of the sanctuary rebuilt by Zerubbabel and the residence of the high priest, who was soon to reach the position of supreme authority. Certainly, there is no absolute distinction between the sacral and the political; after the fall of the local monarchy, the Temple and the priesthood constituted the apex and focus of the nation, and through them God's blessing was expected to come upon all the people. But specifically religious interests dominate to a remarkable extent. The Temple was the cornerstone of the entire restoration. Still shaken by the punishment that had overtaken Israel and

Judah, the priests and Levites sought to organize the new community according to the ordinances of Levitical holiness. This religious movement was directly abetted by the policies of the Persian regime, which had a positive attitude toward the Temple, and indirectly also by the exceptional concern the Iranian priesthood had for purity. Sacral law gained a position of primary importance in the newly reconstituted Judah, as it did everywhere in the Persian Empire. Gradually the "scribes" came to rank with the patricians and priests, replacing the prophets. These scribes were Levitical experts in the sacral law; at times involved in the local government and legal system, at times in teaching, they made themselves indispensable. Scribes may have played a significant role even during the exile (II Chron. 17:7–9; 19:8–11 date them to the reign of Jehoshaphat, 34:13 and 35:3 to the reign of Josiah). Ezra, who is the prototypical scribe, and Nehemiah hastened the development of this group (Neh. 8:4, 7, 13; 13:13) which, later, was largely responsible for the Chronicler's history. The postexilic scribes also played an important role in the transmission, study, and development of the earlier legal traditions. In Jesus' milieu, as in late Judaism generally, they exercised significant power under the title "rabbi." In the period of Ezra and Nehemiah, these legal experts remained subordinate in principle to the high priest and the magnates (II Chron. 17:7; 19:11; Neh. 8:13). But even then, as later, many priests, patricians, and ordinary citizens disregarded the Levitical ideals and consorted with pagan elements (Ezra 9:14—10:44; Neh. 13:1–9; Josephus *Ant.* xi. 297–303). This laid the groundwork for conflict between the cosmopolitan aristocrats and the puritanical scribes, a conflict reflected in the Chronicler's history (cf. Neh. 10:28–30). In the Hellenistic period, this conflict turned into a bitter struggle between two cultures, and provided grounds for the dispute between Sadducees and Pharisees. Nevertheless, Jewish society under the high priest remained essentially a sacral unity. From the time of Ezra and Nehemiah onward, the leadership comprised three classes: the priests, the patricians or "elders," and the scribes, that is, the same groups that made up the Sanhedrin during the time of Jesus and the Apostles (see below p. 146). A unifying symbol was furnished by the palladium of Judaism kept on the fortified hill of the Temple: the sacred vestments of the high priest (Zech. 3:4 f.; Ezra 2:63; Neh. 7:65).

(3) Nehemiah's fortifying of Jerusalem also had great commercial significance for the future. The mere restoration of the cult brought money and workmen to Jerusalem from the Diaspora (Ezra 2:68 f.; 3:7; 7:15–23; 8:31–36). This was even more true of the work on the walls, toward which the wealthy Nehemiah, the patricians, and even the common people contributed (Neh. 5:16–19; 7:70–72). Under Ezra and Nehemiah, we read that Jerusalem and the surrounding countryside contained 42,360 free men, together with 7,337 slaves, 736 horses, 245 mules, 435 camels, and 6,720 asses (Ezra 2:64–67; Neh. 7:67–69). Even if the Chronicler may have based these figures on later circumstances, the statistics do not seem fantastic or exaggerated; they can give us an idea of the economic situation. In addition, Nehemiah is reported to have opposed all commerce on the Sabbath. This story indicates that Jerusalem had gradually become an international marketplace, where merchants from Tyre (which was a prosperous commercial center in the Persian period) and other cities eagerly plied their trade (Neh. 10:31; 13:15–22). Jerusalem was already participating in the trade carried on between the Orient and the Aegean, a trade based on the system of coinage that the Persians took over in Lydia and proceeded to use and spread. It is not by accident that the earliest coin mentioned in the Bible is the daric, coined by Darius I (Ezra 8:27). It became the standard for gold coinage and international trade. In the period of the Achaemenids, the monetary system enabled the world of Greek commerce to exercise its influence on Palestine via Phoenicia and Egypt, as coins minted in Palestine bearing copies of Attic symbols attest.[11] In the fourth century, Jeru-

---

[11] G. F. Hill, *Catalogue of the Greek Coins of Palestine* (1914), pp. lxxxiii–lxxxix; K. Galling, "Denkmäler zur Geschichte Syriens und Palästinas unter der Herrschaft der Perser," *Palästina-Jahrbuch*, Vol. 34 (1938), pp. 74–79; Albright (cited above, p. 19, n. 10), p. 143; Noth (cited above, p. 9, n. 2), p. 341.

salem appears even to have minted its own coins with the inscription "Judah." [12] If this is correct, it provides further evidence that the Persian Empire encouraged local temples to become centers of banking and coinage.[13] One important factor in the development of this system of coinage was the Temple sacrifices, which conventional currency for purchases and expenditures helped to order rationally.[14] Here we have the beginnings of the institution against which Jesus reacted with the cleansing of the Temple (Matt. 21:12 f. and parallels), although by his time the Temple no longer served as a center for coinage, but only as a bank and place of exchange. From the days of Nehemiah onward, the Temple, the nobles, and the merchants profited from Persian and Greek capitalism; but the new monetary system created difficulties for the small landowners (Neh. 5:1–2), and from that time forward, there was an unfortunate conflict between rich and poor.

C. Judaism in the Persian Empire

Nehemiah's successful action in restoring Jerusalem indirectly clarifies the position of the Diaspora Jews under the Persian kings. Under Cyrus the rather obscure Shesh-bazzar, and under Darius the (certainly) more important Zerubbabel, together with their supporters, had been able to promote Jewish interests at the Persian court. This was all the more true of Nehemiah, who filled important offices as royal cupbearer in Susa and as Persian pasha in Jerusalem.

Jewish narratives of the postexilic period reflect the fact that outstanding Jews were successfully associated with the Persian court and government. The story of Daniel, which is reminiscent of the Joseph story, is a typical example. His activity as royal page is connected at first with the Babylonian captivity; then however, it is expressly linked with the Persian

---

[12] The inscription was formerly read *yhw,* but is now read *yhd:* E. L. Sukenik, *Journal of the Palestine Oriental Society,* Vol. 14 (1934), pp. 78 ff.; Vol. 15 (1935), pp. 341 ff.; K. Galling (cited in preceding note), pp. 75 f.

[13] As to Phoenician cities, see Galling (cited above, n. 11), p. 62; as to Hierapolis in Syria, see Albright (cited above p. 19, n. 10), p. 143.

[14] B. Laum, *Heiliges Geld* (1924), pp. 126–51; *idem,* "Geld," in *Die Religion in Geschichte und Gegenwart,* 2d ed., Vol. 2 (1928), cols. 970 f.; G. Lanczkowski, "Münze," *ibid.* (3d ed.), Vol. 4 (1960), cols. 1184 f.

Empire and its satraps (Dan. 6:1–28). According to a Persian
and Greek version of the Chronicler's history, Zerubbabel had
a similar career as a page at Darius' court (I Esd. 3:1—4:63).
According to the Book of Tobit, Ahikar, a wise Jew, even became imperial chancellor in Nineveh (Tob. 1:21 f.). A further example is provided by the beautiful Esther and wise
Mordecai, who attained the highest dignity in the harem and
court of Artaxerxes (Esther 2:17; 8:2). These tales give at-
tractive literary expression to Jewish ideals that could become
social reality in the Achaemenid period.

Despite the return of many Jews to Palestine, the Diaspora
retained its importance. It gradually expanded, as later accounts show, partially through new emigration and partially
through simple population increase. The former captives
and the free emigrants were able to demonstrate their ability
as administrators and businessmen, as tenant farmers and
smallholders, as artisans and entrepreneurs, sharing in the
general prosperity under the Achaemenids. The correspondence of "Murashu's Sons," a thriving banking house in Nip-
pur during the reign of Artaxerxes I and his successors,
provides an excellent picture of the situation.[15] These Babylonian financiers furnished the necessary capital for many
tenant farmers and entrepreneurs; their correspondence
gives the impression that there was a real economic boom. In
particular, their clients included many Jews who wanted to
work their way up.[16]

At this time, Jews were probably found as far east as
Media (Tob. 1:14; 3:7; 9:2; 14:4; Tobit is admittedly a later
source, but it depends on earlier narratives); toward the end
of the Achaemenid period, as the result of a deportation,
even Hyrcania acquired a Jewish diaspora (Eusebius *Chron.*
360, referring to an earlier historian; R. Helm (ed.), p. 121,
ll. 6–10). To the northwest, Jewish slaves appear to have

15 G. Cardascia, *Les archives de Murašu* (1951), p. 8. Murashu's Sons was a
lending institution that used the feudal structure of the Persian Empire to
accumulate enormous capital assets and become a gigantic trust company.
16 B. Meissner, "Die Achämenidenkönige und das Judentum," *Sitzungsberichte der Preussischen Akademie der Wissenschaften*, Phil.-hist. Kl., 38 (1938),
6–32, pp. 9, 11; other studies are cited by Cardascia (cited in preceding note),
p. iii.

been brought to Ionia, in Asia Minor, as early as the Achaemenid period (Joel 3:6 [Hebrew 4:6]), so that the Jewish colony in Asia, which was later to be so important, had its beginning at this time. To the southwest, toward Egypt, emigrants from Israel and Judah had come, during the sixth century, as far as the first cataract of the Nile; there, on the island of Elephantine, the Persians maintained a garrison of Israelites and Jews. The Aramaic Elephantine papyri contain information about these matters. Of course, these were all isolated settlements; but they provided the starting point for the extraordinary expansion of Judaism during the Hellenistic and Roman periods, which was to be very important for the spread of the Gospel. This expansion of Judaism in three directions, as outlined, took place within the framework of Persian hegemony.

Jerusalem remained the spiritual and intellectual center of international Judaism. During a crisis in 410 B.C., for example, the colonists at Elephantine appealed to the holy city (*Pap. Cowley* xxx. 18 f.). On the other hand, the Jewish leaders knew very well that this progress was due, apart from God's grace, solely to the favor of the king (Ezra 9:9), favor which Nehemiah experienced particularly under Artaxerxes I.

3. THE LATE ACHAEMENIDS 424–331 B.C.

We must now briefly describe the situation under the late Achaemenids (424–331 B.C.). On page 26 we present a chronological table, listing Persian provincial governors, Jewish high priests, and some of the brothers of the high priests who wanted to seize power. This table will facilitate our discussion of the Samaritan schism and other problems of this era.

A. THE GENERAL SITUATION

The enormous distances in the Empire and the multitude of pretenders to the throne created many difficulties for the late Achaemenids, but they nevertheless preserved their hegemony to the very end. Danger seemed to threaten the monarchy every time a new ruler acceded to the throne. In

Kings:	Governors:	High Priests:	Brothers of the High Priests:
Darius II, 424–404	Samaria: Deleyah, son of Sanballat I; Judah: Bagoas.[17]	Johanan (Neh. 12:22)	1. Neh. 13:28: an anonymous brother of Johanan was Sanballat's son-in-law; Nehemiah sent him into exile.[17]
Artaxerxes II, 404–358 (the anabasis of Cyrus in 401)	Judah: Bagoas (cf. above) [17]		2. Josephus *Ant.* xi 297–301: Johanan's brother Jeshua was Bagoas' candidate for high priest; he was slain by Johanan, whereupon Bagoas imposed a tax upon the cult for seven years.[17]
	Sanballat II *ca.* 380	Jaddua (Neh. 12:11,22)	3. Josephus *Ant.* xi 302 f., 306–12, 321–25: Jaddua's brother Manasses was Sanballat's son-in-law. The Jerusalem elders forced him into exile. Sanballat wanted to promote him to be high priest, and therefore planned to build a temple on Gerizim during the reign of Darius. He rapidly concluded his work on this temple while the Macedonians under Alexander were advancing in 332 B.C.[18]
Artaxerxes III, 358–338	Hananiah		
Darius III, 336–330	Sanballat III		

[17] The Sanballat mentioned in the second column and in section one of the fourth column is the pasha in Samaria, familiar from Nehemiah 2:10, etc. (see above, p. 18 f.). Three of the Elephantine papyri from the year 407 B.C. (*Pap. Cowley* xxx–xxxii) mention Deleyah, his son and successor, along with Deleyah's brother, as well as Bagoas and Johanan; this means they held office under Darius II. The passage from Josephus cited in section two of the fourth column mentions "the other Artaxerxes"; if this is correct, Bagoas retained his position under Artaxerxes II.

[18] The Josephus passage mentioned in section three tells of a certain Sanballat that was "satrap" of Samaria at a time which can be fixed a century later. Recently discovered papyri from Wadi Daliyeh (nine miles north-northwest of ancient Jericho) mention yet a third Sanballat between these two, who was pasha of Samaria about 380; see F. M. Cross, Jr., "The Discovery of the Samaria Papyri," *The Biblical Archaeologist*, Vol. 26 (1963), 110–21, pp. 120 f. It turns out that the office each time passed to a son and the name to a grandson. Josephus probably was unable to distinguish the three Sanballats.

401, for example, the younger Cyrus led an attack on his brother Artaxerxes II, of which we have a famous account in Xenophon's *Anabasis*. Each time, however, the new ruler succeeded in maintaining his position. The next-to-last king, Artaxerxes III, was in fact an unusually vigorous politician, who successfully asserted his power in the west. Only the amazing military might of the Macedonians, led by Alexander, finally brought about the fall of Artaxerxes' successor, Darius III, and the whole Persian Empire.

The history of Judaism in this period remains obscure. The dating of some Mosaic laws and Davidic psalms in the period of the late Achaemenids rests on uncertain arguments; even those who take this position cannot employ such texts for historical purposes without artificial interpretations. Anachronisms found in the Chronicler's history suggest that it may have been subject to redaction in this period; but at best the narrative depicts only the general setting of the redactor's time, not specific events. The Elephantine papyri furnish details about peripheral matters. The texts from Wadi Daliyeh are now an additional source of information (see note 18 above). Later narratives, like the story of Judith, may have some of their roots in the late Achaemenid period; but we can no longer distinguish these roots. Apart from the Old Testament, Josephus had only legendary traditions to draw on for this era. One may assume, however, that Judaism, now extended over a broad area with the Empire of the late Achaemenids, continued the development begun under the earlier kings. A large number of the Jews probably still profited from the political situation and the universal culture.

B. The Samaritan Schism

The late Achaemenid period does, however, mark a decline in the influence exerted by the restored city of Jerusalem. This decline was still a burning problem at the time of Jesus and the Apostles. Shechem, which had been a cultic and political center for northern Israel until approximately 900 B.C., when Samaria displaced it, now appeared once more as custodian of a temple. Immediately to the southwest of the city, on Mount Gerizim, a temple was built to compete with the Jerusalem Temple as cultic center for the people of northern Palestine.

The circumstances leading to the Samaritan schism are not entirely clear. It seems likely that the schism was mainly due to a reaction on the part of the officials in Samaria and a few aristocrats in Judah against the centralizing (one might say Zionistic) reforms of Nehemiah. As the fourth column of our table on page 26 shows, the references in Nehemiah and Josephus to the schism are contradictory as to chronology; however, they indicate the general situation with unconscious unanimity. All three texts mention a brother of the high priest at Jerusalem; this brother appears as a traitor in league with representatives of the satrapy. In sections one and two, this figure is a brother of the high priest Johanan, sometimes anonymous and sometimes called Jeshua. The former is said to have been exiled by Nehemiah, the latter slain by Johanan. There is no apparent reason to doubt the existence of either of these brothers of the high priest, both of whom are labeled collaborators. There are, however, grounds for hesitation with regard to the tradition in section three of column four. As in the Nehemiah memoirs, Sanballat appears as the father-in-law of the man at enmity with his brother the high priest; but while Sanballat I served under Darius II, this other Sanballat held office under Darius III, and therefore must have been Sanballat III. The similarity of names in itself suggests an anachronism. But there are other grounds for doubt. The latest date that can be assigned to Jaddua is roughly 380 (cf. the table on page 26); it is very unlikely that any of his brothers survived until 332. Above all, the temple on Mount Gerizim was certainly not rebuilt in the twinkling of an eye at the approach of the Macedonians. It seems more likely that it was later enlarged because of the Macedonian colony in Samaria. The tradition recorded by Josephus at this point is clearly tendentious: it is meant to present the detested Samaritan community as the unripe fruit of Hellenistic opportunism. One gains the

impression that Josephus' source originally referred to Sanballat II, who lived around 380 B.C. and served under Artaxerxes II. The assumption that Josephus combined different
traditions furnishes a satisfactory picture. It is readily understandable that even in the period of Nehemiah and the late
Achaemenids some members of the high-priestly family dis-
liked Nehemiah's reliance upon the Levites, because this
policy restricted the freedom of movement enjoyed by the
whole "gilded youth." The satrapy's representatives in
Judah and Samaria used this reaction to repress the priestly
state. The political unrest during Cyrus' anabasis perhaps
provides the best explanation of the circumstances under
which the high priest slew his brother, who had the support
of the royal house. Sometime after Cyrus' defeat in 400,
Bagoas, the commissioner of Judah, taxed the Jewish temple
cult for seven years (Josephus *Ant.* xi. 297–301) . At the same
time, or perhaps a bit later, Sanballat II or other officials in
Samaria may have ordered the building or repair of a temple
upon Mount Gerizim in order to keep resurgent Jerusalem
in check.

Wisely avoiding Samaria, which in Jewish eyes always
bore the stamp of idolatry, they turned to Shechem, and
upon Mount Gerizim chose a site associated with Moses and
with royal and religious traditions (Gen. 12:6; Deut. 11:29;
I Kings 12:25; Jer. 41:5) . Jerusalem Zadokites who collaborated with the Persian authorities provided the new temple
with a priestly dynasty that seemed eminent enough. As the
history of the Samaritan religion shows, the Jewish Pentateuch was borrowed as the basis for worship at Shechem (in
Deut. 27:4, "Gerizim" replaced "Ebal") ; but, out of caution,
the Prophets and Writings were rejected. The new cultic
center, serving the mixed population of northern Palestine,
inevitably took on syncretistic traits.

Against this reconstruction of the beginnings of the Samaritan schism, it should not be said that borrowing of the
Pentateuch suggests a later period. No historical information
about when the redaction of this corpus was completed is
precise enough to be used as a basis for a definite chronology.

The political situation, however, argues strongly for the period suggested. According to Ezra and Nehemiah, the Samaritan representatives of the satrapy and their supporters engaged in constant intrigues against the rise of Jerusalem in order to preserve the supremacy of northern Palestine. The building or restoration of temples formed part of the usual policy of the Persian Empire, as we know from the restoration of the Temple at Jerusalem and also from sanctuaries in Syria. Furthermore, it is much more probable that a high official like Sanballat II undertook to build a temple at Shechem with the help of rebellious Zadokites as a move to block the progress of Jerusalem than that the sudden invasion of Alexander set the huge project in motion.[19]

Ethnically, the new rise of Shechem, like its earlier rise in the days of Jeroboam I (I Kings 12:25), intensified the opposition between the North and the South. In the latter part of the second century B.C., this tension led the Jews to carry out devastating campaigns against the Samaritans (see below, pp. 66 f.) ; and the New Testament period still witnessed many clashes between the two groups. Religiously, the building of a temple on Mount Gerizim had the same result as Jeroboam's earlier institution of sacrifice at Bethel and Dan (I Kings 12:29) : a separate syncretistic Israelite cultic community grew up. This was the community of the Samaritans, which continued to survive for centuries with its own peculiar traditions. In the New Testament period, influenced by Gnosticism, it was at odds with Judea and Jerusalem (Luke 9:53; John 4:9, 20; Acts 8:18–23). It lives on today, a pitiful but venerable remnant, in the vicinity of Mount Gerizim.

C. THE LAST PERSIAN WARS

In the period between 351 and 342 B.C., Artaxerxes III took the field several times against rebels in Syria, Phoenicia, and Egypt. The bloody battles resulted in complete victory

---

[19] For a further discussion of the Samaritan schism, see R. Marcus in, *Josephus, with an English translation by Henry St. John Thackeray*, Vol. 6 (1937), pp. 498–511; G. E. Wright, "The Samaritans at Shechem," *Harvard Theological Review*, Vol. 55 (1962), pp. 357–366; H. H. Rowley, *Men of God. Studies in Old Testament History and Prophecy* (1963), pp. 246–76.

for the king, who punished the rebels severely, particularly Sidon and Egypt. Jews seem to have taken some part in the revolt, for, in addition to the Egyptians, who were deported in masses, Jews are said to have been carried off, being taken to Hyrcania, southeast of the Caspian Sea (see above p. 24).[20] Nothing in the sources, though, suggests that Judah was affected. On the contrary, the Book of Judith may possibly reflect the fact that the Holy Land was spared, as several scholars assume. The evidence is an interesting similarity between two names: Holophernes and Orophernes. The Book of Judith (e.g., 2:4) names the former as the leader of the attack; the latter is mentioned in historical documents as Artaxerxes' general during the Phoenician and Egyptian campaigns. Certainly the Book of Judith came into being later, and its purpose was not to record facts but to summon its readers to courage; yet the legend it recounts may go back to special treatment accorded Judah during Artaxerxes' punitive expeditions.

Achaemenid hegemony came to a sudden end after this manifestation of power. Intrigues on the part of the satraps brought Darius III to the throne. He was not clever and strong enough to stem the tide of the Madedonian state under Alexander. As the Book of Daniel graphically describes, after six years of Darius' reign the wrathful he-goat from the West destroyed the ram who bore the horns of Media and Persia (Dan. 8:7). The famous battles of Granikos in 334, Issos in 333, and Arbela in 331 (in the northwest and southeast of Asia Minor and on the royal highway northeast of Nineveh) spell the downfall of the Achaemenid Empire and the beginning of a new epoch in ancient history.

D. The Effects of Persian Rule on Judaism

For the Jews, as for other nations of the Middle East, the fall of the Achaemenids and the victory of Alexander in 331 did not mean a break with the past. Although political control often changed hands and the various kingdoms were

---

[20] For further details, see Schürer, Vol. 3, p. 6; I. Gutmann, "Artaxerxes III," in *Encyclopaedia Judaica*, Vol. 3 (1929), p. 407.

locked in furious struggles, the Jews of Palestine and the Diaspora generally retained their political position and close social contact. Their cultural and intellectual life also continued to rest on the foundations laid during the Persian Empire; only gradually did Western civilization, introduced by Alexander, superimpose itself upon Eastern culture. This was precisely Alexander's program: to fuse the East and West together both culturally and politically, to bring together indigenous Oriental structures and international Greek elements, as will be outlined below in our discussion of the development of "Hellenism." Alexander and his immediate successors had no intention of violently restricting the individual peculiarity of Judaism. Immediately after Alexander's conquest, the Jewish priests and Levites, elders and scribes, were able to continue the work of Ezra and Nehemiah without interruption.

In addition to the cultic and legal traditions described by the Chronicler as restored together with the restoration of the Temple, the Jewish religion of the period between 539 and 332 B.C. presumably also contained elements deriving from the Persian hegemony, especially in the eastern Diaspora. Only in a few cases can a direct borrowing of Persian traditions be detected, as in the contest between the royal pages in the apocryphal Book of Esdras (I Esd. 3:1—4:42). For the most part we are probably dealing not with influence but with convergence, motifs already present receiving increased emphasis thanks to analogous motifs in the dominant environment. One should also note that the Jews never encountered ancient Iranian religion or any true Zoroastrianism; instead they met a Chaldean-Iranian syncretism transmitted primarily in Aramaic, about which scholars have only rather unreliable information derived from sources that are either very fragmentary or much later. One thing, however, is clear: long after the period of the Achaemenids, Jewish piety still felt a strong bond with the cultural world of Chaldea and Persia, as the Books of Tobit, Esther, and Daniel show. Persian hegemony was most likely the original cause of these contacts.

Several religious motifs of the Judaism of the later postexilic period may well have developed out of earlier conceptions through convergence with Persian syncretism. Among
them are these:

(1) The conception of heaven as a royal court.

(2) A tendency toward dualism, elaborated partially in
material and ethical terms, partially in dramatic and
historical terms.

(3) The doctrine of successive world empires.

(4) The figure of a divine mediator who could be
thought of as primordial man, prophet, and re-
deemer.

(5) Systematic conceptions of angels and demons.

(6) The expectation of a resurrection and retribution.

The importance of these motifs stands out clearly only in
later texts, but it is safe to assume that the hegemony of the
Achaemenids hastened their development. In the later struggle against Greek culture, conservative Jews looked back to
Persian civilization and drew inspiration from the Parthian
kingdom; as a result, elements of Chaldean and Iranian
syncretism were still enriching the Jewish intellectual milieu
in the last centuries before Christ and the first centuries of
the Christian era. It is impossible to decide to what extent it
was the Persian or the Parthian periods that developed motifs of Judaism comparable to Iranian ideas. In general,
however, the political and cultural significance of the Persian Empire for Judaism suggests that the earlier period
exercised considerable influence. In any case, the Jews kept
alive under Alexander an intellectual and spiritual heritage
from the Achaemenid period. This heritage played a significant role for them in the following centuries.[21]

[21] B. Reicke, "Iranische Religion, Judentum und Urchristentum," in *Die
Religion in Geschichte und Gegenwart*, 3d ed., Vol. 3 (1959) , cols. 881–84.

II

JUDEA UNDER HELLENISTIC RULE

332–142 B.C.

1. THE HELLENISTIC SPHERE OF INFLUENCE

> Then a mighty king shall arise.
> . . . And when he has arisen,
> his kingdom shall be broken and
> divided toward the four winds of
> heaven.
>
> Daniel 11:3 f.

A. ALEXANDER'S CAMPAIGN

ALEXANDER, who ruled from 336 to 323, was actually not a Greek at all, but a Macedonian. He was educated as a Greek, however, having Aristotle as his last tutor; when he acceded to the throne in 336 at the age of twenty, he took over from his father the control of Greece. In 334 he set out on his campaign against Persia, a continuation of earlier Greek expeditions to strengthen the eastern colonies, but this time better prepared and more effectively waged. With undreamed success this brilliant and indefatigable commander was able time and time again to put the Persian king to flight and conquer one satrapy after the other. At the same time, Alexander's march through Asia Minor, Phoenicia, Palestine, Egypt, Mesopotamia, Iran, and part of India became the triumphal progress of Greek culture.

The conquest of Palestine took place in 332; the Jews offered no resistance. Alexander first laid siege to Tyre and then marched along the coast to attack Gaza. Meanwhile, Samaria and Jerusalem surrendered voluntarily. Josephus describes Alexander's interview with the high priest of Jerusalem, who comes to the conqueror vested in all his elaborate paraphernalia of office. Alexander tells how, while he was still in Macedonia, this same high priest had appeared to him in a dream and commissioned him in the name of the God of Israel to seize control of the Persian Empire (Josephus *Ant.* xi. 334 f.). This story typifies Alexander's attitude toward the cults of conquered nations. His pilgrimage to the oracle of Amon in Libya is famous: there he arranged to have himself proclaimed the son of the supreme god of Egypt.

With a surprising naturalness Alexander acted everywhere as the divinely appointed ruler of the world. He made no attempt, however, to replace the ruling classes and dominant cultures of the Middle East with Greek and Macedonian elements. Instead, he left the Oriental rugs where they were, so to speak, only making sure that he had his feet firmly planted on them. Temples and cults remained undisturbed; Alexander himself was represented as the ruler chosen by the deity in question. To a great extent Alexander preserved existing institutions, merely appointing governors and garrisons and founding cities at strategic points in order to build up and protect commerce. After the campaign that took him to the Indus, he appeared in the ancient royal residence of Susa as the successor to the Achaemenids and married a daughter of Darius, whom he had conquered. In addition, he had his officers marry daughters of the Persian nobles and recruited Persian horsemen for his cavalry. Alexander plainly aspired to link the Orient with the Occident; the focus of his attention, however, lay in the East. The Macedonians and Greeks opposed these optimistic policies in the Orient, even after the retrenchment Alexander found necessary shortly before his sudden death. Even so, Alexander's campaign brought about a thorough amalgamation of Hellenistic and Oriental cultural elements that lasted for centuries. This phenomenon remained an important factor for the Mediterranean Basin and Asia Minor until the Roman period and beyond, lasting until the division of the Roman Empire in late antiquity.

B. HELLENISM

The civilization of the Mediterranean Basin and the Middle East bore the stamp of Greek (Hellenic) culture until the time of the Roman Empire and, indeed, until late antiquity; modern scholars therefore call this civilization "Hellenism." [1] For the history of Judaism and Christianity, however, this concept alone does not suffice to describe the setting of developments during the first Christian centuries. In certain contexts, Oriental elements played the dominant role in this period, especially in certain powerful religious movements, and also in some aspects of politics. In such cases it might be better to speak of "Orientalism." [2]

Building upon the foundation of Alexander's conquests, Hellenism gradually developed during the last centuries B.C. Its importance for Judaism was both positive and negative. The following institutions were characteristic of it:

(1) The Persian Empire had previously constituted the largest cultural milieu of antiquity (see above, pp. 7 f.). Alexander expanded this milieu by adding to it Macedonia and Greece, together with their colonies. The "coastlands" (Gen. 10:5) had long been in contact with the East through expeditions, foreign representatives, and colonies. Now these same regions, in the days of Alexander the intellectual, commercial, and technical center of the world, could export power and capital, knowledge and culture, to a much greater extent than before. Macedonia, Greece, and Ionia never gained political supremacy; but the Macedonian nobility acquired positions of influence in many places, and civic life in Greece and Ionia set the pattern from the Tyrrhenian Sea to the Indian Ocean. Hellenism itself was enriched by this enormous territorial expansion. Materially, most of the benefits accrued to Aegean trade islands like Delos and Rhodes and

---

[1] The first scholar to use and popularize the term Hellenism to denote the culture of the period from Alexander to Augustus was J. G. Droysen, in his *Geschichte Alexanders des Grossen* (1833–34) and *Geschichte des Hellenismus*, Vols. 1–2 (1836–43). It later became customary to extend the term to the period of the emperors.

[2] As does F. C. Grant, "Hellenismus," in *Die Religion in Geschichte und Gegenwart*, 3d ed., Vol. 3 (1959), col. 210.

Ionian industrial cities like Ephesus. Intellectually, there was definite progress in science and anthropology. On the other hand, the cosmopolitan attitude led unavoidably to gradual breakdown of the ancient Greek way of life.[3]

(2) The numerous cities promoted or founded by Alexander and his successors formed the basis of the enormous Greek influence upon the East. Modeled after a Greek *polis*, a Hellenistic city would often have a marketplace and streets laid out in a grid pattern, government buildings and an official chapel, a gymnasium and a theater, all adorned with works of Greek art. In addition, the surrounding territory belonged to the city. Such administrative and commercial centers of Hellenism are found on the map in close sequence from Ionia through southern Asia Minor and Syria, Mesopotamia and western Iran, as far as the Persian Gulf, and also from Phoenicia through Transjordan and Philistia to Egypt and North Africa.[4] For the most part they lie along the route taken by Alexander; although many of them had existed previously or were founded later, it was Alexander that provided the impetus for this great system of *poleis*. He personally founded the greatest and richest of all the Hellenistic cities, which still bears his name today: Alexandria, in the western portion of the Nile Delta.

At first the population of the Hellenistic cities consisted of an upper class of Macedonians and Greeks along with several lower classes made up of natives, resident aliens, and slaves. The resident aliens often included Jews. As a result of the political and social situation, Greek citizenship and Greek education often appeared extremely valuable to the non-Greek elements.

To be considered a full member of this new society, an individual had to have citizenship (*politeia*) in one of the Hellenistic cities. Citizenship did not mean possession of nationality; by analogy with the Greek and Ionian concept of a *polis,* it meant full participation in the rights and duties

---

[3] H. Bengtson, *Griechische Geschichte von den Anfängen bis in die römische Kaiserzeit*, 2d ed. (1960), pp. 285–506.

[4] Bengtson (cited in preceding note), map following p. 448.

of those belonging to the municipal corporation. Originally it was Greeks who possessed these rights; but, since the Greeks in the East often had to be supplemented with "barbarians," Greek-ness in the social sense became a generally sought privilege. Even where the goal was equality of rights or co-citizenship (*isopoliteia*) without surrender of national difference, as was later true of the Jews in Alexandria, the concept of the Greek citizen furnished the basis. Later, Roman citizenship was also a privilege linked to a city, but felt to be exceptionally valuable, as we see in the case of Paul (Acts 22:28).

Of course, the Hellenistic cities were dependent upon the various monarchies, but the citizens exercised considerable self-government through city council and senate. In addition, the citizens were organized in various bodies for the protection of their interests. The highly developed Greek system of societies achieved considerable importance in the East; in Asia Minor, Syria, and Egypt it helped preserve the awareness of being Greek. In the cities, the gymnasiums especially helped preserve the Greek way of life. Their students, called ephebi, along with former students constituted an academic association; here a man could be sure of full recognition as a Greek citizen (cf. certain exclusive English colleges and American fraternities). Many other associations also structured the life of the city: professional guilds, religious orders, social groups, political clubs. The various bodies stood under the protection of a deity and, whenever possible, a wealthy patron. After the Romans had conquered Greece, Asia Minor, Syria, and Egypt, the Hellenistic system of societies became a rallying point for opposition and nationalism, and under the emperors the societies were outlawed in principle. The early church gradually had to come to terms with this system of religious, political, and social organizations, because its local congregations grew up in the cities (see below pp. 307–10).

(3) The primary means of communication in the vast world of Hellenism was the Greek language, more specifically, *koine,* a simplified form of Attic Greek with Ionic

elements, which began to replace the earlier dialects in the fourth century B.C. The new cosmopolitanism demanded a convenient common language. As the language of officers, notaries, orators, and citizens, *koine* Greek temporarily replaced Aramaic in the Middle East; everywhere it became the common language of politics and government, commerce and instruction. The non-Greek regions, however, maintained their indigenous languages. In such areas many people were bilingual: in Rome the intelligensia, and in Syria, Palestine, and Egypt even the common people, as documents and inscriptions show. Even in the first and second centuries A.D., *koine* still dominated the picture from the Tiber to the Tigris and even beyond. It is no accident, therefore, that the popular writings making up the New Testament were written in *koine* Greek and did not need to be translated until around A.D. 200. But *koine* was also used for rhetoric and literary prose. Rhetoricians of Asia Minor developed a baroque style called Asianism; after the first century B.C., this tendency was opposed by the neoclassical school of Atticism, supported by Alexandrian scholars. After A.D. 150 or thereabouts, Greek began to lose ground: in Italy men were no longer so anxious to learn Greek; in Egypt and Asia Minor, Orientalism contributed to the literary renaissance of Coptic, Hebrew, Syriac, and other indigenous languages.

Hellenism also preserved the old bond between Greek schools and language on the one hand and Greek mythology and literature on the other. Alexander was an ardent reader of Homer, and took Greek writers everywhere he went to record his experiences. Such interests were characteristic of the upper classes throughout the Hellenistic world. In the Greek diaspora, the way of life, religion, philosophy, and ethics all rested primarily on the proud mythological and literary traditions of Greece.

(4) The cities and territories of Hellenism were governed by a monarchy that was ultimately represented as divine. Alexander applied the Oriental ideal of the royal demi-god to himself; his successors, the Diadochi and Epigoni, gradually followed his lead in this matter. The typical likenesses of

Alexander and his successors on coins emphasize divine characteristics: the hair is reminiscent of the sun's rays, the eyes stare into the distance, out of the mouth comes a divine exhalation; on the reverse we find a god like Zeus or Apollo. At first, however, the Diadochi did not take the initiative in promoting the royal cult. The real beginning came when Athens servilely honored the Western Diadoch, Antigonus, and his son Demetrius Poliorcetes as saviors and gods. Other cities soon followed the example eagerly.[5]

In the empire of Alexander royal supremacy embraced mainly military and financial affairs; for these two areas Alexander set up separate organizations. The individual citizen usually came in contact with the imperial power in the form of soldiers and tax officials. For the rest, he could devote himself with considerable independence to affairs of the community and private business. Later the situation changed in the divided empire, where the power of the state sometimes intervened harshly in the life of the community, as happened in Syria and Palestine under Antiochus Epiphanes. The Romans, however, once more made it a standard policy to give tributary lands and cities considerable autonomy.

C. DIADOCHI AND EPIGONI

In broad outline, the political history of the period inaugurated by Alexander runs as follows: Alexander forged Macedonia, Greece, the Persian Empire, and part of India into an empire so vast that even the king himself was unable to hold it together. After his death in 323 B.C., Macedonian and Greek generals engaged in a struggle for power, as Alexander's would-be *diadochi* ("successors"). These included Perdiccas, who was president of the ministry at Babylon, and several governors of Macedonian and Greek districts and of Persian satrapies. Finally, in 301, Alexander's empire was divided in such a way that (1) the Antigonids ruled Macedonia, (2) the Lagids or Ptolemies ruled Egypt and Libya, and (3) the Seleucids ruled Syria and Persia. These three major

---

[5] M. P. Nilsson, *Geschichte der griechischen Religion,* Vol. 2, 2d ed. (1961), pp. 150–54.

territories of Alexander's so-called *epigoni* ("heirs") were later conquered by the Roman state in the course of its systematic expansion, Macedonia falling in 146, Syria in 64, and Egypt in 30 B.C. After 332, Palestine was controlled by Alexander and the Macedonians; in 320 control passed to Egypt, in 200 to Syria, and in 63 to Rome.

2. EGYPTIAN HEGEMONY 320–200 B.C.

> Then the king of the south shall be strong. . . .
>
> Daniel 11:5

At first, Alexander's conquest of the Holy Land in 332 meant no radical change for the local population. There was simply a change of rulers, as there had always been when a new king ascended the throne of the Persian Empire. Judah (called in Greek "Judea") also remained a part of the Transeuphrates satrapy, which was now under the control of Laomedon, one of Alexander's officers. Only some years later, after the death of Alexander in 323, did Ptolemy, who ruled the satrapy of Egypt, draw Judea into the course of world history.

On page 43 a synopsis of the third century B.C. will outline the dynasties of Egypt and Syria and the wars between them, before we go into detail. The names of the Jewish high priests are also included insofar as they are mentioned by Josephus (whose data are not dependable), as well as representatives of the Tobiads, a powerful financial house that strongly influenced Jewish policy after about 260.

A. PTOLEMY I–III AND THE RISE OF EGYPT

Ptolemy I (Macedonian-Greek *ptolemaîos,* "warrior") was one of Alexander's most capable generals; at first, however, he took anything but an aggressive stance. With shrewd foresight he accepted the satrapy of Egypt in 323, avoided the powerful Perdiccas in Babylon, and set about strengthening Egypt as a secure base upon which to build. In 321 he was already strong enough to defeat Perdiccas at the Egyptian border. Because he felt temporarily safe from Babylonian at-

Ptolemies:	Ptolemaic-Seleucid Wars:	Seleucids:	High Priests:	Tobiads:
Ptolemy I Soter (323)306— (285)283	Common war against Antigonus, 320–301 (victory at Gaza in 312)	Seleucus I Nicator 312–281	Onias I	
Ptolemy II Philadelphus (285)283–246	First Syrian War 274–271	Antiochus I Soter 281–261	Simon I the Righteous (?)	
	Second Syrian War 260–253	Antiochus II Theos 261–246	Eleazar, Manasses	Tobias ca. 260–255 (Zenon Papyri)
Ptolemy III Euergetes 246–221	Third Syrian War 246–241	Seleucus II Callinicus 245–225	Onias II	
Ptolemy IV Philopator 221–204	Fourth Syrian War 221–217 (victory for Egypt at Raphia in 217)	Seleucus III Soter 225–223 Antiochus III the Great		Joseph, tax guarantor in place of the high priest ca. 208–187
Ptolemy V Epiphanes (b. 210) 204–181	Fifth Syrian War 202–195 (defeat for Egypt at Paneas in 200)	222–187	Simon II	

tack, he claimed for Egypt the satrapy of Transeuphrates, which included Syria and Palestine; in 320, he deposed its governor, Laomedon. This bold act, however, soon led to attacks from Asia Minor. Between 320 and 301 Ptolemy was forced to fight a series of battles with Antigonus, the satrap of Phrygia, and his son Demetrius; most of these battles took place at sea and along the coasts of Phoenicia, Asia Minor, and Greece. Palestine was also involved; but evidently the elephants and hoplites marched little through Judea and Jerusalem, following instead the roads to the west, south, and east. After Ptolemy's great victory at Gaza in 312, Judea and Jerusalem surrendered to him voluntarily (according to Agatharchides, a Greek chronicler who is quoted in Josephus *Ant.* xii. 5–7). Ptolemy then transferred many Jews and Samaritans to Egypt (Josephus *Ap.* i. 186), presumably carrying out his general policy of military and civilian colonization.[6] Antig-

---

[6] A. T. Olmstead, "Intertestamental Studies," *Journal of the American Oriental Society,* Vol. 56 (1936), pp. 242–57, esp. 243 f.

onus made several counterattacks, but Ptolemy defeated him once more in 306 on the coast of Egypt. Ptolemy then came forward publicly as king; he was hailed as *Sōtḗr,* "Savior," first by the island of Rhodes and then by other regions. He secured his hegemony over the Phoenician coast and, after his allies had overthrown Antigonus at Ipsos in 301, was recognized as master of Phoenicia and Palestine.

The fall of Antigonus was due in large part to another of the Diadochi: Seleucus I, who founded the Seleucid dynasty in Persia, Mesopotamia, and Syria. In 312, with the help of Ptolemy, he had consolidated his rule over Persia and Mesopotamia; this year became the basis of Seleucid chronology, and later of Maccabean. In 301 Seleucus was powerful enough, allied with others, to attack Antigonus. Because of his earlier dependence on Ptolemy, at the distribution of Antigonus' territory Seleucus could claim only Syria. There, in 300, he founded the city of Antioch on the Orontes to strengthen his position and promote commerce. Antioch developed into the greatest Hellenistic city besides Alexandria and Ephesus, and later became the first center for the Christian mission to the Gentiles. In the following period the Seleucids could not restrain their desire to expand toward the Mediterranean. As a consequence, during the course of the third century the successors of Ptolemy I had to fight five wars against the Seleucids. They were able to maintain hegemony over Palestine until 200 B.C., when they were decisively beaten. For the inhabitants of the Holy Land these five Syrian Wars were a frequent source of suffering, although many Jews probably benefited from the situation by serving as soldiers or suppliers.

Culturally, the time of the first Ptolemies represented a period of progress for Hellenism, which benefited even the Jews of the Diaspora. After the defeat of Antigonus in 301, Ptolemy I (openly called "king" after 306), followed by Ptolemy II (co-regent from 285 on and sole ruler after 283) and Ptolemy III (246–221), competing with the Seleucids, built up the ancient land of the Pharaohs until it was the wealthiest portion of the Hellenistic world. The entire land was property of the crown, with feudal lords and colonists, its bureaucratic, financial, and military organization tended to be inflexible, but the country was also a progressive environment for entrepreneurs and settlers. Jews and many others migrated to Egypt, where they also learned Greek. Hellenistic Alexandria thus became a counterpart of modern New York. Through the efforts of Ptolemy I and his successors, Egypt acquired the largest harbor, the strongest fleet, and the most widespread commerce of the Hellenistic world until the rise of Rome. Most important, though, the first Ptolemies aided the development of Hellenism as a spiritual and intellectual force. Ptolemy I personally wrote a biography of Alexander. Museion, the university he founded, with a library containing several hundred thousand scrolls, retained its position of leadership into the Christian era. According to the Jewish-Hellenistic Letter of Aristeas (iv. 10 f.), Ptolemy II ordered the writing of the Septuagint, the Greek translation of the Bible ascribed to seventy scholars. In any case, it is an historical fact that the cultural policies of the early Ptolemies promoted the development of Hellenistic Judaism, which later became extremely important. If the extant sources may be trusted, the acquisition of fantastic crown property by the Ptolemies and their receiving homage as gods at first caused more unhappiness in Athens than in Jerusalem.

B. Jerusalem under the Ptolemies

In itself, Judea had little strategic or commercial importance for Egypt; what was very important, on the other hand, was control of the nearby military and trade routes. This is demonstrated by the fact that Ptolemy II and others fortified and enlarged cities in the vicinity of the Holy Land. Ptolemy II turned Ptolemais (ancient Acco) into an important harbor. Gaza, on the Philistine plain, was of crucial importance for commerce as the terminus for the routes leading to Phoenicia and Arabia, a circumstance which military history also demonstrates. Petra, the Nabatean capital south of Judea, was adorned with monumental buildings in the style of

Egyptian Hellenism. The Nabateans, an Arabian people (simply called "Arabs" by the Bible and by Josephus), had penetrated into Edom-Idumea, Moab, and Ammon; during the Hellenistic period they controlled the caravan routes from Damascus and Syria and from Arabia to Gaza and Egypt. Products of the Orient like spices and cosmetics were transported through their territory. In addition, the Nabateans were brilliant mining engineers, and their aqueducts made possible a civilization that has never been surpassed in the area to the south of the Dead Sea. Ptolemy II Philadelphus built up the ancient city Rabbah of the Ammonites, calling it Philadelphia; it controlled the road to Damascus and Syria. Its great Hellenistic theater is still standing today. The city is now known as Amman, and is the capital of Jordan. The Ptolemies extended their policy of building Hellenistic cites even further in the direction of Damascus. Besides Philadelphia, several settlements in the Decapolis (a league of Greek commercial cities in Gilead and Bashan to the south and east of the Sea of Galilee) go back to these kings.

In contrast to these surrounding cities, one gains the impression that Judea itself was comparatively insignificant in the Empire of the Ptolemies, because most trade took place outside its borders and was channeled by the Nabateans through their own territory to the south and east. There may be some connection between this relative isolation and the religious exclusiveness of Ezra's and Nehemiah's orthodox successors.

Some of the Zenon Papyri from Egypt provide a concrete picture of conditions under Ptolemy II.[7] Zenon was an administrator under the Ptolemaic treasury minister. In his official capacity he traveled through Palestine from the end of 260 to the beginning of 258 B.C. He traveled from Gaza through Idumea and came to Ammonitis by way of Jerusalem and Jericho. In Ammonitis he conducted business with a

---

[7] C. C. Edgar, Zenon Papyri, Vol. 1 (1925), Nos. 59003–05, 59075 f. For a bibliography on this great corpus of papyri, see Claire Préaux, Les Grecs en Egypte d'après les archives de Zenon (1947), pp. 87–91.

certain Tobias. He then visited the Decapolis and traveled through northern Galilee to Ptolemais, finally returning by way of Gaza. Judea was of little interest to him. His actual route took him only through the neighboring regions, and he had Nabateans in his company.[8] Zenon seems to have attached particular importance to the wealthy Tobias in the land of Ammon, who appears in the correspondence as a large landowner, businessman, and tax collector. Josephus describes him as the brother-in-law of the Jerusalem high priest (*Ant.* xii. 160). He was probably a descendant of Tobiah, the Ammonite pasha who intrigued against Nehemiah (Neh. 2:10; *et passim*). In the pre-Maccabean period, the financial house of the Tobiads were prominent as powerful champions of Hellenism (see below pp. 48, 50–53). The ruins of their ancestral palace, called Tyros, between Jericho and Philadelphia (Josephus *Ant.* xii. 233), are still impressive today.[9] The representatives of the Ptolemaic kingdom preferred to deal with liberal semi-Jews of this sort rather than the representatives of Nehemiah's heritage.

Judea lay in the midst of this sphere of Egyptian interest like a sacred enclave; the high priests governed it with considerable autonomy. As in the days of Nehemiah, it remained a relatively unmolested sacerdotal state. The high priests were merely required to pay a tax to the crown on behalf of the people and the land; according to Josephus, this tax amounted to twenty talents per year (*Ant.* xii. 158). The legal status of the land is to be understood as follows: Ptolemaic Egypt was divided into crown lands, temple lands, feudal lands, and, to a lesser extent, privately owned lands.[10] The two categories of temple lands and feudal lands comprised the estates that the king, as owner, had "made over" to someone else for management.[11] Temple lands were en-

---

[8] F. M. Abel, *Histoire de la Palestine depuis la conquête d'Alexandre jusqu'à l'invasion arabe*, Vol. 1 (1952), p. 69, note 2.

[9] 'Araq el-emir, as the central complex is called in Arabic, was discovered in 1818 by two British naval officers, C. L. Irby and J. Mangles; see their *Travels in Egypt and Nubia, Syria, and the Holy Land* (1844), p. 146.

[10] L. Mitteis and U. Wilcken, *Grundzüge und Chrestomathie der Papyruskunde*, Vol. 1, 1 (1912; reprinted 1963), pp. 270–86.

[11] Greek, *gē en aphései*: Wilcken (cited in preceding note), p. 271.

trusted to the appropriate sacral authorities, feudal lands to deserving individuals. Judea was treated as temple land; it remained in principle the property of the deity, which the king as representative of the deity had graciously ceded to the appropriate sacral authorities. On this basis, the high priest had to pay the taxes levied by the crown out of his own resources; what he in turn demanded of the people was his own affair.

C. Ptolemy IV, Ptolemy V, and the Decline of Egypt

Toward the end of the third century, coinciding with the rise of Syria, Egypt began to decline in power. Against all expectations, Ptolemy IV (221–204), an art lover and woman chaser, was able to assert his hegemony over Palestine against the power-hungry Antiochus III (222–187) in the battle of Raphia in 217. But the government and upper class of the Ptolemaic Empire were already showing signs of disintegration. The Jewish high priest Onias II stopped paying the annual tax (Josephus *Ant.* xii. 158). Ptolemy thereupon threatened to make Judea a military fief (*ibid.,* 159). One of the Tobiads named Joseph, a brilliant financier, prevented this from happening by personally paying the tax, not only for Judea, but also for northern Palestine and Phoenicia (*ibid.,* 175). Although the population naturally had to compensate him handsomely, the Jews enjoyed twenty-two years of prosperity until the death of Joseph in 187 B.C. (*ibid.,* 186, 224). One should also remember that the surrounding territory had already been thoroughly hellenized (see above). Religiously speaking, of course, this represented a deficit; Judea lost its special sacral status. Under the control of the tax guarantor, the Ptolemaic temple land looked like any other secular feudal land, all the more so because the people were prospering. It is therefore easy to see how, in the altercations to follow, Judea came to be treated as a purely political entity, the constant object of Antiochus III's aspirations. In 200 B.C. (198 according to a previously accepted chronology), during the Fifth Syrian War, Antiochus defeated the commander-in-chief of Ptolemy V (who was still in his minority) at Paneas, the Caesarea Philippi of the New Testament, near the source of the Jordan, and incorporated Palestine into the Seleucid Empire.

3. SYRIAN HEGEMONY 200–142 B.C.

> [They] shall take away the continual burnt offering. And they shall set up the abomination that makes desolate.
>
> Daniel 11:31

What the eleventh chapter of Daniel tells of the exploits of the king of the south and the king of the north (Dan. 11:5–15) refers to the Ptolemies and the Seleucids down to the battle of Paneas in 200 B.C. The following section of the book deals with the "glorious land" under the Seleucids down to the period of forced hellenization under Antiochus IV (Dan. 11:16–39), whose end is predicted as a sign of the eschaton (Dan. 11:40–45). There is also a hint of the Maccabean revolt (Dan. 11:34), which in 142 B.C. led to Judea's relative independence from the royal house of Syria, now split into a Seleucus line and an Antiochus line.

The table on page 50 lists the rulers and dignitaries of Palestine during the Seleucid period.

A. Antiochus III, Seleucus IV, and Antiochus IV

About 200 B.C., Antiochus III stood at the height of his power. He had fought successfully against the Armenians and the Parthians. Like Alexander, he had even invaded India and been accorded the name "the Great." Now he was impatient to advance westward as well, since he felt called to be defender of Hellenism and protector of the Greeks. His decisive victory at Paneas in 200 and the subsequent withdrawal of the Egyptians from Palestine made it possible for Antiochus to continue his conquests once more into Asia Minor, whence he could then advance upon Thrace and Macedonia. For this reason the Jews, who had surrendered their capital to Antiochus' commander (Polybius *Histories* xvi. 39. 4), were respected politically; their cult was even

Ptolemies:	Seleucids:	Antiochids:	High priests:	Freedom fighters:
Ptolemy V, 205–180	Antiochus III, 222–187		Onias III, to 174	
Ptolemy VI, 180–145	*Seleuco- Demetrids:* Seleucus IV, 187–175			
Ptolemy VIII (brother of Ptolemy VI), coregent 170–164		Antiochus IV, 175–164	Jason I, 174–171	Mattathias, 167–166
Sole ruler 164–163 (afterwards in Cyrene)		Antiochus V, 164–162	Menelaus, 171–161	Judas Maccabeus, 166–160
	Demetrius I, 162–150		Alcimus, 161–159	
		Alexander Balas, rival king 153, sole king 150–145	152–143.....Jonathan, 160–143	
Ptolemy VII, 145				
Ptolemy VIII, sole ruler once more 145–116	Demetrius II, 145–138 (and again 129–125)	Antiochus VI, rival king 145–142	142–134.....Simon, 143–134	

supported (II Macc. 3:2; Josephus *Ant.* xii. 138–146). In addition, Antiochus made the young Ptolemy V his son-in-law and let the income from Palestine continue to flow into the Ptolemaic treasury. The Tobiad Joseph was responsible for paying the tax (see p. 48). Antiochus, however, made a fatal error: his claims in Asia Minor and Hellas, as well as his collaboration with Hannibal, provoked the Romans and led to a violent counterattack. Antiochus was forced out of Hellas and then, in 190 B.C., was defeated at Magnesia in Lydia by Scipio Asiaticus. He was sentenced to pay enormous reparations over the course of twelve years. Thus the wealthy house of the Seleucids suddenly found itself ruined. Antiochus tried to retain his financial position by confiscating temples, which were the central banks of that period; but he was slain at Elymais during one of these episodes.

Seleucus IV (187–175), his son and successor, inherited the huge war debt. It is not surprising that he, too, coveted the rich treasury of the Jerusalem Temple. Besides, the long period of prosperity under Joseph had made Judea a desirable object of taxation (see above, p. 48). Now, however, the temple bank was responsible for the money of the Tobiad Hyrcanus (II Macc. 3:11), the former outcast of the family, who occupied the family palace in Transjordan (p . 47), controlled the surrounding Nabateans, and represented the interests of Egypt (Josephus *Ant.* xii. 186–235). This circumstance, together with a popular demonstration in Jerusalem, caused the Syrian chancellor Heliodorus to forgo the planned confiscation; the Jews celebrated their deliverance as a miracle (II Macc. 3:1–40). Later Heliodorus murdered Seleucus IV, intending to take over the government himself.

In order to rescue the dynasty, Antiochus IV Epiphanes (175–164 B.C.), a brother of the murdered king, hastily made himself king of Syria. After the battle of Magnesia, he had lived in Rome as a hostage. He was captivated by the city, particularly the Hellenism cultivated in diplomatic circles there, reminiscent of the later spirit of the Renaissance. The crown prince (later King Demetrius I), who was not yet of age, had just been brought to Rome as a hostage in place of his uncle. During the journey back to Syria, Antiochus heard of Heliodorus' attempt to seize control; he used the opportunity to usurp the throne in Antioch. Following his natural bent and his admiration for Hellenism, he sought to continue the expansionist policies of his father Antiochus III. From Ptolemy V he borrowed the surname Epiphanes, "manifest," to indicate that he was a manifestation of the deity. Strongly reinforcing a tradition of the Seleucids, he required men to worship him as Olympian Zeus (II Macc. 6:2; also on coins), thereby giving a special Western emphasis to his imperialism and Hellenism. Unlike his father, he was always careful to keep on good terms with Rome and its allies in Asia Minor. The immediate goal of Antiochus IV was to seize control of Egypt, which had lost most of its power. His brother-in-law and sister in Egypt had died and could no longer claim the income from the taxes mentioned above (p. 50).

Naturally the Jews became involved in the struggle, since Antiochus IV needed money for his Egyptian campaigns and also because Judea was an important staging area. Neither reason was anything new in the history of Israel, Judah, and Judaism. In his enthusiasm for Hellenism and in his efforts to unify his empire (I Macc. 1:41), however, he made use of cultural and religious coercion such as had long ago been employed by the Babylonians and Assyrians, but not by the Persians and only to a limited extent by Alexander and his Epigoni. The traditional Jewish cult was to be replaced by a new state cult, the Levitic ordinances by a Hellenistic way of life. Antiochus himself and his counselors certainly looked upon this hellenization of Judea as a comparatively simple matter. The temple lands, of limited extent, were surrounded by Hellenistic regions (cf. the letters of Zenon, pp. 46 f. above); there had long been important men who were collaborators, like the brothers of the high priests (p. 26) and the Tobiads (p. 47); ever since Joseph had taken over responsibility for paying the taxes, Judea had for all practical purposes lost its status as a sacral enclave (p. 48). Quite surprisingly, however, Antiochus' attempts to impose hellenization called forth an heroic reaction on the part of those who remained faithful to the Jewish law. These men began a bitter struggle to preserve the conditions that had developed during the Persian period and had been preserved under the Ptolemies. In Antiochus Epiphanes they saw the worst tyrant of history (Dan. 11:36), while they naturally hoped for an Egyptian victory (II Macc. 5:4).

Antiochus IV undertook his projected hellenization of the Ptolemaic temple land, Judea, a few years before he was ready to march against Egypt. Onias III, the conservative Zadokite high priest, had a progressive-minded brother named Jason, who was an ardent Hellenist and suggested certain hellenizing measures to the King. In 174 B.C., sure that he had found the proper collaborator, Antiochus installed Jason as high priest. Jason thereupon built a gymnasium and an ephebeum below the citadel of the Temple in Jerusalem (II Macc. 4:9). The gymnasium and the ephebeum were establishments for academic sports, music, and military exercises; every ambitious city of the Hellenistic world possessed them. The main participants in such exercises, the ephebi, may be thought of as students who carried weapons and were adherents of a fraternal movement that had begun in Attica but later became international. In particular, the new educational institutions were to gain for the upper class of Jerusalem Hellenistic isopolity in Antioch (II Macc. 4:9, 19; on citizenship in the Hellenistic world, see pp. 38 f.). Now, to the horror of traditionalists, fashionable students turned up everywhere in the characteristic uniform of the Attic ephebi: a broad-brimmed hat (Greek *pétasos,* similar to a Boy Scout hat), a short riding cloak (Greek *chlamús*), and bare legs (which the long Oriental cloak, by contrast, covered decorously). On parade, they carried a lance and a small shield.[12] Reportedly even priests were such enthusiastic spectators at the athletic fields that they would leave the altar and run to the discus when they heard the starting signal (II Macc. 4:14). Jason eagerly arranged a magnificent torchlight procession in honor of Antiochus Epiphanes when the latter made a propaganda visit to Jerusalem before his planned campaign in Egypt. Jason's interest in sports and festivities was purely cultural, however, and in the long run failed to satisfy the aggressive policies of Syria. In 171, Jason was replaced by Menelaus, the brother of a high temple official (see below, p. 148). Menelaus, who was not a priest, had more desire and resources to play politics. With the support of the Tobiads this blatant opportunist purchased the venerable office of high priest from the incarnate Zeus, who had military expenses to worry about. This sharp transaction was to their mutual advantage: the King gained an unscrupulous tool, and Menelaus could rule over his countrymen.

From 170 to 168 Antiochus engaged in the Sixth Syro-Egyptian War, in the course of which he twice marched against Egypt. During the first attack, in 170–169, the eastern

---

[12] For an illustration, see C. Daremberg and E. Saglio (eds.), *Dictionnaire des antiquitées,* Vol. 2 (1892), p. 630.

border fortress of Pelusium, the ancient capital of Memphis, and most of Egypt fell to him; he treated Ptolemy VI as his vassal. The new capital of Alexandria, however, where the Greeks had made the younger brother Ptolemy VIII king, was able to withstand the Seleucid troops. Since the attacker did not want to risk too much, and because of reported unrest in Judea and Phoenicia, he withdrew. Jerusalem was a hotbed of unrest, because Jason was on the point of deposing Menelaus. Antiochus suppressed Jason, confiscated the Temple treasure, and appointed magistrates in Jerusalem and upon Gerizim to strengthen Menelaus' position (I Macc. 1:16–28; II Macc. 5:11–23). In 168, in his second attack upon Egypt, Antiochus marched against Alexandria with even stronger forces, furious at the temporary collaboration between the two Ptolemies. Then "ships of Kittim" arrived (Dan. 11:30): at Eleusis, the eastern suburb of Alexandria, the Roman legate C. Popilius Laenas confronted the King. He handed Antiochus an ultimatum from the Senate (Polybius *Histories* xxix. 2. 1–4), arrogantly drew a circle about him with his staff, and forced him to retire from his campaign on the spot (*ibid.*, 27. 1–8). Antiochus had to retreat to Syria within a specified time, "groaning with displeasure but temporarily yielding to circumstances" (*ibid.*, 27. 9). He was convinced by several factors: the memory of the Roman victory over his father at Magnesia (190 B.C.) and of his own years as a hostage in Rome, and even more the news, which he had just received, of the Roman victory over Macedonia at Pydna (168 B.C.).[13]

B. Religious Oppression

For reasons of political prestige, Antiochus IV next determined to make sure of Palestine's loyalty to himself. Since he claimed to be Zeus Epiphanes, this amounted to a cultic hellenization of the land and the people. For purposes of foreign policy this was not an unreasonable idea, the more so because conservative priests sympathized with Egypt, but progressive capitalists with Syria (Josephus *Bell.* i. 32). One

[13] On the Sixth Syrian War, see H. Volkmann, "Ptolemaios," in *PRE*, Vol. 23 (1959), cols. 1705–10.

must remember that, culturally, the ground had already been prepared for hellenization and that Antiochus had adorned such important cities as Athens and Babylon with Hellenistic monuments. The king was admittedly not a real "Epiphanes"; but the derisive epithet Epimanes ("madman") given him by a well-known supporter of the Romans (Polybius *Histories* xxvi. 1. 1) seems completely unjustified. Maccabean propaganda against the measures taken by Antiochus overlooked the fact that later, under Hyrcanus I, the Jews themselves took strong measures against Idumea and Samaria. Nevertheless, the reign of Antiochus IV definitely marked a break with the policy of religious freedom that had still prevailed under Antiochus III. The result was a religious war that was quite understandable from the Jewish point of view but was to have unforeseen historical consequences.

In 167, as his first move, Antiochus arranged for a military parade on the Sabbath along the north wall of Jerusalem. The troops then marched into the city by surprise, where they occupied and fortified the citadel called the Acra (later the Antonia) at the high northwest corner of the Temple area.[14] This Syrian garrison with its change of guards was long to remain a source of vexation to the Jews (I Macc. 1:29–40; II Macc. 5:24–26) until it could finally be removed in the year 141 (see below p. 65).

In addition, there was a religious outrage that seemed even more vexatious to the conservatives: in order to reinforce the unity of his kingdom (I Macc. 1:41), in 167 Antiochus Epiphanes commanded that observance of the Jewish law cease and ceremonies of the Hellenistic cult be instituted (I Macc. 1:44–53; II Macc. 6:1–9). This religio-political action was not at all intended to be anti-Semitic, but rather anti-Egyptian and pro-Syrian. The contemporary situation and the way in which the order was carried out prove this point beyond all doubt:

(1) An Athenian senator was appointed to direct the

---

[14] According to I Maccabees 1:33—2:31, the "city of David" was the site of the Syrian stronghold. Schürer, Vol. 1 (1901), pp. 198 f., therefore located it upon Ophel, the southeast hill of Jerusalem. Ophel, however, is not strategically suitable; it falls away toward the south from the temple area. I Maccabees probably refers quite generally to the temple hill.

changeover (II Macc. 6:1) ; he probably had the status of a royal Syrian high priest and specialist in the Eleusinian mysteries or the like. Religio-politically, his mission was formally analogous to the earlier mission of Ezra; now, however, the point was to replace the Jewish cult with Hellenistic sacrificial worship. As was usual in Hellenistic religious politics, the government made use of local collaborators for its cultic propaganda (I Macc. 1:51). The Hasmonean high priests of the Jews were later to proceed in similar fashion.

(2) The sources stress the following details of the state cult: (*a*) An altar of Zeus Olympios was set up upon the altar of sacrifice at Jerusalem; sacrifice was offered there on the twenty-fifth of every month, starting with the twenty-fifth of Chislev (December), 167 B.C. (I Macc. 1:54, 59; II Macc. 6:1, 7). Since the twenty-fifth of the month was celebrated as the birthday of Epiphanes, these sacrifices were actually offered to him. Apocalyptic literature called this altar of Zeus "the abomination that makes desolate" (Dan. 11:31; 12:11; Hebrew *šiqqûṣ šômēm,* suggesting the name Baal Shamayim instead of Zeus Olympios; Matt. 24:15 and parallels contain a Greek translation of the Hebrew). The period of the abomination (three years, according to I Macc.; cf. p. 58) was represented as an eschatological period of three and a half years or half a week of years (Dan. 7:25; *et passim*). Hellenistic altars were built and Hellenistic sacrifices instituted in other parts of Judea also (I Macc. 1:47, 54). The Samaritan temple on Gerizim was dedicated to Zeus Xenios (II Macc. 6:2). At the same time, Diaspora Jews living in Syrian cities were forced to take part in the state cult (II Macc. 6:8). (*b*) Besides sacrifices to Zeus, our sources also mention, interestingly, feasts of Dionysus (II Macc. 6:7). These would have involved the sacrifice of pigs; here we may have the religio-historical background of the sacrifice of swine's flesh mentioned with such loathing in I Maccabees 1:47. Probably the Athenian mentioned above was specially responsible for these fertility mysteries; but their institution evidently had anti-Egyptian overtones as well, since Ptolemy IV, who bore an ivy-leaf tattoo, had just declared the worship of Dionysus to be the national religion of Egypt.

(3) The specific purpose of these cultic changes was to blazon forth the supremacy of Antiochus and his gods over Palestine, which had formerly belonged to the Ptolomies. The point was not only to secure possession of the land for Syria, but to win the people's support for the system. In addition, the cultic repression was intended to enable the Syrian government to give portions of the (hitherto protected) temple land in fee to officers and soldiers (I Macc. 3:36). This practice, called "cleruchy," was the usual method of military payment at that time.

C. MACCABEUS, JONATHAN, AND SIMON

> Judas Maccabeus and all his brothers . . . gladly fought for Israel.
>
> I Maccabees 3:1–2

To some extent the Syrian government had achieved success among the Jews with the endeavors outlined above. "But the people who know their God shall stand firm and take action" (Dan. 11:32). The alien religious forms that Antiochus sought to introduce also provoked a popular reaction that demonstrates the profound effects of the restoration achieved by Nehemiah and the Levites.

In the cultural struggle that followed, those who were faithful to the law found energetic leaders in the family of Mattathias, a priest from Modein (northwest of Jerusalem, halfway to the sea), who had five sons. Later literature often calls the family the Maccabees on account of the most famous brother, Judas Maccabeus (Greek *makkabaîos,* which probably does not derive from Hebrew *maqqebet,* "hammer," but from an unknown Aramaic word). Contemporaries, however, called Judas' successors the Hasmoneans on account of an alleged ancestor by the name of Hasmon (Josephus *Ant.* xi. 111; *et passim*). In contrast to the Tobiads, the Maccabeans were a rural family of priests, rich but not aristocratic (I Macc. 2:1), who rejected the Hellenistic-Syrian hegemony. In the ensuing struggle Mattathias and his sons were to have great success; his descendants even achieved the status of high priest and king.

In 167 B.C., Mattathias slew a Jew who was going to offer sacrifice at the heathen altar out of deference to the emissaries of the Syrian cult, who were also slain (I Macc. 2:23–26). He thereby violated the privilege of asylum claimed for cultic sites. With his five sons he fled to the desert of Judah, where guerilla groups formed to fight the Hellenists. They were joined by the Hasidim or Hasideans ("the Pious"), who were devoted to the law (I Macc. 2:42) [see below, p. 67].

Mattathias died in 166, but his third son, Judas Maccabeus, took over leadership of the revolt and continued as its organizer until his death in 160. "He was like a lion in his deeds" (I Macc. 3:4). Not an outstanding religious personality but an imposing military and political figure, he has with good reason become a Jewish national hero.

Antiochus IV was campaigning against the Parthians, and so Lysias, the military governor in the west, had to put down the Jewish rebellion. Lysias was neither willing nor able to commit any sizable forces. In surprise guerilla attacks Judas defeated Syrian units at Samaria, Beth-horon, Emmaus, and Beth-zur (I Macc. 3:10—4:35). He next purified the Jerusalem Temple of the Zeus cult, "the abomination that makes desolate" (see above p. 56). Three years (not three and a half) after the beginning of the abomination, on 25 Chislev (December) 164, he restored the Levitical cult (I Macc. 4:36–58). The date has ever since been celebrated as Hanukkah or the Rededication of the Temple (I Macc. 4:59; John 10:22).[15]

When the King died suddenly in Persia in 164 (I Macc. 6:1–16), Lysias made himself guardian of Antiochus V, then only ten years old (164–162), and undertook to punish the Jewish insurgents severely. He attacked from Idumea, de-

---

[15] On the problem of dating, see W. Kolbe, *Beiträge zur syrischen und jüdischen Geschichte* (1926), pp. 28–42; W. Eichrodt, *Theologie der Gegenwart*, Vol. 20 (1926), p. 265; J. Schaumberger, "Die neue Seleukiden-Liste BM 35603 und die makkabäische Chronologie," *Biblica*, Vol. 31 (1955), pp. 423–35, esp. 434; R. Hanhart, "Zur Zeitrechnung des I und II Makkabäerbuches," in *Zeitschrift für die alttestamentliche Wissenschaft*, Supplementary Vol. 88 (1964), pp. 49–96, esp. 79–84, 93. Hanhart figures the period of the "abomination" as follows (pp. 83 f.): beginning in summer, 167 B.C., lasting about three and a half years (Dan. 7:25; *et al.*), and ending on 14 December, 164.

feated Judas Maccabeus at Beth-Zechariah (southwest of Jerusalem), and laid siege to the capital (I Macc. 6:28–54). The Jews' salvation came in the person of Philip, a rival claimant to the Syrian throne who marched upon Syria from Persia. Lysias had to hasten back to Antioch. To strengthen his position on the southern flank, he had the young King guarantee the Jews religious freedom; they were forced, however, to tear down the walls of Jerusalem (I Macc. 6:55–63).

Soon afterward, an extremely determined Seleucid brought about the downfall of Judas Maccabeus. Demetrius I (162–150), son of Seleucus IV, had been forced while still in his minority to take the place of his uncle Antiochus IV as a hostage in Rome (see above p. 51). He quite rightly considered Antiochus IV and Antiochus V usurpers. In Rome he associated with Hellenistic intellectuals and reformers, primarily the Gracchi, Polybius, and the Scipios, all the while awaiting his chance. Upon the advice of these friends, Demetrius ignored the conservative senate and, in 162, went suddenly to Antioch, overthrew the government, and claimed the throne of his father. He immediately took into his protection the Palestinian Hellenists who came for an audience, and three times sent armies to invade the Holy Land. At the first attack, in 161, a high priest named Alcimus was forced upon the Jews; he was of Aaronic descent, but ideologically a Hellenist. In the course of the second attack, Judas was able to defeat and slay the Syrian colonel Nicanor—on the so-called Day of Nicanor, which later became an annual Jewish festival. During the third attack, however, in 160, Judas went to his death in the terrible defeat at Elasa, near Beth-horon, northwest of Jerusalem (I Macc. 7:1—9:22). Temporarily the Hellenists had the situation under control (I Macc. 9:23–28).

The Syrian pressure, however, was not to last for long. Rome was displeased to see a strong ruler upon the Syrian throne. In accord with their general policy of *"divide et impera,"* the Romans in the following period played off Seleuco-Demetrids against Antiochids, that is, descendants of Seleucus IV and their supporters against descendants of Antiochus IV and theirs. They therefore welcomed a relatively independent status for the Jews. The heroes of the Macca-bean-Hasmonean family skillfully exploited this opportunity.

Egypt in turn supported the Jews against the Syrians whenever possible. Faced with the growing power of Demetrius I and the death of Judas, in 160 B.C. Ptolemy VI let the Egyptian Jews take over an ancient temple in Leontopolis and furnish it properly for their sacrificial cult (Josephus *Ant.* xiii. 70). A certain Onias, a Zadokite, was installed as high priest.[16] Aristobulus, a tutor and philosopher at Ptolemy's court, took charge of the necessary cultural propaganda (II Macc. 1:10; Eusebius *Praep.* xiii. 12). This Jewish temple remained in use for a long time, until the Romans finally closed it down A.D. 72 following the Jewish War (see below p. 289).

Judas' immediate successor was Jonathan, the fifth and youngest brother, who led the nationalists from 160 to 143 B.C. (I Macc. 9:28—12:53). At first he had to be content with being a leader of guerrilla bands in the desert, until he became a sort of judge of the people at Michmash, north of Jerusalem (I Macc. 9:73). Gradually, however, Syrian pressure decreased, because a competitor distracted Demetrius I, namely, Alexander Balas (Baal), who claimed to be an Antiochid and who had the support of the Roman senate. Jonathan hastened to support the newcomer. The two competitors outdid each other with contributions to the Jews, who considered it more promising to continue to support Alexander. They were rewarded: in 152, Jonathan could appear at the Feast of Booths as high priest and commander of mercenaries (I Macc. 10:21).

The struggle to preserve the Jews' freedom of religion and the Levitical temple-state thus became a matter of preserving the Hasmonean dynasty, as Judas' successors were called. Jonathan and the other Hasmoneans fought to extend the rule of their house and their people beyond the borders of the Jewish state. This process began, as was noted earlier,

[16] Schürer, Vol. 3 (1903), pp. 97–100.

when Jonathan, who belonged to a priestly family (I Macc. 2:1) but was not a Zadokite, became high priest in the year 152. The next step took place in 150 B.C., at Ptolemais, where Alexander Balas and Ptolemy VI of Egypt (who then supported Alexander) allowed Jonathan to don purple robes (I Macc. 10:62), an intimation of the royal dignity the Hasmoneans were later to claim (pp. 67–75).

In the following decade, Jonathan achieved great political and strategic gains. He cleverly exploited the competition between Demetrius II and Antiochus VI, the sons of Demetrius I and Alexander Balas. He gained the support of Ptolemy VI, Rome, and Sparta. He acquired some territory from one party and other territory from the other. Money began to flow into his treasury, and his brother Simon gained control of the important coastal plain (I Macc. 11:59). Finally Jonathan and his army of mercenaries ruled over a land that even included non-Jewish regions and fortified cities (I Macc. 12:31–38).

Jonathan's fall, however, was inevitable; for Trypho, the Syrian field marshal who was the power behind Antiochus VI, found the Jewish high priest had grown too powerful. In 143, Trypho defeated Jonathan at Beth-shean (Scythopolis), took him prisoner, and later had him executed (I Macc. 12:39–53).

Leadership of the Jewish resistance passed to Simon, the second oldest of the Maccabean brothers (I Macc. 13:1–16, 17). He led the Jews from 143 to 134 B.C., and, like Jonathan, achieved political and military success. Since the party of Antiochus VI had brought about the fall of his brother, Simon naturally sought an alliance with his competitor, Demetrius II, who granted the Jews tax-exempt status in 142 B.C.

The three most important achievements of the Maccabees are each associated with one of the brothers and came at intervals of about ten years:

> Judas gained freedom of religion in 162 B.C.
> Jonathan became high priest in 152 B.C.
> Simon achieved tax exemption in 142 B.C.

Most important, the history of Judea under the Maccabees and the early Hasmoneans exhibits a gradual advance toward political autonomy. For the first time since the fall of Jerusalem in 597 B.C., thanks to their exemption from taxes, the Jews in 142 B.C. constituted once more an independent state, although the great powers surrounding them could still exert pressure. A new period began, that of seventy-nine years of freedom under Hasmonean rule.

III

THE HASMONEAN RULE

142–63 B.C.

> Thus the yoke of the Gentiles
> was removed from Israel, and the
> people began to write in their
> documents and contracts, "In
> the first year of Simon, the great
> high priest and commander and
> leader of the Jews."
>
> I Maccabees 13:41 f.

THE year 142 B.C. marked the achievement of tax exemption for the Jews (I Macc. 13:39; Josephus *Ant.* xiii. 213), and so they used it as the base for a new chronology (I Macc. 13:42). Simon issued coinage in Jerusalem with the new dates and a legend in Hebrew. Hebrew was also cultivated as the official and cultic language, although Aramaic and Greek continued to dominate everyday life. This Hebrew renaissance is reflected in the literature, particularly in the documents found in the Qumran library (see below pp. 171 f.). The table on page 64 provides a political outline of the new epoch.

1. RULE BY HIGH PRIESTS 142–105 B.C.

A. SIMON AS HIGH PRIEST

Simon, leader of the people since 143, obviously had his own financial resources to draw on, out of which he generously provided arms and the money necessary for diplomacy (I Macc. 13:16; 14:32). He supported a motley army of mercenaries that included some Hellenists; it was far

Ptolemies:	*Seleucids:*		*Hasmoneans:*
	(Seleuco-Demetrids on the left)	(Antiochids on the right)	
Ptolemy VIII (reigned previously 164–163), 145–116	Demetrius II, 145–138 (reigned afterwards 129–125)	Antiochus VI, 145–143	Simon (popular leader from 143), high priest 142–134
		Tryphon, 143–138	
	Antiochus VII, 138–129		Hyrcanus I, high priest 134–105
	Demetrius II (reigned previously, 145–138), 129–125		
		Alexander Zabinas, 128–122	
	Seleucus V, 125		
Ptolemy IX, 116–107 (reigned afterwards 88–80)	Antiochus VIII, 125–113 (reigned afterwards 111–96)		
Cleopatra III, 107–101	Antiochus IX, 113–95 (111–95 in Coele-Syria)		Aristobulus I, king in 104
Ptolemy X, 101–88	Antiochus VIII (reigned previously 125–113), 111–96		Alexander Janneus, king 103–76
Ptolemy IX (reigned previously 116–107), 88–80	Antiochus X against 5 sons of Antiochus VIII, 95–83 [1]		
Ptolemy XII, 80–58, 55–51	(Tigranes ruled Syria 83–69)		Alexandra, queen 76–67
	Antiochus XIII, 69–65		Hyrcanus II, king in 67
	(Pompey occupied Syria in 64)		Aristobulus II, king 66–63

from adhering exclusively to the ideal of Levitical purity. This army helped Simon gain various objectives. Most important, his troops captured Gazara, the former Gezer, for him (I Macc. 13:43–48). Situated on the edge of the rich coastal plain, this city was now Hellenistic. Simon judaized the city by force and put John Hyrcanus, his son, in charge as military governor. Simon even advanced as far as the port

[1] Of the five sons of Antiochus VIII, Demetrius III, who ruled Damascus from 95 to 87, intervened actively in Jewish history (see below, p. 72).

of Joppa (I Macc. 13:11; 14:5). In 141 he removed the
Syrian garrison that had occupied the Acra since the time of
Antiochus IV (13:49–52) and fitted out the fortress as his
palace. Politically, it should be noted, Simon immediately
strengthened the alliances that had been entered into with
Sparta and Rome (I Macc. 14:16–24). The Holy Land thus
became once more a dynamic factor in the political life of
the Near East, which it had not been since the period of the
monarchy. Even during Simon's rule it is possible to speak of
an Hasmonean state, although Judea was still dependent in
principle upon Syria. The Seleuco-Demetrids were engaged
in a constant struggle with the Antiochids (see the table);
each party found it necessary to guarantee the Jewish privileges. Syria's power was obviously declining, while Rome
became more and more influential and the Parthians made
repeated incursions. With the help of Rome and Sparta,
Judea remained relatively independent of the Syrian rulers.

In 140 B.C., the Jews rewarded Simon for what he had done
by acclaiming him high priest, general, and ethnarch ("ruler
of a people," somewhat like a grand duke) for eternity. This
proclamation was immortalized by being engraved on bronze
tablets upon Mount Zion (I Macc. 14:25–49); it was approved by the Roman senate (I Macc. 15:15–24; Josephus
Ant. xiv. 145–48).[2] The "eternal" duration of Simon's
priestly, military, and civil office referred to his family. A new
dynasty had been enthroned, the priestly house of the
Hasmonean princes. The first Hasmonean to claim royal
status was Simon's grandson, but Simon himself appeared on
Mount Zion, in the Temple and in his palace, with the
sumptuous display appropriate to the founder of a dynasty
(I Macc. 15:32 speaks of gold and silver vessels and a crowd
of attendants). He was in a good position to resist the demands of the new Seleucid, Antiochus VII, and mount further attacks upon the Philistine cities (I Macc. 15:25—
16:10).

[2] The passage in Josephus refers to Simon, as is shown by Schürer, Vol. 1
(1901), pp. 250–53; cf. R. Marcus in *Josephus with an English Translation*,
Vol. 7 (1943), p. 524.

In the fashion of Oriental Hellenism, Simon, the patriar-chal capitalist, and two of his sons were murdered at a ban-quet near Jericho by one of his sons-in-law, who was in league with Antiochus VII (I Macc. 16:11–20). The assassin, however, failed to kill John Hyrcanus, Simon's second son, who was military governor of Gazara (I Macc. 16:21 f.). Hyrcanus fled to Jerusalem, where the people gave him refuge from the attack of his brother-in-law and made him high priest (Josephus *Ant.* xiii. 229 f.).

B. HYRCANUS I

Hyrcanus I, who had already gone through his military apprenticeship, was destined to lead his people for many years (134–105 B.C.) and win a great reputation as a military leader and conqueror (Josephus *Ant.* xiii. 229–300). During the early years of his rule, however, he was confronted with enormous difficulties in the realm of foreign relations and was almost deposed. Antiochus VII sought at once to assert his claims to supremacy in Palestine against Hyrcanus I. These claims had been rejected by Simon but supported by Simon's son-in-law. Antiochus recaptured Joppa and Gazara, and held Jerusalem under siege for a con-siderable period. The capital had already capitulated when the Romans forbade Antiochus from encroaching upon their allies (Josephus *Ant.* xiii. 259–66).[3] In 130, Antiochus had to embark on a campaign against the Parthians, in the course of which he died (129 B.C.). Demetrius II was released from captivity by the Parthians and once more ascended the Syr-ian throne; but the situation confronting him was so turbu-lent that he could not begin to think of a show of strength against Hyrcanus.

After the Syrian throne changed hands, Hyrcanus I con-tinued his father's conquests without delay. He took Me-daba, a fortified city in Transjordan, from which he was in a position to disrupt Nabatean commerce. In 128 B.C., he at-tacked Shechem and destroyed the temple of Mount Gerizim (see above, p. 28). He also compelled the pagan Idumeans, who because of Nabatean pressure in Edom had invaded

[3] Schürer, Vol. 1 (1901), p. 261.

southern Judah, to accept circumcision. Finally, in the year 109, Hyrcanus and his sons conquered Samaria, strongly fortified though it was. This took place only after a pitched battle against supporting troops from Egypt and Syria. On the other hand, Hyrcanus had the support of Cleopatra III, the Egyptian queen mother (called sarcastically in Greek "the Red"), who had Jewish sympathies. Samaria, which had been a center first of Persian and then of Hellenistic culture, was destroyed at Hyrcanus' command (Josephus *Ant.* xiii. 254–258, 267–287).

This cruel treatment of Samaria provoked a reaction on the part of those faithful to the law (Josephus *Ant.* xiii. 288–99). Originally, the so-called Hasidim had supported the Maccabean brothers in the battle against Hellenism (see above, p. 58); but they soon had to realize that the policies of the Hasmoneans were taking a Hellenistic turn. Josephus unintentionally shows how the faithful supporters of the law, who had been called "Pharisees" since the time of Jonathan, at first remained on good terms with the Hasmoneans under Hyrcanus. Only after describing the capture of Samaria does the historian find occasion to report that the successes of Hyrcanus and his sons aroused a reaction on the part of the Pharisees and a rapprochement between Hyrcanus and the Sadducees, the party of the wealthy. Finally, however, the tension lessened (Josephus *Bell.* i. 67; *Ant.* xiii. 299). Even at this early date, then, many considered the hellenization and secularization of the high priesthood wrong. Later a permanent rift developed between the Hasmoneans and Pharisees (see below, pp. 71 f.).

Hyrcanus I did not call himself king but stressed the dignity of his position by putting his name at the beginning of the inscriptions on coins. Besides his civil and priestly office, the office of prophet was also ascribed to him (Josephus *Bell.* i. 68 f.; *Ant.* xiii. 299 f.).

2. KINGS 104–63 B.C.

A. ARISTOBULUS I

After the death of Hyrcanus, his eldest son Aristobulus I was chosen to be high priest, while the dead man's widow was supposed to head the civil government. This high priest, however, imprisoned his mother and his brothers and let his mother starve to death. Aristobulus then ruled for a year, 104 B.C., beginning shortly before or after our present New Year's Day. He died suddenly—rumor said he was conscience-stricken because in the meantime he had also murdered one of his brothers. Aristobulus was the first of the Hasmoneans to call himself king in his dealings with other nations (Josephus *Ant.* xiii. 301). For the rest, he was considered friendly to Hellenism, so that Greek authors and Josephus describe him as having a kindly disposition (Josephus *Ant.* xiii. 319). This judgment is hard to reconcile with the acts of cruelty just described; possibly his character was ambivalent.

The most important event of Aristobulus' reign for religious history was his conquest of Galilee, which he judaized by compelling the people to be circumcised. Josephus, following his Greek authorities, describes what happened: Aristobulus "fought against the Itureans, annexed a large part of their land to Judea, and forced the inhabitants to submit to circumcision and live according to the laws of the Jews" (*Ant.* xiii. 318). He is speaking of the Jetureans (Gen. 25:15), who had formerly lived in Transjordan but now, because of the Nabateans, had retreated into the valley between the Lebanon and Hermon-Antilebanon. From this base, at the time of Aristobulus, the Itureans ruled Galilee. They were themselves under the rule of Antiochus IX, Cleopatra III's mortal enemy (see the table on p. 64). This explains Josephus' statement that Aristobulus conquered a part of the Iturean territory and judaized its inhabitants. Ever since the fall of Israel in 722 B.C., Galilee had remained under foreign control and had acquired a generally Aramaic population. None of the Jewish high priests or Hasmonean princes had hitherto been able to exert much influence upon Galilee. With the help of Cleopatra "the Red," Aristobulus succeeded in acquiring this territory for the Jews. In the years to come Galilee was always associated with Judea (Josephus *Ant.* xiii. 322; etc.), even after the death of

Herod, when it was partially subject to other control. Although the larger cities remained Hellenistic, the general population kept the Jewish laws that Aristobulus had forced upon them. The judaizing of the Gailileans, begun by Aristobulus, made constant progress, thanks to resettlement, the activity of the Pharisees, and the building of synagogues; eventually, in the first century of the Christian era, Galilee became the seedbed of the Zealot movement (see pp. 118, 136 f.) . Despite all his acts of cruelty, Aristobulus deserves the credit for having won the home of Jesus and of the first Apostles for the Old Testament faith.

B. JANNEUS

When Aristobulus I died suddenly, he left a widow, Salma or Salome Alexandra. For dynastic reasons, she was married by his oldest surviving brother, Alexander Janneus (Jonathan), who was king of the Jews from 103 to 76 B.C. (Josephus *Ant.* xiii. 320–404) . It was a leviratic marriage, through which the bridegroom, some thirteen years younger than his bride, became king. Following his death twenty-seven years later, Alexandra ruled alone for another nine years. This dynastic continuity demonstrates the influence of Hellenism upon Judaism and the later Hasmoneans, who quite openly promoted Hellenistic institutions. It was not for nothing that Alexander Janneus bore the name of the great Macedonian conqueror. With a desperate heroism rare even in this age of *condottieri* he fought for the power of the Hasmonean house and extended this power in a series of daring ventures, until it covered an area comparable only to the empire of David.

Here we must first take account of the great political and social events of the period, the more so because they were to have far-reaching effects on the future.

(1) Alexandria, still the greatest city of the world, generally dominated the first act of the history of Janneus' reign. The western quarter was inhabited by Egyptians, the center of the city by Greeks, and the eastern quarter by Jews. In the latter half of the second century, while Rome was extending

its power over Greece and Asia Minor, Ptolemy VIII, depending on the Romans, had indulged the growing number of Egyptians in the capital and ousted the leading Greeks. His pro-Roman testament was carried out by his energetic widow, Cleopatra III, "the Red." Ptolemy IX, her elder son, was popular with the Egyptians, but Cleopatra feared Egyptian nationalism; in 107 she got rid of Ptolemy IX by sending him to Cyprus as military governor and promoted instead her younger son, Ptolemy X. Cleopatra associated herself all the more closely with the Jews of Alexandria. With an eye to future military actions, she placed two sons of Onias, the Jewish priest at Leontopolis, in charge of her army and navy and, like the Jews, deposited her wealth at Cos, a banking island loyal to the Romans (Josephus *Ant.* xiii. 349 f.) .

Under these apparently favorable circumstances, Janneus decided in 103 B.C. to pursue the aggressive policies of his father and brother. He attacked Ptolemais, but was forced to retreat by Ptolemy IX, the governor of Cyprus, and defeated at the Jordan. Cleopatra III, however, provided reinforcements. For several years afterward, even after Ptolemy X had slain Cleopatra, Janneus was able to plunder flourishing Hellenistic cities like Gadara in Transjordan and Gaza on the west coast. His mercenary army comprised a mixed lot indeed; not a few of them came from Cilicia and Pisidia, notorious as the homes of thieves and outlaws.

(2) Rome indirectly influenced the second act of the history of Janneus' reign, because social and political upheavals in the Roman Empire had far-reaching consequences for the East. In the capital and in Italy during the nineties there was tension between three social groups. On the right stood the senatorial party of aristocrats called *optimates,* led by Sulla; in the middle, the capitalist party consisting of parvenu knights called *equites;* and on the left, the progressive socialist party. The latter two parties, the *populares,* under the leadership of Marius, the pioneer of the *condottiere* system and tactics based on cohorts, fought for greater rights in the new empire; in 90–89 they partially achieved their

goal. In the eastern provinces and protectorates there had long been a similar tension between the Greek citizens, the Roman entrepreneurs, and many elements of the population that were without privileges, including Jews and other Orientals. This social tension was helpful to Mithradates VI, the Iranian ruler of Pontus on the Black Sea, who desired to expand his power. He entered into alliances with Armenia, Parthia, Syria, and Egypt (Appian *History* xii. 15 f.) ; his Egyptian partner was Ptolemy IX, governor of Cyprus, who represented the Egyptian nationalists. The latter had sent the Seleucid prince Demetrius III from Cnidus to Damascus, supporting Demetrius' claim to the Syrian throne against the other princes. With his southern and eastern flanks thus protected, in 88 B.C. Mithradates occupied almost all of Asia Minor and the islands together with parts of Greece. He everywhere ordered that Romans and Italians be killed, while coming forward as liberator of the Greeks and at the same time promising citizenship to the Asiatics. Ptolemy IX hastened to overthrow his brother in Alexandria and take possession of all Egypt.

This sudden advance of the underprivileged and the Orientals swept the Jews along with it. Even among the Jews of Palestine, three social groups can be distinguished, although the religious situation presented a somewhat different picture. On the political right stood the representatives of the old priestly nobility; in the middle, the Sadducees and the parvenus, people like the Tobiads of the past or the grandfather and father of Herod; on the left, the Pharisees, who succeeded the Hasidim and now represented a popular middle-class party. The radical Pharisees had already shown their opposition to the Hasmonean house as early as the reign of Hyrcanus I (see above, p. 67). About 90 B.C., when the Roman Empire was torn by social unrest, the party of the Pharisees demonstrated against Janneus during the Feast of Booths by pelting him with the lemons used at the festival (Josephus *Ant.* xiii. 327). Such a public demonstration was something new in Jewish history. Then came the campaign of Mithradates in 88, which represented a quite general advance of the underprivileged and the Orientals. Janneus was beaten in Gaulanitis by the camel-cavalry of the Nabateans, fled to Jerusalem, and was there rejected by the "people" (Josephus *Ant.* xiii. 375 f.). This refers to a new political factor: the mob of common people, led on by the Pharisees. In 88, the year of Mithradates (see p. 71), similar factions struggling to improve their position called on Demetrius III of Damascus for aid; he defeated Janneus at Shechem and forced him to take refuge in the hills (*ibid.,* 377–79). Demetrius was unable to capitalize on his victory, but had to return to northern Syria, where his brother defeated him with the help of the Parthians. At the same time, it should be noted, there was unrest among the Jews in Cyrene (Josephus *Ant.* xiv. 114). Obviously there was a widespread reaction on the part of the Jews to the weakness of Rome and the advance of the Orient.

(3) The recapture of control by the Roman nobility constituted the setting for the third act in the history of Janneus' reign. Sulla and the *optimates* were able to restore the status quo in 86–79. Mithradates was beaten back and the control of the Roman senate over Italy and the East demonstrated with renewed power. The popular party was temporarily paralyzed by bloody proscriptions.

Thanks to the collapse of Mithradates' designs in Asia, Janneus, the Jewish priest-king, was also able to restore himself to power. After the departure of Demetrius in 88, Janneus once again won supporters, attacked the popular party, and carried out a proscription of his opponents, in the course of which he had eight hundred of the leaders crucified in Jerusalem while he banqueted with his harem on the roof of the palace (Josephus *Ant.* xiii. 380). Eight thousand insurgents are reported to have fled abroad to escape the tyrant (*ibid.,* 383). These may have included the community of the Damascus Document, which has Pharisaic traits (see below p. 172), provided that their flight to Damascus is to be understood literally and not symbolically (the Pharisees had just established communication with this city). In foreign relations, too, Janneus once more became rich and powerful. He did still have some trouble with the Nabateans, and in 85 built palisades on the Philistine plain in a vain attempt to keep Antiochus XII, the last of the Damascus Seleucids, from passing through to attack the Nabateans (*ibid.*, 391). Somewhat later Antiochus fell, and the Nabateans occupied the empire of Damascus, inflicting a defeat upon Janneus in the process. After this, however, they left the Jewish king in peace, probably because Tigranes of Armenia controlled Syria and Phoenicia after 83 B.C. Janneus grasped as much as he could lay his hands on in the immediate vicinity of Palestine; as a consequence of his successes, the Jewish people received him once more with jubilation around 80 B.C. It looked for a time as though the Davidic kingdom had sprung up once more. Janneus and the Jews even ruled cities and territories belonging to the Hellenistic Phoenicians, Philistines, Idumeans, Nabateans, and Syrians (Josephus *Ant.* xiii. 395–97):

on the sea, Strato's Tower, Apollonia, Joppa, Jamnia, Ashdod, Gaza, Anthedon, Raphia, Rhinocorura;

in the interior, Adoraim, Marisa, all of Idumea, Samaria, Carmel and Tabor, Scythopolis, Gadara;

in Gaulanitis, Seleucia and Gamala; in the region of the Decapolis, the Cilician valley and Pella, the latter being destroyed because it refused to accept Judaism; in Moab, Hesbon, Medaba, Lemba, etc.

From the Levitical temple territory in the mountains of Judah that Ezra and Nehemiah were permitted to organize under Persian sovereignty, it was an immense step to the land of the Hasmoneans that Simon made independent in 142 and finally the militant kingdom of the priestly *condottiere* Janneus.[4] The Jews now controlled practically all of Palestine west of the Jordan from Idumea to Iturea with the sole exception of Ptolemais and Ashkelon, and also considerable territory east of the Jordan from Mount Hermon to the Dead Sea. This area included several wealthy cities

[4] The appended map, "Palestine in the Period of the Maccabeans and Hasmoneans," shows how the Hasmonean kingdom roughly quadrupled in size between 142 and 80 B.C.

with Hellenistic culture, which Janneus either destroyed or repressed. Though his policies are reminiscent of those of the Renaissance popes, a cultural comparison is impossible.

C. ALEXANDRA, HYRCANUS II, AND ARISTOBULUS II

The Jewish namesake of the Macedonian conqueror Alexander is said to have advised his wife Alexandra before his death in 76 to yield to the popular party of the Pharisees (Josephus *Ant.* xiii. 400). If she would negotiate with the leaders of this party (Greek *stasiôtai,* "partisans"), he told her, she would be able to count on the support of the "people."

In any event, during her reign (76–67) Alexandra sought to establish a positive relationship with the party of the Pharisees and succeeded in this aim. Hyrcanus II, Janneus' elder son, became high priest. He was notoriously indolent, and, with respect to the new demands of the masses, must have seemed innocuous enough. The Pharisaic tribunes with their oratory led the masses in the desired direction and promulgated new laws directed against the upper classes. They also began a proscription of Janneus' supporters (Josephus *Ant.* xiii. 405, 408, 411). As in Rome at the time of Pompey and Spartacus, the middle and lower classes were in ferment, with the difference that under Alexandra a party of Puritans influenced the course of events.

Naturally the government of the Pharisaic tribunes in Jerusalem provoked the opposition of the Sadducaic jurists and aristocratic officers. At the very beginning of the proscription the Jewish *optimates* (Greek *dunatoi*) sent a delegation to the palace. Among them was Aristobulus, the King's younger son, who, like his father, dreamed of military glory and despised government by a woman. He and other young soldiers were put off with military advancement. Later, however, when Alexandra fell ill, Aristobulus seized control of the eastern border fortresses.

After Alexandra's death in 67, Hyrcanus II made himself king. Aristobulus II immediately marched against his elder brother, defeated him at Jericho, and claimed for himself the priestly and royal dignity, although he let his brother retain the revenues (Josephus *Ant.* xiv. 6). He was able to hold power from 66 to 63 B.C.

In this period there took place again what happened in 88 during the conflict between Janneus and the Pharisees: a foreign ruler was called upon for help, this time from the south. Hyrcanus II himself, it is true, did not take the initiative. But behind him there appeared a *homo novus* seeking to make a political name for himself in the spirit of the age: Antipater, whose Idumean father had collaborated with Janneus and served as governor of Idumea, and who was himself father of the later King Herod. A political climber of the first order, Antipater calculated that helping to restore Hyrcanus to the throne could only help his career. Hyrcanus II became the tool of a clique of capitalists led by Antipater, and agreed to having Antipater persuade the king of the Nabateans to march against Aristobulus and lay siege to him in the Temple. This was too much for respectable Jews (Josephus *Ant.* xiv. 21–28), but it was impossible to lift the siege. Aristobulus II turned to the Romans for support and summoned the quaestor Scaurus, who had come to Damascus at Pompey's request because of a new war with Mithradates. A mere threat from Rome sufficed to make the Nabateans withdraw.

This action did not, however, resolve the quarrel between the two brothers, the more so because the struggle was associated with a tension between social classes that was general in this period. Antipater encouraged the contest for personal reasons. It seemed that only a greater power could put an end to the civil war. This power was Rome, whose general Pompey was now seeking to extend Roman control over all of the Near East, pursuing the interests of the Metropolis and the capitalists.

IV

PALESTINE UNDER ROME AND HEROD

63–4 B.C.

1. THE ROMAN SPHERE OF INFLUENCE

A. The Rise of Rome as a World Power

THE republican city-state of Rome, working and progressing methodically, was governed by a hierarchy of magistrates both elective and honorary. The public career of a Roman included not only civil but also priestly and military positions. At the head of the government stood two consuls, elected annually, who took office on 15 March or, after 153 B.C., on 1 January.

Two privileged classes achieved special prominence in the Republic:

(1) The governing body was the senate, a municipal assembly of elders consisting of three hundred members, and, from the first century B.C. onward, of six hundred. Originally the heads of the patrician families (*patres*) held seats; after the fifth century B.C., the heads of some plebeian families were admitted (as so-called *conscripti*), because these families were important although they did not have a very lengthy tradition; after the first century B.C., even parvenus were admitted, the criterion in this case being governmental experience as well as descent. This Roman "House of Lords," whose members wore purple boots, togas trimmed with a purple border, and gold rings, consisted primarily of rich landholders. As the leading magistrates came from their circles, they ruled the entire Republic until other forces seized control in the first century B.C.; in the following cen-

tury, however, they were still the advocates of a republican oligarchy in opposition to the Emperor.

(2) After 129 B.C. the members of the official aristocracy were not allowed to engage in commercial pursuits. They now faced competition from a new class based on wealth: the industrial and commercial entrepreneurs who profited from the newly-opened trade routes. If these businessmen entertained social ambitions, they could start their sons on a public career by enrolling them as reserve officers in the cavalry, for which the only necessary qualification was considerable resources. The recognized reserve officers constituted the class of so-called equestrians (*equites,* "knights"). One may think of them as Roman citizens with sufficient wealth to ride with the cavalry in wars or on parade; after 129 B.C., the aristocracy were also excluded from this kind of service. Thus the equestrians did not constitute a nobility like the knights of the Middle Ages, who were associated with some prince. As citizens who occasionally served in the armed cavalry, the Roman equestrians are somewhat comparable to the Greek ephebi, although in the case of the equestrians the basic qualification was not education but wealth. In 123 B.C., Gaius Gracchus obtained for them political privileges that served to further the interests of capitalism (see below, p. 80). As a sign of their position they wore a toga with a purple border narrower than that of the senators; after the time of Vespasian, they also wore a gold ring (see below, p. 268). By profession they were mostly businessmen. In the period when Rome became a power in the Hellenistic world, Roman society was dominated by a bitter contest between the senators (who belonged to the nobility) and the wealthy equestrians; the latter also began to compete with the citizens of the Hellenistic cities.

Rome always took care to extend its power quietly and methodically. In 275 B.C. it had beaten off the attacks led by King Pyrrhus of Epirus, that aggressive proponent of Hellenism, and was henceforth undisputed master of subjects and allies in central and southern Italy. During the Punic Wars, the Roman fleet developed its capabilities; the effectiveness of the army was increased by new weapons, including the javelin and rapier, and a more mobile formation than the Macedonian phalanx. Under the leadership of the brothers Scipio Africanus Major and Scipio Asiaticus, Rome first defeated Hannibal in 202 west of Zama, in Numidia, and then Antiochus III in 190 at Magnesia in Lydia (see above, p. 50). The entire Mediterranean world thus came under the control of the city on the Tiber. After the battle of Pydna in 168 (see above, p. 54), Macedonia was divided into four parts and made a vassal state; in 148 it became a Roman province, which also included Greece after the destruction of Corinth in 146. In the same year Carthage was destroyed by Scipio Africanus Minor. The growth of Roman interests in Egypt, along with traditional hostility to Phoenicia and Syria, paved the way for the senate's declaration of solidarity with the Hasmoneans and the Jews (see above, pp. 59–66). In 133 the Hellenistic kingdom of Pergamum fell to the Romans by bequest and was organized as the province of Asia. With this eastward expansion of its influence, Rome suddenly found itself the greatest power in the Hellenistic world. Roman aristocrats such as the Scipios and the Gracchi gladly accepted the ideals of Hellenism; and, although Latin was still used in daily life, the cosmopolitan citizens and politicians of Rome made great efforts to acquire the Greek language and culture, particularly Asiatic rhetoric and Stoic philosophy. In 155 B.C., three leading philosophers from Athens had come to Rome and there gained students among the young men of the upper class: Carneades, Critolaus, and Diogenes, the first a leader of the Academic school, the second, of the Peripatetic school, and the third, of the Stoic school.

In the last third of the second century B.C., class warfare brought Rome's expansion to a halt. The old social order was not suited to the circumstances of a world empire. It was defended by the aristocratically minded *optimates,* but attacked by the more democratic *populares.* We can distinguish three parties. (1) The aristocratic party of conservative property-owners, comprising the senatorial nobility and other members of the aristocracy, tried to prevent any restrictions of their political, social, and economic privileges. (2) The businessmen's party, consisting of equestrians who had acquired wealth through trade, along with their colleagues, fought hard for increased status and power, trying to gain acceptance as *optimates*. Opportunism or idealism occasionally allied them with the lower classes and various peripheral groups, and they appeared in that case as *populares*. (3) The oppressed or disadvantaged groups included the numerous townspeople of Rome, farmers in the country either ruined or struggling along, and entrepreneurs living far from Rome. They aspired to increased political rights and other advantages, and depended on the help of democratically minded aristocrats and citizens, with the result that a popular party appeared whose composition differed from time to time.

The leaders of the *populares* were two brothers, Tiberius and Gaius Gracchus, who had been much influenced by Stoicism. Both of them brought about social reforms, Tiberius aiding the small farmers and Gaius aiding the moneyed equestrians. The two brothers were slain, one in 133 and the other in 122 B.C.; but many of the reforms continued in effect. In particular, the equestrians were able to increase their wealth by acting as *publicani* or government agents in charge of the tax system in the province of Asia and of road construction in Italy.

The aristocratic party, which returned to power after the death of the Gracchi, demonstrated their incompetence in two wars that affected Italy: the war against Jugurtha in Africa and the war against the Cimbri and Teutons in Gaul. Now a member of the businessmen's party saved the military honor of Rome: following Hellenistic example, Marius recruited drifters to serve as mercenaries, and between 106 and 101 B.C. defeated the enemies both in the north and in the south. From this time forward Rome more and more gave up the general levy in favor of professional soldiers, who were more versatile and useful in the conduct of war and defense. Several aspirants to political power, however, hit upon the idea of organizing private armies of mercenaries with which to attack their political opponents. Marius' reform of the army thus inaugurated a period of civil wars that continued until Octavian's victory at Actium in 31 B.C.

Despite his victories, Marius did not have enough political power to make further progress in association with the popular party, but had to place his businessmen's party under the protection of the conservative party of the nobles, headed by Sulla. He was not made supreme commander in Asia Minor, where he hoped to wage a war profitable for the equestrians against Mithradates, the aggressive king of Pontus. Much against his will, Marius had to fight in Italy against Roman allies who were demanding the right of citizenship. At the end of the Social War (91–89 B.C.), Roman citizenship was extended to the municipalities of the Italians allied with Rome. Mithradates capitalized on this domestic political crisis, engaging Rome in the First Pontic War (88–85 B.C.), which began with his conquest of Asia and Hellas. At the same time, the capital of the Roman Empire was embroiled in a civil war that involved both the contest between the senators and the equestrians for command in the East and the efforts of left-wing politicians to have the rights of citizenship extended to more people. Sulla ejected Marius from Rome and then, at the senate's request, marched against Mithradates. Marius and the radical Cinna made themselves consuls by force, but in January of 86 Marius died of old age. In the meanwhile, Sulla drove the Pontic troops out of Greece, forced Mithradates to come to terms in 85, and in 84 reorganized the province of Asia. The Second Mithradatic War (83–81 B.C.) left the situation unchanged. After a prolonged struggle in Italy, Sulla restored senatorial control in Rome. We have described above how Janneus put down a Pharisaic rebellion in Palestine at this time and then increased the authority of the Sadducees (see above, pp. 71 ff.). Sulla became dictator, restored the aristocratic constitution, and then withdrew from politics.

Even so, tensions continued to disrupt Roman politics, both domestic and foreign. The needs of the businessmen and underprivileged had been met only in part. Above all, pirates interfered with the Oriental trade so important for Rome; and in 74 Mithradates, allied with Tigranes of Armenia, began the third Pontic war, which lasted until 64. In this situation two leaders appeared: first Lucullus, a member of the party of the nobility, who was noted as a patron of the arts and who ably championed Roman authority in the East; and then Pompey, who in the last phase of the war had gone over to the businessmen's party. The latter secured Roman power in the Levant on a capitalistic basis and extended this power over the former Seleucid Empire, including Palestine.

B. Pompey Occupies Palestine

> Pompey made Jerusalem tributary to the Romans, but separated the cities of Coele-Syria that the Jews had taken and put them under the command of his legate.
>
> Josephus, *Antiquitates* xiv. 74

At the age of twenty-three, Pompey (106–48 B.C.) gathered a mercenary army with which he took the field on behalf of Sulla and the nobles. In 70 B.C. he went over to the businessmen's party of the millionaire Crassus and the advocate Cicero, and contributed to certain reforms in Sulla's constitution to benefit neglected groups of people in Italy and Roman financial interests in the provinces. To back up the Roman coinage, Pompey was given unlimited authority to subdue the Mediterranean pirates with his troops; he then took the place of Lucullus, who was about to terminate the war against Mithradates of Pontus and Tigranes of Armenia. Pompey carried out both tasks brilliantly, and came to Damascus in 64 to organize Seleucid Syria, formerly controlled by Tigranes, as a Roman province.

In Damascus Pompey received representatives of the three Jewish parties: (1) Aristobulus II, accompanied by several reactionary aristocrats flaunting their parade uniforms, who must have reminded Pompey of Catiline and his fellow revolutionaries; (2) Hyrcanus II, with a host of wealthy individuals summoned by Antipater; (3) the representatives of "the people," who vowed they would hear nothing of monarchy, but, at most, of a hierarchy (Josephus *Ant.* xiv. 41–45). Pompey would have preferred to see how things were with the Nabateans first; but military threats by the extreme rightists forced him to take Aristobulus prisoner and march at once against Jerusalem. The defeatist Hyrcanus opened the gates, and naturally it was not hard for the experienced soldiers of Pompey to make siege devices and storm the Temple area, defended by the priestly nobility. In 63 B.C., on a feast day, probably the Day of Atonement, Pompey and his staff, as a symbol of Roman occupation, entered the Holy of Holies (*ibid.,* 66, 72). Hyrcanus was rewarded by being allowed to remain high priest.

Judea thus became once more a small temple land under foreign domination. Just as earlier it had belonged to the Persian satrapy of Transeuphrates and to Hellenistic Egypt and Syria, so now in 63 it was made by Pompey a part of the Roman province of Syria, whose major cities were Antioch and Damascus. The territory that Hyrcanus II was temporarily allowed to govern as a client of Rome was restricted to Judea, Perea, and Galilee. Since the latter two areas had been so effectively judaized under the Hasmoneans, they could no longer be accounted part of the Hellenistic world, but rather as belonging to the Jewish Temple. But the *poleis* in the west, in Samaria, and in the east, captured and for the most part destroyed by Hyrcanus I, Aristobulus I, and Janneus, were taken away and added to the province of Syria. Pompey and his successors had them rebuilt, for after the Mithradatic Wars the Romans considered the culture of the Hellenistic cities their best political and commercial instrument for controlling the East. This restoration of Hellenism under Pompey meant that Judea, Perea, and Galilee, the regions in which John the Baptist, Jesus, and the first Apostles lived, were surrounded or split by strings of Hellenistic commercial and cultural centers which were felt to be alien.

Strategically, the Holy Land was henceforth important to

Rome. Previously the land had lain on the military route from Persia, Mesopotamia, and Syria to Egypt; again and again it had been pulled back and forth in a tug-of-war that ran from northeast to southwest. Now, together with Syria and Phoenicia, Palestine furnished the land bridge between Asia Minor and Egypt, two spheres of interest essential to Rome's supply system. In addition, the still undefeated Nabateans occupied Transjordan and the south, and continued to control caravan trade between Asia and Africa. And yet another danger bore watching: ever since the fall of the kings of Syria, Pontus, and Armenia, the Parthian advance toward the Mediterranean was becoming more and more threatening. It was therefore very important for the Romans to retain control of the Holy Land.

2. TRIUMVIRS, ANTIPATER, AND HEROD 63–4 B.C.

The era of Jewish history that begins with the Roman occupation of Palestine in 63 B.C. is dominated by the relationships between Palestinian usurpers and the Roman triumvirs. It was quite generally a period of usurpers and power-seekers. By means of skillful intrigue Antipater laid the groundwork for Herod's kingship, but both father and son were absolutely dependent on the great individuals who dominated the world: Pompey and Caesar, Antony and Octavian. The most important names and dates of this period, down to the death of Herod in 4 B.C., are given in the table on page 85.

A. ANTIPATER

> Antipater had much capital at his disposal; he was a man of action, and a partisan.
>
> Josephus, *Antiquitates* xiv. 8

Under Roman hegemony the Idumean counselor of Hyrcanus II, Antipater, continued to exercise his influence on the high priest. From the Roman occupation in 63 until 55, he was the unofficial *effendi* of the land, and from 55

Selected Roman Rulers:	Selected Commanders in the East:	Selected Governors of Syria:	Rulers of Palestine:	Selected high priests:
Pompey and Crassus in 70 (representing the businessmen's party)	Pompey, 67–61	Scaurus, 65, 62	Antipater, 63–43; procurator after 55	Hyrcanus II, 76–40
First Triumvirate (a coalition of capitalists and socialists): Pompey, Crassus, Caesar, 60–53		Gabinius, 57–55 Crassus, 55–53 Cassius, 53–51		
	Caesar, 48–46		Hyrcanus II, ethnarch 47–40	
Caesar, dictator 46–44				
	Cassius, 44–42		Phasael and Herod, generals 43–40	
Second Triumvirate (to continue the work of Caesar): Antony, Lepidus, Octavian, 43–36	Antony, 41–31		Antigonus, king 40–37 Herod I, king 37–4	Anael (from Babylon), 37–36 Aristobulus III (brother of Mariamne I), 35
Octavian (after 27, Augustus), *Imperator* and *Princeps*, 30 B.C.— A.D. 14	Agrippa, 23–20, 17–13			Anael (again), 34–? Simon Boethus (from Alexandria; father of Mariamne II), *ca.* 24–*ca.* 4

until 43, when he was slain, he was Roman procurator in Jerusalem and then over the entire country. At times he was even able to exercise control over the Jews in Egypt. Such love of power on the part of a capitalist was not unusual in the period of the triumvirs. Nor was Antipater, who was considered a semi-Jew and was every bit as unpopular as his son Herod, anything but self-seeking. He nevertheless played his political cards with great skill and good fortune; despite the changing constellations in the Roman sky, he always remained on good terms with those in power, and was able to gain important advantages for the Jews, even those living in the Hellenistic world (Josephus *Bell.* i. 159–226; *Ant.* xiv. 80–283).[1]

Pompey took Aristobulus and his family to Rome as prisoners of war, leaving Scaurus as legate in Syria. In 62, Scaurus embarked on the interrupted punitive campaign against Petra and the Nabateans, which was essential for the maintenance of the caravan trade. In the earlier civil war, Antipater had induced the Nabateans to attack Jerusalem; now, residing in Idumea, he was very useful to the Romans, first providing supplies for their troops and then helping to arrange the Nabatean ransom.

The right-wing party at Rome criticized Pompey's policies in the East, thereby inducing Crassus and Pompey, in the year 60, to form the so-called "first triumvirate," an official coalition of these two middle-of-the-road politicians with Caesar, the crafty leader of the left. When Gabinius, their protégé, became proconsul of Syria, a rebellion broke out in Judea that he had to put down three times between 57 and 55. The first and third times, its instigator was Alexander, the eldest son of Aristobulus II; the second time, it was Aristobulus himself, who had escaped from Rome. Their right-wing conspiracies were doomed to failure; but there was more behind them than a mere reminiscence of Catiline: the senators opposing Pompey supported such conservative elements. With the full support of Antipater, Gabinius and his daring cavalry commander Mark Antony (later a member of the second triumvirate) each time suppressed the rebellion, and finally sent Aristobulus and his younger son in captivity back to Rome. During the first campaign, the proconsul utilized the opportunity to speed the rebuilding of the Hellenistic cities in Palestine; during the second, Hyrcanus' rights were restricted and the temple land was divided into five dioceses; in 55, during the third campaign, Antipater, who had recently helped Gabinius in connection

[1] U. Wilcken, "Antipatros, 17," in *PRE*, Vol. 1 (1894), cols. 2509–11.

with a change of regime in Egypt, was made Roman procurator (Greek *epimelētēs*) in Jerusalem (Josephus *Ant.* xiv. 127).

Crassus, the enormously wealthy protector of Gabinius, replaced his protégé in 55. To compete with Pompey in Syria and Caesar in Gaul, he wanted to gain honor by conquering Parthia. Jerusalem had to surrender the treasure of the Temple to provide arms. In this connection Josephus, following Strabo, describes the far-flung community of Diaspora Jews and proselytes from "all the world," even Asia Minor and Europe, who had long contributed to the fabulous wealth of the Temple (Josephus *Ant.* xiv. 110–18). Crassus, however, was born more for financial than for military triumphs; in 53 B.C., at Carrhae, near Abraham's old home, he lost the Roman standards and then his life. Syria was saved for Rome by Cassius, the man who later assassinated Caesar; Antipater managed at the same time to have an Aristobulid rebel executed.

Gaius Julius Caesar (100–44 B.C.) was leader of the socialistic (though not democratic) popular party. Following the fall of Crassus in 53 B.C. and his own victory in Gaul over Vercingetorix in 52, he felt compelled in 49 B.C. to cross the Rubicon, in northern Italy, and seize power in Rome. He also had the enthusiastic support of many of the old aristocrats with radical leanings. The senate in terror called on Pompey for help, but he had to evacuate Italy and make Greece his base of operations. Having occupied Rome, Caesar liberated a number of prisoners, including the Hasmonean Aristobulus II, whom he sent to Syria to fight against Pompey. Pompey's supporters, however, soon eliminated Aristobulus and his elder son Alexander; the younger prince, Antigonus, revolted nine years later (see below, pp. 92 f.). In 48, Pompey was defeated at Pharsalus in Thessaly and hit upon the unfortunate idea of seeking refuge with his ward, the thirteen-year-old Ptolemy XIII of Egypt. This little man had just dismissed his twenty-one-year-old sister, Cleopatra VII (the famous Cleopatra of literature) from her position as co-regent; he was now to take the life of one great man of that age and endanger the life of the other. The moment. Pompey landed and set foot on shore he was slain by the ministers of Ptolemy. Caesar rushed to Alexandria and occupied both the city and the land, summoning Ptolemy and Cleopatra and keeping the former in his palace as a hostage and the latter as a concubine.

But the new ruler of the world had reckoned without Egyptian nationalism: the soldiers of the Egyptian army and the Egyptians of Alexandria began the Alexandrian War, which lasted from autumn of 48 until the spring of 47. Caesar was besieged in the Greek quarter and was barely able to hold out because of lack of water and troops; the reinforcements summoned from Asia Minor and Syria were delayed; nor did the release of Ptolemy XIII to the Egyptians help, since the youth himself soon took the field against Caesar. In this position of mortal danger Caesar sent a certain Mithradates to Syria to get reinforcements, whereupon Antipater appeared as *deus ex machina* (Josephus *Ant.* xiv. 127–36). With a combination of friendly influence on Syrian neighbors, speedy intervention of Jewish troops, and pressure on the Egyptian Jews, he contributed to Caesar's victory at the crucial moment, thus making it possible for the popular Roman hero to continue his rise to dictatorship (Caesar *Bellum alexandrinum* xxvi. 1–3; Caesar does not mention the Jews, however). Morally the outcome of the Alexandrian War was a defeat for the Egyptians, but a victory for the Greeks and Jews in Alexandria and elsewhere.

In grateful repayment for this assistance, Caesar granted a series of privileges to Antipater and the Jews while he was returning through Syria and Asia Minor (*"veni, vidi, vici"*) and then when he was dictator in Rome. These privileges remained extremely important even in the New Testament period, because Antony and Octavian, Caesar's successors, were prepared to continue his policies.

Thus in 47 B.C. Hyrcanus II became ethnarch of the Jews. He was entitled to one of the seats of honor at gladiatorial games, etc., so that he achieved some political status again.

Antipater was granted Roman citizenship—a highly prized privilege, which referred to the city, not the state—and became procurator of the Roman Republic over the territory of the Jews. He named his eldest sons, Phasael and Herod, military governors (*stratēgoi*) of Judea and Galilee. The taxes to be remitted to Rome by way of Sidon were reduced, henceforth being levied only upon Jerusalem because it was permitted to rebuild its walls, and upon Joppa because it was given to the Jews outright; there was a corresponding increase in the Levitical taxes paid to the priests. In addition, several towns in the valley of Jezreel were added to the land. Jewish territories were to be exempt from the usual obligation of providing auxiliary troops. Under Caesar and his successors, a whole series of Greek cities and even Rome itself hastened to show favor to the Jewish clients of the mighty dictator (Josephus *Ant.* xiv. 190–267). In many places, within the framework of their synagogues, the Jews were allowed to exercise their own jurisdiction, hold communal banquets, and establish communal financial institutions—in short, to enjoy a legal and commercial, religious and social freedom of movement that was exceptional in the Greek cities for reasons of civil defense and in the Roman Empire because of the law against associations promulgated in 55 (p. 308). One should not overlook the significance this freedom was later to have for the spread of the Gospel, which took place in and through the synagogues of the Diaspora, including their membership and adherents. No wonder that when Caesar was assassinated in 44, of all the foreign nations the Jews mourned at his grave with special fervor (Suetonius *Caesar* 84 says they mourned continuously for several nights).

After Caesar's death, another collaborator grasped the opportunity to poison Antipater in 43. Now the two centers of power in the land confronted each other directly: on the one hand, the patricians, who favored oligarchy, and the priests, who profited from the new tax system; and on the other, Herod, as the dictatorial military governor of Galilee. Herod had already shown the high assembly that, like Caesar in conflict with the senate, he was prepared to disregard the aristocrats (Josephus *Ant.* xiv. 168–84) .[2]

B. Herod I

> Authority passed to Herod, the
> son of Antipater, who was de-
> scended from a plebeian house
> and a common family.
>
> Josephus *Antiquitates* xvi. 491

The right-wing extremists who murdered Caesar did not find the popular approval they had expected for a restoration of the Republic. Many preferred to see the dictatorship continue; Antony, Caesar's field marshal and co-consul (82–30 B.C.) , stood ready to satisfy their wish. To block Antony, the senate sought help from Caesar's legal heir, the nineteen-year-old Octavian, who attacked Antony from the rear at Mutina. However, when Lepidus came to the aid of his colleague Antony, Octavian broke with the senate and joined with Antony and Lepidus, the opponents of Caesar's assassins. In 43 they formed the second triumvirate, which can be thought of as an officially recognized continuation of the dictatorship. After obtaining money by means of large-scale proscriptions, they marched against the assassins, who had made the rich Orient their base. Planning to rule the East himself, Antony led the campaign.

In the Holy Land the political movements of the Roman Empire were reflected in a microcosm. Just as after the assassination of Caesar in 44, when the aristocratic senators in Rome were in conflict with the military triumvirs, so also, after the assassination of Antipater in 43, there was an intensification in the Holy Land of the enmity between the patrician members of the assembly and the military governors Phasael and Herod (see above, pp. 89 f.) , who sought to continue the dictatorship of their father in Judea and Galilee as a sort of "duumvirate."

[2] A picture, painted in 1611 by Hans Bock for the courtyard of the city hall at Basel, depicts the scene from the point of view of the assembly.

Herod (*ca.* 73–4 B.C.), now about thirty, won the contest through flexibility and sureness of purpose. Through thick and thin, he constantly managed to retain the confidence of successive Roman rulers (Josephus *Bell.* i. 227–85; *Ant.* xiv. 283–389). He finally replaced the oligarchy with a monarchy which had no roots among the Jews but depended on Antony's command of the East and then on Octavian's world empire. This royal satellite, whose name has been made famous by Christmas stories and plays, stifled all local resistance, imagined or real, with inhuman ferocity and displayed a disgusting servility toward his Roman masters. In view of this, his common epithet "the Great," which may originally have meant "the Elder" (Josephus *Ant.* xviii. 130, 133, 136), appears undeserved.[3] The energy displayed by this upstart, however, is as impressive as that of any Renaissance prince. Josephus, for example, though basically hostile to Herod refers to one of Herod's early opponents and says that his possession of the strongest fortresses "was of no avail against the might of Herod" (*Bell.* i. 238). Herod appears personally unattractive because of his cruelties and sycophancy, but as a politician and soldier he is an imposing figure to the eye of the historian. Though his reputation is bad among both Jews and Christians, he made some culturally valuable contributions; he beautified and enlarged many cities in Palestine and elsewhere, and, by clever maneuvering, built up the financial strength of the Jews.

To curry favor as a Roman collaborator, Herod first concentrated his efforts on Cassius who, after the assassination of Caesar, had come to Syria with a large army. With surpassing swiftness Herod collected from his land the monies demanded for support of the legions, thus becoming a "friend" of Cassius. Thanks to this Roman protection, Herod was able to put down his Sadducean opponents and to become betrothed to a Hasmonean princess, Mariamne I, the daughter of the Alexander whom the supporters of Pompey had executed (see above, p. 87).

After the triumvirate defeated Caesar's assassins at Phi-

[3] W. Otto, "Herodes," in *PRE*, Supplement 2 (1913), cols. 145 f.

lippi in Macedonia in 42, Antony, now ruler of the East, marched by stages through Asia Minor to Syria.[4] Everywhere embassies from Eastern governments and parties sought audience with him. Jewish aristocrats tried to rid themselves of Herod; but Herod was able to protect himself by playing on Antony's acquaintance with his father (see above, p. 86) and by stressing his new connection with the family of Hyrcanus II. Quite apart from these considerations, Antony was generally inclined to continue Caesar's policies. He confirmed the privileges granted by Caesar to the Jews, and gave Antipater's sons, Phasael and Herod, the status of tetrarchs—"ruler of a fourth," roughly equivalent to a duke—over the land of the Jews.

Shortly afterward a catastrophe endangered the further rise of Herod; ultimately, however, it hastened his advancement. In 40 B.C., Antigonus, the surviving son of the frequently rebellious Aristobulus II (see above pp. 86 f.) , saw his chance to eliminate the Idumean upstart and restore the Hasmonean monarchy. In this year the Parthians invaded Syria, where they were greeted as deliverers from the power of Rome. Antigonus fomented a rebellion in Jerusalem and persuaded the Parthians to send cavalry to his aid; he soon controlled the capital and great areas of the countryside, and was able to appear as the last Hasmonean king of the Jews (40–37 B.C.) . The coins of Antigonus carry patriotic symbols like the table for the Bread of the Presence; he wanted to represent the traditional nationalistic party in opposition to the house of Antipater. The aged high priest and protégé of Antipater, Hyrcanus II, was taken prisoner, along with Antipater's elder son Phasael. The former had his ears cut off so that he would be unfit for cultic office; the latter took his own life in Galilee. Herod escaped, and after many adventures made his way to Rome.

Antony and Octavian received Herod in Rome as the protector of Roman interests in Palestine. At a meeting of the senate in 40 B.C. on the Capitol, Herod was named King

[4] H. Buchheim, *Die Orientpolitik des Triumvirn M. Antonius* (1960) , pp. 60–74.

over Judea. Striding out of the hall between Antony and Octavian, at the head of the assembly, he was allowed to witness the sacrifice of ratification. In return for special tribute he was later granted the right to call Samaria and other territories part of his kingdom.

Herod, thus made a rival king with the support of the triumvirs and the Roman senate (Josephus *Bell.* i. 282–673; *Ant.* xiv. 381–xvii. 199), was temporarily a king without a country. His first task was to gain control of his kingdom. Despite aid from the Romans, this turned out to be difficult because Antigonus, the Hasmonean king, had the powerful support of the aristocrats and Sadducees in Jerusalem and elsewhere. Herod had to fight for three years (39–37) before he could regain control. Since Antigonus posed a constant threat, he was crucified and beheaded in Antioch; in addition, Herod ordered the execution of some forty-five priests of the Sadducean aristocracy. Shortly before the fall of Jerusalem in 37 B.C., Herod had married Mariamne I, a Hasmonean, in Samaria. This relationship by marriage to the ancient royal house helped secure his position.

As a Roman client king in Palestine, Herod enjoyed far-reaching domestic and foreign privileges. He had the right, for example, in some cases to wage war against foreign nations. But he was responsible to the Romans, and had to furnish troops on demand and render tribute for certain territories.

On the whole, the period of Herod's reign, which lasted from 37 to 4 B.C., was a time of both dynastic contention and cultural achievement. This period may be divided into three parts: 37–27, 27–13, and 13–4. In the first and third periods, attacks upon real or supposed enemies claimed most of the King's attention; in the second, large-scale public works were uppermost in his mind.

(1) During the first period, from 37 to 27, Herod followed the Oriental custom of devoting himself in domestic affairs primarily to the task of trying and executing the members and supporters of the old royal house for high treason. We may pass over the details of this sadistic story. The victims

included the young high priest Aristobulus III, Herod's brother-in-law, whom Herod had murdered in the bath at Jericho; one of Herod's uncles; the aged Hyrcanus II; his own Hasmonean wife, Mariamne I, whom he suspected of unfaithfulness; and, above all, his mother-in-law, who had long vexed him by her intrigues with Cleopatra VII until, after the downfall of the influential Ptolemean woman, he was able to have her executed with impunity.

In foreign affairs, during the first few years Herod was forced again and again to pay regard to the ambitious Cleopatra VII. Seeing that Antony was fond of playing the part of Dionysus, she won him for herself at Tarsus in 41 by coming to him on a magnificent boat, dressed as Aphrodite. Both of them wanted to put together a Hellenistic empire with Alexandria as its center. For the moment the Parthian War prevented this, but, after Antony had forced the Parthians to retreat, Cleopatra endeavored to restore the rule of the Ptolemies over Syria and Palestine. Herod then stood in her way. She sought to incite Antony, who was dependent on her, and also the Hasmonean ladies of Jerusalem against Herod. The proud King was several times forced to retreat and render services. With heroic self-control he obeyed, and was thus able on the whole to maintain his position under Antony; he also refused the Queen when she came to him from Syria and tried to win him over with her personal charm. After the battle of Actium in 31 and the subsequent suicide of the two lovers, Herod ceased to be threatened from this quarter; in Rome, too, there was rejoicing over the downfall of this dangerous woman (Horace *Odes* i. 37: *"nunc est bibendum"*) .

Octavian (63 B.C.—A.D. 14) won the battle of Actium in 31 through a combination of superior forces and cautious strategy; even without this success he would soon have defeated Antony and Cleopatra, for his financial ability guaranteed him enough soldiers, while his opponents lost many supporters as a result of their insolence. After his victory, Octavian exercised clemency in the East, as befitted his cautious nature, and preserved for the most part the political arrangements made by Antony. Greek cities and Oriental princes continued undisturbed and were allowed to profit from the *Pax Romana,* provided that they had not fought with absolute devotion on the side of Antony and Cleopatra.

When the victorious triumvir returned to Rome, his principate was established in the Roman commonwealth between 30 and 27 B.C.[5] Its characteristic elements were these: (*a*) Octavian remained *imperator,* generalissimo, by retaining the *imperium* or command that belonged to him as triumvir. It is true that in 29 he celebrated his triumph in Rome, shut the Temple of Janus, and formally relinquished his *imperium* two years later. In actual fact, however, he remained supreme commander of the legions; this made him protector of the provinces, which needed a military guard. Egypt, the wealthiest area of the Roman world, was not put under Rome's control, but was made subject directly to Octavian, who appointed a prefect to administer it. (*b*) Drawing on the income from the provinces, Octavian created a new state treasury, the imperial *fiscus,* which stood at his disposal. Beside this new treasury, the old senatorial *aerarium* became meaningless. (*c*) In order to preserve the fiction that he shared his power with the senate, Octavian accepted a whole series of municipal offices. In particular, in 28 B.C. he became *Princeps* of the senate, a title that he bore from that time on; it refers to the most distinguished member of the senate, who had the privilege of speaking first when a vote was taken. (*d*) Following the Hellenistic custom, Octavian encouraged the provinces to worship him as a god, usually together with the city goddess Roma. In the capital, popular opinion seemed averse to such a cult in honor of the sovereign; in Rome, therefore, Octavian merely required worship of his *genius.* Moreover, in 28 B.C. he allowed the senate, acting on the motion of Munatius Plancus, to confer on him the title "Augustus," which sounded archaic and religious (to be derived from the root *augere,* the title means "exalted"; it

---

[5] P. Sattler, *Augustus und der Senat. Untersuchungen zur römischen Innenpolitik zwischen 30 und 17 vor Christus* (1960), pp. 34–57.

was translated into Greek as *sebastós,* "revered"). The senate also made him the eponym of the sixth month (which was henceforth called August). Octavian nevertheless took great pains not to violate the ancient Roman traditions. A similar deference to Roman patriotic feelings led to propaganda on behalf of Roman customs and the Roman language; even today the "Augustan age" of Latin literature is a standard term. (*e*) Octavian bore the family name "Caesar," but never used the name as a title meaning "emperor" (Luke was here more accurate than several translators of his gospel, for in 2:1 he says that Caesar Augustus, not the Emperor Augustus, decreed the census). Merely through his control of the provinces and his authority in Italy Octavian laid the groundwork for the empire of the Roman Caesars. His successors at first were chosen from his immediate family, and his titles and names gradually became the official style of the emperors: *Imperator, Princeps, Caesar, Augustus.* Domitian later added the designations *Dominus* and *Deus.*

In 31 B.C., immediately after Octavian's victory at Actium, Herod was confronted with the question whether the new ruler of the world would let him keep his throne, since he had been a protégé of Antony. He had been appointed by the senate in Octavian's presence and had always taken a firm stand against Cleopatra; moreover, Octavian did not seem to be planning many changes in the East. It was nevertheless a tense situation for Herod. Furthermore, an earthquake struck Palestine in 31, leaving many places such as the Essene community at Qumran (see below, p. 171) in desolation, the population discouraged, and the whole land open to pillage by the Nabateans. To be on the safe side, Herod slew the aged Hyrcanus and hastened to be of service to Octavian. He captured some of Cleopatra's gladiators for Octavian, at an audience with the triumvir on Rhodes declared that he had advised Antony to murder Cleopatra, contributed generously to the support of Octavian's troops when they were marching against Egypt, and accompanied the *Imperator* to Egypt and then on his return to Antioch. This diplomatic initiative paid off, because Octavian's mind was not moralistic but pragmatic. Herod was allowed to keep his throne. As a reward for his services, he was even granted several territories, some of which he had been obliged to cede to Cleopatra, others of which he had never possessed, such as Hippos and Gadara, wealthy Hellenistic cities east and southeast of the Sea of Galilee. In the year 23, the *Princeps* gave Herod three additional extensive territories east of the Sea of Galilee: Batanea (Bashan), Trachonitis, and Auranitis. Later, Herod also received the territory of Paneas, at the source of the Jordan. In the New Testament period, these territories belonged to the tetrarchy of Philip. Octavian's purpose was to secure the route between Damascus and the Decapolis against Nabateans and Bedouins. The appointment of Herod's younger brother, Pheroras, as tetrarch of Perea in the year 20 was also part of Octavian's anti-Nabatean policy. At the same time, these grants of territory also show how well Herod succeeded in gaining, preserving, and increasing the confidence of Octavian, even after the battle of Actium. Politically, the position that Herod attained under Octavian was a brilliant one. These successes continued to benefit the Jews of the Roman Empire throughout the New Testament period and contributed greatly to the conversion of proselytes.

(2) In the second period of Herod's reign, 27–13 B.C., the item of greatest interest is a number of magnificent public buildings that he constructed, which witness to the high financial and cultural status of the king. They enhanced the reputation of Judaism greatly. Herod had the means to adorn his kingdom sumptuously with examples of Hellenistic and Roman architecture. He also went far beyond the borders of his own country, taking part in the restoration of cultural centers in Greece and elsewhere. The ruins of Herod's enterprises in Palestine remain spectacular to this very day.

He enlarged Samaria, for example, the ancient royal capital of the Northern Kingdom, adorning it with a temple of Augustus, a magnificent throughfare, a forum, etc.; in honor of Augustus it was renamed Sebaste, i.e., Augusta. Strato's

Tower, an ancient Phoenician site on the coast, he made into an extremely important harbor. It was named Caesarea, again in honor of the *Princeps,* and contained a temple of Augustus. It was also furnished with the usual embellishments of a Hellenistic city: a palace, a theater, an amphitheater, a stadium, and a hippodrome. Caesarea later became a fit residence for the Roman procurator. In addition, Herod built or added to a whole series of cities and fortresses; as an example, we may mention Masada, an incredibly strong fortress on the west shore of the Dead Sea.

His most impressive buildings, however, Herod built in Jerusalem. In the western quarter, south of the present-day Gate of Jaffa, he built his palace. Imposing remnants of its mighty towers are still standing, especially the Tower of Phasael, built as a memorial to Herod's brother. The Acra, the old fortress at the northwest corner of the Temple area, was fortified and renamed the Antonia, in honor of the triumvir of the same name. This is presumably the site of The Pavement (John 19:13), so that the trial of Jesus took place alongside the Antonia, where a Roman cohort was garrisoned and where Paul was later taken prisoner (Acts 21:31–34). The southern quarter of the city received a theater, an amphitheater, and a hippodrome; games were to be held every four years. The devout, however, refused to attend these games because of their connection with the state cult.

Herod's greatest accomplishment was the Hellenistic rebuilding of the Jerusalem Temple, which had been constructed by Solomon and restored after the exile by Zerubbabel, but was now beginning to deteriorate. Work on the third Temple was begun in 20 B.C. After nine and a half years, the structure of the temple proper was finished; the rest of the Temple precinct took longer (more than the forty-six years mentioned in John 2:20). The whole complex was not officially consecrated until A.D. 63. Tragically, the Herodian Temple stood in all its glory for only a few years, being destroyed in A.D. 70, at the end of the first Judaeo-

Roman War. Herod's additions to the south and east enlarged the Temple precinct so greatly that it came to occupy twice the area of the Solomonic Temple. A person walking around the Temple area, one of the largest of the ancient world, would have been greatly impressed by its proportions and adornments, as the enthusiastic comments of Jesus' disciples indicate (Mark 13:1: "What wonderful stones and what wonderful buildings!"; Luke 21:5: ". . . how it was adorned with noble stones and offerings").

The substructure, which reached a depth of thirty-five meters, was invisible; but the height of the Temple must have filled every visitor with awe. The Temple proper was itself twice as large as it had formerly been. Its exterior length was fifty meters, the same as the width of the entrance hall to the east, which was attached like the crossbar of a "T" to the main building, whose long axis ran from east to west. Over the gate of the entrance hall Herod placed the resplendent gold eagle of the sun god, which shocked the Jews. Otherwise he respected the religious sensibilities of the people. Images and distracting symbols were prohibited, even on the local coins. Gentiles were forbidden under penalty of death to enter beyond the outer court of the Temple precinct. This so-called Court of the Gentiles was a terrace surrounding the raised inner precincts of the Temple. The terrace was provided with beautiful colonnades: on the east, the Portico of Solomon, where Jesus and the Apostles spent considerable time (John 10:23; Acts 3:11 ff.) ; on the south, the Royal Portico, which had five rows of pillars.

Signs in Greek and Latin, of which fragments have been found, prohibited all who were uncircumcised, on pain of death, to climb the steps leading to the inner area of the Temple precinct, the Sanctuary (Greek *tò hierón*) in a specific sense. The New Testament calls the main gate, leading into this inner area from the east, the Beautiful Gate (Acts 3:10; because he was ritually defective, the lame man mentioned in this passage could be brought only as far as this boundary between the Court of the Gentiles and the Sanctuary). The so-called Sanctuary contained first the Women's Court and then west of it the Men's Court, each court constituting a higher terrace.

Finally, at the western end of the Temple precinct, came the plateau on which stood the Temple proper, with an imposing flight of stairs before its eastern façade. In front of the Temple, on the terrace of the Men's Court, stood the great altar of burnt offerings surrounded by other sacred implements. The structure occupied an area marked off by a fence; this area was called the Priests' Court. Here the sacrificial priests carried out their bloody service (see below, pp. 165–68).

The whole complex resembled a model of the familiar world-mountain of ancient Near Eastern cosmology, on which the four classes of mankind—priests, Jews, Jewish women, and Gentiles—each had its allotted terrace. Above all, this Temple with its splendid buildings and imposing gates was an impressive monument of the Jewish people, for whom Herod had gained an important place in the civilized world. Whether it was also a fit dwelling place for the God of the fathers was disputed by some inhabitants of the land, among them the members of the Qumran community (CD iv.) and the followers of the teacher of Nazareth (Acts 7:48; I Cor. 10:20). Awed by this magnificent edifice, however, most of the Jews forgot all their reservations concerning Herod and Hellenism; they venerated the sacred site, visited, enriched, and adorned it, and, in three wars (A.D. 66–70; 115–17; 132–35), defended it fanatically.[6]

Herod also sought to gain a reputation throughout the Roman world as a patron of culture, which for him meant Hellenistic civilization. This benefited the Jews, especially in the Diaspora. He followed the usual custom among Hellenistic princes of making a name for himself as a benefactor (Greek *euergétēs*) by means of public bequests. A whole string of Hellenistic cities along the coast of Palestine and

[6] Photographs of Herod's important edifices can be found in A. H. M. Jones, *The Herods of Judaea* (1938), plates 1–6: the citadel, Samaria, the Temple area, a warning sign, the Wailing Wall, and Kidron Valley. Cf. also plate 7: illustrations of Temple implements on the Arch of Titus.

Phoenicia came to enjoy the generosity of this king in the form of buildings and monuments: Ashkelon, Ptolemais, Tyre, Sidon, Berytus, Byblos, and Tripolis, as well as the Syrian capitals Damascus and Antioch. Herod even extended this cultural beneficence to Asia Minor and Greece: he built a temple of Apollo on the island of Rhodes and public colonnades on Chios; he donated monuments to Athens and Sparta, and contributed to the adornment of Nicopolis, a triumphal city built by Augustus at Actium (probably mentioned in Titus 3:12). Herod set great store by being hailed as a benefactor by all these famous cities.

It is not hard to guess that this large-scale cultural activity cost the Jews a considerable sum in taxes. Yet it brought considerable advantage to the Jews themselves. Representatives of this nation were now scattered throughout the Roman world; they had synagogues and social organizations in every important city, at least in the eastern parts of the commonwealth. Jews could pursue their business undisturbed, and were able to acquire powerful patrons and numerous adherents. The exceptionally vigorous expansion of the Jews, together with their freedom of movement within the framework of Augustus' world empire and the *Pax Romana*, which are important considerations in the New Testament period, had of course long been in the making, especially under Caesar. But they would not have been possible to such a great extent without the favorable relations that obtained between Herod and Augustus and Herod's splendid contributions to Hellenistic civilization. The heartless King (Matt. 2:13–23) thus quite unintentionally paved the way for the spread of the Gospel, for the mission of the primitive church utilized the Jewish colonies and the elaborate Jewish proselytizing structure throughout the Roman Empire.

Herod also sought to raise the level of education; again, as with his buildings, he followed Greek models. His own education was desultory, but he saw to it that his sons received a Hellenistic education from court philosophers, and even sent some of them to Rome to complete their studies under famous Greek professors. The most famous of Herod's court philosophers and counselors was Nicolaus of Damascus (b. 64 B.C.), a Peripatetic (Aristotelean) thinker and scholar, who was particularly important as an historian. Josephus made use of his writings, which Herod had commissioned and published in large part as propaganda for the Jewish nation. The king also used Nicolaus as a diplomat, sending him as ambassador to Rome and asking his counsel in dynastic strife.

Herod's internal administration of the country was autocratic and arbitrary, as one would expect of an Oriental despot. Relatives, friends, and others who had his approval he appointed to offices, military positions, or administrative posts; he exerted a tyrannical influence upon them all. As the mood struck him, he appointed Jews to offices and then removed them again. This was particularly true for the office of high priest and for the Sanhedrin; in the face of venerable traditions to the contrary, these offices were made subject to royal appointment. The first high priest appointed by Herod came from Babylonia. After a year in office, he was replaced by Aristobulus III, a handsome youth; after the murder of Aristobulus, the original incumbent returned. Later Herod appointed an Alexandrian as high priest, a certain Boethus whose daughter Mariamne II he had married. Admittedly, however, Herod restored order to the land and enabled the people to enjoy the *Pax Romana* that Octavian Augustus had brought to the Mediterranean world.

Financially, Herod's regime benefited the land; his buildings provided the clearest evidence of this. Newly established contacts promoted trade with other parts of the Roman commonwealth, especially via the new port of Caesarea, but also quite generally via the wealthy Hellenistic cities and large territories that Herod received from Augustus. A typical example of the relative prosperity was the fishing industry on the Sea of Galilee, mentioned in the New Testament. Commercial firms shipped the dried or salt fish even to foreign countries. One such center of the fishing industry was Mag-

dala or Tarichea (Greek *taricheúō,* "to salt") on the western
shore of the Sea of Galilee, which is known to have been a
home of men working in this industry at least since 53 B.C.
(Josephus *Ant.* xiv. 120). The fishermen of Galilee formed
partnerships (Luke 5:10) and were able to acquire comparatively expensive equipment (Matt. 13:47–50); they should
not be thought of as primitive. Furthermore, there were
some wealthy capitalists in Palestine (as Luke 16:1–13 suggests). Thus we may reckon in the New Testament period
with an increase in Jewish income that was due in part to the
achievements of Herod. It is undeniable that many were
poor and that the people had to pay rather high taxes to
Herod and his successors in order to finance their expenditures. On the other hand, in 24–23 B.C., which were years of
scarcity, Herod assisted his people with generous contributions and relinquished considerable amounts in taxes when
the economic system worsened.

Nevertheless, Herod was not loved by the people. To many
he was simply too much a foreigner and a usurper: he did
not belong to the legitimate royal house; in fact, he was not
even a Jew. In addition, he represented Roman force and
Hellenistic culture, which clashed with the popular ideals of
political freedom and ethnic purity. There were Jewish circles which considered Herod a new Antiochus Epiphanes.
The Pharisees in particular, with whom he had a good relationship at the outset, became increasingly hostile. Herod's
policy of promoting Hellenistic culture prevented them from
inculcating Levitical purity and priestly observance of the
law among the people.

The situation with the Sadducees was the reverse. Originally, as representatives of a businessmen's party of political
realists, supporting the Hasmoneans, they detested and opposed the upstart, particularly during the Parthian War,
40–37. When he finally gained power, he executed several of
the Sadducees and constantly replaced the important
officials, particularly the high priest. By these means Herod
robbed the Sadducees of their power, so that they finally

became his obedient instruments. To some extent they were even impressed by the King's regime, since they were always politically minded and open to Western ideas.

Herod also had his supporters among the people (Josephus *Ant.* xiv. 450), who appear as the Herodians during the reign of his son Antipas (Matt. 22:16; Mark 3:6; 12:13).[7] Universal enthusiasm for Herod is said to have gripped the people when Augustus sent his old school companion, son-in-law, and representative in the East, Marcus Agrippa, to Jerusalem; this Roman admiral sacrificed a whole hecatomb (one hundred oxen) in the Temple and multiplied the wealth of the sacred precincts with his lavish gifts. On this occasion the people are reported to have accompanied the pro-Jewish viceroy to the harbor, strewing flowers and marveling at his piety (Philo *De Legatione ad Gaium* xxxvii).

In other words, feelings were mixed; Herod and Rome had both friends and enemies. Toward Augustus and Agrippa, Herod always showed himself obedient, loyal, and obliging. It strikes us as disreputable that he constantly and eagerly sought audience with the mighty to submit to them his humble requests. That was the usual practice in this period, however, and necessary conduct for a vassal. It really shows that Herod was a cautious and adaptable ruler. Later, however, Herod was to create anxiety for the Roman *Princeps* with his renewed dynastic conflicts, which colored the final third of his reign.

(3) During the third period of Herod's reign, 13–4 B.C., domestic conflicts flared up again, this time because the King's sons had grown old enough to be politically significant. Over a period of years, Herod's ten wives bore him several male heirs. At his sister's instigation, he now charged Alexander and Aristobulus, his two sons by Mariamne I who were Hasmoneans on their mother's side, with high treason, and had them executed in Samaria in 7 B.C. This made Herod's son by his first marriage, Antipater, heir presumptive to the throne, and he was so designated in the

[7] W. Otto, "Herodianer," in *PRE*, Supplement 2 (1913), cols. 200–202.

King's testament. He also bore the same name as Herod's father. Soon, however, this son also came under suspicion, and Herod wrote a new testament, naming a younger son as his successor, namely, Herod Antipas, who is familiar in the New Testament as tetrarch of Galilee.

Herod was then almost seventy years old and seriously ill. He still had strength enough to arrest some Pharisaic students of theology who, at the instigation of their professors, had removed the golden eagle from the Temple; they were executed by torture. But the King himself was afflicted with terrible pains which could not be relieved, even by an extended rest cure at the baths of Callirhoe, east of the Dead Sea. He returned to Jericho to make provision for the succession. Because Antipater had been making premature gestures as though he were already on the throne, Herod hated him so violently that he got Augustus' permission to have this, his eldest son, executed also. After this he became more favorably disposed toward his other sons, even those who had received nothing in the second testament, and determined in a third testament that all three should divide his kingdom. Five days after Antipater's execution, Herod I died, shortly before Passover in 4 B.C. He was interred with great splendor in the Herodium; its site is the conspicuous tell southeast of Bethlehem that contains the ruins of Herod's palace and mausoleum.

Herod was certainly, after David, the most powerful ruler of the Holy Land. But he was never popular with his Jewish contemporaries, although he benefited the land and the people by his building activities and by the expansion of trade. His Jewish critics found several grounds for complaint: his descent, his ten wives, his collaboration with the Greeks and Romans, his arbitrary treatment of laws and traditions. Many people hoped for a new form of government after the death of their powerful ruler; they wanted to be rid of the house of Herod and either put the land in the hands of the *Princeps,* as was the case in Egypt, or gain its freedom with the aid of a popular hero. These two movements led unavoidably to dissension.

C. The Date of Jesus' Birth

According to the Gospel of Matthew, Jesus was born in Bethlehem in the days of Herod (Matt. 2:1). This verse undoubtedly refers to Herod I, for later the return from Egypt is said to come during the reign of his successor in Judea, Archelaus, who ruled from 4 B.C. to A.D. 6 (Matt. 2:22). This means that Jesus was born in 4 B.C. at the latest. Luke presupposes the same facts in the first chapter of his Gospel: the Baptist's birth took place in the days of Herod (Luke 1:5) and Jesus was six months younger (Luke 1:26); Jesus was therefore born under the rule of the same king. In his second chapter, however, Luke associates the birth of Jesus with a census or enrollment for taxation that was ordered by Augustus and carried out at the time of Quirinius (Luke 2:1 f.). The only such enrollment for which we have evidence took place in A.D. 6 (see below, pp. 135 ff.); in this context, therefore, Luke apparently suggests a date at least ten years later for Jesus' birth. The long scholarly debate over this point make it questionable whether the conflict can ever be resolved. Possibly such a property census also took place under Herod and was later associated by Christian tradition with the tax enrollment under Quirinius. Luke 2:4 states that Jesus' parents, whose residence was in Galilee, had to travel to Bethlehem in order to record property that they owned there. This is most easily explained if the enrollment took place under Herod, when the kingdom was not divided. It is highly implausible that, after the division of the kingdom, taxpayers under Antipas took part in the taxation of Quirinius, for this latter taxation applied only to the former territory of Archelaus (Josephus *Ant.* xvii. 355; etc.). In short, the date of Jesus' birth is best placed in the last period of Herod's reign.

Of course, the earliest Christians were not concerned with the date, but only with the fact of their Messiah's birth. For a while, their chronology was very simple: "In the fifteenth year of the reign of Tiberius," and the like (Luke 3:1). Hellenistic Judaism often based its chronology on the Seleu-

cid era, beginning on 1 October 312 B.C. (see above, p. 44) ;
postbiblical Christianity often used the Roman era, beginning on 1 January (earlier 1 March), 753 B.C. (the traditional date of Rome's founding being 21 April of the same
year). Christian chronology was introduced in A.D. 526 by a
Scythian monk in Rome, Dionysius Exiguus. He had been
commissioned to standardize the calendar of church feasts,
and fixed the incarnation of Christ on 25 March of the
Roman year 754, which was selected as the year 1 of the
Christian era, beginning on 1 January. Dionysius overshot
Herod's reign by five years; but this does not mean that our
familiar system should be changed.

V

PALESTINE AT THE TIME OF JESUS AND THE APOSTLES

4 B.C.–A.D. 66

JESUS and the Apostles lived and carried on their work in the period between Herod's death in 4 B.C. and the outbreak of the First Jewish War in A.D. 66. The historical books of the New Testament therefore refer primarily to the first two-thirds of the first century of the Christian era. Within this period, Jewish history, Roman history, and the history of the Gospel each in itself constitutes a relatively complete and independent unit.

(1) After the death of Herod in 4 B.C., the *Princeps* and the emperors after him placed Palestine under the administration of Herod's sons and of procurators. The officials were sometimes Roman, sometimes native; but the system of government and the boundaries of the land remained generally the same. This external political order was preserved until the outbreak of war in A.D. 66; after the fall of the capital in 70, Judaism also ceased to have an independent domestic political life.

(2) By about 4 B.C., Augustus had finished most of his constitutional reforms in the Roman Empire, and the Roman system of government was fixed for the next several decades. This stability is typified by the succession, which remained in the Augustan line until the suicide of Nero A.D. 68. Politically, this was the period of the *Pax Romana* throughout the Empire. Augustus' inauguration of an Age of Peace at the *Ludi Saeculares* in 17 B.C. (Horace *Carmen saeculare*) was not an empty gesture. In the Roman Empire proper, this period of peace remained comparatively undis-

turbed until the time of Nero. Like two harbingers of revolution, however, a fire broke out in Rome in 64 and a war at Zion in 66; after Nero's death, the whole Roman Empire was ablaze and at war during the year 69. The same *homo novus* who conquered the Jews, Vespasian, was soon able to restore the power of the emperors, but upon a new foundation.

(3) Jesus lived in the first third of the century, appeared toward the end of this period in Galilee, Perea, and Judea, and was crucified, probably in the year 33, by the Jewish high priest and the Roman procurator. In the second third of the century, the Apostles continued to proclaim his message, and brought the Gospel from Jerusalem to Syria and Asia, Hellas and Italy. This apostolic period, A.D. 33 to 66, is defined at the beginning by the death of Jesus and at the end by radical changes in the entire situation. The circumstances and events appearing in the final act include the pressure of Jewish nationalism; the martyrdom of James, the brother of the Lord, in 62; the subsequent scattering of the primitive community and decentralization of Christianity; the martyrdom of Peter and Paul in 65; and the outbreak of the Zealot revolt in 66. These events made it necessary for the church to change its orientation both toward Judaism and toward the power of Rome. With the exception of "the disciple whom Jesus loved" (John 21:20), the generation of the Apostles now belonged to the past. As a result, the year 66 marks the beginning of the subapostolic age, which comprised the last third of the century, under radically changed circumstances.

1. THE DIVISION OF HEROD'S KINGDOM 4 B.C.

Caesar Augustus gave half the kingdom to Archelaus, with the title of ethnarch; the other half he divided into two tetrarchies, which he gave to two other sons of Herod, one part to Philip, the other to Antipas.

Josephus, *Bellum Judaicum* ii. 94

According to his final testament, Herod I wanted to divide his kingdom among three of his surviving sons. Augustus ratified this decision, with certain modifications, and so Herod's kingdom was distributed among the three princes named in the following table (and seen in a wider framework in the table on p. 128) .

Herod I
King 37–4 B.C.

Fourth wife: Malthace, of Samaria		Fifth wife: Cleopatra, of Jerusalem
Archelaus	*Herod Antipas*	*Philip*
Born about 25 B.C. Ethnarch of Judea and Samaria, 4 B.C.—A.D. 6. Banished to Vienna (Vienne), where he died prior to A.D. 18	Born about 23 B.C. Tetrarch of Galilee and Perea, 4 B.C.—A.D. 39. First wife a Nabatean princess; second wife: Herodias, daughter of his Hasmonean half brother Aristobulus, whom Herod had executed in 7 B.C. She had been married to his half brother Herod Boethus, to whom she bore Salome. Banished to Lugdunum (Lyon) in 39, where both later died.	Born about 24 B.C. Tetrarch of northern Transjordan, 4 B.C.—A.D. 34. Wife: Salome, Antipas' stepdaughter. Died A.D. 34 without offspring.

The father of these princes had already executed three of their older half brothers. A half brother of the same age, Herod Boethus, the son of Mariamne II, had been accused of making common cause with the last half brother executed; despite his ambitious wife Herodias, who later married Antipas, he withdrew from political activities and lived the rest of his life as a private citizen, probably in Caesarea. There were a few young sons of Herod, but they were still children and therefore unimportant as far as the question of succession was concerned.

In his second testament, Herod had chosen Antipas alone to be his successor. In the third, however, he showed favor to all three: the kingship would pass to Archelaus, while Antipas and Philip would merely become tetrarchs. As usually happened in the East, internal dissension broke out immediately upon Herod's death. People either wanted to be rid of

111

the Herodian dynasty or to have a different distribution of the power (Josephus *Bell.* ii. 5–79; *Ant.* xvii. 206–99).

The unrest that flared up expressed more than the dissatisfaction of those who had been less favored in Herod's testament. Large sections of the Jewish people were also gripped by a latent frenzy for liberty. The military ardor of the Maccabean period and the successes of the Hasmonean period had abundantly nourished the hopes formulated in the Holy Scriptures. During the Roman occupation and the Herodian tyranny these forces had been repressed; now the resulting explosion was all the more violent, and was repeated, in various forms, over a considerable period.

Immediately after Herod's death in 4 B.C., there was so much unrest in the Holy Land that Varus, the Roman governor of Syria (6–3 B.C.), had to enter the land with three legions. This is the same Varus who later became famous on account of his catastrophic defeat in the Teutoburg Forest in A.D. 9. He had hardly put down the unrest in Jerusalem when an actual revolt broke out in several places. In Jerusalem especially there was violent opposition to the plans of the interim Roman procurator to confiscate Herod's wealth. The procurator was confined to Herod's palace after a bloody struggle, in the course of which portions of the Temple were burnt. In Judea, a muscular shepherd by the name of Athronges came forward to claim power. In Perea, east of the lower Jordan, it was the Pharisees who instigated the uprising; their candidate was an imposing slave from the court of Pheroras named Simon, who succeeded in burning Herod's palace at Jericho. Galilee, however, was the most important center of the freedom fighters. It already had a long history as the home of various rebel leaders. The commonest practice was for groups to gather around a specific family in which the office of pretender to the role of Messiah was considered hereditary. After the death of Herod, the self-declared Messiah was Judas, the son of a certain Hezekiah, a famous rebel who had been executed by Herod. All three of these freedom fighters are said to have put on the royal diadem, which indicates that each wanted to be the chosen ruler of the people. Theirs was not the ideal of a suffering Messiah, as was later advocated by Jesus; they were influenced, rather, by the ideal of a victorious Messiah, triumphant over the foe. As previously under the Maccabees and later under the Zealots, members of the occupying forces and collaborators were murdered whenever possible. The serious new disturbances brought Varus to Palestine once more, and this time his legions were reinforced with Nabatean troops. He pacified Galilee and destroyed Sepphoris, the strongest fortress of Judas, the Galilean leader, then marched through Samaria to Jerusalem, dispersed the turbulent mob, and ordered the crucifixion of about two thousand Jews throughout the land. This fanatical uprising in 4 B.C. was the first revolt of the Jews against Rome. It is not as famous as the Zealot revolts of A.D. 6 and 66–70; account must be taken of it, however, if one wishes to understand the political tensions of Jesus' day.[1]

In the meantime, Herod's testament was being discussed in Rome. After the burial of the powerful ruler, almost the entire royal house set out for Rome with the utmost speed; for each member wanted to represent his own interests personally before Augustus. The first two of this host of petitioners were Archelaus, the presumptive king, and his brother Antipas. Since the latter had been slighted in the third testament in favor of his brother, he tried to represent the testator as being no longer responsible. The disputants also included Herod's sister, Salome, who had exerted great influence in recent years and was unwilling to yield to her twenty-one-year-old nephew. A delegation from the Jewish aristocracy also showed up in Rome, expressing their desire to be rid of the house of Herod, especially Archelaus, and subject directly to Augustus (Josephus *Ant.* xvii. 304–14) ; this wish was granted ten years later, but the Jews had not reckoned with the Roman procurators and tax officials (see below, pp. 134–37). Despite this disagreement among the princes and the nobility, Augustus decided to sanction Herod's

[1] W. R. Farmer, "Judas, Simon and Athronges," *New Testament Studies,* Vol. 4 (1958) , pp. 147–55.

113

testament. Still, he was unwilling to make Archelaus king immediately; instead, he made him ethnarch until further notice.

In 4 B.C., then, Augustus divided the kingdom of the Jews among the following men, thus establishing the regime that existed in the first years of Jesus' life and, in part, for some years thereafter:

Archelaus, under the title of ethnarch (i.e., "ruler of a nation"), was put in charge of Judea, including Idumea and Samaria. He had reason to believe that he would later become king if he conducted himself properly.

His younger brother, Herod Antipas, who appears several times in the New Testament simply as "Herod" (e.g., at the execution of the Baptist and at Jesus' crucifixion), was made tetrarch ("ruler of a fourth") of Galilee and Perea. His uncle, Pheroras, had previously been tetrarch of the latter region.

Their half brother Philip became tetrarch of the parts of northern Transjordan that Augustus had given to Herod I in 23 and 20 B.C.: Batanea, Auranitis, Trachonitis, and Paneas; in addition, he also received Gaulanitis.

Salome and the other relatives were apportioned regional possessions and financial benefits. In so doing, Augustus relinquished some of the income to which he had legitimate claim; he saw a good opportunity for demonstrating his famous generosity vis-à-vis the Herodians, who came forward with quite petty demands.

It is noteworthy that Augustus treated the Herodians as a dynasty. Herod I was an upstart; always a vassal, he was not granted a successor of royal rank. Nevertheless, with Augustus' consent, the government of Palestine remained in the hands of Herod's family. For Herod himself and his host of children the idea of a dynasty had become a firm conviction. The primary reason the offspring of the Idumean usurper strove so zealously to gain the royal inheritance was that their father had convinced them that royal blood flowed in their veins. For this reason they contracted dynastic marriages among themselves and also with princely houses in

Asia, Syria, and Armenia, and shared gladly in the sybaritic life of the Roman capital. Jesus and the Apostles lived at a time when the Jews found themselves confronted with this snobbish family of princes which the Romans, even long afterwards, considered among the Eastern royalty.

We shall now examine in detail the development of each of the three parts of the Herodian kingdom from their separation in 4 B.C. to their reunification under Agrippa I in A.D. 41. Following in broad outline the story of Jesus' life, we shall proceed from north to south.

2. GALILEE-PEREA AND NORTHERN TRANSJORDAN AT THE TIME OF JESUS

A. ANTIPAS' TWO TERRITORIES

> Herod the tetrarch built the city Tiberias, named after Tiberius, which he established in the loveliest part of Galilee, on Lake Gennesareth.
>
> Josephus *Antiquitates* xviii. 36

Herod Antipas (tetrarch from 4 B.C. to A.D. 39), according to the terms of his father's will, took control of two sections of the land, Galilee and Perea (southern Transjordan). These two regions were separated by Samaria and the Decapolis (central Transjordan), two strongly Hellenistic territories that controlled the trade routes; Samaria was apportioned to Archelaus, while the Decapolis constituted a league of free cities. The only common bond between Galilee and Perea was their adherence to Judaism, which had gradually been brought about by resettlement and conversion, in Galilee since the time of Aristobulus I, in Perea since the time of Janneus and, most recently, under Pheroras (see above, p. 97). The major reason for giving Antipas these two regions was to balance the power of Archelaus. Some parts of Galilee and Perea were fertile, however, and other parts capable of development, so that Antipas was not at a complete disadvantage.

(1) Galilee in particular was a densely populated and productive territory, where trade and the fishing industry flourished (Josephus *Bell.* iii. 35–43). The comparatively high level of material civilization there is indicated by the Hellenistic building projects that Antipas, following his father's example, was able to undertake. He rebuilt the Greek city of Sepphoris, which Varus had destroyed in the course of his campaign in 4 B.C., fortifying it with strong walls. In particular, Antipas built a new capital, beautifully situated on the west shore of the Sea of Galilee, which he named Tiberias in honor of Tiberius, the reigning emperor (14–37). The Jews, however, declared that the site was an ancient burial place and therefore unclean (Num. 19:16). For this reason Antipas had to make up the population of his capital out of Gentiles or nonobservant Jews, while all the strict Jews stayed away. Jesus and his disciples also seem to have avoided Tiberias, despite its importance. Among the Gospels, John is alone in mentioning the city, but without letting Jesus and his disciples visit it (John 6:23). From the commercial point of view, this city, built on Hellenistic lines, was admirably situated. The opposition of the Jews gradually disappeared, so that Tiberias also came to have synagogues. From around A.D. 200 onward, it was the center for the Sanhedrin and one of the four holy cities of Judaism, thanks to the local study of the law, which led to the Masoretic text of the Hebrew Bible and the compilation of the Mishna.

(2) In itself, Perea was not such a flourishing territory (Josephus *Bell.* iii. 44–47). As a defense against the Nabateans, it was provided with a fortified city by the name of Livias, later changed to Julias (Josephus *Bell.* ii. 168). The fact that here, too, Antipas found opportunities to continue the building operations of his father points to a reasonably good financial situation.

B. JESUS' HOMELAND

Galilee, with its green hills and blue lake, was also the home of Jesus. In Our Lord's day, the whole countryside, fertile, well-watered, and intensively cultivated, looked like a garden (Josephus *Bell.* iii. 42). The plain of Gennesareth, then as now, was of legendary beauty.[2] Its name probably goes back to the Old Testament Chinnereth, in the tribe of Naphtali (Josh. 19:35); this name is connected with the Hebrew word for lyre (*kinnôr*), but almost certainly not on account of the shape of the coast, which is visible only from the air. Gennesareth is a section of the coast on the northwest shore of the Sea of Galilee, about a mile wide and three miles long. It has a subtropical climate. Situated at the foot of the mountains 690 feet below sea level, it is protected from the wind. It was also an important commercial site, for at the time of Jesus the *Via maris* passed through Gennesareth. This is the "way of the sea" (Isa. 9:1 [Hebrew 8:23]; Matt. 4:15), the caravan route from Damascus through northern Transjordan and "the land of Naphtali" (*ibid.*) to Caesarea by the Sea. Not far from the border of Philip's tetrarchy in northern Transjordan there was located therefore a military post and customs station: Capernaum (Matt. 8:5–13; 9:9–13; and parallels). In addition, the plentiful supply of fish in the Sea of Galilee made possible the development of a food industry, the size of which is suggested by the city of Magdala or Tarichea, on the west shore of the lake (see above, pp. 102 f.). Jesus therefore proclaimed the kingdom of God in a delightful natural setting and an environment filled with activity; these earthly things, however, flowers and fields, farmers and fishermen, he saw only as an image of heavenly things.

Ever since the Assyrian conquest of Israel in 722 B.C., the population of Galilee had been quite mixed. Arameans and other peoples had settled here, so that there seems to be good reason for the biblical expression "Galilee of the Gentiles" (Isa. 9:1; Matt. 4:15). Since the time of Aristobulus I, however, Jews had migrated to Galilee and the population had gradually become judaized (see above, pp. 68 f.). Matthew and Luke presented Jesus as belonging to one of these families that had immigrated from Judea; his genealogy is traced

2 C. Kopp, *Die heiligen Stätten der Evangelien* (2d ed.; 1959), pp. 212–87.

117

back through Judean names to Judah and David (Matt.
1:1–17; Luke 3:23–38). Mary is said to have visited relatives
in Judah (Luke 1:36, 39), and we read that Joseph came to
Bethlehem to be enrolled, i.e., for assessment of the land tax.
Jesus himself came forward not as an alien, but as the
teacher and savior of the Jews (John 4:9, 22). The materials
contradict any so-called Aryan descent; at most, one might
think of an admixture of some other Near Eastern elements,
such as would be suggested by the Synoptic genealogy, which,
with the exception of Mary, mentions only such foreigners as
Tamar, Rahab, Ruth, and Bathsheba among Jesus' female
ancestors (Matt. 1:3, 5–6). We have no precise data, however, about the racial composition of Galilee.

As to the spiritual and intellectual climate in Galilee,
there developed in the course of time a surprising enthusiasm for the Jewish law once the land had been judaized;
the people were easily persuaded to join protest movements
directed against foreign influence. After the death of Herod
I, serious unrest arose in Galilee. As a representative of
Hellenism and Romanism, Antipas was always hard put to
avoid a civil war; that there were no uprisings against him
must be credited to his prudence. The activists opposed the
Romans all the more violently in 6 A.D., when Quirinius
began the tax enrollment of Judea and Samaria; at this time
the Zealots, a party of extreme nationalists, came into being
in Galilee (see below, pp. 136 f.). This party later played such
an important role in Galilee that, to the people round about,
"Galilean" sounded roughly equivalent to "anarchist"
(Matt. 26:69; Mark 14:70; Luke 13:1 f.; 22:59; Acts 5:37:
"Judas the Galilean"). As the Zealots fought on behalf of the
Mosaic law, there can be no doubt that popular religion in
Galilee had to a large extent become law-centered Judaism.
The statements in the Gospels about synagogues and Phari-
sees in Galilee confirm this assumption. On the other hand,
there was probably at least this difference between Galilee
and Judea: there were not quite as many Pharisees and
scribes active in Galilee as in Judea. On some occasions
Pharisees and scribes had to come to Galilee from Judea in

order to dispute with Jesus (Matt. 15:1 and parallels).
Apocalyptic circles, on the other hand, seem to have been
especially well represented in Galilee. In any case, we are
dealing only with differences in degree; this apart, the religious situation in Galilee at the time of Jesus was probably
about the same as in Judea, although the situation in Samaria was different (see above, pp. 27–30).

C. THE SYNAGOGUES

One of the essential institutions for the religious life of
Galilee was the synagogue (Aramaic *kništâ;* Greek
synagōgé, "assembly," or *proseuché,* "place of prayer"). This
type of community center and place of worship was undoubtedly borrowed from the Diaspora, where the social and religious need for a common meeting place was especially great
and the environment furnished certain models.

Jewish exiles in Babylonia may possibly have been familiar with some kind of predecessor of the synagogue (Ezra
8:17; Ezek. 11:16 [?]). The temple built at Elephantine by
Jewish colonists in Upper Egypt, which was in existence
around 525 B.C. (see above p. 25), is comparable in some
respects to the synagogues; the worship carried on there,
however, was of a different nature. The earliest historical
evidence of a synagogue is an inscription from Lower Egypt,
which states that the Jews of Schedia, near Kafr el-Dawar,
fourteen miles east-southeast of Alexandria, built a place of
prayer about 225 B.C. in honor of Ptolemy III and his family.[3] The first extant literary reference to a synagogue is
associated with the next of the Ptolemies (III Macc. 7:20).
The passage is legendary, but the mention of a synagogue in
this context is not accidental. Most of the references to pre-
Christian synagogues come from the Ptolemaic Kingdom;[4]
Alexandria in particular was distinguished by its possession
of a large number (Philo *De Legatione ad Gaium* 132).
Essentially, then, the Jewish synagogue system can be derived

[3] W. Dittenberger, *Orientis graeci inscriptiones selectae,* Vol. 2 (1905) p.
467, no. 726.
[4] S. Krauss, *Synagogale Altertümer* (1922), pp. 261–65; *idem,* "Synagoge," 2,
in *PRE,* II, Vol. 4 (1932), cols. 1306 f.

from Ptolemaic Egypt, where the Hellenistic associations, with their meeting places, influenced its development.[5] Shortly after 200 B.C., the Jewish colony in Syrian Antioch built a magnificently decorated synagogue (Josephus *Bell.* vii. 44 f.). In Palestine, too, synagogues came into being, first as Jewish centers in border cities like Lydda and Caesarea or at Jerusalem, the goal of pilgrimages (Acts 6:9; 24:12), then later throughout the whole land as places of assembly for the community. The building was expected to be situated on the highest spot available (*Tosefta Meg.* iv. 23, 227). In the Diaspora, where the synagogues served as centers for the Jewish colonists, they developed quickly since Caesar granted them the legal privileges of associations (see above, p. 89). In the time of Herod and the apostolic period they were to be found in every important city from the Tigris to the Tiber (Acts 15:21).

Galilee shared actively in this development. There, too, in the second century B.C. there were probably fraternal organizations of Jewish minorities, similar to the later synagogues of Babylonian Jews in Sepphoris and Tiberias.[6] During the judaization of Galilee in the first century B.C., the Jewish scribes obviously found this system, developed in the Diaspora, to be of value in teaching the law to the Galileans, in the manner prescribed by the Chronicler (II Chron. 17:9; Neh. 8:7 f.). By the time of Jesus, at any rate, Galilee had been won to Judaism, and a network of synagogues had been built (Matt. 4:23) in which scribes from Jerusalem often supervised the conduct of worship (Luke 6:7). Originally colonial and missionary institutions, these synagogues developed into community centers. The gospels mention by name the synagogues of Capernaum (Mark 1:21) and Nazareth (Luke 4:16), though no trace of them remains (the impressive ruins at Capernaum date only from the second century A.D.). After the political downfall of Jerusalem in A.D. 70, Galilee gradually became a center of synagogal Judaism; in

---

[5] F. Poland, "Synagoge," 1, *ibid.*, col. 1285: "There seems to have been a tendency in Egypt to hand over temples to the associations for purposes of assembly."

[6] Billerbeck, Vol. 2, p. 662.

the third century, Tiberias is said to have possessed thirteen synagogues.[7]

The synagogue buildings in Galilee often took the form of a basilica with three doors at the southern end, a long tripartite room, and perhaps a gallery for the women. During worship and other transactions, the members of the community and the worshipers sat on benches in the front part of the nave; the elders or rulers sat on chairs further back in the choir, facing the people. The last section, the Holy Place, contained the so-called ark, a container for the scrolls of the law and the Prophets. Two men were responsible for the building and its worship: a "ruler of the synagogue" (Greek *archisynágōgos;* Mark 5:22; etc.) and an "attendant" (Hebrew *ḥazzān,* Greek *hypērétēs;* Luke 4:20). At least ten persons had to be present at worship, which was often held on Monday and Thursday as well as every Sabbath and feast day.

The normal worship on the morning of the Sabbath included the following components (Mishna *Meg.* iii/iv. 1–5) :

(1) The Jewish kerygma "Hear, O Israel" (Hebrew *šᵉmaʿ*), consisting of three biblical pareneses (Deut. 6:4–9; 11:13–21; Num. 15:37–41), preceded and followed by benedictions, was recited in chorus.

(2) A leader appointed by the ruler of the synagogue, wearing a prayer shawl, stepped before the ark and in a loud voice recited the beginning and conclusion of the Eighteen Benedictions (Hebrew *šᵉmōneh ʿesrēh*), so called because it consisted of eighteen parts (some of which are reminiscent of the Lord's Prayer), while the congregation stood up and responded "Amen." If the leader was a priest, he would then recite the Aaronic blessing, hands extended horizontally toward the congregation.

(3) The attendant next solemnly took out the law, i.e., a scroll of the Pentateuch, from the ark. The ruler of the synagogue had appointed three, five, or seven readers—priests or Levites if possible, otherwise any men or even boys. Standing at a reading desk they took turns reading the ap-

pointed pericope from the Pentateuch, which was determined by a three-year lectionary. (The Hebrew term for this
pericope was *sēder;* in Babylonia, where there was a one-year
cycle, the selection was called a *pārāšâ*). Everyone had to
read from the scroll, and it was not permitted to recite any
selection by heart. Because the people were no longer able to
understand Hebrew texts, a trained translator (Aramaic
mᵉturgmān) presented an Aramaic paraphrase verse by
verse. Unlike the reader, he was forbidden to make use of a
manuscript. In the first Christian centuries and later, however, detailed examples of such Aramaic paraphrase were
recorded; they are extant in collections called "Targums."
(*a*) For the Pentateuch, these are the Babylonian Targum
Onkelos; the fragmentary Targum Jerushalmi II, supplemented by the newly discovered Targum Neofiti; and the
Targum Jerushalmi I, ascribed to a certain Jonathan. (*b*)
For the historical and prophetical books, we have the Babylonian Targum Jonathan. (*c*) For the Hagiographa, there
are various smaller Targums.

(4) On the morning of the Sabbath and on feast days, the
attendant fetched the Prophets, i.e., a scroll from among the
historical and prophetical books, from the ark. The leader of
the prayers, the last man to read from the Torah, or someone
else was appointed to read a section from the Prophets (Aramaic *haptārâ*). In Jesus' day it was evidently still possible to
choose a text at will, for in Nazareth the Master read passages from Isaiah that do not appear in the official lists [8] (Isa.
61:1–2; 58:6, according to Luke 4:17–19). Later instructions
also state that whoever read from the Prophets could skip
from passage to passage,[9] though not backward, as Jesus
decided to do when he read. If a translator joined in the
reading, he translated the prophetical reading into Aramaic
in groups of three verses.

(5) "And he [Jesus] closed the book, and gave it back to
the attendant, and sat down" (Luke 4:20); that is, he sat
down on the special preaching seat of the synagogue (called

[8] Billerbeck, Vol. 4, p. 170.
[9] Billerbeck, *ibid.*, p. 167.

"Moses' seat" in Matt. 23:2) in order to deliver a sermon (Aramaic *dārāšâ*, "research"; cf. the word *midrash*) based on the reading (Luke 4:21–27). Technically this scene at Nazareth corresponds to the usual course of synagogue worship, except that Jesus provided not scribal wisdom but messianic revelation. Such an extemporaneous thematic address was not uncommon, and could either be delivered independently of the Pentateuch pericope or as an exordium to its interpretation, in which case the speaker would choose arbitrary passages from Scripture as his point of departure. The rabbinic tradition actually contains more details about thematic preaching than about expository sermons, although at least in the Christian era the latter type was no doubt considered primary; because it was obvious, there was no need to describe it.[10] Luke provides a vivid description of a service in Antioch in Asia Minor, which agrees with Jewish tradition: after the readings, the rulers asked the congregation whether anyone wanted to deliver a word of exhortation (Greek *lógos paraklḗseōs;* Acts 13:15) ; Paul responded, and delivered a thematic address punctuated with various scriptural quotations (Acts 13:16–41). Such thematic synagogue sermons provided a liturgical point of departure for the Christian kerygma. The analytical expositions of texts, however, especially when delivered by scribes, contained more didactic material; they may be thought of as one of the sources of Christian didache. It should be noted that a famous scholar generally preferred to preach in Hebrew, bringing with him an interpreter to translate into Aramaic; the former would speak softly while sitting, the latter aloud while standing. We hear nothing of such a practice in Jesus' case, but Papias describes a similar practice of somewhat later date, referring to the missionary activity of the Apostles: Peter, he says, was accompanied by Mark as an interpreter, probably to translate his sermons into Greek, and Mark later published the expositions of the Apostle which are referred to as instructions (Eusebius *Hist.* iii. 39. 15).

(6) There is no evidence for any special concluding ri-

---

[10] Billerbeck, *ibid.,* pp. 171–84.

tual. According to a pre-Christian source, the high priest concluded the sacrificial worship of the Temple with the Aaronic blessing (Ecclus. 50:20) ; the rabbinic sources, however, state that in synagogue worship a priest would recite this text earlier, at the end of the Eighteen Benedictions.

In addition to religious worship, the synagogue also provided a center for social service; in fact, the distinction between a place of prayer and a community center seems to have been rather vague. In particular we read about instruction of children and care of the poor (Mishna *Shab.* i. 23; *Pea* viii. 7) . The synagogue officials were also concerned with such juristic matters as flogging and excommunication (Matt. 10:17; Luke 6:22) .

At the time of Jesus, the synagogues in Galilee were controlled to some extent by Judean scribes and Pharisees (Matt. 23:2; Mark 3:22; Luke 5:17) . This Judean interference in community life might well have disquieted the tetrarch of Galilee. Since, however, he had gained support from the Pharisees in opposition to Archelaus during the dispute over Herod's testament in 4 B.C., he let them have their way. Occasionally the Pharisees even sought out contact with the Herodians, Antipas' supporters, in order to attack Jesus (Mark 3:6; 8:15; 12:13) .

D. The Reign of Antipas 4 b.c.—a.d. 39

At the outset Herod Antipas followed the policies of his father, although he ruled with much less violence (Josephus *Ant.* xviii. 27, 36–38, 102–105, 109–125, 240–255) . Like his father, he was a supporter of Hellenistic culture, a tendency he expressed most strongly in his building activities, which often offended the sensibilities of the devout. Antipas nevertheless sought to take Jewish piety into account: he put in an appearance at the festivals in Jerusalem; he issued coinage without images; he later rejected Pilate's attempt to place gold plaques with the name of the Emperor in Herod's Jerusalem palace (see below, p. 190). In this way Antipas steered a middle course between the various interests, and was able to rule for three decades without any disturbances.

The last ten years of his reign, however, took a form less happy and serene. Antipas was under the influence of a very ambitious woman, Herodias, infamous for her part in the execution of John the Baptist. Herodotus exaggerated greatly in finding women to be behind the wars between East and West (Herodotus *Pers. bell.* i. 1–5), but he would have been right in the case of Antipas' woes. Antipas had married a Nabatean princess, but divorced her in favor of his sister-in-law Herodias. As the granddaughter of Herod I and Mariamne I, Herodias had inherited the drive for power of the Herodians and the Hasmoneans, and was dissatisfied with her politically idle husband Herod Boethus (Mark 6:17 confuses this Herod with Philip, who later married Herodias' daughter Salome). The levirate marriage of Antipas and Herodias was consummated while her first husband was still alive, and therefore aroused the criticism of John the Baptist (Matt. 14:4; and parallels). Antipas even feared a popular revolt led by the successful prophet (Josephus *Ant.* xviii. 118), who was certainly suspected of having Nabatean connections because of his stay in the frontier region. For this reason, John, whose activity is said to have begun in A.D. 28 (Luke 3:1), was put in prison; around A.D. 32 he was executed (Matt. 14:3–12 and parallels). In the meantime, the Nabatean king, Aretas IV, was preparing to go to war for the sake of his divorced and humiliated daughter. In 36, he attacked Antipas and defeated him so thoroughly that Vitellius, the Syrian legate (see below pp. 190–93), was forced to mount a counterattack, temporarily rescuing Antipas. Herodias was soon to cause his final downfall, for she could not stand Caligula's naming her brother Agrippa I king over the newly independent tetrarchy of Philip in 37, and she drove Antipas to contend for equal rank. The capricious Emperor deposed him in 39 for being too power-hungry, and banished him and his wife to Lugdunum (the modern Lyon), in Gaul, where both of them died.

The intrigues of Agrippa I contributed greatly to Antipas' ignominious end. This daredevil brother of Herodias had gained the ear of the tyrant Caligula and was named king over Philip's tetrarchy in 37. By the year 40 he was also allowed to take over the tetrarchy of Antipas (see below).

E. The Land and Rule of Philip

> Philip built the city of Pan at the sources of the Jordan and named it the City of Caesar. . . . Caligula placed the diadem on the head of Agrippa and made him king over the tetrarchy of Philip.
>
> Josephus, *Antiquitates* xviii. 28. 237

Philip (tetrarch from 4 B.C. to A.D. 34) was between his half brothers Archelaus and Herod Antipas in age; but by the terms of his father's testament, he had to be content with northern Transjordan (Josephus *Ant.* xviii. 28, 106–108). His interests were decidedly Hellenistic, and it was therefore just as well that his tetrarchy did not include any strictly Jewish territories. The population of the tetrarchy was mostly Aramaic and Greek; the territory was located on the routes by which cultural influence passed from Damascus to Tyre, Caesarea by the Sea, and the Decapolis. Philip, who was not as ambitious and underhanded as his half brothers, was able to further trade and culture in peace and quiet, following his own plans. His regime was therefore extolled for its liberality and tranquillity. Like his father and brothers, he left imposing monuments. In particular, he enlarged two important cities, which are also mentioned in the New Testament: Caesarea Philippi and Bethsaida-Julias. Caesarea was built on the site of Panium, the ancient city at the sources of the Jordan; it was modernized, enlarged, and renamed in honor of the ruler of the world, with the addition of Philippi to distinguish it from the famous Caesarea by the Sea. In the territory of this *polis,* Jesus received Peter's confession of faith (Matt. 16:13 and parallels). Bethsaida was a fishing village located where the Jordan flows into the Sea of Galilee; it was rebuilt and made a Hellenistic commercial center. In honor of Julia, the daughter of Augustus, it was named Julias. The first miracle of the loaves and fishes is said to have taken place nearby (Mark 6:45; Luke 9:10). Even on his coins Philip showed his readiness to honor the sovereign of the Empire, for he had them stamped with the likenesses of Augustus and Tiberius, which aroused no hostility in his territory. Philip was married to Salome, the daughter of Herodias, who danced at the execution of John the Baptist; their marriage remained childless.

After Philip's death in A.D. 34, his tetrarchy was joined to the province of Syria for a few years. Upon Caligula's accession in 37, it was made the kingdom of Agrippa I, the brother of Herodias and a friend of the Emperor. Agrippa's singular career will be described in the context of the history of Judea, the major scene of his activity (see below, pp. 195–202).

3. JUDEA AND SAMARIA IN THE TIME OF JESUS AND THE PRIMITIVE CHURCH 4 B.C.—A.D. 41

The ethnarchy of Judea-Samaria, which had been given to Archelaus, lasted for ten years. Jesus' only contact with it was a brief visit in early childhood (Matt. 2:22). The first procuratorship, however, which followed the ethnarchy and lasted for thirty-five years, was of crucial importance for him and the Apostles. The history of these regions must therefore be studied in detail. We shall be concerned with the persons and events listed in the table on page 128, and in addition with social and religious factors in Judea.

A. THE TWO TERRITORIES OF ARCHELAUS

(1) In the first place, Archelaus gained control of Judea, religiously and historically the most important territory, where the violent alternation of mountain and valley seems to suggest a dramatic past. Judea comprised the following regions, added in different periods:

(*a*) Postexilic Judah constituted the nucleus. This was essentially Jerusalem and its environs, corresponding geographically to the ancient tribal territories of Benjamin and

Emperors:	Important Legates of Syria:	Judea-Samaria:	Galilee-Perea:	Northern Transjordan:	Selected High Priests:	Significant Events:
Augustus, *Princeps* until A.D. 14	Varus, 6–3 B.C.	Archelaus, ethnarch 4 B.C.—A.D. 6	Antipas, tetrarch 4 B.C.—A.D. 39	Philip, tetrarch 4 B.C.—A.D. 34		Disturbances in Palestine, 4 B.C.
	Quirinius, A.D. 6–11	*Procurators:* Coponius, 6–9 Ambibulus, 9–12 Rufus, 12–15 Valerius Gratus, 15–26			Annas (Ananus I), A.D. 6–15	Tax census; Zealotism, A.D. 6
Tiberius, 14–37		Pontius Pilate, 26–36			Caiaphas, 18–36	Crucifixion of Jesus, probably 33
	Vitellius, 35–39	Marcellus, 36		Under Syria, 34–37	Jonathan, 36–37	Martyrdom of Stephen, 36
Caligula, 37–41	Petronius, 39–42	Marullus, 37–41	Agrippa I, king 40–44	Agrippa I, king 37–44	Theophilus, 37–41	Disturbances in Alexandria, 38
Claudius, 41–54		Agrippa I, king 41–44				Martyrdom of James the son of Zebedee, *ca.* 42

northern Judah. In other words, it included only the northern part of the old kingdom of Judah. Ezra and Nehemiah had built up Judah as a temple land; the Maccabees and Hasmoneans had given it renewed political and national power. This rocky land has the shape of a peaked roof interrupted by steep valleys on either side; its ridge runs from north-northeast to south-southwest, attaining an elevation of 2500–3000 feet above sea level. Its eastern slope reaches 1300 feet below sea level before its stony flank vanishes beneath the light blue surface of the Dead Sea. High above on the watershed lie the religiously important cities of Bethel, Jerusalem, and Bethlehem, roughly forming a straight line. The capital, today the holy city of Jews, Christians, and Moslems, attains an elevation in its northwest portion of 2600 feet above sea level, and in its southeast portion of 2400. Only some fifteen miles to the northeast lies Jericho, 820 feet below sea level at the mouth of Wadi el-Qelt. Herodian Jericho lay southwest of Old Testament Jericho, at the foot of the Judean upland. Since it was the eastern gateway to the land, it possessed a customs station (Luke 19:2). Its tropical fecundity also made it an important city; Archelaus had a special liking for his residence there.

(b) Jonathan and Simon advanced toward Sharon in the northwest, conquering and judaizing the regions of Arimathea, Lydda, and Joppa, which had previously been Samaritan and Philistine (I Macc. 11:34; 13:11). From that time forward, Judea included a portion of the rich plain and a city directly on the coast; the New Testament, too, considers Arimathea, Lydda, and Joppa as Judean (Matt. 27:57, and parallels; Acts 9:32, 36). Here the border between Judea and Samaria, which Janneus fortified, went past the military outpost called Antipatris. This was as far as a military guard had to accompany Paul to protect him from the Jewish conspirators (Acts 23:31). Farther to the south lay the territory of Jamnia, which did not belong to Archelaus and Judea, but rather to Herod's sister Salome and later to the imperial family; nonetheless, after the destruction of Jerusalem in 70, it became the residence of the Sanhedrin. Ashkelon and Gaza remained free cities throughout the entire period.

(c) Hyrcanus I extended Judea by adding to it Idumea, which, before the exile, had constituted central and southern Judah (see above, pp. 66 f.). In the north there is the cultural center of Hebron, and in this vicinity the highland reaches an elevation of 3000–3500 feet; toward the south, it drops gradually into the Negeb (the "dry land"). The downfall of the kingdom of Judah allowed the Edomites to penetrate from the south. In Greek they were called Idumeans. Hyrcanus forced them to accept Judaism and be circumcised. This did not always mean that they were considered Jews, as Antipater and Herod were to learn; but for the most part they and the Jews formed a single ethnic community.

The fertile area of Judea was limited almost entirely to the environs of Jerusalem and Hebron, the Jordan depression, and the plain of Sharon. Joppa, Lydda, Jericho, and Jerusalem, however, were also important centers of commerce, especially Jerusalem, as the goal of pilgrimages, with a regular population of some fifty thousand which would often more than double on the festivals.

(2) Samaria, with its fruitful hills and prosperous cities, was added to the regions listed. This was a commercial advantage for the ethnarchy of Archelaus and later a political advantage for the Roman procurator; historically, however, the unification was hardly a matter of course.

(a) Samaria corresponds geographically to the major part of the kingdom of Israel. After its conquest by the Assyrians in 722 B.C., however, it had acquired a mixed population which, in the postexilic period, came to bear the stamp of Persian and later Macedonian and Greek elements. Its center was the pass between Mount Ebal and Mount Gerizim (2850 ft.). Shechem, which was located there, again became the religious center at the time of the Samaritan schism (see above, pp. 27–30), while Samaria, to the northwest, remained the political center. In the Achaemenid Empire, Samaria outranked Jerusalem by virtue of being the residence of the Persian governor; after Alexander's victory it became a Macedonian military colony and helped pave the way for Hellenism. As custodian of the temple upon Gerizim, Shechem was in fierce competition with Jerusalem and later became an important center for the Seleucids' campaign of hellenization (II Macc. 6:2: Zeus Xenios; see above, p. 56). Constant intercourse with the Hellenistic cities of the Decapolis, which also included an area west of the Jordan in the vicinity of Scythopolis, heightened the tendency toward syncretism in Samaria.

(*b*) Hyrcanus I conquered this land, now thoroughly Gentile, destroying Shechem in 128 and Samaria in 109 B.C. (see above, pp. 66 f.). It remained in Jewish hands until the fall of the Hasmonean kingdom; in contrast to Galilee, however, which was occupied even later, it could never be judaized. In 63 B.C. Pompey added Samaria to the province of Syria and restored Hellenism. From that time on, the Decapolis and Samaria, much to the annoyance of orthodox Jews, constituted a Gentile and semi-Gentile enclave between Judea and Galilee. The mutual hatred of the Jews and the Samaritans, who worshiped at the Gerizim temple, was notorious in the time of Jesus (Luke 9:53; John 4:9).

(*c*) Herod I was at first allowed to govern Samaria in return for payment of tribute; in 30 B.C. it was made his feudal property. He promoted Hellenism through large-scale building in the old capital and the new harbor; in honor of Augustus he named the former Sebaste and the latter Caesarea. For the population the commerce that focused on Caesarea was very important; here was the terminus of the routes from Damascus through Galilee, from the Decapolis through Pella and Scythopolis, and from the lower Jordan through Sebaste. Culturally and commercially Samaria had the advantage over Judea, and it was no accident that Caesarea later became the residence of the Roman procurator. It was all the more galling for Judea to be separated from judaized Galilee by Samaria and the Decapolis (Luke 17:11).

B. THE REIGN OF ARCHELAUS 4 B.C.—A.D. 6

Archelaus was ethnarch of Judea and Samaria from 4 B.C.

to A.D. 6; his reign was neither long nor happy (Josephus *Bell.* ii. 1–116; *Ant.* xvii. 196–355). From the very outset he had to contend with domestic opponents who, within a few years, brought about his fall.

His personal characteristics were probably unattractive. But the major reasons for the opposition he encountered were in part the jealousy of the other Herodians, who would have preferred to see the cautious Antipas become ruler, and in part the desire of the Sadducees and Pharisees for greater freedom of movement than they could expect under this son who most resembled his father Herod. Archelaus was at first supported by the military; later, however, some units that he was no longer able to pay rose up against him.

The obsequies of Herod I, which Archelaus performed with great splendor, were hardly finished when the popular party of the Pharisees demonstrated against the remarkably imperious conduct of the heir apparent to the throne; on the Passover, they instigated a riot in the Temple. Archelaus had to depart for Rome in order to protect his interests as set forth in his father's testament. There Antipas and the other Herodians attacked him before the Emperor. In the meantime Varus, the Roman legate in Antioch, quelled the popular uprisings and then returned to Syria. The Roman procurator in Caesarea, Sabinus, took advantage of this vacuum to support the financial interests of Augustus in Jerusalem all too openly. As a result, in 4 B.C. during the Feast of Weeks the above mentioned revolt broke out in the capital, and soon messianic movements filled the whole land (see above pp. 112 f.). Varus had to return and put down the revolutionaries. Upon this new display of Roman power, it seemed wise to the upper-class party of the Sadducees and property owners, with the consent of Varus, to send a fifty-man delegation to Rome requesting direct annexation to the province of Syria; these men had the support of the more than eight thousand Jews in Rome (Josephus *Bell.* ii. 80–91; *Ant.* xvii. 301–314). At this point, however, the Herodians were almost ready to back Archelaus. Augustus finally decided to ratify

Herod's testament with only one reservation: Archelaus temporarily became ethnarch and had to earn subsequent promotion to the status of king. Because of this restriction on his power, Archelaus, despite his royal ambitions, was never able to overcome the resistance of the Jews.

The Synoptic Gospels reflect the general antipathy toward this power-hungry successor to Herod. Joseph and Mary, we read, did not settle in Judea after their return from Egypt because they heard that Archelaus had come to power (Matt. 2:22), so that they feared a repetition of Herod's persecution. Later, in the Parable of the Talents, which Jesus told near Jericho, Archelaus' city, he was probably alluding to the difficulties surrounding Archelaus' succession (Luke 19:11–27) : the nobleman had to go to a far country to receive kingly power, his subjects hated him and let it be known through a delegation that they did not want him as king—none of these details are really essential to the parable itself.

Archelaus was far from idle. Like his father, he erected impressive buildings, restored the palace at Jericho, provided aqueducts for the palm groves in the area, and founded the city of Archelais a bit to the north.

Nevertheless the leading Jews hated their ethnarch with a passion. They were angered by his deposing of two high priests from the house of Boethus. They likewise considered it intolerable when, for dynastic reasons, Archelaus married the widow of his half brother Alexander, who had been executed in 7 B.C. Questions of obedience to the law played a subsidiary role; the really important factor was the interests of the patricians, capitalists, and Sadducees. These circles were even able to persuade the leading Samaritans to join in a counteraction. In A.D. 6, the upper classes of both regions sent new delegations to Augustus to lodge complaint against Archelaus, who had to appear at Rome. His considerable property was confiscated by Augustus; the ethnarch himself was exiled to Vienna, in Gaul (the modern Vienne on the Rhône south of Lyons). He probably died there some ten years later.

C. The Establishment of the First Procuratorship A.D. 6

> Coponius, a member of the class of equestrians, was appointed procurator of the Jews, with general authority. Quirinius also came to Judea . . . to assess the resources of the Jews.
>
> Josephus, *Antiquitates* xviii. 2

In the course of the debate over Herod's testament in 4 B.C., the Sadducees and property owners, who were thinking in terms of a republican oligarchy, had suggested to the *Princeps* that Judea should be directly annexed to Syria and do without any local prince. When Archelaus was deposed in A.D. 6, Augustus followed this suggestion; he even went a step further and made Samaria, Judea, and Idumea his own mandated territory, the first imperial procuratorship of Judea, which lasted from A.D. 6 to 41 (Josephus *Bell.* ii. 117–177; *Ant.* xviii. 1–100).

A similar fate befell Commagene, a kingdom in Syria, which was annexed to Syria from 17 to 38 at the request of the local nobility but against the wishes of the people (Josephus *Ant.* xviii. 53 f.). The procuratorship of Judea, however, was to be directly under the *Princeps;* the new procurator Coponius and his successors were to govern it as Augustus' personal representatives. Accordingly, the land was not made a part of neighboring Syria; the Syrian legate Quirinius was only commissioned to make the initial tax assessment, and his successors intervened only in the case of large-scale popular uprisings. Like the prefecture of Egypt, Judea became Augustus' personal protectorate. As in the Ptolemaic period, it was also treated as temple territory under the control of the high priest, not as property of the crown. To be sure, the *Princeps* confiscated the wealth of Archelaus without further ado, and he attached great importance to claiming the taxes and customs duties for the imperial treasury or fisc, although this change dismayed the Jews. But not until much later was the new procuratorship treated like an ordinary province; Roman colonists were not settled there until after the Jewish defeat in the year 70.

In A.D. 6, then, Quirinius had to take charge of the enrollment or tax registration in Judea-Samaria mentioned by Luke (Luke 2:1 f., where "all the world" is simply the popular expression for "the whole land"; see also Acts 5:37). He was the newly appointed legate for the imperial province of Syria with his residence in Antioch; he thus held one of the highest offices in the Empire, with the title *Legatus Augusti pro praetore,* which can be thought of as a legion commander who represented Augustus and bore the rank of a praetor. The imperial provinces, of which Syria was one, had a military government; they were controlled by a general descended from the highest senatorial nobility, who in this case commanded three legions (brigades) of professional soldiers, totaling some 18,000 men. The senatorial provinces, in contrast, had a civilian government (see below, pp. 229 f.). A civilian government was also planned for the imperial procuratorship of Judea, although the procurator also had to have the support of troops. First, however, Quirinius, the highest-ranking dignitary and military commander in the East, was instructed to lay the groundwork for the organization of the Judean and Samaritan tax structure. In line with earlier practice the new procuratorship was divided into toparchies or tax districts, and every *pater familias* was required to file a financial declaration at the district center, so that the population and economic situation could be determined. Because wealth consisted for the most part of real estate, the Jews were generally enrolled in the city near which they owned land.

We have already touched on the problem of the date of Christmas, which is connected with the divergent statements made by Matthew and Luke (see above, p. 106). Some scholars seek to resolve the conflict between the dating in the time of Herod (Matt. 2:1; Luke 1:5, 26) and that in the time of Quirinius (Luke 2:2) by referring to documents that mention an earlier governorship held by Quirinius. Despite the fragmentary evidence, this earlier period in office is not absolutely improbable. In that case, however, Luke would be referring to an enrollment that took place at the time of Quirinius but not at his instigation, for in Herod's kingdom the king was responsible for such matters. It is simpler to assume, as we have done above, that the Lukan tradition associated an enrollment under Herod with the later one under Quirinius, which everyone knew of.

Quirinius' tax enrollment in A.D. 6 affected only those areas of the Holy Land that had formerly belonged to Archelaus (Josephus *Ant.* xvii. 355; *et al.*), and yet it brought about a surprisingly violent reaction on the part of the popular party in Galilee, where some Pharisees now promoted the ultranationalistic Zealot movement.

The circumstances surrounding the growth of Zealotism deserve notice. In the interests of oligarchy, the genteel party of the Sadducees had just succeeded in transforming Judea from an Herodian principality into a Roman procuracy. The popular party of the Pharisees was not prepared to show its opposition by fighting for the house of Herod on behalf of the monarchy, but its theocratic principles made domination by the Romans seem even worse. Once again, Commagene is comparable: the aristocracy there preferred Roman to royal government, while the people as a whole would have preferred the indigenous monarchy (see above, p. 134). For the Pharisees, of course, the religiously motivated struggle against Hellenistic culture and paganism was central. In addition, how shall we account for the fact that "Galilee of the Gentiles" became the birthplace of the Zealot movement, and this in consequence of a tax enrollment affecting only Judea? In the first place, Jewish devotion to the law had increased markedly in Galilee; the many immigrant Jews had obviously become superpatriots, as can easily happen with colonists. In the second place, the political atmosphere was freer under Herod Antipas than in Judea, where the legionaries of Quirinius could smother any emotional outbursts in a moment.

And so the circumstances of the first Zealot revolt become clearer. Two men of Pharisaic background, aided by gangs of young hotheads based in Galilee, sought to force the people in Judea to sabotage the enrollment (Josephus *Bell.* vii. 253–256; *Ant.* xviii. 3–10, 23–25) . These two were Judas, a scribe from Gamala, east of the Sea of Galilee, who was also called Judas "the Galilean," i.e., the revolutionary (Acts 5:37) , and Zadok, a Pharisee. Their activity is reminiscent of the enthusiasm for the law shown by Mattathias of Modein (I Macc. 2:24) . The high priest and the conservatives were able to dissociate Judea from the revolt; in addition, the presence of the Romans had a restraining effect. Beneath the surface, however, the flame continued to burn, especially in Galilee. This situation is still reflected at the trial of Jesus, where a Jewish girl quite naïvely used the term "Galilean" in a sense roughly equivalent to "anarchist" (Matt. 26:69) . According to Josephus, this nationalistic movement in Galilee, led by Pharisees, laid the groundwork in Judea for the powerful popular party of the Zealots or "fanatics."

Despite the uprising, Quirinius carried out the tax enrollment, reorganizing the tax and customs structure in such a way that the tribute money and assessments accrued to the *princeps.*

This process was also furthered by the romanization of the coinage. Coins continued to be minted locally, and without a portrait of the ruler because of the Jewish prohibition of images; they were, however, Roman coins. Foreign coins also circulated, often with the head of the emperor, as archaeological discoveries show. Jesus' answer to the question about tribute put to him by the Pharisees in Jerusalem (Matt. 22:15–22 and parallels) assumes that, despite the prohibition of images, one of the questioners had with him a denarius with the portrait of the emperor. One may think of one of the widespread silver *denarii* of Tiberius, a large proportion of which were minted in Lyon.[11]

---

[11] For pictures of the Tiberius *denarii,* which are found as far away as India, and a discussion of them, see F. W. Madden, *Coins of the Jews* (1881) , pp. 291 f.; C. H. V. Sutherland, *Coinage in Roman Imperial Policy 31 B.C.—A.D. 68* (1951) , pp. 190 f.; pl. vi, 5; M. Grant, *Roman Imperial Money* (1954) , pp. 133 f.; *idem, Roman History from Coins* (1958) , pp. 83 f.; pl. 32, 4.

D. ROMAN GOVERNMENT A.D. 6–41

After Quirinius had carried out his special commission, the procurator, Coponius, was entrusted with responsibility for the fiscal affairs and social order of Judea. His residence was in Caesarea by the Sea, a place that had the advantage of being easily accessible, having Hellenistic buildings, and being religiously neutral.

Procurator means "financial agent" or "supervisor" (Greek *epitropos,* "trustee," in the New Testament *hēgēmón,* "principal," translated in the RSV as "governor"); such an office would be entrusted to equestrian members of the capable and ambitious upper-middle class. As representatives of the *princeps,* they were to oversee the revenues flowing into the fisc from the imperial domains and provinces. Augustus promoted this ambitious group of salaried officials in order to have loyal civil servants and to enable members of the second class to pursue a public career, which could see them rise as high as prefect of Egypt or co-prefect of the Praetorian Guard. Imperial revenues from a procuracy comprised many kinds of taxes and tolls, including per capita taxes and levies on land as well as the despised border customs, marketplace tariffs, and excise taxes.

The task of collecting these numerous tributes was delegated by the procurator to private companies and entrepreneurs, the tax contractors, who were often accused of avarice. As early as the time of the Ptolemies a wealthy Tobiad had paid the taxes as a lump sum and then collected them in his own name (see above, p. 48). We now find a well organized profession, not uncommonly rapacious and therefore detested: the equestrian publicans and their humbler colleagues, the so-called *conductores.* Ever since the second century B.C., the Roman East bemoaned the presence of the publicans (Latin *publicanus,* "state contractor"), i.e., members of the Roman capitalist class who were organized in large companies and were allowed to exercise a monopoly on the collection of taxes in the provinces. Caesar had somewhat restricted the extent to which such tax contractors could exploit the Jews (Josephus *Ant.* xiv. 201). It is at least conceivable that Herod, Archelaus, and Antipas also employed Roman tax contractors for the benefit of the fisc in Jerusalem and in Tiberias. To be sure, such taxes and tolls were collected for the most part by indigenous entrepreneurs, who, according to Roman terminology, would have been called *conductores*. But seeing that people in Galilee classed their Jewish "tax collectors" (Greek *telónai*) with Gentiles and sinners (Matt. 5:46; *et pass.*), it is also possible that they were associated with the detested publicans; and since the procurator in Caesarea was responsible to the fisc in Rome and was himself a member of the capitalist class, it is reasonable to assume that he employed Roman publicans. Out of respect for the sensibilities of the people, however, he saw to it that for the most part those who actually collected the taxes were Jews. This explains why in the New Testament the tax collectors are generally Jews whom the Pharisees and nationalists shunned as collaborators, so that Jesus' association with them appeared repugnant (Matt. 9:11; *et pass.*). Judean tax collectors were therefore not public officials but rather local entrepreneurs similar to the *conductores,* with hired assistants. This system had begun to supplement the function of the Roman publicans in the second century B.C. We meet such a figure in the wealthy Zacchaeus, at Jericho, who is called a chief tax collector (Luke 19:2) because he contracted for the border and sales taxes of the region and hired assistants to collect them. Later on, another Jew appears in Caesarea as tax collector and spokesman for the local Jews (Josephus *Bell.* ii. 287); he was probably the agent of the procurator. In the other passages where the New Testament mentions tax collectors, we may frequently consider them subordinate assistants to the tax contractor; they were business agents, not public officials. As a consequence, the people's hatred of the tax collectors rested on two grounds: first, their collaboration with the occupying forces; and second, the often unjust opportunities this class had to turn a profit (Luke 3:13; 18:11; 19:8).

In order to put down potential uprisings, the procurator also had soldiers at his disposal. Since no legions were stationed in Palestine, these soldiers were auxiliaries, light-armed militia units made up of provincials; Jews were given the opportunity to join, but were not compelled to. As a high-ranking reserve officer, the procurator had something like a regiment under his command; this force usually consisted of five cohorts, each of which comprised some six hundred men, which is roughly equivalent to a modern battalion. Each cohort was commanded by an officer who, like the procurator, belonged to the bourgeois middle class (John 18:12; Acts 21:31—25:23); this officer was called a tribune (Greek *chiliarchos,* "major"). His subordinates, drawn from the common people (Acts 10:1; *et pass.*), bore the title "centurion" (Greek *hekatóntarchos,* "sergeant"). The troops were garrisoned at Caesarea (Acts 25:23), but units were also transferred elsewhere as needed, for instance to Jericho and the fortresses in the Dead Sea region. One cohort was stationed permanently at Jerusalem, in the Antonia, as Herod renamed the fortress at the northwest corner of the Temple area. The local garrison included a cavalry unit (Acts 23:23); it was therefore one of the *cohortes quingenarii equitatae,* consisting of about five hundred foot soldiers and one hundred horsemen. Augustus exempted Jerusalem from the usual requirement that the standards bear the portrait of the emperor. At the great feasts the procurator often came to Jerusalem with his escort, which would approximately double the military force in the capital. While the procurator was in Jerusalem, he and his bodyguard lived in the palace built by Herod on the west side of the city, which therefore was given the Roman name *Praetorium* (Matt. 27:27). The procurator, however, also came to the Antonia for official business, as Pilate probably did at the trial of Jesus (see below p. 184).

As regimental commander, the procurator of Judea was also the highest military tribunal. He exercised *ius gladii* over the Roman soldiers, and was also empowered to pass the death sentence in the case of the civilian population (John 18:31). Thus Jesus was executed at Pilate's command under the supervision of a centurion (Matt. 27:26, 54 and parallels). In other cases, too, the procurator acted as a superior court by virtue of his military position, as Felix had to do in the trial of Paul (Acts 23:24). This official could also intervene at times in administrative matters, as for example, when Pilate ordered that an aqueduct be built (see p. 176).

E. THE JEWISH ADMINISTRATION

In domestic affairs, meanwhile, the Jews preserved a large measure of autonomy. This was particularly true in the field of religion, but also in questions of jurisdiction and administration.

Augustus was familiar with the Jews' love for their cultic and ethical traditions. In the field of religion he therefore refrained from too strong an assertion of Roman supremacy. The military standards in Jerusalem were not to bear the picture of the emperor. The Jews were not required to participate in the cult of the ruler; the emperor was content to have sacrifice offered on his behalf in the course of the two daily burnt offerings at Jerusalem (Philo *De Legatione ad Gaium* 157; Josephus *Bell.* ii. 197). Nothing was done to force the Roman religion on the people; quite the contrary, Augustus took the temple cult into his personal protection and saw to it that the prohibition against Gentiles' entering the Temple remained in force. It was also religiously significant that Jewish men could not be recruited into the army by force.

In the East the Romans preferred to leave jurisdiction and administration to local authorities, especially the Greek democratic assemblies with their long tradition. Since the Jews also possessed traditional organs of government and since their aristocrats had proposed the procuratorship for the very purpose of introducing a pro-Roman oligarchy, Judea, like the Greek cities and territories, was allowed to keep its social organizations. The Hellenistic cities of Caesarea and Sebaste, with their environs, retained separate administrations; but the rest of the land, with Jerusalem as its center, was treated as a *polis*, i.e., a city with its surrounding territory.

F. The High Council

Under the procurators, the highest organ of domestic authority was the High Council at Jerusalem; it functioned as the senate of the Jewish *polis*. In consequence, the Romans addressed official correspondence to the "rulers, senate, and people of the Jerusalemites" (Josephus *Ant.* xx. 11).

Historically, the Jerusalem High Council or Sanhedrin derived from the assembly of dignitaries that came into being under Ezra and Nehemiah (see above, p. 21). At the time of the Seleucid conquest, around 200 B.C., it appears again as a representative assembly of elders (Greek *gerousia*), mentioned even before the priests (Josephus *Ant.* xii. 138, 142). Even at this time real power lay in the hands of the elders: these were the patricians or heads of families, as in Greek municipal assemblies and the Roman senate. In the period of the Maccabees, we hear of two groups: the rulers (*árchontes*) and the elders (I Macc. 1:26). We may think of the former as those with special functions and the latter as patricians in general. The assembly of patricians, now called the Sanhedrin, put itself forward as the legal government of the entire country in opposition to the arrogant young military governor of Galilee, Herod (Josephus *Ant.* xiv. 167–179). When he became king, however, Herod repressed both the patricians and the priestly aristocracy, turning the Sanhedrin into a docile instrument for carrying out his policies (*ibid.*, xv. 173; *et pass.*). Under the procurators this governing body was now restored, becoming a kind of parliament with a domestic importance even greater than before. This took place, with Quirinius' approval, under the leadership of Annas, whom he installed as high priest (Josephus *Ant.* xviii. 26).

1) *Annas as Princeps*

Ananus I, or Annas, held the office of high priest from A.D. 6 to A.D. 15. He was head of a priestly family that, upon his accession, began to supplant the family of Boethus, which was related to the house of Herod and had hitherto dominated the priesthood (Josephus, *ibid.*). Quirinius probably chose him to be high priest because he was one of those Sadducees and men of substance who for years had been advocating a Roman regime, and also because he had played a leading role in the fall of Archelaus; it was a political appointment tendered to a man whom Quirinius trusted. Not only did Annas reorganize the High Council at Jerusalem and preside over it during his period in office, he also dominated it from the time he was removed from office in 15 until his death in 35. This lifelong leadership in domestic politics he owed to his tactical shrewdness and patriarchal power. From his wealthy family six others eventually rose to the high-priestly dignity: a son, a son-in-law Caiaphas, and then four more sons (Josephus *Ant.* xx. 198). Annas was the real power behind the first two of his successors. Just as Augustus was *princeps* of the Roman senate (see above, p. 95), so at the time of Jesus and the first Apostles one might say that Annas was honored as *princeps* of the Jewish senate, the member whose opinion must be heard first (Matt. 26:3 and parallels; Luke 3:2; John 18:24; Acts 4:5–6). As everyone well knew, he was the moving force behind the reorganized Sanhedrin, which constituted the executive, the parliament, and the supreme court for the Jews throughout the New Testament period until the fall of Jerusalem.

2) *The High Priest as Praeses*

Under Annas and his successors, the official high priest once more stood at the head of the Jewish state. Now, however, this religious dignitary was not a sacerdotal prince, as in the Hasmonean period, but an aristocratic *praeses* of the Council.

The most important figures to hold this office during the time of Jesus and the Apostles were:

Ananus I (Annas)	6–15
Caiaphas, Annas' son-in-law	18–36
Jonathan, Annas' son	36–37
Ananias, a powerful financier	48–58
Ananus II, Annas' son	62

The Romans took special care to limit the power of the high priest. From 6 to 36 the high-priestly vestments were kept by the garrison in the Antonia. At any time the officials could depose a high priest and appoint a new one; many stayed in office only a few years. The procurators of the period were authorized to appoint the high priest; after the end of the first procuratorship this right passed to the later Herodian client-kings: Agrippa I (41–44), Herod II of Chalcis (44–48), and Agrippa II of Chalcis, later northern Transjordan (50–66).

Despite these restrictions, during the first procuratorship (6–41) the high priest was the most powerful man in Idumea, Judea, and Samaria after the procurator; during the second procuratorship (44–66) this power extended also to Galilee. By virtue of his office he presided over the High Council; in this capacity he headed both the permanent cabinet or consistory of "high priests" (see below, pp. 146–49) as well as the whole assembly, which functioned as parliament and supreme court (Matt. 26:3, etc.; Acts 5:21; 22:5). According to rabbinic tradition, prominent scholars headed up the presidium in turns; this statement, however, is an anachronism (Mishna Ḥag. ii. 2).[12]

At the time of Jesus and the Apostles the high priest generally had the following three duties as a consequence of his traditional religious significance and newly regained political position:

(1) He represented all the Jews before the God of Israel, especially at the annual festivals: the Day of Atonement, the Feast of Booths, Passover, and the Feast of Weeks. Whenever possible he performed liturgical functions on other occasions also, and supervised the Temple worship and the sacrificial system with their attendant priests and Levites.

(2) He represented the people of Judea before the procurator, and at least symbolically represented all the Jews of the Empire before the *imperator*.

(3) He presided over the domestic administration, jurisdiction, and political life of Judea.

[12] Schürer, Vol. 2 (4th ed., 1907), pp. 202–205.

As leader of the priestly aristocracy, the high priest was a political authority for the patricians and Sadducees (Acts 5:17), who constituted the ruling party during the first and second procuratorships. In addition, the high priest had spiritual authority over the priesthood and, indirectly, over the Jews throughout the entire world.

3) *The Members of the Council*

In addition to the high priest, the High Council comprised seventy members, so that the whole assembly consisted of seventy-one councillors. The scriptural command "Gather for me seventy men" (Num. 11:16) was cited; Moses was counted in addition, so that there were "seventy-one altogether" (Mishna *Sanh.* i. 6b).

For plenary sessions, a hall in the southwest portion of the Temple area, near the Xystus Valley, was used (Josephus *Bell.* v. 144).[13] The members of the Council, vested in their robes, sat in semicircles, as in a theater, with the high priest in the center and next to him the "men of high rank" (Mishna *Sanh.* xv. 3a); these latter probably included the members of the consistory of "high priests" (see below, sec. *a*). For legal proceedings, the plaintiff and defendant stood before the president, the defendant being dressed in mourning. The witnesses were heard in turn (*ibid.,* iii. 5); the matter was then discussed in the absence of the parties concerned (Acts 5:34). When a vote was taken, court secretaries noted the result (Mishna *Sanh.* xv. 3b). Students (*ibid.,* 4) and auditors (Tosefta *Sanh.* vii. 8. 426) were allowed to stand at the rear and listen to the proceedings; an audience of this sort swelled the tumult directed against Stephen (Acts 7:54, 57). A plenary session was required only in especially serious cases, such as the condemnation of a false prophet (Mishna *Sanh.* i. 5). Because the assembly also included a group of laymen, called "elders" (see below, sec. *b*), the high priest obviously could not summon it at a moment's notice. This may have been possible, however, at the time of

---

[13] Schürer, *ibid.,* p. 211; H. St. John Thackery, *Josephus with an English Translation,* Vol. 3 (1928) pp. 242 f., note; also map III.

the annual festivals, as in the case of Jesus' trial, which Mark 15:1 says involved a plenary session.

Smaller portions of the Council would also hold session, or there might even be an audience before the high priest in private. These were a substitute or a preparation for a plenary session. In simple cases such a session sufficed (Mishna *Sanh.* i. 1–3; i. 4, 6 describes committees of 3, 10, and 23 members). The high priest had certain members at his disposal almost constantly: the members of the consistory of "high priests" (see below, sec. *a*), and the most zealous of the "scribes" (see below, sec. *c*); according to rabbinic tradition, the scholars spent each day in the Temple area (Tosefta *Sanh.* vii. 1. 425). During the conspiracy against Jesus these two groups stood beside the high priest (Mark 14:1; Luke 22:2). After Jesus was taken prisoner, they and some of the elders came to the small night session at the palace of the high priest (Matt. 26:57 and parallels), which preceded the final plenary session the next day (Mark 15:1).

The seventy-one Jewish senators of the New Testament period were divided into three groups, which the Gospels and Acts regularly distinguish (see, for example, Mark 11:27 and Acts 4:5). These groups were: (1) the "high priests" (Greek *archiereîs;* RSV "chief priests") or the "rulers" (Greek *árchontes*); (2) the elders (Greek *presbýteroi*); (3) the scribes (Greek *grammateîs*). The first two groups are known from the Maccabean period (see above, p. 142), and they are here supplemented by the indispensable legal experts, the scribes.

a) *The High Priests as a Consistory*

In the New Testament, the plural "high priests" refers, contrary to a common misapprehension, in typical Hellenistic fashion to a consistory made up of priests and laymen.[14] Such a committee of the assembly of elders is first mentioned in a diplomatic note from Jerusalem to Sparta about 144 B.C.

---

[14] A body with a fixed membership; this was first shown, on the basis of rabbinic texts, by J. Jeremias in his *Jerusalem zur Zeit Jesu,* II B 1 (1929), pp. 33–40.

(Josephus *Ant.* xiii. 166), where it is called "council of the priests" (Greek *koinòn tôn hieréōn*). To what extent this document is an invention (it goes beyond I Macc. 12:6–18) is unimportant in this context; the terminology, however, is significant, the more so because a degree of precision is attempted with respect to the official titles of Sparta. Greek analogies confirm that the so-called high priests were a common administrative board responsible for the temple and sacrificial system of the particular region, such as, "the high priests of the island" (*scil.* Cyprus); "the high priests of Asia" (cf. Acts 19:14); "the high priests of the Galatian league." [15] Because supervision of the temple and sacrificial system at Jerusalem was complicated after the time of Herod, the high priest on duty was supplemented by such a consistory, which was given the usual technical name, "the high priests." As a consequence of the broad impact of the cultic law and the service of the altar, the authority of the Jerusalem consistory extended to various areas of domestic politics in general. Its members were therefore also called "the rulers" (I Macc. 14:28; Acts 4:5, 8; Josephus *Bell.* ii. 405, 407). Another term for this governing body was "the ten foremost men" (Josephus *Ant.* xx. 194), an expression that shows it was composed of approximately ten wealthy and distinguished citizens. This suggests yet another Hellenistic analogy, for several Greek and Roman cities had a ten-man committee of wealthy and distinguished, primarily aristocratic councilors (Greek *dekaprôtoi,* Latin *decemprimi*); this was even true of Tiberias, the capital of Galilee (Josephus *Vit.* 69. 296). [16] In other words, the "high priests" at Jerusalem made up an aristocratic committee of the High Council, a consistory that functioned as the executive government of the Judean temple-state.

In this period, the actual high priest presided over the governing consistory as well as over the entire High Council. At the trial of Jesus, this high priest was Caiaphas, who was

---

[15] C. G. Brandis, "Archiereus," in *PRE,* Vol. 2 (1896), pp. 471–483, cols. 471–478.

[16] Schürer, Vol. 2 (4th ed., 1907) pp. 172, 201 f.

dependant on Annas (Matt. 26:3; John 18:24) ; [17] at the trial of Paul, it was the wealthy Ananias (Acts 23:2; 24:1) .

The following dignitaries were consistorial councillors, i.e., members of the board of high priests and colleagues of the high priest in cultic and legal administration:

1. The captain of the Temple (Aramaic *s^egan*, "governor"; Greek *ho stratēgòs toû hieroû*) , who plays a significant role in the New Testament as commander of the temple guard (Acts 5:24, 26) ; a priest of the highest aristocracy, he was often a candidate for the position of high priest (Palest. Talmud *Yom.* iii. 41a. 5) .

2. Some five additional aristocratic priests, including the following in the early years of the primitive church: Annas, the *princeps* of the assembly; Caiaphas, the *praeses;* and some other aristocratic priests, two of whose names have been preserved by tradition (Acts 4:6; rabbinic tradition, idealizing in the style of Chronicles, describes instead a whole court of Temple functionaries) .

3. Three or four priests or laymen as treasurers (Neh. 13:13; Josephus *Ant.* xiv. 106; Tosefta *Sheq.* ii. 15. 177) ; at the time of Jesus and the Apostles, these treasurers were experienced businessmen, because significant amounts of merchandise and money passed through the Temple.

This consistory of about ten prominent and wealthy men dealt with current problems that, in a modern society, would be the responsibility of the ministries of public worship, justice, and finance.

1. As adjutant of the high priest, the captain of the Temple kept order in the Temple proper and the surrounding area. He commanded the temple guard, a sort of military police made up of Jews. Because all popular movements were feared, this force participated in the capture of Jesus and the Apostles (John 18:3, 12; Acts 5:26) and also was responsible for guarding the tomb of Jesus (Matt. 27:65) .

---

[17] The repeated statement made by John's Gospel that Caiaphas was high priest in that year (John 11:49, 51; 18:13) does not mean the author thought of an annual election of the high priest, but only that he is emphasizing the special responsibility attaching to the highest Jewish office in the year of Jesus' death.

2. The other aristocratic priests of the consistory dealt with religious questions but also with judicial matters (e.g., Matt. 27:6; Acts 5:17). The high priests of the New Testament period could even claim judicial authority over Jews in other lands. Jesus came from the tetrarchy of Antipas, and yet, as a pilgrim accused of fomenting unrest, he was brought first before the high priests (Luke 22:66) ; only later was the procurator asked to confirm the sentence of death (Luke 23:1). Paul performed voluntary police duty at the execution of Stephen (Acts 7:58), and then asked the high priest for authority to bring followers of Jesus by force from Damascus to Jerusalem (Acts 9:2). In such cases the high priest obviously claimed to preside over a tribunal with authority over all Jews.

3. The three or four treasurers were responsible for the temple property, as well as for the income from the sacrifices and the wages of the priests and workmen. Similar functionaries are known from the pre-Christian period. Nehemiah appointed a four-man committee to oversee the administration of the temple stores and the payment of the workers; it consisted of a priest, a scribe, a Levite, and a layman (Neh. 13:13). Elsewhere we read of an individual in charge of administration, who is once called the commissioner of the high priest (II Chron. 24:11) and once the prefect (Greek *prostátēs*) of the Temple (II Macc. 3:4) ; under the authority of the high priest he was to administer the finances and furnishings of the Temple. In one case he was clearly a businessman (II Macc. 4:23), and was responsible for the temple bank and the market tax (II Macc. 3:4, 10 f.). During the New Testament period, this office was once again divided among several officials, primarily because Caesar's regulation of income (see above, p. 89) and Herod's reconstruction of the Temple had brought about a rapid increase in the volume of business. Consequently the treasurers had to be capable businessmen, whether they were priests or laymen. In the latter case they are sometimes called rulers (Greek *árchontes*) in a narrow sense, to distinguish them from the priestly councillors (Luke 23:13; 24:20).

b) *The Elders*

The second category belonging to the High Council, the elders, consisted of the leaders of the aristocratic families. As in the Greek assemblies and the Roman senate, these aristocrats had formerly constituted the High Council; for this reason Josephus, writing of the period around 200 B.C., called it the assembly of elders (see above, p. 142). In the New Testament period, however, the patricians no longer played a decisive role, because, on the one hand, the administrative consistory of high priests and, on the other hand, the scribes trained in theology and law were more competent to deal with the questions of the day. The assembly was therefore no longer a House of Lords, but a general parliament. Nevertheless, the elders, representing the priestly and financial aristocracy, remained a significant force, because they provided the government and also shared the conservative views of the Sadducees.

c) *The Scribes*

The last class to be accepted into the High Council, the scribes, were experts in interpretation of the law, and were therefore both theologians and jurists.

As the term "scribe" (Hebrew *sōpēr*, Greek *grammateús*) suggests, the historical precursors of this division of the High Council were the secretaries and notaries of the Oriental kings and governors,[18] with whom the Jews became particularly familiar in the Persian Empire (*Pap. Cowley,* "Words of Aḥikar" 1; cf. Tob. 1:22; I Esd. 2:15 f.). The Chronicler took it for granted that those kings of Judah who had long before developed a hierarchy and bureaucracy like that of the Persian Empire employed skilled notaries drawn from among the Levites (II Chron. 19:11; 24:11; 34:1, 3, 15–20). Conditions in Egypt and Greece made officials of this class seem absolutely indispensable in the Ptolemaic kingdom (Zenon Papyri, above, pp. 46 f.; III Macc. 4:17). Contacts with the Roman world probably also impressed the Jews with the

---

[18] H. Kees, *Ägypten* (1933), p. 369, *s.v.* "Schreiber."

role played by the *scribae,* who came from the equestrian class and were organized into guilds.

To the Chronicler, and, later, to all Jews, the ideal scribe was Ezra, the reformer who had come to Judah as a Persian official and Jewish legal expert (Ezra 7:6) in order to instruct the people in the law and to appoint judges (Ezra 7:10, 25). Levites were appointed to carry out the instruction (Neh. 8:7). Thus a Jewish scribe was to serve as government official, as teacher, or as judge; in each case, his authority derived from special familiarity with the Mosaic law. According to old traditions, the ideal scribe was also to be the guardian of secular wisdom (*Pap. Cowley,* "Words of Aḥikar" 1); this combination is not found in Chronicles, but it is in later texts (Ecclus. 38:24; I Cor. 1:20; *Pirqe Abot* i. 4; etc.).

Jewish scribes of the postexilic period were therefore qualified jurists [19] with an education that may be thought of as a combination of theology, jurisprudence, and philosophy. For the most part they were occupied with studying the Scriptures and developing traditions of sacral law, with instruction and jurisdiction. They were organized in guilds that were called synagogues (I Macc. 2:42; 7:12 f.). If they did not belong to the paid bureaucracy, they taught, like the Greek philosophers, out of enthusiasm for the system they represented; many also had an ordinary profession. The most highly regarded scribes were surrounded by disciples, who often served as amanuenses. Some of these disciples, like Paul and Josephus, were seeking an ordinary religious education by attending Pharisaic schools; others were studying for an academic degree. At this time the Jewish professor lectured sitting on a chair while the students crouched on the ground before him; this is why Paul says that he had sat at the feet of the famous Gamaliel (Acts 22:3). The student diligently learned by heart what the professor presented in his lectures, riveting his attention on every word and every gesture of the master. Recognized scholars were given the

[19] Schürer, Vol. 2 (4th ed., 1907), pp. 320.

honorary title "rabbi," which means "teacher." Jesus was also honored with this title, as well as being called "teacher" and "master" (Matt. 8:19; 26:25; Luke 5:5), although he had no academic license (John 7:15). The usual titles of scholars were simply applied to him loosely, as a token of personal respect for this great teacher. For his own disciples, however, the master of Nazareth rejected all boasts of learning (Matt. 23:6–10).

In the postbiblical period we read of solemn ordination of Jewish scribes and their acceptance into a professional guild (Mishna *Sanh.* i. 3a; Babyl. Talmud *Sanh.* 13b; Palest. Talmud *Sanh.* i. 3; Schwab X. 236).[20] The titles given reflect a chronological differentiation. Jewish authorities of the pre-Christian or early Christian period were now thought of collectively as the real "scribes," descended from the professional guild of the "Great Synagogue" founded by Ezra *(Pirqe Abot* i. 1–2); individually, they were given the title of "rabbi" *honoris causa*. The ordained scholars of the postbiblical period were spoken of collectively as the "wise"; individually, they received the title "rabbi" as a mark of the degree they had earned through pursuing regular studies.

G. Sadducees and Pharisees

Among the scribes there had long been various parties, corresponding to those into which much of Jewish society was divided. We shall first discuss two groups frequently encountered in the Gospels and Acts: the Sadducees and the Pharisees. Luke calls each of them a "party" *(hairesis;* Acts 5:17; 15:5; 26:5), and Josephus usually treats them similarly;[21] in the Mishna they appear as different schools of scriptural interpretation (Mishna *Yad.* iv. 6; etc.).[22] In addition, Josephus (though strangely not the New Testament) mentions the Essene movement and in Hellenistic fashion he introduces all three groups as schools of Jewish philosophy (Josephus *Ant.* xiii. 171–73), though he is not referring to

---

[20] Billerbeck, Vol. 2, pp. 648–61.
[21] The relevant passages from Josephus are listed in Schürer, Vol. 2 (4th ed., 1907), pp. 382–84.
[22] The passages are listed *ibid.*, pp. 384–86, 409 n. 16.

metaphysics, but to political and jurisprudential theories. Now, the Essene movement was also related to the scribal tradition, but it was not represented in the High Council, basing itself more on the priestly ideal; we shall therefore discuss it later in connection with the priesthood.

1) *The Genteel Party: the Sadducees*

Whether the term "Sadducee" (known in Aramaic only through the Syriac *zadduqāyā;* Greek *saddoukaîos;* late Hebrew *ṣᵉdûqî*) derives from a proper name or an adjective remains disputed. The high priest Zadok has often been suggested as the eponymous ancestor of this school, because his descendants were represented as the legitimate priests of the new Jerusalem (Ezek. 40:46; etc.), and because Ezra (Ezra 7:2) and above all the high priests of the postexilic and pre-Maccabean period (I Chron. 24:3; Hag. 1:1; Ecclus. [Hebrew] 51:12) sought to refer their ancestry to him. But the sources never indicate that the Sadducees claimed priestly succession from this Zadok or spiritual affinity to him. Quite the contrary: the Sadducees supported the non-Zadokite dynasty of Annas (Acts 4:1; 5:17). If any group claimed to be the spiritual sons of Zadok, it was the Essenes (1QS v. 2; CD iv. 3 f.). The modern equation of Zadokites with Sadducees therefore does not correspond to any historical evidence. A rabbinic tradition has also been cited according to which the Sadducees trace their origin to a scholar named Zadok who was active in the second century B.C. (*Abot R. Nath.* 5). But as this Zadok is set in parallel to a certain Boethus, in whom one can recognize the ancestor of the Boethus priests who were in competition with the Annas priests (see above, p. 142), the passage cited is merely an etiological legend. Until there is solid evidence for a proper name, we may return to the old derivation from an adjective.[23] Whereas the vowels do not correspond to the Hebrew

23 T. W. Manson, "Sadducee and Pharisee," *Bulletin of the John Rylands Library,* Vol. 22 (1938), pp. 144–59, emphasizes that the derivation from a proper name is improbable. In his opinion, *Sadducee* derives from the Greek *syndikos,* "legal counsel," *Pharisee* from the Aramaic *parsa'a,* "Persian" (*ibid.,* pp. 147–56). These derivations do not explain satisfactorily the vowels of the

ṣaddîq, "being right," it seems that by formal analogy to *ḥannûn,* "practicing graciousness," a hypothetical form *ṣaddûq,* "doing right," would be a natural basis for the term. This derivation would also fit with the strict legalism of the Sadducees.

Josephus provides many details that illustrate the essence of Sadducean ideology; we can describe it as an immanentist conception of righteousness. The theory behind the Saducees' program was a doctrine of duties and punishments that emphasized law and order; this theory was relentlessly put at the service of a politically conservative and hardheaded administration of government. To the Sadducees, the written laws were the only legal norm; unlike the Pharisees, they would admit no recourse to supplementary traditions or scholarly opinions (Josephus *Ant.* xiii. 297; xviii. 16). In addition, a man was supposed to be absolutely responsible for his actions (Josephus *Bell.* ii. 164; *Ant.* xiii. 173); each individual must make good his transgressions during his earthly life, since there was no soul to survive or return after death (no "angel" according to Acts 23:8; in addition, see Josephus *Bell.* ii. 165; *Ant.* xviii. 16). As a consequence, the Sadducees were strict in their jurisdiction (Josephus *Bell.* ii. 166; *Ant.* xx. 199), while as judges the Pharisees inclined toward popular leniency precisely because they took into account the factors rejected by the Sadducean camp. All these factors predestined the Sadducees to the role of a conservative party, both theoretically and in practice supporting the authority of the aristocrats and the discipline of the people.

The Sadducees make their first appearance in the history of Judaism alongside the Pharisees and Essenes in an account by Josephus of a legation sent about 144 B.C. to Rome and Sparta in the name of Jonathan and the assembly of elders (Josephus *Ant.* xiii. 171–73). Here we find, unexpectedly, a description of the Jewish parties formulated in philo-

---

words as found in the New Testament and Josephus or the consonants as found in the rabbinic sources. Manson has, however, emphasized some historically important facts.

sophic terms but intended to be political, perhaps because
Josephus' source was seeking to call attention to certain analogies to the struggle between *Optimates* and *Populares* that
was then dominating the Roman Republic (see above, pp.
70, 79 f.). In any case, from this time on the Sadducees
clearly appear as a group in association with the patricians
and the wealthy parvenus. At the outset the Maccabean
brothers, who did not come from the nobility, had nothing to
do with them. Even the hardheaded Hyrcanus I at first surrounded himself with teachers and counselors belonging to
the popular party of the Pharisees, until they censured him
for his cruel conquest of Samaria in 109 B.C. He then joined
forces with the genteel party of the Sadducees (Josephus *Ant.*
xiii. 288–98), although he later appeased the Pharisaic opposition (*ibid.,* 299). Janneus (104–76 B.C.) provoked a violent
political struggle which lasted until the time of Herod, as we
have noted above (pp. 71 f., 75, 93). On the one side were
ranged the reactionary aristocrats and Sadducees, who supported and later admired the military regime of Janneus,
and on the other the common people and Pharisees. The
revolt of the nobility under Aristobulus II (66–63) and again
under his son Antigonus (40–37) therefore ushered in the
heyday of the Sadducees. Herod, who represented the opposite party, suppressed the Jewish magnates; his rebuilding of
the Temple and his reform of the sacrificial system, however,
strengthened the priesthood once more, with the result that
later a wealthy priestly aristocracy stood ready to take control of domestic government under the Roman procurators.
This gave the Sadducees their great chance: nothing could
suit them better than using theological and juristic arguments to support the sovereignty of the Roman *princeps* and
the Jewish aristocracy. Members of the aristocracy, whether
priests or laymen, were disciples of the Sadducees (Josephus
Ant. xiii. 298), and preferred to elect Sadducean scribes as
counselors (xviii. 17). Although in the minority, under the
first procuratorship the Sadducees were the governing party.
Annas and his colleagues were so closely associated with the
Sadducees that Luke equated the supporters of the high

priest with the party of the Sadducees (Acts 5:17). This explains why the Sadducees passionately opposed every popular movement that seemed to threaten the power of the imperial officials and the high priests. They attacked Jesus in collaboration with the high priests and even, by way of exception, with the Pharisees (Matt. 16:1; etc.); they attacked the Apostles only in association with the high priests (Acts 4:1; 5:17) and in part against the wishes of the Pharisees (Acts 5:34; 23:6–9).

2) *The Popular Party: the Pharisees*

The term "Pharisee" (Aramaic and Syriac *p⁶rišâ*, Greek *pharisaîos*, Late Hebrew *pārûš*) is as disputed as the term "Sadducee." It derives from Hebrew *pāraš*, Aramaic *p⁶raš*, "to separate." In the Bible, this verb means "to explain"; according to an earlier view, therefore, "Pharisee" originally meant "examiner, interpreter" (of the scriptures).[24] In rabbinic literature, though, the verb usually means "to separate," and Pharisee is repeatedly taken to mean "one who has been separated." One can agree with the many scholars who presuppose some such meaning even for the pre-Christian period. It is wrong, however, to understand Pharisee as meaning "dissident" or "separatist." On occasion *pārûš* can mean "dissident" but then it does not refer to Pharisees (Talmud Babli *Pes.* 70a). Both in the New Testament and in Josephus, as well as in the overwhelming majority of the rabbinic passages, the Pharisees appear as the very opposite of an isolated sect: they are a most expansive popular party, with highly developed social relationships and structures. In rabbinic literature, the context in which the name appears suggests a meaning such as "puritan," a zealous proponent of ritual purity (Mishna Ḥag. ii. 17; Talmud Yerushalmi *Ber.* ix. 14b, 40; Schwab I. 169).[25] Since this interpretation agrees

---

[24] Despite C. Steuernagel, "Pharisäer," *PRE*, Vol. 19, 2 (1938), col. 1826, this etymology, proposed by H. Graetz and others, is quite possible. It is analogous, for example, to the formation of *pariṣ*, "housebreaker," from *pāraṣ*, "to break in."

[25] The rabbinic material is conveniently assembled, though in part misleadingly interpreted, in J. Levy, *Chaldäisches Wörterbuch*, Vol. 1 (1867), pp. 302 f.; *idem, Neuhebräisches und chaldäisches Wörterbuch*, Vol. 4 (1889), pp. 142 f.; Schürer, Vol. 2 (4th ed., 1907), pp. 384–86 (the important Mishna passages); Billerbeck, Vol. 4, pp. 334–39, 344–52.

with the passages from the New Testament and Josephus (such as Matt. 15:2; Josephus *Ant.* xviii. 12–15), we may assume the same meaning for the pre-Christian and early Christian period. The basic concept was therefore not that of separation from the rest of the people, although we sometimes hear loud laments about the ignorant masses (John 7:49), but rather separation "from the pollutions of the peoples of the land" (Ezra 6:21; 9:1; 10:11; Neh. 9:2; 10:28) and "from the nations of the world with their abominations" (Mekilta *Exod.* 19. 6, 71a).[26] In this sense the Pharisees may be thought of as puritans.

The Pharisaic ideology was accordingly characterized by a transcendent concept of purity, which appears to some extent in the Old Testament, in the New Testament, and in Josephus, but in greater detail in the rabbinic literature. This fundamental theory of the Pharisees found expression in a system of ritual observances based entirely on revelation and rigorously applied to society, coupled with optimistic and idealistic social policies intended to realize the covenant demands. God had revealed the norms of purity through holy scriptures, traditions, and scribes; the Pharisees sought to develop this revelation and make it applicable to society, so that every Jew could realize the ideal of the covenant people. This basic idea appears as early as the Nehemiah covenant (Neh. 10:29–30):

> All who had separated themselves from the peoples of the lands to the law of God . . . joined their brethren, their nobles, and entered into a curse and an oath to walk in God's law which was given by Moses the servant of God, and to observe and do all the commandments of our lord Yahweh and his ordinances and his statutes.

To preserve and develop the purity of this Levitical covenant people, the scribes had to master and interpret the commandments and statutes exactly, according to the model of Ezra and his Levites (Neh. 8:7—9:13).

In scrupulous detail the Pharisees analyzed and discussed

---

[26] The Mekilta passage is translated in context by Billerbeck, Vol. 3 (1926), p. 789. L. Baeck, *Das Wesen des Judentums* (6th ed., 1960), p. 45, rightly calls it a classic witness.

the books of the Bible, which provided the legal norm (Josephus *Bell.* ii. 162; *Pirqe Abot* i. 1; etc.). This exegetical discussion was called "midrash" (Heb., *midrāš*, "investigation"); seven basic methods of it were introduced by Hillel about 20 B.C. In addition, this same term was later used for commentaries on the individual books of the Bible.[27] Among the Pharisees, the biblical material furnishing the legal norm was supplemented more and more, and eventually almost replaced, by the exegetical tradition itself, the "tradition of the elders" (Matt. 15:2 and parallels; Josephus *Ant.* xiii. 297; *Pirqe Abot* iii. 11). The earlier scholars were even revered personally as vehicles of revelation (Josephus *Ant.* xviii. 12; *Pirqe Abot passim*). For different reasons, the Sadducees (see above, p. 154) and Jesus himself (Mark 7:8, 13) reacted against certain tendencies to relativize the Scriptures and prefer traditions or authorities. But the basic purpose of the Pharisees was to discover for every conceivable situation a reference to relevant passages from the Bible, together with authoritative explanations of their meaning and application. Thus above and beyond the analytic Midrash there developed a systematic exegetical tradition made up of two elements: the tradition of observances or *halākâ* ("walking"), based on the legal material of the Bible; the tradition of edification or *haggādâ* ("narration"), based on narrative and parenetic material. The literature of the systematic tradition is preserved in the Talmud ("teaching"). This comprises two collections: (1) the Hebrew Mishna ("instruction"), containing sixty-three tractates, which was assembled about 200 A.D. in Tiberias; (2) the Aramaic Gemara ("supplement"), containing commentaries on thirty-six (or thirty-nine) tractates of the Mishna, being preserved in a Palestinian version dating from about A.D. 400 and a Babylonian version dating from about A.D. 500, Talmud Yerushalmi and Talmud Babli. Like the Mishna, but more copious, is the Tosefta ("addition"), edited about A.D. 250. These

[27] For a good explanation of this concept, see E. Gross, "Midrasch," in *Die Religion in Geschichte und Gegenwart*, 3d ed., Vol. 4 (1960), cols. 940 f. H. L. Strack, *Introduction to the Talmud and Midrash* (1931), part II.

gigantic collections of legal material came into being at about the same time as the elaboration of the Roman law and the constitutions of the ancient church. To a modern reader, their crabbed and casuistic pedantry will no doubt seem capriciously Oriental. These traits, however, are intimately associated with the Pharisaic conception of God and his people: God predetermines, in every detail, Israel's destiny or "Heilsgeschichte"; but the people must contribute to its own sanctification and perfection through precise fulfillment of the law (Josephus *Bell.* ii. 162 f.; *Ant.* xiii. 172; xviii, 13).

Pharisaism, then, was an attempt to transfer concretely to the covenant people the purity revealed by God through scripture and tradition. The Pharisees therefore not only took part in government, administration of justice, and legal instruction, but also formed associations dedicated to the practical realization of the Levitical ideals. Such corporate bodies are behind the rabbinic term for an adherent of organized Pharisaism: *ḥābēr,* "associate, comrade," i.e., a member of a *ḥabûrâ,* an "association," which lived according to Levitical and Pharisaic law and custom. During a period of probation, which lasted for a month according to Hillel but sometimes for a year according to his contemporary Shammai, the novices had to demonstrate their obedience to the ritual prescriptions governing purity. Then, upon taking an oath, they were received into the association by a scribe—later by three associates (Josephus *Vit.* 10; Tosefta *Dem.* ii. 10—13:48).[28] After such a period of study under Gamaliel I, Paul became a Pharisaic lay brother (Acts 22:3; 23:6; 26:5; Phil. 3:5); he may even have intended further study leading to the examination that would qualify him as a scribe. Among the obligations of the Pharisaic brethren were strict observance of cultic purity (Mishna *Dem.* ii. 3), such as the washing of hands (Matt. 15:2 and parallels), as well as scrupulous obedience to the commandments. Conspicuous phylacteries were worn on the left upper

---

[28] Billerbeck, Vol. 2, pp. 502 f., 505 f., 508; Jeremias (cited above, p. 146, n. 14), pp. 120 f.

arm and tassels on the four corners of the cloak (Matt. 23:5) ; such trifles as mint, dill, and cummin were tithed (Matt. 23:23) . Special meals on the Sabbath constituted part of the observance (Luke 14:1) , as well as diligent execution of works of charity, including participation in family meals of joy or mourning (Tosefta *Meg.* iv. 15, 226) .[29] In this sense the Pharisaic movement with its associations may be called "social" (Josephus *Bell.* ii. 166: the Pharisees emphasize mutual love and a social disposition) . They did not take political ideas as their models, however, but rather the Mosaic ideal of the covenant community, including the ordinances of the Pentateuch relating to groups of one hundred, fifty, or ten associates under one scribe (Exod. 18:25; Deut. 1:15) . The Hellenistic system of religious societies (see above, p. 39) may also be considered an analogy.

Because they were concerned for the sanctification and perfecting of the covenant people, the Pharisees included eschatology in their *Heilsgeschichte*. They taught survival of the soul, resurrection of the dead (Acts 23:8; Josephus *Bell.* ii. 163; *Ant.* xviii. 14) , a last judgment (Josephus, *ibid.*) , and a world to come (*Pirqe Abot* ii. 8, quoting Hillel) .

As to the history of the Pharisaic scribal tradition, we may assume that its roots lie among the Jews deported to Babylon and the reformers in Jerusalem; Babylonia and Jerusalem remained the centers of Pharisaism as long as it continued to exist. In any event, the Pharisees developed the scribal ideal represented in the Chronicler's description of Ezra and the Levites (e.g., Neh. 8:7—9:13; 10:29 f.) . Only later, however, do our sources mention the Pharisees by name as a particular party. At the beginning of the Maccabean revolt in 167 b.c. (see above p. 58) , we read of a group of Hasidim or pietists (Hebrew singular *ḥāsîd,* "pious") who had pledged themselves to obey the law and consequently opposed the hellenizing policies of Antiochus IV and joined the Maccabean movement (I Macc. 2:42) . In 161, some outstanding scribes belonging to this group were deceived by Alcimus, the Hellenistic high priest (I Macc. 7:12–18) ; this

[29] Schürer, Vol. 2 (4th ed., 1907) , pp. 387 f., 397–403; Billerbeck, Vol. 2, pp. 494–519; Vol. 4, pp. 607–10; Jeremias (cited above, p. 146, n. 14) , pp. 118 f.

forced them once more into association with the Maccabees. Scholars are wont to consider these Hasidim the predecessors of the Pharisees, or even a parallel or particular group of them. This view is in harmony with the Pharisees' appearance at the end of the century as a school still closely associated with the house of the Hasmoneans. Hyrcanus I was educated at court by Pharisaic tutors. He surrounded himself with Pharisees as counselors, until one of them criticized him and the high priest went over to the Sadducees (see above, p. 67). In the following period, however, the Pharisees appear as a popular party who governed the masses through their tribunes and opposed dictators as well as *optimates,* though often seeking the support of influential women. Thus, the Pharisees instigated a popular revolt against the military government of Janneus (104–76 B.C.; Josephus *Ant.* xiii. 400–404). Alexandra (76–67) then gave them seats on the High Council (*ibid.,* 408–10). As soon as possible they instituted proscription against their wealthy opponents, meeting the desperate opposition of Aristobulus II (67–63) and the reactionary aristocrats (see above, pp. 74 f.). Hyrcanus II took over the protection of the Pharisees, one of whom courageously stepped forward in the High Council to oppose the military dictatorship of the youthful Herod in Galilee (see above, p. 90). When he became king, Herod at first opposed the *optimates;* but he was later forced to combat conspiracies on the part of the Pharisaic *populares.* He ordered the execution of ten Pharisees who had formed a *ḥabûrâ* with the intent of assassinating him (Josephus *Ant.* xv. 282–89), as well as some of the Pharisees, said to number more than six thousand, who had intrigued against the king with princesses and courtiers (xviii. 41–46), and finally two professors and several students of theology for destroying the eagle affixed to the Temple (*ibid.,* 148–67; see above, pp. 99, 105). In the first and third instances, the zeal shown on behalf of the law anticipates the rise of the Zealots.[30] The unrest that broke out after the death of Herod (see above, pp. 112 f., 132) also began when Pharisees incited the common people, and afterward the pilgrims, at Jerusalem to demonstrate against the

[30] M. Hengel, *Die Zeloten* (1961), pp. 265 f.

third execution (*ibid.,* 206–18). It is not surprising that when Quirinius began his tax registration a Pharisee and a scribe appeared as instigators of the rebellion and as founders of the Zealot movement, the roots of which therefore lie in Pharisaism (see above, pp. 136 f.).

During the first procuratorship, Annas was able to reorganize the Sanhedrin along aristocratic and Sadducean lines; but he and his successors needed the support of the Pharisaic scribes, who constituted the majority of the professional lawyers and largely controlled public opinion (Josephus *Ant.* xvii. 298; xviii. 15 f.). In the days of Jesus and the Apostles, then, the Pharisees, and especially the Pharisaic scribes, had two sources of power: first, their position as members of the High Council; and second, their position as functionaries and authorities among the common people.

How are we to explain the Pharisaic opposition to Jesus? As the Synoptics tell the story, the members and adherents of this school could not abide having many people consider Jesus' words and deeds a superior revelation (Matt. 7:29; 12:23 f. and parallels). Neither could they abide his rejection of the Pharisaic traditions (e.g., Matt. 9:11 and parallels) and his criticism of the power belonging to the Pharisaic scribes (Matt. 23:2–31 and parallels). In their opposition to the teacher of Nazareth, the Pharisees are said not to have disdained the assistance of the Herodians (Mark 3:6) and Sadducees (Matt. 16:1) in Galilee or the high priests in Jerusalem (according to Matt. 21:45 f., shortly before the Passion; according to John 7:32 even earlier). Jesus fell victim to this constellation of factions. The temporary opposition of the Pharisees to a religious movement (Luke 19:39) and their support of the political status quo (Matt. 22:15 and parallels) was also due in part to Tiberius. In A.D. 31 he dismissed his anti-Jewish confidant Sejanus and ordered the provincial governors to treat the Jews with more respect, which made them less hostile toward the Romans (see below, p. 183). According to Luke in the book of Acts, however, the Pharisees took a more favorable attitude toward the Christian community after Jesus' death. First the famous Pharisaic professor Gamaliel I came forward in the High Council to oppose the arrest of the leading Apostles (Acts 5:34). His disciple Paul, with the authority of the high priest, persecuted the Hellenistic Christians with great zeal (Acts 9:1 f.; Phil. 3:5 f.); but the primitive community soon included many Pharisaic members (Acts 15:5), and later on, Pharisaic scribes in the High Council spoke up in Paul's behalf (Acts 23:9).

During the Apostolic period, the Pharisaic scribes exercised greater and greater influence on the High Council and the government (Josephus *Ant.* xviii. 17). They were especially powerful from 41 to 44 under Agrippa I. It is true that after the year 50 they had to yield some of their popularity to the Zealots; personally, however, they resisted the excesses of these nationalists. After the fall of Jerusalem in A.D. 70, they succeeded in reestablishing the High Council as a legal academy in Jamnia, an imperial city on the Philistine plain. The scholarly work of the Pharisees, which moved to Galilee in the second century, laid the groundwork for the Mishna (see above, p. 158). Pharisaism therefore had a substantial influence on post-Christian Judaism.

H. PRIESTS AND ESSENES

Whereas the Sadducees and Pharisees were basically two schools of scribal interpretation, both revering the law, they differed politically. There were two other groups in the population that were dedicated to worship, but had different ideas of religion. On the one hand, there were the priests, appointed to serve in the Jerusalem Temple. On the other hand, there were the Essenes, living together in colonies like monks, according to priestly ideals. As the discoveries at Qumran show, despite the silence of the New Testament, the Essenes played a significant role in the environment of Jesus and the Apostles.

1) *The Temple Service of the Priests*

Since all Jews looked upon Palestine, and Judea in particular, as a temple land, government and the administration of justice were indissolubly linked with supervision of the cult. The most important duty of the high priest was to carry out the sacrificial worship; one basic function of the ruling consistory was to supervise the Jerusalem Temple and its employees. Because the high priest was only occasionally and to a limited extent able to participate in the many cultic activities (Ecclus. 50:1–21) , the ordinary priests had to assist him and often functioned in his stead.

The ordinary Jewish priests were not a ruling body like the high priests nor a class of leaders like the elders and scribes, but a particular group of the people, considered as a cultic community. Nevertheless, they alone had the right to enter the Court of the Priests to serve at the altar of burnt offering and in the Temple proper, like the father of John the Baptist (Luke 1:5) . In this regard they were able to represent the high priest; they in turn had Levites at their disposal to serve as doorkeepers, musicians, etc. The Levites also had special status in the Temple, but were not allowed to enter the Court of the Priests.

As was frequently the case in the ancient world, cultic office was hereditary in Judaism. Certain family groups were entrusted with the sacrificial worship. Proper descent made a man a priest or Levite; theological studies were not required at this time. Nehemiah is said to have attached great significance to the genealogies (Neh. 7:5–65) , and the Chronicler generally illustrates the interest of postexilic Judaism in family trees. Three Old Testament figures played special roles in this regard: Levi, Aaron, and Zadok (priest under David and Solomon) ; the latter two became ancestors of special groups, each standing one rank higher than its predecessor in the list. Thus there arose this genealogical ideal of the hierarchy; the chief priests, who were supposed to be Zadokites (I Chron. 24:6) ; the ordinary priests, regarded as Aaronites (I Chron. 24:1) ; the subordinate cultic functionaries, who were Levites (I Chron. 24:20) .

In other words, priests and Levites formed one genealogical unit divided into three classes. After the radical changes made by Antiochus IV and Jason (174–171 B.C.; see above pp. 52 f.) , the high-priestly office ceased to follow the Zadokite line; it was filled by a series of different families. Foremost among them were the Hasmoneans and, in the New Testament period, the dynasty of Annas. But the idea of a special priestly aristocracy was retained (Acts 4:6) .

Only the actual high priest, the captain of the Temple, and the members of the consistory had permanent duties in the Temple during their term of office. These duties were mostly of supervisory nature. The captain of the Temple was responsible for supervising the performance of the sacrifices; the high priest was obliged to intervene only on major occasions.

The rites were performed in the name of the high priest by successive divisions of ordinary priests, assisted by Levites. All these priests and Levites had their own profession and place of residence (Luke 10:31 f.; Acts 4:36) ; they had only a quasi-military obligation, analogous to that of the Egyptian priesthood, of serving periodically in Jerusalem.[31] According to I Chronicles 24:1–31, both categories were arranged in twenty-four divisions, similar to regiments ("unto this day," according to Josephus *Ant.* vii. 367) . Each division (Hebrew *mišmār*, "watch"; Greek *ephēmería*, "[daily] division," Luke 1:5) would send a company to stand watch at Jerusalem from one Sabbath to the next; this meant in practice that each individual served roughly twice a year. If the company having the watch needed some 300 priests and 400 Levites, as the cultic regulations seem to assume, there may have been about 7200 priests and 9600 Levites; [32] the companies, however, may have differed considerably in size. The priests were housed in guardrooms north of the Temple proper (Mishna *Tam.* i. la) . The white uniform of the officiants, which was kept in the Temple, consisted of turban, cloak, and breeches (Ezek. 44:17–19) ; these were worn only during actual performance of the ritual (Mishna *Tam.* i. lb) . A professional functionary, probably a subordinate representative of the captain of the Temple, chose by lot each

[31] J. M. Meyers, *I Chronicles* (1965) , pp. 167 f.
[32] Jeremias, (cited above, p. 146, n. 14) , pp. 61–66.

day those who were to officiate and introduced them to their service (*ibid.*, i. 2b–3a).

The major cultic acts performed by the priests in the Temple under supervision of the captain of the Temple and his representative were the following:

1. Twice a day they carried out a censing (Hebrew *qᵉṭōret*) of the "holy place," the main room of the Temple. This took place in the morning before the first of the two burnt offerings (see below), and in the afternoon after the second (Exod. 30:7 f.; Philo *De Specialibus Legibus* i. 17; Mishna *Tam.* vi. 1–3; *Yom.* iii. 5). During the censing the Levites intoned certain psalms (*Tam.* vii. 4).

2. Twice a day they performed a burnt offering (Hebrew *ʿôlâ*) on behalf of the community; for the Jews this offering was, so to speak, the *ordinarium* (Hebrew *tāmîd*, "permanent"). They performed this offering at the altar of burnt offering in the courtyard before the east façade of the Temple by slaughtering a yearling lamb at dawn and another at the ninth hour (about three o'clock; Acts 3:1) and burning all but the skin (Exod. 29:38–42; Mishna *Tam.* iii. 2–5; iv. 1–12). In addition, there were offerings made on behalf of the Emperor (see above, p. 141), as well as cereal offerings (Hebrew *ḥabittîm*, "baked goods") on behalf of the high priest (Lev. 6:14; Mishna *Tam.* i. 3d; iv. 12b) and other food offerings. During the *ordinarium*, the Jewish kerygma "Hear O Israel" (Hebrew *šᵉmaʿ*) was recited; in the biblical period it consisted of a blessing, the decalogue, and three pareneses (Deut. 6:4–9 ["Hear O Israel"]; 11:13–21; Num. 15:37–41), together with two prayers and the blessing of Aaron (Mishna *Tam.* v. 1). In somewhat different form, this kerygma was recited in synagogues (see above, p. 121) and private homes (Mark 12:29), as is still customary, with slight changes, even today. When the high priest himself took part in the *ordinarium,* the captain of the Temple let him perform some of the concluding acts. In this case, at the end of the ceremony the high priest would pour some wine at the foot of the altar, to the accompaniment of trumpets and cymbals

(Ecclus. 50:12–16; Mishna *Tam.* vii. 3). Here, too, the Levites intoned psalms (*ibid.,* vii. 3g).

3. At the annual festivals (New Year in the fall, the Day of Atonement, the Feast of Booths, the Dedication of the Temple, Passover, and the Feast of Weeks) many people visited the Temple. Then the priests were responsible for additional community offerings (following Lev. 23:8–20, for example). These demanded an increased number of guards; often the whole division was required, supplemented if necessary by priests coming to the festival as pilgrims.

4. There were also private communion sacrifices (Hebrew *šelem,* "peace offering"). The worshiper would bring the sacrificial animal on his shoulders into the Men's Court, where he would slaughter it himself or have a Levite slaughter it; he would then bring it to the north fence of the Court of Priests (the altar area), where one of the priests would receive the blood. The blood, fat, and meat would then be treated in various ways, depending on the kind of sacrifice involved. The following types were the most important: a. For a private sin offering and a guilt offering, the priest poured out the blood and burned the fat on the altar of burnt offering. Then he cooked the meat and ate it, together with his colleagues (Lev. 4:27–35; 6:24—7:7). b. A special form of private communion sacrifice was the Passover sacrifice, for which yearling male lambs or kids were used. To deal with the thousands of animals slaughtered at the same time, the priests stood in lines between the fence and the altar, passed bowls holding the blood, and had their colleagues at the end of the lines empty the bowls at the foot of the altar (Mishna *Pes.* v. 6). Then the worshiper's lamb was flayed and carried out in its skin; it was roasted on a spit within the city and eaten in a room after sundown. Ten to twenty people shared the meal, having joined together for the festival as a household, according to the law (Exod. 12:4; Matt. 26:18 and parallels; Josephus *Bell.* vi. 423).[33] On this occasion, in addition to the fifty thousand or so regular

[33] Billerbeck, Vol. 4 (1928), pp. 41–76.

inhabitants, there were probably more than one hundred thousand pilgrims in the city, which could certainly lead to practical difficulties.[34]

The high costs of maintaining the Temple and providing for the sacrifices were met by taxes and gifts. From all parts of the Jewish world the annual temple tax flowed to Jerusalem (Matt. 17:24–27). It was a head tax imposed upon all males over twenty, with the exception of priests, and amounted to half a shekel or stater (Exod. 30:13),[35] which in the New Testament period represented a double drachma, about a dollar (Matt. 17:24). The Temple also received a large income from gifts and offerings. Since the ancient (Tyrian) Temple money was no longer available for making payment, the taxpayers had to go to an official money changer (Matt. 21:12; Greek *kollubistés*) in the provinces or in the Temple and let him exchange their money, paying him agio (Greek *kóllubos;* Mishna *Sheq.* i. 3.; ii. 1; *Bek.* viii. 7). Obviously the high priest and priestly aristocracy, who were in charge of the money and real estate of the Temple, had many opportunities to turn a profit.[36] The ordinary priests, however, were not wealthy capitalists, but simple farmers or the like. As compensation for their cultic performances they were supposed to receive portions of the sacrifices, as well as firstlings and tithes (Neh. 10:35–37; Num. 18:21–32); they did not always receive their due, however.[37] In the New Testament period what proportion went to non-priestly Levites remains obscure (Heb. 7:5 refers to ordained priests). There were probably also special perquisites.

2) *The Community Life of the Essenes*

Although the Essenes constituted a special priestly and monastic community, they rejected the temple cultus. They claimed spiritually to represent the priesthood of Zadok, to

---

[34] Jeremias (cited above, p. 146, n. 14), Vol. 1 (1923), p. 96, estimates 55,000 inhabitants and 125,000 pilgrims.

[35] Nehemiah 10:32 sets the tax at a third of a shekel, but this was later changed to the half shekel of Exodus 30:13.

[36] Jeremias, (cited above, p. 146, n. 14), Vol. 2A (1924), pp. 13 f.

[37] *Ibid.*, pp. 21–24.

which Ezekiel and the Chronicler had given prominence (Ezek. 40:46; I Chron. 24:4). In their eyes, ever since the high priest Onias III had been deposed in 174 B.C., this priesthood had been expelled from the Temple and had to live in exile. They therefore looked upon themselves as an exiled community led by the true Zadokite priests, and considered the high priests who followed Onias III, along with their supporters, as profane usurpers. Certainly the priests of the temple at Leontopolis in Egypt were also such a community in exile, but the Essenes remained for the most part in Judea and did not build a new temple and altar. They were organized, rather, like the Pharisees, for they, too, had scribes in positions of authority and lived in precisely determined associations. On the other hand, they remained more strictly apart from the rest of society than did the Pharisees. Ideologically, the Essenes had even higher goals than the Pharisees. Legal purity of the covenant people did not satisfy them; they sought instead to realize socially the cultic holiness of the priesthood. Therefore the Essenes wore the white robes of priests, and therefore they accorded leadership in their communities to a priesthood of their own, which they considered both biblical and Zadokite.

The concurrent terms "Esseans" and "Essenes" (Greek *essaîoi* in Philo, but usually *essēnoi* in Josephus; Latin [Pliny] *esseni*) can be derived by way of two Syriac plural forms (*ḥasēn*, emphatic *ḥasayyâ*, "holy ones") from two different forms of an Aramaic word for "holy." The substance of Essenism was a quite exclusive concept of holiness (Josephus *Bell.* ii. 119). Organized and living together like votaries of a monastic order, the Essenes sought to establish the cultic purity and spiritual perfection of each member (general descriptions are given by the Qumran texts mentioned below as well as by Philo *Quod Omnis Probus Liber* 75–91; Josephus *Bell,* ii. 119–61; *Ant.* xviii. 18–22; Pliny *Hist.* v. 17).

The historical basis of Essenism lies in Judaism, as the original Essene texts discovered at Qumran prove. There are striking analogies to Persian dualism and Greek idealism, but these analogies do not extend to either terminology or organization, and should therefore be considered more as formal convergences; the Essenes themselves considered only the Holy Scriptures of Judaism authoritative. Their study of Scripture and their common life exhibit striking similarities to Pharisaism. But whereas the Pharisees, following Levitical ideals, devoted themselves more exoterically to carrying out the law within the framework of existing society, the Essenes, following priestly ideals, devoted themselves more esoterically to the secrets of apocalyptic, looking forward to a spiritual deliverance. But even so the Essenes merely represented an intensification of Jewish ideals, a concentration on the Holiness Code and the idea of the holy remnant. Like the Pharisees, the Essenes were probably somehow associated with the Hasidim (see above, p. 58) of the period around 167 B.C. (1QS i. 8 speaks of *b*°*rît ḥesed,* "covenant of piety") ; at the start they may have taken part in the Maccabees' struggle against the Hellenists (1QM) . There is also a clear connection with "those who are wise" (in apocalyptic regard) mentioned in the Book of Daniel (Dan. 12:3, 10; cf. 1QS iii. 13; etc.) ; this book, with supplements, was in the Essene library at Qumran (see below, pp. 171 f.) , along with other apocalyptic literature (I Enoch, etc.) . Josephus, too, considered apocalyptic teaching based on study of the Scriptures to be typical of the Essenes (Josephus *Bell.* ii. 159) .

The first documentary evidence for the name "Essene" refers to the time about 144 B.C.; Josephus, as we have seen, mentions the philosophy of the Sadducees, the Pharisees, and the Essenes in connection with negotiations carried out by the High Council with Rome and Sparta about this time (*Ant.* xiii. 171–73) . According to him, in the realm of politics the Essenes ascribed absolute significance to God's plan ("fate") but none at all to human measures; this description agrees with the apocalyptic interest just mentioned. Whenever individual Essenes appear in Josephus' history, they function as prophetical counselors to Hasmoneans and Herodians (Josephus *Bell.* i. 78–80 [= *Ant.* xiii. 311–13]; *Ant.* xv. 373–79; *Bell.* ii. 113) . The first of these passages tells of an Essene prophet active around 104 B.C., who instructed his students in the art of prognosis, teaching in the Temple area. One of the gates of Jerusalem was also called the Essene Gate (Josephus *Bell.* v. 145), probably because Essene scribes gave similar instruction there. As a consequence, these pietists also had connections with the government and capital.[38] Because they were also associated with an order, they can be likened to the modern Jesuits.

On the other hand, the Essenes developed a communistic colony life more reminiscent of the modern Israelite kibbutzim. Their communism was not conceived socialistically, however, but according to priestly ideals; it served as a means for individual sanctification and spiritualization. Just as in Pharisaism, the Holy Scriptures were of crucial importance; the Essene communities were like the Pharisaic associations, but more radical and more exclusive.

In 1949 a large settlement of the Essenes was discovered at Qumran, on a plateau on the northwest shore of the Dead Sea. The site was later excavated by Dominican scholars and others. Its center was a large monastery, which included plumbing and baptismal basins, a fortified tower, a long assembly room in which were found eating utensils and writing material, as well as a pottery shop and several smaller chambers. To the east a cemetary of some 1100 graves was discovered. To the west, in the rocks, twenty-six caves were examined in which the Qumran community had deposited in tall jars their Hebrew (and sometimes Aramaic) documents. The first of these caves (designated 1Q) was found in 1947 by Arab shepherds from the vicinity of Bethlehem. Coins and other articles enable us to fix the following dates in the history of the monastery: (1) It was founded about 165 B.C. (a coin of Antiochus IV), (2) enlarged about 100 B.C., (3) and destroyed by an earthquake in 31 B.C. (see above, p. 96). (4) Having been restored shortly before the year 1, (5) it was destroyed by the Tenth Roman Legion during the First Jewish War in A.D. 68. The caves in the vicinity have yielded (1) canonical and deuterocanonical

---

[38] B. Reicke, "Official and Pietistic Elements of Jewish Apocalypticism," *Journal of Biblical Literature,* Vol. 79 (1960), pp. 137–50.

books of the Old Testament; (2) midrashic and apocalyptic commentaries on these books; (3) previously unknown collections of community regulations, psalms, and apocalypses. The most important is the somewhat misnamed Qumran Manual (1QS), better called the Community Rule. A strikingly similar document was discovered in Cairo shortly before 1900 and published in 1910; this is the so-called "Damascus Document" (CD); several fragments of it have also been found at Qumran. If the emigration to Damascus described in this document was not meant metaphorically, we may think of a missionary community there whose origin can possibly be traced to the reaction of the Pharisees against Janneus and their association in 88 B.C. with Demetrius III of Damascus (see above, p. 72). The *halākā* of the Damascus Document is especially reminiscent of Pharisaism. The Qumran Manual, on the other hand, shows clear points of agreement with the statements of Philo and Josephus about the Essenes, and there is no doubt that Qumran and Essenism represent the same movement in different stages of development.

According to the Qumran documents, the "Teacher of Righteousness" enjoyed particularly great authority. Scholars have made attempts to identify this figure with all sorts of historical persons, although the texts present him as the ideal of an inspired scribe. He was opposed by the Wicked Priest, representing the secularized high-priesthood, apparently that of the Hasmoneans.

To become the comrades of the true sons of Zadok, those destined to join the Essene community had to pledge themselves to asceticism, that is, strict obedience to the law and self-control. Being the Sons of Light, they must repel the forces of darkness and fill their being with light and spirit. Acceptance into the community therefore demanded even more difficult tests and stricter vows than among the Pharisees (1QS v. 7–24; vi. 13–23; Josephus *Bell.* ii. 137–42). The regular members formed communities under the supervision of priests; they held all goods in common and did not marry,

although some had women for the purpose of bearing children (Josephus *Bell.* ii. 161 f.). On working days they contributed to the support of the community by farming, herd-
ing, and other occupations. At specified times during the day
and on festivals they donned their white priestly clothing
and took part in sacred baptismal rites, meals, and prayers.
The cultic regulations of the Essenes even extended to gestures of the hand, relieving oneself, and other such physical
details. At the same time, the Essenes had a tendency toward
spiritual mysticism; because of their philosophic-sounding
idealization of religious knowledge (e.g., 1QS ii. 3; iii. 15)
they may be considered precursors of Jewish Gnosticism.

The Essene movement played no discernible role in politics, as the Sadducees and Pharisees did; but it can illuminate the background of the Gospel by similarities as well as
by differences. 1. John the Baptist grew up in the desert of
Judah (Luke 1:80) and baptized people in the Jordan not
far from Qumran. His eschatological preaching suggests a
possible connection with the Essenes, for in both quarters
spiritual purity was required (1QS iii. 4–9; Josephus *Ant.*
xviii. 17) and on both sides the prophecy "In the wilderness
prepare the way of the Lord" (Isa. 40:3) was quoted (1QS
viii. 14 and Matt. 3:3 and parallels). On the other hand,
John's baptism was unique, and therefore differed from the
repeated ablutions of Qumran. 2. Jesus shows no dependence
on the Essenes, despite frequent assertions to the contrary
ever since the period of Romanticism; at most, he came into
contact with them through John. In his teachings one may
possibly find points of agreement or disagreement with traditions held by the Essenes and their followers, including his
attack upon the legalist in the case of the animal in the well
(cf. CD xi. 13 f.; Matt. 12:11 and parallels); peripheral
points of contact are therefore not out of the question. 3.
Above and beyond these few points, the Qumran literature is
of value for understanding the New Testament if this literature is employed, not to demonstrate a mechanical influence,
but to illuminate the general background. In this regard, the

discoveries cast new light especially upon the Jewish background of Johannine and Pauline theology.[39]

I. PILATE, GOLGOTHA, THE PRIMITIVE CHURCH

As our survey of the internal situation during the first procuratorship has shown (secs. C–H), life in Judea bore the stamp of powerful religious movements and national aspirations. The procurator and the officials were in a very difficult position: on the one hand, they represented the supreme Roman authority; on the other, they had to take into account Jewish idiosyncracies. In general, the Jewish people was not hostile to Rome, although in 4 B.C. and A.D. 6 messianic Zealots had come forward to foment unrest, and similar forces continued to be at work underground. But the Jewish organizations and movements were all rooted in sacred traditions and therefore continually promoted the spirit of nationalism.

Significant conflicts arose between the procurator and the representatives of the people under Pilate (26–36), who sought to emphasize Roman supremacy. He was even prepared to deliver Jesus to death in order to stifle the new Galilean revival movement. Yet this movement continued to grow in Jerusalem; and in the following period, despite losses in the year when Pilate was deposed, in the following period it rapidly spread beyond the borders of Palestine and Judaism. Details of this story, which furnishes the basis for Christianity, will be discussed in three sections.

1) Gratus and Pilate

Augustus had his procurators in Caesarea serve terms of approximately three years, but the Emperor Tiberius (A.D. 14–37) introduced a new policy. He was of the opinion that higher colonial officials should remain in office for an extended period, for this policy would reduce their exactions. As an old soldier, he referred to flies that suck their fill at a

---

[39] For convenient summaries of the material and the literature, see O. Betz, "Dead Sea Scrolls," *The Interpreter's Dictionary of the Bible*, Vol. 1 (1962), pp. 790–802; *idem*, "Zadokite Fragments," *ibid.*, Vol. 4 (1962), pp. 929–33; W. R. Farmer, "Essenes," *ibid.*, Vol. 2 (1962), pp. 143–49.

wound and then stay there, keeping other flies away (Josephus *Ant.* xviii. 174). In addition, from 18 to 31 Tiberius let Sejanus, the prefect of the praetorians in Rome, nominate men for colonial office. Sejanus was the most prominent member of the equestrian order, from which the procurators were drawn, and stood for strictness toward the Jews, as various of his measures demonstrate. The two procurators of Judea under Tiberius, Gratus and Pilate, must be considered obedient tools of Sejanus; their dependence on him for promotion explains their inclination brutally to demonstrate Roman authority over Jerusalem from Caesarea (Josephus *Bell.* ii. 169–77; *Ant.* xviii. 33–35, 55–62, 177).

Valerius Gratus (15–26) undertook many experiments with the high priests. He appointed and deposed these dignitaries nearly every year, until about A.D. 18 he found one who had appeared both reliable and representative to Roman eyes: Caiaphas, Annas' son-in-law, who is famous as *praeses* of the consistory and the Sanhedrin during the trials of Jesus and the first Apostles. This tractable man suited Pilate, too, and remained in office until Pilate was deposed in A.D. 36.

Pontius Pilate (26–36) is a name often read mechanically in the Gospels and the creed, without much idea of his position and policies. Edifying stories have much to say about his character that cannot be demonstrated historically. Josephus' account, however, shows that the supreme authority of Rome was his guiding star (Josephus *Bell.* ii. 169–77; *Ant.* xviii. 55–62, 85–89).

At the very outset of his term in office, Pilate showed the Jews that he would support relentlessly the principle of Roman sovereignty. He ordered the cohort that was to occupy the Antonia to march into the city at night, without laying aside the standards decorated with the image of the Emperor, as was usual (see above, pp. 140 f.). This action provoked an uproar, during which great mobs of Jews marched to Caesarea and besieged the procurator for five days, refusing to withdraw even though the Roman soldiers threatened to use their swords. Against his will, Pilate had to order the removal of the imperial standards. Then there was a second demonstration against Pilate in Jerusalem when he made the basically reasonable decision to draw on the Temple treasury in order to build an aqueduct from the pools of Solomon to Jerusalem. This time he held the mob in check by means of soldiers in mufti armed with truncheons, and the project was completed (see map IV, bottom left).

2) The Last Passover of Jesus

In obvious conformity with the policy of Roman supremacy, which Pilate followed first out of obedience to Sejanus and then after Sejanus' deposition, he had Jesus crucified at a Passover festival. At the annual festivals it was always easy to foment unrest; for this reason the procurator usually went to Jerusalem with a military escort before the festival. Shortly before this Passover, Pilate had condemned an agitator named Barabbas and two other robbers to death. Then the high priests handed over to him a man taken prisoner by the temple guard, Jesus the Galilean, described him as an anti-Roman agitator (Luke 23:2), and demanded in exchange that Barabbas be released, a man with whom they obviously had connections (Matt. 27:20 and par.). Pilate gave in and sentenced Jesus to crucifixion, the Roman form of capital punishment for traitors, insurgents, and the like.

a) The Date of the Last Supper and Crucifixon

How are we to determine the date of the Last Supper and Jesus' crucifixion? The sources contain only two points of reference: the Jewish day of the week and the sacral day of the month. These do not suffice to fix the day of the solar calendar precisely because each year the calendar commission of the High Council established the first day of the month, according to observations of the moon.[40] With regard to the year, there are no mathematical calendar dates, but only a few historical references to serve as clues.

Judaism quite generally had a rather simple system for keeping track of the days and hours. Although usage varied,

[40] Quotations illustrating how these factors could vary are given by Billerbeck, Vol. 1 (1922) pp. 745 f., 1031 f.

the day began officially at sunset, about 6:00 P.M. on the average. The night was divided into three (Luke 12:38) or four watches (Matt. 14:25 and parallels; Mark 13:35; Acts 12:4), depending on whether the division was based on the practice of the Jewish temple or the Roman army. Then the day proper, beginning at sunrise, 6:00 A.M. on the average, was divided into twelve hours (John 11:9); these could not be measured precisely, but consisted of between forty-nine and seventy-one minutes, depending on the time of year.

Without going into exhaustive detail, we may point out the following circumstances as relatively clear for dating the Last Supper and the crucifixion, taking into account that the day began in the evening, just after 6:00 P.M.

1. According to both Synoptic and Johannine tradition, Jesus held the Last Supper in the early part of the night from Thursday to Friday. According to both sources, the arrest took place later the same night and then, during the day, which is expressly called Friday, the crucifixion (Mark 15:42 and John 19:31: "the day before the Sabbath," i.e., Friday). Concerning the duration of the crucifixion the accounts vary by a few hours: either from about 9:00 A.M. to about 3:00 P.M. (Mark 15:25 together with Matt. 27:46 and parallels) or from about 1:00 P.M. to about 5:00 P.M. (John 19:14: sentencing about noon; John 19:31: burial before sundown). Later, analogous dating of the removal of Jesus' body from the cross and the resurrection confirms once more that Friday was the day of his death: Joseph laid him in the tomb before the night of the Sabbath (Mark 15:42; John 19:31–42); the women visited the tomb on Sunday morning (Matt. 28:1 and parallels; John 20:1).

2. How is this Friday of the Last Supper and the crucifixion related to the days of the official Passover week? Since we are dealing with members of the Council and priests of the temple, not with sectarians, our inquiry concerns the official festival calendar of Judea. As defined by this calendar, the date in question, consisting of the night and the following day, turns out to be a Day of Preparation for the Sabbath that was on this occasion also a Day of Preparation for

Passover (see below), i.e., 14 Nisan, roughly equivalent to April. Without attempting to harmonize the differently constructed accounts of the Synoptics and of John, one can determine by close analysis that both accounts are basically oriented around this date. After a few remarks about the Jewish Day of Preparation and Eve of Passover, we shall examine the manifold relationships between the Last Supper and crucifixion and this Day of Preparation.[41] The Jewish Day of Preparation (Hebrew *'ēber*, "evening"; Greek *paraskeuē*, "preparation") was the day before a Sabbath or festival. During this day all necessary work had to be taken care of and everything prepared, so that the holy day could be celebrated solemnly and without labor. In Pharisaic circles, an ordinary Day of Preparation for the Sabbath concluded with a meal to consecrate the Sabbath; this meal was later called *qiddûš*, "consecration," and is still celebrated in Jewish families. It is not inconceivable that devout Galileans such as Jesus and his disciples consecrated the Day of Preparation for Passover with such a *qiddûš*; several scholars make this assumption in order to date the Last Supper more easily on the night of the Day of Preparation for Passover (as John 13:1 in particular suggests). Although the Mishna contains no evidence for a *qiddûš* introducing the Day of Preparation, a *qiddûš* of this kind would have been natural for Jesus because, according to the same source, the Jews of Galilee considered the Day of Preparation itself as a Sabbath (Mishna *Pes.* iv. 5c). For the people of Judea, however, the night and morning of the Day of Preparation, up to twelve noon, were treated as part of an ordinary workday (*ibid.*), which seems reasonable in view of the swarm of pilgrims and the activity of Passover. Within this space of time, until the slaughtering of the animals for Passover began at noon, everything necessary had to be taken care of. According to the halakic regulation that "no judgment must be passed [on a feast day]" (Tosefta *Yom t.* iv. 4, 207), the arrest and condemnation of Jesus were clearly items that the high priests,

---

[41] For material on the Jewish Passover regulations, see Billerbeck, Vol. 2 (1924), pp. 812–53; Vol. 4 (1928), pp. 41–76.

elders, and scribes had to finish before the slaughtering began on the Day of Preparation at the latest. Afterward many of them had to help with the slaughtering between noon and 5:00 P.M.; then all had to observe the sacred evening.

In the Mosaic laws, the evening of Passover (on which a meal lasting from about 7:00 P.M. until midnight inaugurated the festal week) is first dated 14 Nisan (Exod. 12:6, 8, 18) ; later passages, however, give the date as 15 Nisan (Lev. 23:5 f.; Num. 28:16 f.), and the latter date became general throughout Judaism (Bk. Jub. 49:1). On this evening one ate lying at the table rather than sitting (Talmud Yerushalmi *Pes.* x. 37b, 53). The head of the family blessed and distributed the following—to name the most important (Mishna *Pes.* x. 1–7) : wine, bitter herbs, freshly-baked matzos, i.e., cakes of unleavened bread (Hebrew plural *maṣṣôt*, "squeezed bread"; Greek *ázuma*, "unleavened bread"), and a lamb or a kid roasted whole (Aramaic *pasḥâ*, Greek *páscha*). Provided that Jesus died on a Friday, and that this Friday was not only a Day of Preparation for the Sabbath but also for Passover, as the Fourth Gospel suggests (John 19:14, 31, 42) and as seems probable from the circumstances, then in the year of Jesus' death the official evening of Passover was also a Sabbath evening. Even apart from this juxtaposition the Passover meal inaugurated an extremely sacred day on which work was absolutely prohibited: the first day of the week of Unleavened Bread, i.e., 15 Nisan, on which no one must engage in any secular occupation (Exod. 12:16; Lev. 23:7; Num. 28:18). The fourth evangelist knew this day as a "high Sabbath" (John 19:31), and Pharisaic rabbis called it simply "the Sabbath" in determining the date of Pentecost (following Lev. 23:11, 15) .[42] During this night and the following day such a coup d'état as the arrest and condemnation of Jesus would have been a scandalous violation of the Sabbath. Even if the Jewish politicians feared and hated the Galilean teacher, it is inconceivable that the high priests, with their well-founded fear of a riot (Matt. 26:5 and parallels) , and the Sadducees, with their renowned caution

[42] Billerbeck, Vol. 2 (1924) , pp. 598–600, 847–50.

vis-à-vis the law (see above, p. 154), would have let themselves become guilty of such a shocking desecration of the sacred evening and the day of Unleavened Bread, on which all labor was prohibited.[43]

It follows that Jesus held the Last Supper with his disciples not on the evening of Passover, but during the previous night.

This is basically also the view of the Synoptics, although they use misleading terminology and do not distinguish the Last Supper of the disciples from the Passover meal of Judaism as clearly as does John.

Special note should be taken of the official instructions, emphasized by Matthew and Mark, for the arrest and condemnation of Jesus: "Not during the feast" (Matt. 26:5 and parallels). The evangelists would hardly have retained this quotation if they had thought the limit was transgressed. Luke, too, states that Jesus' betrayer wanted to avoid the multitude that would be at the festival (Luke 22:6). The following account of the preparations for the Last Supper only apparently contradicts this schedule, because the Synoptic reporters do not use the Jewish terms in a technical way. They are well aware, however, what day was involved.

We are first told that the preparations for the Last Supper took place on "the first day of Unleavened Bread" (Matt. 26:17a); this Jewish term is then explained for Gentile readers by means of a more familiar concept: "when they [the Jews] usually sacrificed the passover lamb" (Mark 14:12; Greek *éthuon,* imperfect of customary action), or even more clearly: "the day . . . on which the passover lamb had to be sacrificed" (Luke 22:7). The purpose of the evangelists is not to suggest that the disciples or the Jews had by this time already begun to sacrifice; they are merely trying to inform a wider circle of readers that the day in question was 14 Nisan

---

[43] In favor of 15 Nisan as the date of the crucifixion, Billerbeck (Vol. 2, pp. 824–27) quotes a statement made by Rabbi Aqiba that mentions the possibility of an execution "during the festival." But since the Pentateuch passages just mentioned prohibited all trials and punishments on the first day of Unleavened Bread, Aqiba must have been referring to a lesser festival. In addition, his statement is an isolated phenomenon.

and the Day of Preparation. This nontechnical dating is based on the first Passover text in the Old Testament, the well-known account in Exodus, which designates the fourteenth day of the month of spring as the day of paschal sacrifice and also the first day of Unleavened Bread (Exod. 12:6, 8, 18). The Synoptics did not bother about the later, more usual dating, which separated the sacrificing on 14 Nisan from the eating on the night of 15 Nisan (Bk. Jub. 49:1). If one reads the text simply with Jewish concepts in mind, the subsequent account creates confusion once more, since Jesus and the disciples speak of preparations for the Passover meal (Matt. 26:17b, 18b, 19 and parallels). But this passage mentions only the room, and there is no hint of any lamb to be sacrificed at the Temple. The point is instead just this: on the evening of the day in question (Matt. 26:20 and parallels), to the astonishment of his disciples, Jesus held a covenant meal similar to the Passover meal but nevertheless novel. There was nothing remarkable in Jesus request that the room be made ready on the evening of the Day of Preparation; in view of the Galilean sanctification of this day (see above, p. 178), a common meal held on that very night to inaugurate the Passover hardly seemed revolutionary to the disciples, the more so because sacrifices of communion on 13 and 14 Nisan were common (Mishna *Zeb.* i. 3; Tosefta *Pes.* iii. 8, 162). Surprisingly, however, this nocturnal common meal was so structured that Jesus announced his coming betrayal and, with that in mind, established a new sacrificial covenant (Matt. 26:20–29 and parallels). Here again we must avoid any mechanical association with Jewish concepts. In fact, not one word in the Synoptic accounts suggests that for the Last Supper Jesus had a Passover lamb slain and roasted (*páscha* in Luke 22:15 f. does not refer to a lamb but to the meal; only on this interpretation are the following words comprehensible: "I shall not eat it again until it is fulfilled"). The absence of all mention of a lamb can hardly be dismissed as accidental; for, in view of the many ceremonial details of the account, such carelessness with regard to a major aspect of the Passover festival would be most strange. In fact, the symbolic offering of Jesus' blood at this point (Matt. 26:28 and parallels) appears to exclude the presence of a ritually sacrificed Passover lamb, because this lamb would be eaten without blood and would therefore not lend itself to such symbolism. Apart from all other considerations, the remarkable absence of the Passover lamb can best be explained by assuming that Jesus celebrated the Last Supper during the night of the Day of Preparation and before the day when the Passover lamb was sacrificed. Furthermore, this very vacuum gives a liturgically reasonable form to the establishment of the new Passover sacrifice: Jesus himself can now appear as the Paschal Lamb, as John and Paul represent him (John 1:29; I Cor. 5:7). Although this means that the paschal sacrifice proper did not take place until the next day, according to the Synoptics Jesus at the Last Supper anticipated several elements of the Passover (Matt. 26:20 and parallels): a dish (to dip the bitter herbs in), flat cakes of bread, a cup of wine; the motif of haste (according to Luke 22:15); blessing and distribution; flesh and blood as sacrifices of communion; establishment of a covenant, reconciliation; singing of the Hallel, and readiness to march (according to Luke 22:36). Jesus' appended declaration that he will not live to drink of the wine again (Matt. 26:29 and parallels) appears to be an explanation for this anticipation of paschal elements on the Day of Preparation: Jesus will not live to see the coming feast day.

John's chronological data about the farewell meal of Jesus are easier to deal with. Although the Johannine account differs from the Synoptic in many details, it points directly to the night of the Day of Preparation. The farewell meal is explicitly said to take place "before the feast of the Passover" (John 13:1); and when Jesus' betrayer rises from the table, the disciples think that he is going to buy something for the feast (13:29) —at the bazaars, which are still open. When Jesus is finally handed over to Pilate, John again says, "It was the day of Preparation for the Passover" (19:14). The Johannine farewell meal differs in many respects from the Synoptic Last Supper; at important points, however, we find once more a few anticipated paschal fragments: a dish for dipping (the bitter herbs) and a morsel of bread (John 13:26) ; the symbol of the vine (15:1) . In any case, the chronology is in notable agreement with that of the Synoptics, without recourse to any textual emendation, transposition, or adaptation.

It follows from all this that Jesus was arrested somewhat later the same night, 14 Nisan, the Day of Preparation, and then tried and condemned on the morning of the same day. The high priests, elders, and scribes considered it important for legal reasons to have the trial finished before the ritual sacrifices began at noon. Then the soldiers of Pilate had to carry out the crucifixion, which took place in part while the paschal sacrifices were being presented at the Temple (John 19:36 quotes Exod. 12:46, which refers to the paschal lamb) . A baraita of the Talmud also mentions this time: "On the Day of Preparation for the Passover Jesus the Nasorean was hanged" (Talmud Babli *Sanh.* 43a) .

3. For the reasons mentioned above, 14 Nisan in the year of Jesus' death cannot be determined exactly according to our solar calendar. We can calculate only an approximate date in the middle third of the month of April.

4. With regard to the year of Jesus' death, we have no usable astronomical data at our disposal. Certain historical references, however, suggest A.D. 33 as the most likely year. First, John the Baptist appeared A.D. 28 (Luke 3:1) . His execution, which took place perhaps a year before that of Jesus (Matt. 14:12 and parallels) , would be hard to date prior to 32; for it was brought about by the divorce of Herod Antipas (see above, p. 125) , which itself probably took place not long before the Nabatean War, of which it was the cause (see below, pp. 191 f.) . Second, in 31, Tiberius deposed the dictator Sejanus, who was hostile to the Jews, and then, presumably in 32, ordered the provincial authorities to treat the Jews more considerately (Philo *De Legatione ad Gaium* 161) . If the drama of Golgotha is dated in 33, this imperial edict provides a good politico-historical explanation for the remarkable fact that on this occasion "the kings of the earth"

and "the rulers" of the people had *united* against the "Anointed One" (Acts 4:26). It is otherwise hard to explain why, in the Jewish criminal proceedings against Jesus, the formerly authoritarian Pilate was ready to oblige the High Council, and on the other hand why so suddenly not only the conservative high priests and Sadducees but even the nationalistic Pharisees were eager to show their loyalty to Tiberius, even on the question of taxes (Luke 23:2), and in their attack upon Jesus demanded the assistance of the governor against whom they had formerly struggled (John 19:12). The political situation around A.D. 33 provided the necessary circumstances.[44]

b) The Drama of Golgotha

Jesus was probably condemned to death at the Antonia, the fortress at the northwest corner of the Temple area, because the cohort garrisoned there was responsible for detention (Acts 22:24) and because both the surrender of the prisoner and the demonstrations of the mob could very easily take place there (Matt. 27:2, 20 and parallels). The execution, on the other hand, was the responsibility of the procurator's guard (Matt. 27:27a); after Jesus was condemned, he was therefore brought to the Praetorium (Matt. 27:27b and parallels). *Praetorium* means "commander's quarters"; the word therefore refers to the palace of Herod in the western part of the city, now called the citadel, where during festivals the procurator and his guard were quartered. The Fourth Gospel prefers the setting of the Temple for its account. With less precision, it calls the Antonia the Praetorium (John 18:28), and has Pilate condemn the King of the Jews there at the same time the paschal sacrifices began nearby (John 19:14), after which Jesus went directly from the Antonia on his Via Dolorosa (John 19:16). According to the Synoptics, after Jesus was condemned, the procurator's military escort—which, as we have seen, was billeted not in the Antonia but in the palace of Herod—began a saturnalian

---

[44] The popular modern question of responsibility for having condemned Jesus to death is anachronistic: it was Jews and Romans who killed him, not Israelis and Italians.

ridicule of the new King of the Jews (Matt. 27:28–31a). The soldiers were easily provoked to this anti-Jewish demonstration, because in the palace of Herod they were reminded of the former Jewish monarchy, and there had been compelled to lay aside the insignia of the Emperor.

Jesus therefore probably began his walk to death at the palace of Herod; what is today pointed out as the Via Dolorosa, which runs from the Antonia southwest to the Church of the Holy Sepulchre, corresponds only to the fact that, after he was condemned, Jesus was first brought from the Antonia to the palace of Herod. The hill on which the crucifixion took place, however, is most probably to be found in the vicinity of the traditional Golgotha, i.e., somewhere near the Church of the Holy Sepulchre, which is located about 1000 feet north-northeast of the palace of Herod. Such a Roman place of execution would probably lie not far from the governor's residence, though outside the city wall (Matt. 28:11; John 19:20); the traditional location meets both conditions. Aelia Capitolina, the new city ordered by Hadrian in 130, also included this area, and when Constantine dedicated the Church of the Holy Sepulchre among the monumental buildings that had sprung up here, it was not outside the walls; but such data are irrelevant for the topography of the Gospels.[45] In this area, even if not directly beneath this once magnificent church, we may assume that the hill of the crucifixion was located.[46] On his way from the Praetorium to the place of crucifixion, Jesus, as was customary, had to carry the transverse beam (Latin *patibulum*) of the cross between the rows of spectators, while the upright (Greek *staurós,* "post"; Latin *palus, stipes*) stood in place at the execution site and was used over and over again. According to the Synoptic tradition, a certain Simon who happened to be present was forced to carry the beam (Matt. 27:32 and parallels), but

[45] General C. G. Gordon took the Turkish wall as his point of departure when he inaugurated a new Place of the Skull north of the old city. There the Garden Tomb was built, which at least has artistic merit.

[46] J. Jeremias, *Golgatha* (1926); A. Parrot, *Golgotha et le Saint-Sépulcre* (1955), trans. E. Hudson, *Golgotha and the Church of the Holy Sepulchre* (1957).

hardly out of pity for the King of the Jews; the Johannine account says that the Son of God himself bore the cross (John 19:17). Before the condemned man, or by him, there was carried a small tablet with a brief statement of the charge (Latin *titulus*); this was later fastened to the cross. Pilate ordered that the charge read "Jesus the King of the Jews" (Matt. 27:37 and parallels); he may have added the sectarian term "Nazorean" (John 19:19), which must be distinguished from the geographical term "Nazarene" (as Acts 24:5 shows). Whether quoted verbatim or not, the charge confirms that Pilate crucified the Master, like the two thieves, for political reasons. Jesus was described as a Galilean agitator; and Pilate, who had depended until quite recently upon Sejanus, thought it appropriate to impress Roman authority once more upon the pilgrims by means of a public crucifixion.

The execution itself was a military punishment. Pilate had pronounced judgment as regimental commander; the punishment was carried out by an execution squad under the command of a centurion, who then had to report to the procurator (Matt. 27:54 and parallels; Mark 15:44). Some of the soldiers (four, according to John 19:23) were to guard Jesus and crucify him (Matt. 27:36); others were in charge of the two thieves; a general detachment was to control the crowd (Luke 23:36).

The details of the crucifixion can be reconstructed as follows. Upon the hill stood several permanent uprights, doubtless strong, but no more than about ten feet high. In the middle was a kind of wooden seat (Latin *sedile*). At the top, or a little beneath it, there was a groove to receive the transverse beam; in the first case, the cross had three arms (like a "T"), in the second case, four arms (Latin *crux commissa* or *immissa*). The condemned person was sometimes offered a narcotic; in accordance with Jewish tradition (Ps. 69:22a; Prov. 31:6), Jesus was offered sweet wine mixed with gall but refused to drink it (Matt. 27:34 and parallels). The prisoner was stripped and his arms were tied to the transverse beam; nails were sometimes driven through his hands (here, again, according to John 20:25). He was then placed on the seat, the transverse beam and his feet were tied to the upright, and the notice of the complaint was attached to the top (Matt. 27:35–37 and parallels). The victim was to hang in this agonizing position until released by death, which usually came about through difficulty in breathing and stoppage of circulation, not so much through loss of blood. If it took too long, the end was often hastened by means of a club or poison. This time, however, a Roman soldier (unconsciously echoing Ps. 69:21b) sought to revive Jesus (Matt. 27:48 and parallels; conative imperfect) by giving him a little sour wine (Greek *óxos*, "sour drink"), the usual remedy for thirst. In jest the soldier reached for his comrades' drink in order to allow more time for Elijah to come and rescue the victim. Jesus, however, died at that very moment (Matt. 27:50; John 19:30).

The usual Roman practice was for the officials to leave the body of a crucified person until it rotted; according to Jewish law, however, the body of a hanged man had to be buried on the day of execution to prevent the land from being defiled (Deut. 21:23). Since a holy day was approaching (Mark 15:42), the Jews asked the procurator to have the bodies taken away (John 19:31–37). Joseph of Arimathea, a wealthy member of the Council, saw to Jesus' burial in a tomb that belonged to him (Matt. 27:57–61 and parallels; John 19:38–42); Jesus was therefore given "a grave with the rich" (Isa. 53:9). On this occasion there was no funeral procession, otherwise an important ceremony during which the corpse, covered with a cloth, was carried on a bier (as in Luke 7:14, at Nain); a coffin would possibly be used in the grave, but usually there was none at all (John 11:44, in the case of Lazarus). The precise location of Jesus' tomb is unknown, but it was probably a cave of the type familiar from Judean family tombs (John 11:38): a door shaped like a millstone, set in a groove, opened by being rolled aside; a central chamber with side passages; niches in the walls to receive the bodies. The corpse was wrapped in a shroud and then bandages soaked with resin were wound around the hands and feet; a cloth, the sudarium, was placed over the face (John 11:44). Finally, the tomb was shut.

Immediately after the subsequent Sabbath came the morning of the Day of First Fruits, which had to be observed by the presentation of a sheaf (Hebrew '*ōmer*) in the Temple (Lev. 23:11) and which was also the day from which the Feast of Weeks, celebrated fifty days later, was calculated. On this morning some women sought to show their respect to the Lord by bringing spices and perfumes, but found that he was no longer in the tomb (Matt. 28:6; John 20:2). Here, the limits of secular history, which studies worldly factors, are reached; there remains only salvation history, which deals with divine actions. In any case, the intended ceremony at the tomb became pointless. Neither could there be any *ossilegium* for Jesus, a ceremony that otherwise took place a year after death, at which the bones were laid in a decorated *ossuarium*, a chest about twenty inches long.

3) *The Pentecost Season of the Church* A.D. *33–41*

Inspired by the unexpected discovery of the empty tomb and the post-Easter appearances of the crucified Jesus, the company of the Apostles looked upon itself enthusiastically as the people of the promise. This consciousness was strengthened by a spiritual experience fifty days after the Day of First Fruits (Lev. 23:15), in the setting of the joyous Feast of Pentecost, when Jews and proselytes from the whole Diaspora were present (Acts 2:1–41). To be sure, the appearances of the Lord and the pouring out of the Spirit are also realities that are not accessible to secular history, but only to salvation history. Nevertheless, these experiences of the community after Easter and at Pentecost profoundly influenced the consciousness of the believers, especially in the years of the church's initial growth, A.D. 33–41. It is a drama that can be divided into three acts: (1) a period of peaceful development; (2) a violent persecution in A.D. 36; (3) a period of further expansion.

a) *The Development of the Apostolic Community*

At the trial of Jesus, various factions had joined together to oppose the new Galilean revival movement: (1) the governing circles and the Sadducees; (2) the Pharisaic scribes, for the moment eager to display civic virtue because of a new edict of the Emperor favoring the Jews (see above, p. 183) ; (3) Pilate, though only at the request of the Jews. The Apostolic community that subsequently appeared in Jerusalem was no longer opposed by this coalition, but was left for a while undisturbed. An influx of enthusiastic adherents caused it to grow rapidly (Acts 2:47). Luke's account is literary and stylized, but the general course of development confirms its basic outline.

The priests in power, led by Annas and Caiaphas, together with the Sadducees, gradually reacted against the success of the Apostles and ordered the arrest of Peter and John, and perhaps others (Acts 4:1 ff.; 5:17 f.) ; however, the enthusiastic support of the people forced them to free the Apostles once more.[47] No date is given, but circumstances suggest the years 34 or 35. For one thing, the party of Annas stood in political isolation at this time. Then too, the Pharisaic scribes were clearly unwilling at this time to oppose the movement of the Nazorean, as they called Jesus, although radical legalists soon afterward achieved a new hostile coalition. Finally, the situation with Pilate had grown cloudy once more (see below, p. 190). This time, therefore, the high priests had to refrain from strong intervention.

Gamaliel I, then the leading scribe of the Pharisees, is said to have spoken in the High Council in favor of releasing the arrested leaders of the community (Acts 5:34–39). Whether the speech is authentic or not, the course of his argument agrees with one basic tenet of Pharisaism, that God alone determines destiny (Josephus *Bell.* ii. 162; see above, p. 159) , so that political sanctions did not seem suitable. On the basis of this separation between politics and religion, adherents of the Pharisaic party were gradually able to join the Christians (Acts 15:5). Even in the years when the Zealot movement reached its height, Pharisaic members of the Council would incline toward a favorable opinion of Christianity (Acts 23:9). Judean Pharisaism of the Apostolic period therefore

[47] B. Reicke, *Glaube und Leben der Urgemeinde* (1957) , pp. 55–114.

included moderates who no longer desired to oppose the Galilean movement that preached the kingdom of God, although attacks were still launched by zealous legalists.

b) The Deposition of Pilate and the Persecution of Stephen

After the fall of Sejanus and Tiberius' edict of favor toward the Jews (see above, p. 183), Jewish national sentiment increased. The monarch's interest in local cultures and the provinces, as well as his antipathy toward fashionable Hellenism, no doubt contributed to this development. In the Diaspora the Jews were very sensitive to such changes of policy because of their competition with the Greeks, as events in Alexandria show (see below, pp. 195 f., 205). The strong Jewish colonies in Nehardea and Nisibis, Mesopotamia, offered military resistance to the Persian satrap (Josephus *Ant.* xviii. 310–69).

Nationalism in Judea, Samaria, and Galilee was soon directed against Pilate, who no longer had Sejanus to protect him. The demands of Herod's sons and the family of Annas forced the procurator to remove from the palace of Herod several golden shields decorated not with images but with the name of the Emperor and of Pilate, who had donated them himself (Philo *De Legatione ad Gaium* 299–305). Later, when his soldiers tried to disperse a mob that had gathered on Mount Gerizim to hear a prophet, indignation grew so great that Vitellius, the new legate of Syria (see above, p. 125), deposed Pilate in 36. All sorts of legends (e.g., *Acta Pilati*) recount the subsequent fate of this man, notorious among both Jews and Christians, and Philo is said to have described his violent death in a lost work (Eusebius *Hist.* ii. 5, 7); objective accounts, however, are no longer available.[48]

Vitellius, the imperial legate in Syria from A.D. 35 to 37, was also entrusted with the tetrarchy of northern Transjordan after the death of Philip. He favored the Jews in his policies because the Parthians were once more laying claim to the old Seleucid Empire. Because of the critical situation,

[48] Schürer, Vol. 3, 4th ed. (1909), p. 527.

Tiberius granted extraordinary authority over the whole Near East to this patrician, whose son later became emperor (see below pp. 262–65). Upon his return from the first campaign against the Parthians, Vitellius felt it advantageous to gain the good will of Annas' sons and the Jews. It was for this reason that he deposed Pilate in 36. He chose as his representative in Caesarea one of his protégés, Marcellus, who possessed no imperial authority but was only the tool of the general. The real power in the land was the Jewish high priest. Without hesitation, Vitellius replaced the compliant Caiaphas with a dynamic son of Annas named Jonathan. The high-priestly vestments, which Herod and the earlier procurators had kept in the Antonia and handed over only on festivals, were now placed completely at the disposal of the priests. Then the legate proceeded east once more for negotiations with the Parthians at the Euphrates. Herod Antipas, under the threat of a Nabatean war (see above, p. 125), contributed to these negotiations with a striking obsequiousness (Josephus *Ant.* xviii. 90–105).

In 36, during this interregnum under Marcellus, the martyrdom of Stephen took place, as the following details show. 1. The Diaspora Jews, organized in Jerusalem synagogues, who came forward to accuse Stephen, were motivated by a Zionism and a devotion to the law similar to that of the Zealots (Acts 6:9, 11, 13). With the zeal of youth, a student of the Pharisees named Saul or Paul (Saul being his Pharisaic name, Paul his name as a Roman citizen) joined in (Acts 7:58). He later described his conduct then as that of a Zealot (Acts 22:3; Gal. 1:14; Phil. 3:6). 2. The hostile members of the Council were led by a powerful high priest (Acts 7:1), who later employed Saul to persecute Christians in Jerusalem and even in Damascus (Acts 8:3; 9:1 f.). 3. The high priest did not bother to have his decision ratified by the procurator, but rather let the stoning and persecution go ahead without consulting the Roman authorities (Acts 7:58; 8:1). These measures, by no means natural and obvious, depended on the new sense of freedom that we may assume followed Vitellius' restoration of the high-priestly vestments to the power-hungry Jonathan and the legate's departure for the Euphrates.

Execution by stoning was the sacral form of capital punishment among the Jews (Lev. 24:10–16; Deut. 17:2–7; Mishna *Sanh.* v. 3—vii. 5). The criminal was taken outside the city, placed upon a wall or rock, and thrown upon his back from a height of twelve to fifteen feet. If the fall did not kill him, the two witnesses, and sometimes the whole crowd as well, dropped heavy stones on his chest. In cases of blasphemy, the body was hung on a stake. Before nightfall, however, the corpse had to be thrown into a cave.

At the execution of Stephen, Paul of his own accord played the role of a policeman (Acts 7:58b). In the subsequent persecution, this Pharisaic zealot, supported by the Jerusalem authorities, played havoc with the Hellenists of the primitive community (Acts 8:3; 22:4–5a; 26:10) and even sought to arrest the Christians of Damascus in the name of the high priest (Acts 9:1 f.; 22:5b; 26:12). This campaign on behalf of Jewish national ideals, led by the high priest and carried out by Pharisees, took on astonishing proportions; but in the Marcellus interregnum of 36 it was possible because no imperial procurator was in Judea and Vitellius gave the leading Jews considerable freedom of action.

c) *Caligula's Reign and the Spread of the Gospel*

Vitellius successfully resolved the Parthian question, but afterward the position of the Jews and Christians changed because of new political events. As a consequence of his divorce from his Nabatean wife (see above p. 125), Herod Antipas was attacked by the Nabatean king Aretas who, during the Roman campaign against the Parthians, defeated the troops of Antipas decisively. Much against his will, Vitellius had to rescue the tetrarch from a difficult situation. In the spring of 37, he marched with two legions and their auxiliaries from Ptolemais through the plain of Jezreel and the Jordan Valley, intending to continue through Moab to Petra. Out of deference to the Jewish people he did not let his troops enter Judea, but went up to Jerusalem with Antipas and a few adjutants to offer sacrifice at the Passover. While there, however, Vitellius replaced Jonathan as high priest with his brother Theophilus (A.D. 37–41), evidently because Jonathan had grown too independent and because the situation once more permitted assertion of Roman supremacy.

Almost at the same time news arrived that Tiberius had died and Caligula (A.D. 37–41) had succeeded him. This put an end to the campaign which Tiberius had ordered against Aretas (Josephus *Ant.* xviii. 109–126a). Vitellius was willing to support the Jews only when it seemed politically expedient, and this was no longer the case. He left the Galilean tetrarch and the Judean high priest with their authority considerably reduced. The new emperor was as famous for his adherence to Hellenism as his predecessor was for his opposition to it, and so a reverse was to be expected for the recently kindled flame of Judaism. Caligula also hastened to place Judea once more under an imperial procurator, this time by the name of Marullus (A.D. 37–41).

The anti-Hellenistic persecution of Stephen itself gave new impetus to Christian missionary activity; then the pro-Hellenistic change of regime provided favorable circumstances for a few years. During the persecution, it is true, the community in Jerusalem was scattered: only the Apostles and Jewish Christians were allowed to remain, while the proselytes of Hellenistic background, already numerous, were slain or exiled (Acts 8:1). The very dispersal of the Hellenists, however, led to a spread of the Gospel in Judea, Samaria, Philistia (Acts 8:4–40), and even as far as Damascus (Acts 9:2). It was at Damascus during this period that Paul ceased persecuting the Christians and became their colleague (Acts 9:2, 27); he soon began his missionary work in the neighboring regions of the Nabatean Empire (II Cor. 11:32; Gal. 1:17, "Arabia"). When Jonathan the high priest was deposed, persecution in Jerusalem ceased. In 38, therefore, Paul was able to visit Peter in Jerusalem under the protection of Barnabas, a Christian Levite (Acts 9:27; Gal. 1:18 says "after three years," counting, as usual, the initial year). Paul stayed there incognito, and the brethren sent him as quickly as possible to his homeland of Cilicia (Acts 9:30; Gal. 1:21), where he presumably took up his missionary work again, for the moment at an isolated frontier. In the meantime, the church in Judea, Samaria, and Galilee was able to secure its positions (Acts 9:31). Peter, too, set to work as a missionary, going through Sharon as far as Caesarea (Acts 9:32—10:48). Some of the scattered Hellenists went even further, preaching in Phoenicia and Cyprus, and in Antioch even among Gentiles (Acts 11:19–24). Barnabas, sent from Jerusalem to Antioch, summoned Paul to assist him (Acts 11:25). Now the Gentile mission of the church had begun in good earnest. The center of this new activity, during the subsequent missionary journeys of Paul, was not the capital of Palestine, but Antioch, the imperial residence and military capital of Syria, which had more than half a million inhabitants and was the third largest city of the Roman Empire, surpassed only by Rome and Alexandria. Here the name "Christians" (Acts 11:26) first came into use (Greek *Christianoi,* "followers of Christ," formed analogously to such words as Latin *Caesarianus,* "follower of Caesar"). On occasion the community at Antioch also contributed to the support of the community at Jerusalem (Acts 11:27–30); but they devoted themselves for the most part to the conversion of the Hellenistic world (Acts 13:1–3; etc.). In the Acts of the Apostles, Luke described this extraordinary growth and development as the work of the Spirit; his account, however, is basically historical and not legendary. The expansion was not only triggered by the persecution of Stephen and the Hellenists, but was also hastened by the change of course associated with the deposition of the high priest Jonathan and the accession of the Emperor Caligula. Despite the inept political conduct of this vain emperor, the situation during his reign and until the persecution of James around A.D. 42 (see below, pp. 200 f.) was favorable to the church.

d) Agrippa's Rise and the Cultural Struggle

For the Jews, the accession of the pro-Hellenistic emperor Caligula meant a setback in their cultural defense but an improvement in their political situation. These contrary aspects of the change were both associated with Agrippa I, a grandson of Herod, who, through personal connections with Caligula and later with Claudius, was able to piece together once more the kingdom of Herod.

Agrippa I (the king of Philip's tetrarchy after 37, of Antipas' tetrarchy after 40, and of all Palestine from 41 to 44), whom Luke in popular fashion called "Herod," after his grandfather (Acts 12:1–23), was the black sheep of the Herodian family before his rise to power. He went to school in Rome with emperor's sons; afterward he lived the careless life of a dandy among all kinds of fortune hunters. Deep in debt, he returned to Idumea and tried to commit suicide. His wife and his sister Herodias, however, obtained for him a sinecure in Tiberias with Antipas. He soon fell out with his brother-in-law, made himself detested in Antioch, borrowed money with the help of his wife, and tried his luck once more in Rome. There he found monetary and diplomatic support from a powerful woman: Antonia, the grandmother of the expected heir to the throne, Caligula, and mother of the later Emperor Claudius, with whom Agrippa had attended school. The forty-six-year-old Herodian became adjutant to the twenty-four-year-old crown prince. He flattered the prince so audaciously that Tiberius imprisoned him for six months in the praetorian barracks. In 37, after Tiberius' death, Caligula ascended the throne with the aid of the Praetorian Guard; as soon as possible he made Agrippa vassal king of the tetrarchy of Philip, with the addition of Abilene on the Antilebanon. Caligula loved princely splendor, and also reintroduced the Hellenistic kingship of Commagene, in northern Syria.

In the course of his journey to his small kingdom in the summer of 38, Agrippa seized the opportunity to parade his magnificence before the Jews of Alexandria. This incited the

Greeks to persecute the Jews; the cultural conflict between
the elements constituting this metropolis had long been notorious (see above, pp. 69 f.) . Isidore, the rabidly Hellenistic
rector of the gymnasium, had his students trot out an imbe-
cile representing the King of Israel, whom they called
"Lord" in pseudo-Aramaic. Historians of religion have compared this parody to the mocking of Jesus; but in this case
Agrippa, the spokesman of the Jews, was being derided.
Then the Greeks, knowing Caligula's love of the Hellenistic
emperor cult, declared that images of the emperor had to be
set up in the synagogues. When the Jews refused, their
houses were robbed and burned. Agrippa complained to
Gaius Caligula, as did a delegation of Alexandrian Jews led
by the philosopher Philo, whose books *In Flaccum* and *De
Legatione ad Gaium* discuss this important struggle. Caligula gave more favorable audience to the delegation of Alexandrian Greeks under the rhetor Apio, against whom Josephus' later polemic *Contra Apionem* is directed. The
Emperor could not understand why all men should not
worship him as god.

This interracial strife, brought about by Agrippa's visit to
Alexandria, continued to rage for a long time in the capital
of the East and spread throughout other portions of the
Judaeo-Hellenistic world. With respect to Alexandria, newly
discovered papyri, the so-called "Acts of the Alexandrine
Martyrs," show the efforts made by Claudius and later Emperors to restrain the Hellenists there. In some ways IV
Maccabees is a Jewish counterpart to these Greek martyr
documents, provided that its story enables it to be dated
in the period of Caligula. With regard to other parts of the
Empire, under Caligula the Jews were persecuted even in
distant Mesopotamia (Josephus *Ant.* xviii. 370–79) .

Upon the arrival of the new king Agrippa I in Palestine in
38, the Greeks in the imperial city of Jamnia in the Philistine plain set up an altar to Caligula, which the Jews tore
down. In a rage, Caligula commanded the legate of Syria,
Petronius, to have an image of the Emperor set up in the
Jerusalem Temple in 39. Such an image was fabricated in

Sidon while Caligula was on campaign in Gaul and Germany. Petronius delayed action because the Jews demonstrated violently. Then, however, in the summer of 40, the Emperor returned to Italy without military successes and showed himself all the more impatient in the matter of the statue. Agrippa, who had overthrown Antipas shortly before Caligula's German campaign, hastened to the Emperor to intercede. On this occasion he first saw to it that the tetrarchy of Antipas was formally handed over to him. Then, when the self-willed Caligula mentioned the image in the Temple, Agrippa fell into a mock faint and moved the Emperor to suspend the project (Philo *De Legatione ad Gaium* 261–333). Caligula still requested that voluntary actions in support of emperor worship be encouraged (*ibid.*, 334–37), but was soon slain by a senatorial conspiracy. Thus the Jews escaped with a bad scare. But the strenuous efforts of the Greeks and the Emperor to force an image cult upon them had a lasting effect upon the Jewish mind and later colored Christian thinking (Wisd. of Sol. 14:16; II Thess. 2:4; Rev. 13:14 f.).

In January of 41 Caligula was assassinated; the intervention of monarchistic praetorians gave the throne to Claudius, his uncle. Agrippa was still in Rome and gave his nervous school companion moral support against the senate. In return he was allowed to extend his royal power and add Judea to the tetrarchies of Philip and Antipas, so that for the next several years the kingdom of Herod was restored.

4. PALESTINE IN THE TIME OF JAMES AND PAUL
A.D. 41–66

The table on page 199 places some important events in the history of the church in relation to Agrippa's reign, the second procuratorship, the activity of Paul, and the Roman authorities in Syria and Palestine. For the history of the church the chronology must remain relative, since we have no absolute dates. The following points of reference are more or less definite: (1) the Apostolic Council at Jerusalem, following the first missionary journey, which Paul dates fourteen (by modern reckoning thirteen) years after his conversion in 36, i.e., A.D. 49 (Gal. 1:16; 2:1; the three years of 1:18 must be included) ; (2) the second missionary journey of Paul, in the course of which he was accused before Gallio in Corinth (Acts 18:12) ; according to an inscription, Gallio was proconsul there in 51–52, so that the journey can be dated A.D. 50–53. The other events must be so distributed over the particular years that they harmonize externally with the dates of Roman and Jewish history and, internally, yield a natural course of development.

A. AGRIPPA I AS KING OF JUDEA A.D. 41–44

> Herod [Agrippa] put on his royal robes, took his seat upon the throne, and made an oration to them.
>
> Acts 12:21

1) *Agrippa's Patronage of Pharisaism*

We have seen that Agrippa I became king over Philip's tetrarchy in 37, over that of Antipas in 40, and over all Judea in 41 (see above, pp. 195 ff.); he ruled until his death in 44. In his political conduct he exhibited a character completely different from that which he had exhibited as a private citizen. He had conducted himself as an adventurer and man of the world; now he sought to carry out the observances of Judaism and gain the respect of the Pharisees. Thus his regime brought about a flowering of Pharisaism like that in the previous century, when Pharisaism flourished under Alexandra (76–67 B.C.) . Josephus and the Talmud also picture King Agrippa as a great hero. We read, for instance, that he led an unexceptional life, kept the ordinances of the fathers, and offered sacrifice daily (Josephus *Ant.* xix. 328. 330 f.) . In fact, he understood how to win the affection of the people, who were controlled by the Pharisees. For him, however, this was not a matter of religious conviction but of political expediency: the king considered it opportune to support Jewish interests. It was worth pursuing a pro-Jewish policy because of Claudius' efforts to resolve the conflict

Emperors:	Selected Legates in Syria:	Rulers in Palestine:	Selected High Priests:	Significant Events (relative chronology):
Claudius, 41–54		Agrippa I, king of all Palestine, 41–44		Martyrdom of James I, ca. 42.
		The Seven Last Procurators, 44–66:		
		Cuspius Fadus, 44– ca. 46		Revolt of Theudas, ca. 45
		Tiberius Alexander, ca. 46–48		Famine, 46
				First missionary journey, 47–48
		Ventidius Cumanus, 48–52	Ananias, 48–58	Apostolic Council, 49
				Second missionary journey, 50–53
				Zealot disturbances, 50–52
				Expulsion of Jews from Rome, 50
		Antonius Felix, 52–60		Persecution of Christians in Palestine, 52
Nero 54–68				Pro-Hellenistic Emperor, 54
				Zealot terrorism, 54–66
				Dispute between Paul and Peter at Antioch, 54
				Third missionary journey, 54–58
				Revolt of the Egyptian, ca. 55
				Paul arrested, 58
	Corbulo, 60–63	Porcius Festus, 60–62		Paul taken to Rome, 60
		Lucceius Albinus, 62–64	Ananus II, 62	Martyrdom of James II, 62
	Gallus, 63–66	Gessius Florus, 64–66		Emigration of the primitive community, ca. 64
				Martyrdom of Peter and Paul, 65 (?)
		(The Jewish War, 66–70)		

between Jews and Greeks in Alexandria. The *Epistula Claudiana* (*Pap. Lond.* 1912), discovered in 1921, is the chief evidence for Claudius' benevolent attitude toward the Jews.[49] Agrippa also made concessions to Jewish patriotism by beginning to construct a third wall for Jerusalem a bit north of Herod's palace; upon the command of the legate of Syria,

[49] H. I. Bell, *Jews and Christians in Egypt* (1924), pp. 1–37; S. Lösch, *Epistula Claudiana* (1930).

however, he had to leave the project half finished. In addition, Agrippa kept up diplomatic relations with Oriental princes who, like him, were dependent on Rome and at the same time had regional interests. It meant a great triumph for Judaism when King Izates of Adiabene, in northern Syria, and his mother Helen were converted to Judaism, took Jerusalem as their favorite residence, and selected a site for their tomb there; the imposing "royal tombs" half a mile north of the Damascus Gate are Hellenistic funerary monuments of Adiabene's dynasty. Agrippa finally succeeded in bringing together a string of Roman vassals from Syria and Asia Minor at Tiberias for a conference. The intervention of the Roman legate of Syria also brought his project to naught; the plan shows, however, that Agrippa's pro-Jewish attitude was coupled with political calculation.

Like his grandfather before him, the luxury-loving Agrippa I appeared outside of Judea as a friend of Hellenistic culture, which he promoted with considerable energy. In particular, he provided the resources for adorning the Phoenician city of Berytus (modern Beirut) with majestic buildings. In addition, he sponsored gladiatorial games and theatrical entertainments in many cities, even Caesarea. His coins that were stamped in Caesarea or Tiberias bore the image of the King or the Emperor.

2) *The Martyrdom of James, the Son of Zebedee*

As a consequence of his pro-Jewish policies, Agrippa I considered it necessary in Palestine to avoid or even oppose whatever seemed advantageous to Hellenism. He saw to it that the coins minted in Jerusalem bore no image, and treated the Hellenistic cities of the region, Samaria and Caesarea, with conspicuous reserve.

To oblige Pharisaic interests Agrippa also undertook a persecution of the Christians (Acts 12:1–19), during which the Apostle James, the son of Zebedee, was slain with the sword and Peter was cast into prison. Like the persecution of Stephen in 36, this persecution of James about 42 was due to a feeling of prosperity and expansion among the Jews, which made them want to repress all elements that seemed alien to the nation. The removal of the leading Apostles, James I and Peter, was an attempt to cripple a movement that by now had many associations with Hellenism. This action was a severe blow to the church in Palestine. Peter was rescued, but he was no longer able to show himself as leader of the primitive community. Instead, he let the responsibility devolve upon James II, the brother of the Lord, and withdrew to a place unnamed (Acts 12:17).

3) *The Death of Agrippa I, and His Survivors*

The provocative diplomacy of Agrippa I would probably have alarmed the Romans in short order, had death not removed him in 44. Here the accounts of the New Testament and Josephus agree on certain details: he was stricken by a stomach ailment while attending public games at Caesarea, where his claqueurs acclaimed him as a god (Acts 12:19–23; Josephus *Ant.* xix. 343–50). The latter incident suggests a certain interest in the Hellenistic ruler cult.

Agrippa I, whom Josephus calls a "great king," left at his death an elder brother, Herod II, who ruled Iturean Chalcis in the Antilebanon from 41 to 48; three daughters; and a young son. Two of his daughters were married for a time to Oriental princes; the New Testament mentions them in passing upon their encounters with Paul in Caesarea about 58 and 60. These were Drusilla, Agrippa's third daughter, who was then married to the procurator Felix (Acts 24:24), and Bernice, his first daughter, the widow of their uncle Herod II (Acts 25:13). The son, Agrippa II, was seventeen years old at his father's death; he did not become king of the Jews. Because of the nationalistic policies of the dead King, the Emperor's officials advised him against entrusting the kingship to the youth. Later, however, Claudius made Agrippa II king over adjacent territories, which he ruled from 50 to about 94.[50] In 50, after the death of his uncle and brother-

---

[50] Hardly until 100, as a statement by Photius has led scholars to assume. For details, see O. Stählin, "Die hellenistisch-jüdische Literatur," in W. Schmidt and O. Stählin, *Wilhelm von Christ's Geschichte der griechischen Literatur* ("Handbuch der Altertumswissenschaft," VII, 2:1) 6th ed. (1920, reprinted 1959), p. 593, n. 1.

in-law Herod II, he received the territory of Chalcis. In 52, he exchanged it for the tetrarchy of Philip and some border areas. Here he enlarged Caesarea Philippi and renamed it Neronias. In addition, about 56, Nero granted him Tiberias, Tarichea, and some cities in Perea (Josephus *Bell.* ii. 252; *Ant.* xx. 159). Like his uncle before him, Agrippa II kept the investment of the high priest under his control. He was important as a Roman confidant in Jewish questions; for this reason he appeared at Paul's trial in Caesarea, accompanied, as usual, by his sister Bernice (Acts 25:13—26:32).

B. THE SECOND PROCURATORSHIP, THE ZEALOT MOVEMENT, AND THE CHURCH A.D. 44–66

> Under the procurator Cumanus [48–52] unrest began. . . . Under Felix [52–60] the bandits threatened to kill all who desired to obey Roman authority.
>
> Josephus, *Bellum Judaicum* ii. 223, 264
>
> Festus [60–62] found Judea laid waste by the bandits . . . ; the *sicarii* were by this time exceedingly numerous.
>
> Josephus, *Antiquitates* xx. 185 f.

In 44, the Emperor Claudius (A.D. 41–54) brought to an end the kingdom of Judea, restored under Agrippa I from 41 to 44. In line with his general policy of developing the administration of the provinces, he placed the land directly under Roman control. Thus came into being the second procuratorship, which differed from the first in comprising Galilee as well as Judea and Samaria. It lasted through the outbreak of the Jewish War in 66, but was replaced in 67 by the regional military government of Vespasian and in 70 by the imperial province of Judea.

1) *Patriots and Zealots in Judea*

Josephus depicts the procurators of the period between 44 and 66 as barbarians and extortioners, but they were hardly worse than the general run of Roman colonial officials. The surprisingly violent Jewish reaction was more likely due to the political situation. The glory of Herod's kingdom, restored according to strict religious principles under Agrippa I, had suddenly to vanish. From the very outset, therefore, the Jews detested their new guardians. To this anger must be added the turbulent struggle between Greek and Jewish culture. About 50, Claudius had the Jews banished from Rome. In 52, however, he took the part of the Jews in the East against the Greeks. After the year 54, the world had in Nero an aggressively Hellenistic ruler. The Jewish nationalists gradually developed a burning hatred of foreign domination. Aristocratic patriots on the one hand and demagogic Zealots on the other set the mood and gradually succeeded in inciting the population to rebel.

Thus, the period from 44 to 66 prepared inevitably for the first war between the Jews and the Romans, 66–70. The popular insurrection grew almost exactly in step with the seven changes of procurator during this period (see below, sec. 2). At stake were the freedom and purity of Judaism, for which the Temple and the law were two sacred palladia. The nation looked back upon its earlier independence under the line of David, the Hasmoneans, Herod I, and Agrippa I. With the courage born of despair, it also sought to bring about fulfillment of the prophecies of salvation. Because this latter attempt was often direct and concrete, we may call it a "materialization of eschatology."

Zealotism led to all kinds of complications, not only for the Greek residents and the Roman authorities, but also for the Christian congregations (see below, sec. 3). For the church, the period of the second procuratorship bore a double stamp: on the one hand, the loyalty to Israel of James II; and on the other, the Gentile mission of Paul. Theological and personal differences hardly suffice to explain this polarity; we must rather examine the historical circumstances under which the Jewish Christians and Gentile Christians lived.

2) The Seven Procurators and the Growing Terror

a) Fadus, Alexander, Cumanus, and Felix to A.D. 54

Already during the regime of the first of the new procurators, Cuspius Fadus (44–*ca.* 46), questions of prestige led to altercations. Fadus wanted to place the vestments of the high priest once more in Roman keeping, evidence of Claudius' more vigorous moves against the Jews. Admittedly, the emperor did allow Herodian control of the high priests to continue: after the death of Agrippa I, his elder brother Herod II, king of Chalcis, was commissioned to select the high priest and supervise the Temple; after his death, this right passed in 48 to Agrippa's son, Agrippa II (mentioned above, pp. 201 f.). But Fadus was certainly instructed to keep firm control. The reaction of the Jews was inevitable, and even assumed messianic forms: about 45, a prophet named Theudas tried to part the Jordan miraculously and march through Jerusalem against the Romans with his band of followers: Fadus, however, had him beheaded in time (Josephus *Ant.* xx. 97–99).[51]

The second of these procurators was a distinguished Alexandrian Jew, Tiberius Alexander (*ca.* 46–48), a nephew of the Hellenistic Jewish philosopher Philo of Alexandria. He had also engaged in philosophy and had published a book stating that animals were devoid of reason. Against this materialistic nephew, Philo wrote his idealistic study *Alexander*. In the eyes of the Jewish nationalists, Alexander was an unscrupulous apostate in the service of tyrants. He also suppressed Jewish nationalism by having two representatives of the Zealot party crucified (Josephus *Ant.* xx. 102); both were the sons of Judas the Galilean (Acts 5:37), the pioneer of the Zealot movement (see above, pp. 118, 136 f.). Alexander was later made prefect of Egypt (see below, pp. 261, 263).

The third holder of the procuratorship after the death of

---

[51] According to Luke, Gamaliel addressed the High Council about ten years earlier concerning a false Messiah named Theudas (Acts 5:36). If this refers to the same man mentioned by Josephus, the anachronism is readily intelligible: Luke wanted to embellish Gamaliel's speech with some familiar examples of frustrated messianic movements, and had also heard of Theudas.

Agrippa, Ventidius Cumanus (48–52), found the Jews peaceful at first. After the year 50, however, they became restive again, in connection with riots that took place in Rome and Alexandria. At times Cumanus crushed the repeated uprisings too brutally; but for the most part his conduct was too weak, and his negligence finally resulted in a civil war of the Jews, led by the Zealots, against the Samaritans, who were considered half Gentile (Josephus *Bell.* ii. 223–46) .

Cumanus did not know what position to take in the struggle between Greek and Jewish cultures, for here, as elsewhere, Claudius seemed to vacillate. Suetonius reports that, in the year 49 or, rather, 50, Claudius issued an edict banishing the Jews from Rome for a time because they were engaged in strife over the Messiah (Suetonius *Claudius* xxv. 4; the expression *"impulsore Chresto tumultuantes"* confuses the occasion of the strife with the instigator) . On account of this edict of Claudius, the Jewish Christians Aquila and Priscilla left Rome and came to Corinth (Acts 18:2) . At the same time, the struggle between Greeks and Jews in Alexandria flared up once more. This brought the dilemma of Cumanus in Palestine to a head. In the year 52, the Emperor summoned new delegations from both camps; Agrippa II represented the Jews (*Acta Alexandrinorum* iv. c, col. ii. 21–24) .[52] Claudius decided both the Alexandrian (*ibid.,* iv, A, col. ii. 16 f.) and the Palestinian question (Josephus *Bell.* ii. 254) in favor of the Jews, and Cumanus was banished.

At the suggestion of the former high priest Jonathan, who had slain Stephen (see above, pp. 191 f.) and now led the patriotic party of Annas, in the year 52 a favorite of the Roman administration by the name of Antonius Felix was appointed procurator in Caesarea by the Sea. In place of Chalcis, Agrippa II received the tetrarchy of northern Transjordan and became a Roman client king in Caesarea Philippi (see above, pp. 201 f.) . For the Jews, both changes meant new successes in the struggle against Greek culture and improvement

[52] H. A. Musurillo, *The Acts of the Pagan Martyrs: Acta Alexandrinorum* (1954) , pp. 23, 124.

in the political situation. These developments further encouraged the patriots and Zealots.

Unlike the earlier procurators, Antonius Felix (52–60) was not an equestrian, but rather a freedman of Antonia, the Emperor's mother, from whom he received his forename. Claudius made a policy of employing such court servants in his administration. Felix was even the brother of the Minister of the Treasury, Pallas, and the husband of a Roman princess descended from Antony and Cleopatra; he therefore had the ear of the central government and a place in higher diplomatic circles. After taking office in Caesarea, Felix was able to conclude another favorable marriage, this time with the beautiful Jewish princess Drusilla (Acts 24:24). Agrippa II allowed his sister to marry the Roman without the usual requirement of circumcision, a sign that he considered the match very advantageous. All this established friendly relationships between the Romans and the Jews in the first two years of Felix' procuratorship. Claudius had taken the part of the Jews in their contest with the Greeks, and despite his physical weakness he functioned, so to speak, as "the restraining one" (II Thess. 2:7) with respect to the coming lawlessness, until his death in A.D. 54. But hosts of Zealots stood ready to intervene against foreigners and enemies.

b) Felix after A.D. 54, Festus, Albinus, and Florus

The young hellenophile Nero had scarcely been proclaimed emperor in 54 when the Zealots rose up against Greeks and even Romans in Palestine. An organized campaign of terrorism began which led to war twelve years later. The explosion of anarchy was not due to the despotism of this infamous emperor, which he did not evidence until the sixties, but rather to 1. his support of Hellenism; 2. his changes in the government; and 3. disturbances caused by the Parthians. 1. Nero claimed the title "Son of Apollo," and appeared ostentatiously in this role. 2. Pallas, the brother of Felix and Minister of the Treasury, was forced out of the government; this left Felix out on a limb. In addition, Felix had to surrender several territories to Agrippa II (see above

p. 202) ; he remained in power only because Agrippina, the Emperor's mother, was still able to protect Pallas from ruin. 3. Agrippa II, along with other Oriental rulers, was ordered to support the legate of Syria against the Parthians, who were once more on the warpath; the Roman troops in the East, however, were at that time not battle-tested. Because the Jews were no doubt accurately informed, they saw in this situation an advantage for their Greek rivals and a reverse for their local Roman authorities.

On the basis of personal reminiscences, Josephus describes how the Holy Land became filled with anarchists ("robbers") and fanatics ("conjurers") just after Nero's accession (Josephus *Ant.* xx. 158, 160). Felix could do little about this disorder. He ambushed and imprisoned Eleazar Dinaei, who for twenty years had led the militant Zealots and had caused much trouble for Cumanus. He also ordered the assassination of Jonathan, the high priest in the year 36 (see above, pp. 191 f.) , who had contributed to the appointment of Felix (see above, p. 205) , and now, as leader of the party of Annas, headed the aristocratic patriots. But these measures of the procurator only drove the resistance movement to greater violence. The young Zealots in Jerusalem organized themselves as assassins or *sicarii;* they kept a short Persian saber (Latin *sica,* "dagger") under their cloak and slew those of their countrymen that had been singled out as collaborators with the Greeks and Romans. Around 55, a popular leader called "the Egyptian" came out of the desert with thousands of *sicarii,* encamped on the Mount of Olives, and sought to take Jerusalem. Though the Roman troops were able to disperse them, belief in his return persisted (Acts 21:38) . In addition, the Jews in Caesarea by the Sea denied the local Greeks the right of citizenship on the grounds that Herod I had founded the city; the Jewish Zealots thus finally acknowledged the Idumean to be Jewish. As in the case of the contention in Alexandria under Caligula and Claudius, representatives of both ethnic groups in Caesarea had to appear before the Emperor. It goes without saying that Nero decided in favor of the Greeks. Furthermore, in 59 he murdered his influential mother and confiscated the wealth of her protégé Pallas; then he could depose Pallas' brother Felix with impunity. As the two-year trial of Paul demonstrates, for the past few years Felix had been almost incapable of independent action (Acts 24:27). This political situation and Pauline chronology suggest that Felix was deposed in the year 60. Some theologians, basing their conclusion on the chronicle of Eusebius, prefer the year 56. But this early date yields an impossibly short time for Paul's long journeys; it is also excluded by statements of Luke and Josephus (Acts 24:10 says that Felix had been in office "for many years"; Josephus *Vit.* 13 mentions Jewish magnates kept hostage in Rome since the time of Felix and set free in 62).

Felix was succeeded in Caesarea by a certain Porcius Festus (A.D. 60–62). Luke and Josephus depict him as a politician capable of prudent and speedy action (Acts 24:27—26:32; Josephus *Bell.* ii. 271; *Ant.* xx. 182–96). There is no mention of him in other contemporary sources; but he presumably belonged to the equestrian order, as did later bearers of the name Porcius.[53] Unlike Felix after Nero's accession, Festus had the support of the Roman government; he was able to send the captive Paul at once to the Emperor and hold the rebellious Jews in check. Agrippa II was brought in as a consultant, in part with regard to Paul's trial (Acts 25:13) but more on account of the problem of the Jewish nationalists (Josephus *Ant.* xx. 193). Another desert prophet and his followers were overthrown. Festus also joined with Agrippa in opposing the high-priestly patriots, who were engaged in building a high wall to separate the sanctuary from the Antonia and the palace on the Xystus, and in collecting the tithes, at the expense of the rural priests, to finance some future actions. Felix had already forced these Jewish magnates to send ten representatives to Rome as hostages. Quite unexpectedly, the wall was left standing and the hostages were freed, because Festus died in

---

[53] M. Lambertz in *PRE,* Vol. 22, 1, cols. 219 f. Our Porcius is dealt with *ibid.,* cols. 220–27; nothing is given, however, besides chronological data and what the New Testament records.

62 and the Empress Poppaea intervened on behalf of the Jews. The patriots found a clever agent in Josephus, who was born in 37 the son of an aristocratic priest and who claimed to have studied the doctrines of the Pharisees, Sadducees, Essenes, and Baptists successively (Josephus *Vit.* 10–12a). He later claimed to be a Pharisee, but only for diplomatic reasons (*ibid.,* 12b). In 62, Josephus and some other patriots waited upon Poppaea and succeeded in having the Jewish magnates freed. Once he ascribed her benevolence to her fear of God, another time to her friendship with a Jewish actor (Josephus *Ant.* xx. 195; *Vit.* 16).

The sudden decease of the Roman procurator in 62 brought renewed vigor to the patriotic party of Annas in Jerusalem. Ananus II, a son of the powerful Annas (Ananus I) and himself an ardently patriotic Sadducean high priest, used the interregnum of about four months before the arrival of a new procurator to get rid of popular leaders suspected of not following the patriotic line. One of these was James II, the brother of the Lord, who had been a leading figure since about 42 and the highest authority of the Palestinian church since about 50; he was accused and stoned (see below pp. 215 f.). In the autumn, however, when the new procurator finally began his journey, Jewish legitimists hastened to him and demanded legal protection, while Agrippa II deposed the autocratic high priest (Josephus *Ant.* xx. 197–203).

In the year 62 Rome went through another change of regime, which was to be disastrous for the Empire and also for the Jews. Burrus, the sagacious prefect of the Guard and adjutant of the Emperor, died of a throat disease. He was replaced by the barbarous Tigellinus, who fanned the Emperor's lust for power. Up to this time Seneca had mediated between the Emperor and the senate, but he was now ousted from the political arena. Nero attacked several outstanding representatives of the senatorial party, surrounding himself instead with disreputable careerists from among the equestrians or dubious characters from the Hellenistic world. While he wanted to come forward as a classic artist and superman, he conducted foreign policy like a dilettante and played havoc with the finances of the Empire. Both in Italy and in the provinces powerful movements gathered against him. These first erupted in Judea, where the Zealot movement, hatred of the Greeks, and the manipulations of robbers contributed to it.

After some delay, Festus was succeeded as procurator by Albinus (A.D. 62–64). He represented the brutal type of government official that Tigellinus brought to power while Nero tried his luck as charioteer and opera singer. Because of the Parthian question and other difficulties, as well as the extravagances of the tyrant, the government needed great sums of money; as procurator of Judea, Albinus seized every opportunity to fill the imperial coffers as well as his own (Josephus *Bell.* ii. 272–76; *Ant.* xx. 197–215). These financial activities soon earned him a promotion, and he became governor of Mauretania (see below, p. 261).

His successor, the last procurator of Judea, was Gessius Florus (A.D. 64–66). While at Rome he had been, thanks to his wife, a protégé of the pro-Jewish Poppaea(Josephus *Ant.* xx. 252). In Judea, however, he aroused violent opposition through his continued and increased exactions (Josephus *Bell.* ii. 277–83). In complete despair, the Jews complained to the commandant at Antioch, Cestius Gallus; but Gallus did not dare take any measures against the financial agent of the Emperor. The social structure of Palestine was disintegrating; competing for the plunder were the procurator, patriotic aristocrats, Zealot rebels, and desperados of all sorts. At the same time, one must also consider the anarchical tendencies that soon became evident in other parts of the Empire. The first Jewish War in 66 was not an isolated phenomenon, but the harbinger of a general revolution. In 69, on the other hand, it became the background of Vespasian's restoration of the imperial dignity, while in 70 it led to the downfall of the Jewish commonwealth.

3) *The Church's Mission to Jews and Gentiles A.D. 44–66*

In the period of the second procuratorship, 44–66, two opposing forces dominated the apostolic church: loyalty to the Jews, conscious of their role as God's chosen people; love for the nations, which were interpreted as standing in need of salvation. These interests were represented characteristically, though not exclusively, by two Apostles, the one a leader in Jerusalem, the other in the mission field. These were James II, the brother of the Lord, and Paul, the Apostle to the Gentiles. Their life and work reflect the political and ethnic problems of the period.

Despite the Zealot movement, the church thought it theologically and politically important to maintain a positive relationship with Jerusalem and Judaism, until the martyrdom of James in 62, the growth of terrorism, and the first Jewish War finally forced a break with organized Judaism. This long association elucidated the connection between the Old and the New Covenant. It also facilitated the conversion of Jews and the growth of the Christian community in the Roman Empire, where, from the time of Caesar to that of Nero, the prohibition of associations did not apply to the Jews and therefore also not to the Christians (see pp. 89, 101, 226 f., 239, 291, 294, 308).

Ever since the first day of Pentecost, and particularly after the persecution of Stephen, the church had also directed its attention to the non-Jewish world, which was viewed as consisting ethnically of Hellenes and barbarians and politically of the Roman Empire and the Parthian Empire. Apocryphal legends of the Apostles describe the mission to the Parthian Empire; the evangelization of the Roman Empire from centers established at Antioch, Ephesus, Corinth, and Rome can be followed in the Acts of the Apostles, the letters of Paul, and other documents. After the martyrdom of James at Jerusalem in 62, Rome, the most important stopping place of the Apostles Peter and Paul, came to the fore; and even after their martyrdom there, which probably took place about 65 (see below, p. 218), the capital of the Empire remained in the limelight for the church. Despite the threat posed by the power of the state, the church's long-term goal was the religious conquest of the Roman Empire; during the following centuries, this plan was carried out on a grand scale.

The history of the church between 44 and 66 can therefore

be thought of as an ellipse, whose foci were two cities: until almost the end of the period, Jerusalem; and, during the concluding phase and afterward, Rome.

a) *James, the Brother of the Lord*

Originally, the leading figure of the Jerusalem congregation had been Peter, together with James I and John, the two sons of Zebedee. About A.D. 38, however, James II, the brother of the Lord, seems to have been second in authority, directly after Peter (Gal. 1:19). After the martyrdom of James I about A.D. 42 and the temporary departure of Peter, James II played the leading role in Jerusalem (Acts 12:17). At the Apostolic Council in 49, Peter appears on almost equal footing with James, the brother of the Lord (Acts 15:7–11 has Peter speak first, but in Acts 15:14–21 James gives the decision; in Gal. 2:9 James is mentioned first), but in the year 54 followers of James determine Peter's conduct in Antioch (Gal. 2:12). James retained this position of leadership in Jerusalem until his martyrdom in 62.

The persecution about 42, which was inspired by Pharisees and conducted by Agrippa I, had crippled the Jerusalem congregation severely (Acts 12:1–17). The second procuratorship at first brought a few years of political peace, because the new procurators Fadus and Alexander held the Zealot movement in check between 44 and 48. Furthermore, the efforts of Claudius to resolve the conflict between Jews and Greeks in Alexandria, which we know from the *Epistula Claudiana* (see above, p. 199), contributed to the relative calm. This helped the church, which, ever since the persecution of Stephen, had been suspect in the eyes of the Judaists because of its association with Hellenists. In addition, the animosity of Judaism toward Hellenism was restrained for a few years around 46 by an economic crisis and subsequent famine that struck the eastern Roman Empire (Josephus *Ant.* iii. 320 f.; xx. 51 ff., 101; Eusebius *Hist.* ii. 12. 1). Foreigners saved the Jerusalemites from misery by gifts of bread and money: the Jews received help from Helen and Izates of Adiabene (see above, p. 200), the Christians from

Barnabas and Paul, who were based in Antioch (Acts 11:27–30; 12:25). For the moment, the primitive community did not have to fear reprisals on account of its Hellenistic ties. On the contrary, it gained new adherents from the Pharisaic camp (Acts 12:24; 15:5).

After the relief work just mentioned, the Christians at Antioch sent Barnabas and Paul on a missionary journey during which they passed through Cyprus and Asia Minor in 47 and 48 (Acts 13:1—14:28). In the course of this journey, numerous proselytes, God-fearers, or Gentiles were received into the church. This disturbed the Christian Pharisees in Judea (Acts 15:1, 5), where Judaism was beginning to gather courage once more under the unstable procurator Cumanus (A.D. 48–52), and so the relationship between Jewish and Gentile Christians became a burning issue.

Peter and James discussed this problem with Barnabas and Paul at the Apostolic Council in Jerusalem in 49 (Gal. 2:1: fourteen years after Paul's conversion, in 36, counting the first year). Paul and Luke left divergent accounts of the Council (Gal. 2:1–10; Acts 15:1–29), not because they were thinking of different occasions, but because they differed in their estimates of the Jerusalem "pillars": Paul relativized them, Luke idealized them. According to Paul, the Apostolic Council, with James at its head, decreed that missionary work among the Jews and Gentiles should pursue parallel courses, provided only that the missionaries to the Gentiles continued their collection for the Jerusalem community (Gal. 2:9 f.); according to Luke, however, James saw in the mission to the Gentiles a special form of the mission to the Jews, and, in the so-called Apostolic Decree, suggested a minimal observance of the Mosaic law for Gentile proselytes (Acts 15:16, 20). However this may be, the primitive community, despite the Pharisees, decided to allow the missionary activity to continue as before, the mission to the Jews based in Jerusalem, and the mission to the Gentiles based in Antioch; Gentile converts did not have to be circumcised. Joy in missionary success and concern for the unity of the church may have contributed to this agreement on the part of the primitive community. The historical background, however, must not be overlooked: the year of the Council, 49, was preceded by the years 44–48, a period of political calm but economic crisis. There was little fear of Jewish reprisals against the church on account of its Hellenistic ties; aid from abroad, however, like that now to be undertaken by Barnabas and Paul (Gal. 2:10), was all the more welcome. After the Council, from the year 50, the pressure of Judaism increased once more, help from abroad no longer appeared necessary, and so in 54 James and Peter were forced to give in to particularism (see below). As a consequence, the agreement of the Apostolic Council, despite ecumenical ideals, remained a product of peculiar circumstances.

The political events of the following years made it rather impossible for the "pillars" in Jerusalem to maintain an ecumenical attitude, because the Hellenistic mission of the church exposed it once more and in greater degree to the Judaism of the Zealots. Let us recall the victory in the struggle against Hellenism which Agrippa II, Jonathan the high priest, and, in the background, the Zealots were able to celebrate in A.D. 52 thanks to Claudius' good will (see above, p. 205). In the same year, the Christians in Palestine were harassed by the Jews, a situation over which Paul lamented bitterly during his second missionary journey (I Thess. 2:14–16). And after Nero's accession in 54 and the outbreak of the fearful Zealot violence and terrorism of the *sicarii,* directed against all supposedly alien elements, accomodation of the church to the tradition of legal observance and circumcision seemed the only way to preserve the Jewish Christians from destruction. On account of the dangerous Zealot campaign against everything Greek, a few Christians close to James II persuaded both Peter and Barnabas while in Antioch to refrain from eating with uncircumcised Gentile Christians, to Paul's great indignation (Gal. 2:11–13). Since this Antioch episode obviously did not follow directly upon the Apostolic Council (Acts 15:35), it must be dated after the second missionary journey, i.e., in the year 54 (Acts 18:22; Gal. 2:9 f.). At the same time, the circumcision propaganda of the Jewish Christians spread to Galatia (Gal. 5:2), once again as a consequence of the judaizing and Zealot movement (Gal. 1:14 states that Paul had been a Zealot; 4:17 says that the false preachers were active as Zealots). Upon returning from his third missionary journey in 58, Paul found the primitive community in Jerusalem dominated by thousands of Jewish Christians who were ardent Zealots on behalf of the law (Acts 21:20). James II had to caution Paul to avoid disturbance and accommodate himself to their Zionism and love of the Mosaic law (Acts 21:24); this measure proved insufficient, however. Only the Roman garrison could rescue the Apostle to the Gentiles from the irritation of some Diaspora Jews concerning the Temple and from the xenophobia of the mob.

For the moment, the Palestinian community of Jewish Christians obviously remained immune. James was even held in high regard by devout Jews (Josephus *Ant.* xx. 201), the more so because he came forward as a Nazirite and priest, and prayed for Israel in the Temple (according to biographical data of some value given by the Christian Jew Hegesippus about 150, cited in Eusebius *Hist.* ii. 23. 3–9, 17–20). Thanks to the brother of the Lord, and despite the Zealots, there was in the years around 60 no popular animosity toward the Christians in Palestine, as there had previously been on the occasion of the martyrdom of Stephen in 36, the execution of James, the son of Zebedee about 42, and the troubles around A.D. 52 just mentioned.

In A.D. 62, however, James, the brother of the Lord, was martyred in connection with the attack by the patriots upon various popular prophets, which Ananus II, as leader of the party of Annas, instigated during an interregnum (see above, p. 209). About twenty-eight years before, the high priests and Sadducees had been responsible for the very first attacks upon the leaders of the Christian community in Jerusalem (Acts 4:1 ff.; 5:17 f.); the situation now repeated itself, in the final act of the history of this congregation. From his ultra-patriotic and Sadducean point of view, Ananus II found James suspicious; he had the scribes stamp James' confession of Christ as anti-Jewish propaganda and stone the universally admired prophet (a legend of his martyrdom, with an historical nucleus, is related by the same Hegesippus, according to Eusebius *Hist.* ii. 23. 10–16).

Of course many Jews lamented and censured the murder of the brother of the Lord; but his martyrdom upset the relationship between Judaism and Christianity in the Holy Land, and the clash of the Zealots' arms made the situation continue to deteriorate. The primitive community was no longer headed by any of the apostolic "pillars," who might have made it possible to remain in Jerusalem. Peter was no longer in Jerusalem but off on his journeys; after the martyrdom of James, the brother of the Lord, he probably settled with the Roman community (see below). Since the political and social situation of the mother community was becoming more precarious with each passing day and there was a real threat of annihilation, in the last years before the war the church abandoned Jerusalem. Eusebius states that, as a result of Prophets' warnings, Palestinian Christians emigrated before the war (66–70) and found a new center in Pella (Eusebius *Hist.* iii. 5. 3); this city lay in the neutral territory of the Decapolis, which bore the stamp of the Hellenistic culture of Syria. In reality there was probably no single organized emigration, but rather spontaneous and gradual flight, culminating in the years 64–66. Furthermore, it is hardly likely that all Christians left, particularly not those in Samaria; neither did they all go to Pella. With these reservations however, in view of the terrorism of the Zealots, it seems reasonable to believe that during the years before the war the Christian communities in Jerusalem, Judea, and Galilee finally broke up and resettled for the most part in the East.

Later writers also mention Transjordan and Syria as regions where sects of Jewish Christians spread. Two of the most important of these sects bore names that are reminiscent of primitive Christianity: 1. the Ebionites or "the poor," a term of honor applied in the New Testament to the primitive community (Rom. 15:26); they had a theology with Jewish traits (Eusebius *Hist.* iii. 27. 1–6) ; 2. the Nazoreans (Greek *nazōraîoi*) ; this term originally had nothing to do with the place-name Nazareth, but was a Jewish sectarian term for Jesus and his disciples (Matt. 2:23; Acts 24:5).[54]

Such groups of Jewish Christians remained very much apart from Western Christendom; they increasingly accepted Jewish and Gnostic teachings, and also became an important influence on Mandeans, Manicheans, and Moslems.

Later, after the defeat of the Zealot movement in 70, communities of Christian Jews gradually reappeared in Palestine, but only sporadically. To succeed James as bishop in Jerusalem they are said to have chosen a young cousin of Jesus by the name of Simon (Eusebius *Hist.* iii. 11. 32). In the nineties two grandsons of Jude, a brother of the Lord, are said to have enjoyed great esteem as sons of David (*ibid.*, iii. 19. 1—20. 6). Nevertheless, the Palestinian church of the postapostolic period remained fragmentary. Ignatius of Antioch does not even mention it in his letters (about A.D. 115).

In general it is true to say that, after the murder of James, the brother of the Lord, in the year 62 and the flight of the primitive community, contemporary Jerusalem and Judaism were no longer the gateway to the Christian temple in the Roman Empire.

b) Paul, the Apostle to the Gentiles

For the church as a whole, the leading spokesman for the Gentile Christianity during the time of the second procuratorship was Paul, although certain groups of Jewish Christians attempted to play Peter off against him (at Antioch, according to Gal. 2:11, and at Corinth, according to I Cor. 1:12). Even after his arrest in Jerusalem in 58, Paul continued to exert authoritative influence through his letters and disciples, as is shown by the captivity letters written by him (Philippians and Philemon) or perhaps in his name (Ephesians and Colossians). About this time Peter had broken

---

[54] For a general discussion of these movements, see H. J. Schoeps, *Theologie und Geschichte des Judenchristentums* (1949).

with Jewish Christianity (Gal. 2:11) and was engaged in
missionary journeys (I Cor. 9:5), in the course of which he
came to Rome and there, like Paul, became an authority for
Gentile Christianity, as the letters bearing his name assume
(especially I Pet. 5:13, "Babylon"). Finally, according to
important traditions of the church, Peter and Paul were both
active at Rome (Ignatius, Romans 4:3), where they died as
martyrs under Nero (I Clement 5:2–7 mentions Peter and
Paul; John 21:19 and Ascension of Isaiah 4:3 mention
Peter). Their martyrdom can be associated with the persecution of the Christians in Rome ordered by the Emperor in 65
(see below, pp. 249 f.). The shape of Gentile Christianity was
therefore dominated by Paul from about 46 to 60, and by
Peter and Paul from about 61 to 65.

After his conversion in 36, Paul had first labored in the
region of Damascus and in Cilicia (see above, pp. 193 f.); later
he became a missionary in Antioch, and, about 46, helped
provide aid for Jerusalem (see above, pp. 212 f.). The missionary center of Antioch, which comprised Christian Jews, proselytes, and Greeks, then sent Paul on three journeys into the
Hellenistic world of Asia Minor and Greece during the conflicts in Judea under the procurators Alexander, Cumanus,
and Felix. He was to make converts of Jews, proselytes, and
Greeks. One speaks in this connection of the three journeys of
Paul, although he had journeyed as a missionary twice previously, and although in spite of the great distances and
difficulties the journeys did not consume as much time as
Paul's stops at various places. On his journeys, he made great
use of the Roman imperial roads; when he stopped, he often
took up residence with Jewish colonists and proselytes.

(1) The first journey took place roughly A.D. 47–48; it was
led by Barnabas, a former Levite. Barnabas first went to the
island of Cyprus, his homeland (Acts 13:1–12). Paul then
persuaded him to sail to Asia Minor and go to the cities
along the Roman military road that ran through the south-
central section of the land, through Pisidia and Lycaonia,
passing Antioch, Iconium, Lystra, and Derbe (Acts
13:13—14:26). On this journey, the "door of faith" was

opened to the nations (Acts 14:27) ; this disturbed the Pharisaic Christians and necessitated the Jerusalem council in 49 (Acts 15:2).

(2) On his second journey, A.D. 50–53, Paul was accompanied by Silvanus and, later, Timothy (Acts 15:36—18:22). He wanted to strengthen the congregations he had founded in Asia Minor, but the little band marched much farther than they had originally planned. Paul undertook a journey rather like Alexander's campaign in reverse: from the Cilician Gates diagonally through Asia Minor and across the Hellespont to Macedonia, where he travelled along the east-west Roman road known as Via Egnatia, visiting Philippi and Thessalonica. He then went to Greece to preach in Athens and Corinth. Everywhere he made conquests for the King whose kingdom he was to spread with the support of the Christians at Antioch.

(3) During his third journey, A.D. 54–58, Paul spent most of his time in Ephesus and the vicinity (Acts 18:23—19:40), sending Titus to Greece as his ambassador (II Cor. 2:13; etc.). Ephesus, the venerable Ionian port, was at this time the fourth largest city of the Mediterranean world, surpassed only by Rome, Alexandria, and Antioch. With respect to trade, industry, administration, and religion, it was the capital of Roman Asia. Paul achieved great success, but was attacked by the worshipers of Artemis. He then visited Macedonia and Greece once more, collected alms for the primitive community, and returned with the money to Jerusalem, going through Troas, passing by Ephesus because of the unrest there, and arriving by way of Miletus and Caesarea (Acts 20:1—21:16).

James and the elders of the primitive community feared that Paul had offended Jewish nationalism through his preaching of the Gospel apart from the law. At their suggestion, he offered sacrifice in the Temple; there, however, the Apostle to the Gentiles was attacked by Jewish agitators as a collaborator and defiler of the Temple. The Roman cohort took him into protective custody, but a Zealot conspiracy threatened his life, and so he was brought to the procurator

Felix in Caesarea (Acts 21:27—23:35). Felix had Paul present his defense, but did not dare to hand down a decision. Seeing that Festus, who replaced Felix in 60, had greater support from Nero and the government, Paul at once exercised his rights as a Roman citizen by appealing to the Emperor (Acts 25:11). In the autumn, he was transported to Rome (Acts 27:9; 28:14); this is referred to as Paul's fourth journey. There the Apostle remained for two years in a private dwelling under police supervision; he was able to converse unhindered with pupils or visitors (Acts 28:16, 30).

Afterward, as a consequence of Nero's administrative changes in the year 62 (see above, p. 209), Paul was probably set free once more. Since the Emperor now came forward openly as an autocrat and supporter of Hellenism, he really had little concern for such legal questions. In the same year, he freed the Jews whom Felix had sent as hostages (see above, pp. 208 f.), and certainly saw even less reason to sanction the fanaticism of the Palestinian Jews against the apostle of Greece. The concluding remark of the Lucan we-source (Acts 28:30) regarding Paul's two-year house arrest probably confirms this dropping of charges against him. With regard to later journeys of Paul and another captivity, many scholars have claimed to find hints of such in the Pastoral Letters (I and II Timothy, Titus); others dispute this evidence. In any case, it remains problematical whether the places cited in these letters refer to the third and fourth journeys (which is possible for Troas in II Tim. 4:13, Crete in Titus 1:5, and Rome in II Tim. 1:17) or point to later activity (which is possible in the case of Nicopolis, Titus 3:12). But as we have already noted (see above, p. 218), well-attested noncanonical tradition suggests that Paul, like Peter, fell victim to the Neronian persecution of the Christians in Rome in A.D. 65, and this persecution was not connected with his earlier trial.

In his daring expeditions to spread the lordship of Christ, Paul took orders only from heaven. His home base was Antioch, but he always considered Jerusalem the headquarters of the Christian forces. He first came to know the name of

Jesus and followers of Christ in Judea (Acts 9:5); in the saints of the Jerusalem community he saw the spiritual nucleus of the new people of God (Rom. 15:27), and, despite well-founded fear of the Zealot movement, after he finished taking up the collection, he returned to the poor of the primitive community, for whom he had special regard (Rom. 15:31). Thus for Paul, too, the mission to the Jews was the first and ultimate task of the church. Only on account of the Jews' temporary obduracy was the mission to the Gentiles the greater task for the time being (Rom. 11:25). Furthermore, justification of the nations, without their being bound to Jewish law and nationality, was merely a consequence of the promise made to Abraham (Rom. 4:17: "the father of many nations").

Paul's elliptical concept of the church, which he attached to Jerusalem as well as to Hellas and Rome, was on a spiritual plane and irreconcilable with all human ecclesiastical politics. All attempts at centralization and claims for authority emanating from Jerusalem he therefore rejected and combatted as materialistic ways of thinking. Such attempts were in fact made, ever since the thirties when Peter and John had interceded to subordinate the missionary work of the evangelist Philip in Samaria to the apostolate in Jerusalem (Acts 8:14). In the Book of Acts and in the Pauline letters we can follow the gradual advance of such centralism or ultramontanism as it is subsequently spread over the congregations founded by Paul, although the extant documents mention only a few of the missionary territories. The ethnic situation made it easy to link this centralization to judaizing tendencies. During his second journey, in the year 52, Paul first heard of the pressure of Judaism upon the Christians in Palestine (I Thess. 2:14). On his third journey, 54–58, he was confronted with the fact that judaizing propagandists for centralization had infiltrated the congregations he had founded or built up; these men and their followers played off first Peter and then an Alexandrian Jew named Apollos against the Apostle to the Gentiles. The process began at Antioch in 54 with the partisans of James, who had persuaded Peter to distinguish between Jewish and Gentile Christians (Gal. 2:11). After this, Paul found Christian Galatia under the influence of judaizing ultramontanists, who claimed to derive their authority from dignitaries in Jerusalem (Gal. 1:7–14), insisting upon circumcision and works of the law (Gal. 3:2; 5:12); Paul considered them Zealots (Gal. 1:14; 4:17). Coming to Ephesus in 55, Paul found this offshoot of Judaism again: Apollos, with his rhetorical and philosophic brilliance, had promoted in the synagogue there a baptist movement oriented more toward Judaism than Christianity, before he left for Corinth with written credentials (Acts 18:24, 27; 19:1). Paul stayed in Ephesus and the vicinity for some time, legitimizing his apostolic commission through extraordinary workings of the Spirit (Acts 19:6, 11). In 56 or 57, however, he learned that the congregation in Corinth, which he had founded, was now split on account of Jewish Christian centralism (I Cor. 1:11). While some adhered to Paul, others would recognize only Apollos or Peter as their apostle (I Cor. 1:12), and demanded of Paul written credentials from the proper authorities, such as Apollos had been able to present (Acts 18:27; II Cor. 3:1; etc.). Further subordination of the local communities to dignitaries and central authority was effected by traveling commissions, which Paul sarcastically calls "superapostles" (II Cor. 11:5; 12:11). These used their Jewish ancestry and metaphysical sophistry for propaganda purposes. Since in the fifties the nationalism and Jerusalem-centered politics of these circles could easily lead to Christian involvement in the Jewish Zealot turmoil, Paul spoke not theoretically but on the basis of painful experience when he wrote his Letter to the Romans in 58: in the first part, he warns against pride in the Jewish law (Rom. 2:17–29); in the second, he urges obedience to the Roman government (Rom. 13:1–7) and rejects combativeness and "zeal" (Rom. 13:13, RSV, "jealousy"). Soon afterward, in Jerusalem, he was forced to discover that thousands of Jews who belonged to the church were also zealous for the law (Acts 21:20). The Jewish Zealots almost killed him then, and because of them he had to spend several years in prison. The Christian Zealots, in the meanwhile, became more and more influential in the mission congregations. In the letter to Philippi, written during his captivity, Paul's ire at their ardor for circumcision and their ecclesiastical politics reached its apogee (Phil. 3:2, 19 f.). The rising curve of Paul's admonitions runs parallel to the growth of the Jewish Zealot movement during the second procuratorship.[55]

c) *Peter's Move from Zion to Rome*

Ultimately, however, the course of events in Palestine proved the apostle to the Gentiles correct. All evidence suggests that the Zealot madness converted Peter, too, to Paul's point of view. After the episode at Antioch in 54, there is nothing more to suggest that Peter represented the exclusive ecclesiastical policies of the circle of James in Jerusalem. The First Letter of Peter shows him, rather, as opposed to Zealot encroachments (I Pet. 3:13) and supporting Pauline stability (I Pet. 2:13). The letter itself turns out to be a missionary document sent from Rome at Peter's behest by Paul's companion Silvanus (I Pet. 5:12 f.). The Second Letter of Peter, written later, also contributes to this picture by its emphatic reference to Paul's restraining admonitions (II Pet. 3:15). Quite apart from the question of authorship, the Petrine letters confirm the ecclesiastical tradition according to which Peter finally labored and died at Rome together with Paul (see above, p. 218). Peter appears to have come to Rome between 63 and 65: the Book of Acts mentions Paul alone there down to the year 62 (Acts 28:30 f.); on the other hand, the martyrdom of both is dated to the reign of Nero, probably in 65. The most important source on this point states briefly and clearly that several times during his life Zealots or fanatics round about Peter got him into difficulties (I Clement 5:4). Thus while Zealot persecution brought Paul to Rome, Peter probably went there in reaction against their intrigues. Furthermore, the martyrdom of both Apostles is ascribed to Zealotism in their environment (I Clement 5:1-7). This strange statement is comprehensible only

[55] B. Reicke, *Diakonie, Festfreude und Zelos* (1951), pp. 240–319.

against the historical background. Many people in Jerusalem were zealous for the law, and exerted pressure that spread to ever more distant Christian communities. Paul experienced this pressure in various places, and had to fear it in Rome, also. As the Petrine letters suggest, Peter, too, was upset by the Zealots and went from Judea to Italy in order to help bring peace. Finally, it seems reasonable to assume, these Zealot agitators provoked the Neronian persecution, to which Peter and Paul probably fell victim (see below, pp. 246–51) .[56]

However vague the details, the shift of the first Apostle from James to Paul, from Zion to Rome, can symbolize the course of church history during the turbulent final years of the second procuratorship. Political crisis made the exclusive mission to the Jews impossible, and the leading Apostles therefore finally labored together on behalf of the expanding mission to the Gentiles, which also included the mission to the Jews, though without Zionistic overtones (Rom. 11:13, where Paul discusses his own people; I Pet. 2:9, where Silvanus, writing in Peter's name, speaks of the people of God) .

Between 61 and 66, therefore, Jerusalem was replaced by Rome as geographical focus of the life of the church, though authoritarian church government came into being in Rome only much later. On the other hand, from the time the kingdom of God was first proclaimed, Rome had always been the intended focus of the Gentile mission, for it dominated the world as it was known to Jesus and the Apostles. The community bearing the stamp of Jerusalem was surrounded by the Empire bearing the stamp of Rome. This meant additional political problems, which had gradually been developing from the days of Jesus until the death of Peter and Paul, but then suddenly assumed overwhelming importance.

---

[56] On the significance of I Clement 5:1–7, see O. Cullmann, *Petrus* (1952) , pp. 96–119; 2d ed. (1960) , pp. 101–23; on Peter in Rome, see also F. V. Filson, "Peter" in *The Interpreter's Dictionary of the Bible*, Vol. 3 (1962) , pp. 754 ff.

VI

THE ROMAN EMPIRE IN THE TIME OF JESUS AND THE APOSTLES

4 B.C.–A.D. 66

[To discuss Herod's testament, in 4 B.C.] Augustus called a meeting of the Roman magistrates and his confidants in the Temple of Apollo on the Palatine.

Josephus *Bellum Judaicum* ii. 81

[To account for the conflagration in A.D. 64, Nero] fastened the guilt on others, and punished with exquisite tortures those people, detested on account of their crimes, whom the populace calls Christians.

Tacitus *Annales* xv. 44. 2

A SHORT list will outline once more the years in power of the rulers of the Roman Empire from Augustus to Nero, who will concern us in this chapter. They are the five representatives of the Julio-Claudian dynasty (cf. pp. 128, 199):

Augustus	30 B.C.—A.D. 14
Tiberius	A.D. 14–37
Caligula	37–41
Claudius	41–54
Nero	54–68

1. THE EMPIRE, THE JEWS, AND THE CHRISTIANS

The historical background of the relationship between the Gospel and the Empire lies in the division of Herod's kingdom in the year 4 B.C., which bound the small princes of Palestine very closely to the *Imperator*. On account of the complaints about Archelaus in A.D. 6, Augustus found it quite natural to change the major portion of the land (Samaria, Judea, and Idumea) into a Roman procuratorship. Indirectly the Jews of the Holy Land were then the subjects of the Emperor. In Judea, Jesus had to debate the question of whether tribute to Tiberius was legal (Matt. 22:15–22; and parallels); despite his neutral position, he was accused of inciting to rebellion (Luke 23:2). In the apostolic period, the relationship between Jerusalem and Rome was always a problem for both Jewish and Gentile Christians. Until the year 66, however, the problem was usually peripheral, because Judaism furnished protection for Christianity in the social sphere. This held true not only in Palestine, but also in the missionary regions. Throughout the apostolic period, the Roman officials considered the followers of Christ as emigrant Jews and proselytes. Two experiences of Paul in Corinth confirm this observation. In A.D. 49 or, more likely, 50, Claudius expelled the Jews from Rome because they were creating a disturbance about the Messiah (see above, page 205); this brought the Jewish Christians Aquila and Priscilla to Corinth in the year 51 (Acts 18:2). In 52, Gallio refused to intervene officially on behalf of the Jews at Corinth that were demonstrating against Paul, because he considered the matter an internal question of the Jewish law (Acts 18:15). Without this connection with Judaism the Christian communities would have found themselves in a legally dubious position; for in the Roman Empire, since the time of Caesar and Augustus, the formation of new associations had been prohibited (Josephus *Ant.* xiv. 215 f.; Suetonius *Julius* 42.3; *Augustus* 32. 1).[1] The Jewish synagogues, however, were

[1] M. Radin, *Legislation of the Greeks and Romans on Corporations* (1910), pp. 89–122.

excepted (see above, pp. 89, 101, 211) .[2] Only with the Neronian persecution was a temporary distinction made between Jews and Christians before the law. Since the time of Tiberius, however, outside this Jewish enclave the question of the relationship between church and state had been smouldering, especially in the large cities. The fire had been capable of blazing up at any moment; finally, at the end of Nero's reign, came the conflagration.

2. AUGUSTUS AND TIBERIUS 30 B.C.—A.D. 37

About 4 B.C., Augustus (see above, pp. 95 f.) had passed a series of laws and reforms that secured his system of government, in theory diarchic but in practice monarchic. Now, almost sixty years old, he was concerned with the question of who should succeed him. Tiberius, who became his successor, endeavored to maintain the same system.

A. Augustus' System of Government

It was typical of the Augustan state that the seat of government was moved to the Palatine. On this hill Augustus had built himself a palace (the word derives from the name of the hill). Beside it he constructed a temple of his favorite god, Apollo, adorned with gold and marble, where he convoked meetings and assemblies. Since he was *imperator,* i.e., supreme commander of the legions, he controlled most of the provinces and the government income; the senate retained mostly local and symbolic significance. Augustus aspired for a moral strengthening of the Roman aristocracy, but his authority kept the primacy of the Julian house undisputed.

The important question of succession to the throne caused Augustus personal concern, though he was able to suppress it stoically. His stepson, Tiberius, would have been the obvious candidate since he was a superb general and the husband of Augustus' daughter Julia. But he withdrew from politics in 5 B.C.—because Augustus gave preferment to a son of Julia by his deceased friend Agrippa—and instead pursued academic studies at Rhodes. Soon afterward, Augustus had to banish

[2] *Ibid.,* pp. 122–24.

Julia because of her profligate behavior, and the young crown prince was mortally wounded on a campaign in the East. Lacking other male offspring, Augustus was forced to adopt Tiberius and declare him his successor. Dynastic succession appeared necessary in any case.

B. THE PROVINCES UNDER AUGUSTUS AND AFTERWARD

By 27 B.C., Augustus had kept some provinces under his personal control as *imperator* and assigned others to the senate. With few changes this division of the Empire continued throughout the apostolic period; it was important for both Judaism and Christianity (see map V).

1) *Imperial Provinces, Including Syria and Galatia-Lycaonia*

The imperial provinces had a military government; the emperor himself was the supreme commander of the legions stationed in them. Among them were the following countries, which had large Jewish colonies and were therefore visited early by Christian missionaries:

Syria, including Phoenicia and eastern Cilicia, with its center at Antioch (see above, p. 44). Ever since it was conquered by Pompey in 64 B.C., this had been the eastern outpost of the Roman Empire; it was of such importance militarily that its commandant functioned at times as a sort of vice-king for the Orient. Antioch, Damascus, and the Phoenician cities were important centers for Eastern commerce. Tens of thousands of Jews lived in Damascus, where a large proportion of the women had become followers of Judaism (Josephus *Bell.* ii. 560 f.); in Antioch, too, the Jews were strongly represented (*ibid.*, vii. 43).

The commander of such military provinces as Syria was a senatorial nobleman in charge of a legion, who bore the title *legatus Augusti,* i.e., general commissioned by the *imperator.* Syria, being an important border province, was assigned three legions, and even four in the time of Jesus and the Apostles. Since every legion (roughly the equivalent of a brigade) comprised about six thousand professional soldiers, together with auxiliary personnel, concubines, purveyors, etc., the social life of an imperial province bore the stamp of a large military contingent. The legionnaires also constituted an upper class, because they either possessed the right of Roman citizenship or hoped to gain it through military service.

Sometimes the general had temporary authority over the procurators, who were financial agents drawn from the class of the industrial equestrians. This was true of Quirinius, for example, when Coponius was appointed procurator of Judea (see above, pp. 137 f.). Often, however, the procurators were responsible directly to Rome, since they looked after the interests of the imperial fisc. This was the normal situation in Judea.

Galatia-Lycaonia, which had been a Roman province since 25 B.C., with Ancyra (the modern Ankara, capital of Turkey) as its administrative center. This imperial province, which was put together *ad hoc,* comprised the central section of Asia Minor: in the north, the region of Galatia, whose name derived from the Galatians, three Celtic tribes that immigrated in the third century B.C.; in the south, the regions of Lycaonia, Pisidia, and other territories. Ethnically and historically, this province was not a single unit; during the New Testament period it did not even have a name, but was referred to in decrees and inscriptions by listing its components: "Galatia, Pisidia, Lycaonia," etc. For convenience, later geographers and historians would call the province "Galatia"; in our period, however, Galatia was still the region in the northern part of central Anatolia. In the Letter to the Galatians, therefore, Paul was referring to Galatia proper, in the north (Gal. 1:2), as supporters of the "north-Galatian" theory assume. Whoever would include Lycaonia, in the south, suggests that Paul committed a gross blunder by referring to the "Galatians" (Gal. 3:1).

2) *Senatorial Provinces, Including Asia, Cyprus, Macedonia, and Achaea*

The senatorial provinces of the Augustan Empire retained their traditional civil administration. They were used to supplement the wages of former consuls or praetors, who were allowed to govern them as proconsuls for some length of time. Since most proconsuls had to improve their financial position after expensive years in Rome, the senatorial provinces were often subject to ruthless taxation. This class of province included the territories where Paul founded his most important congregations and to which most of the apostolic letters of the New Testament are addressed, as well as the letters of the prophet John, namely:

Cyprus, previously controlled by Phoenicia and Egypt but in Roman hands after 58 B.C., and after 22 B.C., a senatorial province. Its capital was the eastern seaport Salamis, where the Jews were organized into more than one synagogue (Acts 13:5). Barnabas was originally a Levite from Cyprus (Acts 4:36). On the first missionary journey, he and Paul encountered the Roman proconsul Sergius Paulus and his Jewish astrologer Bar-Jesus in the western seaport Paphos (Acts 13:6–12).

Asia, particularly the Greek territories of Ionia and Lydia in western Asia Minor, which the king of Pergamum had bequeathed to the Romans in 133 B.C. Its production of fruit and wine, its industries, and its commerce made it a goldmine that suffered greatly under the Roman publicans until Augustus made better conditions possible. Its leading city was Ephesus, the most important port and industrial center on the Aegean Sea and the golden gate to Asia at the end of the ancient royal road running from Persia through Babylonia, Syria, and Asia (see above, p. 12). Ephesus was especially proud of being guardian of a temple (Greek *neōkóros*), for cults and temples were popular throughout Asia, as was the ruler cult established by the indigenous kings. The shrine of Artemis of Asia, which crowned a hill to the northeast, was considered one of the wonders of the world. The ancient Ionian temple, adorned by Croesus, is said to have been burned to the ground by Herostratus in 364 B.C. and later restored to its former glory. It was also important as a banking institution. Paul's success put a severe crimp in the souvenir industry of the temple; he was therefore attacked by Demetrius, the master of the guild of silversmiths, as well as the workmen (Acts 19:24).

Since the time of Augustus, several cities of the province competed for the honor of being allowed to construct, with the consent of the senate, a temple of Roma and Augustus. Pergamum was granted the privilege under Augustus, Smyrna under Tiberius, and Ephesus under Claudius. The so-called Asiarchs were responsible for the administration of such provincial temples and the arrangement of festivals (Acts 19:31). Some of these Asiarchs could attain the rank of high priest of a specific temple (Acts 19:14; see above, p. 147). They constituted a diet for the entire province, called *koinòn Asías*, which held annual deliberations and festivals in a series of cities: Pergamum, Smyrna, Ephesus, Cyzicos, Laodicea, Philadelphia, and Sardis. Almost the same list of cities constituted the seven churches of Asia for the prophet John (Rev. 1:4), except that the more centrally located Thyatira (Rev. 2:18) replaced Cyzicos, which lay far to the north.

The former kingdom of Macedonia was divided into four Roman clientary kingdoms in 168 B.C. In 148, it became a senatorial province, which included northern Epirus and, until 27 B.C., Greece. After a period of brutal taxation, Macedonia was allowed to recover by being given the status of an imperial province from 15 to 44; it then became a senatorial province once more. The Via Egnatia was of military and commercial importance as the road linking East and West, going from Byzantium through Philippi, Thessalonica, and Pella to Epirus, where several ports serviced the trade with southern Italy. Philippi was re-founded by the father of Alexander the Great and named after him. The Roman Republic made it the capital of the eastern district of Macedonia; after the battle of Actium, Augustus made it a military colony with the right of Italian citizenship (Acts 16:12). Here there lived an Italian upper class acutely conscious of their citizenship; the Jews had set up their place of prayer outside the city (Acts 16:13). Thessalonica, however, was chosen as the residence of the proconsul; it was the largest port of Macedonia, with a beautiful frontage on the sea. It was located in the middle of the Via Egnatia and at the end of the northern road coming from the Danube region. It was re-founded in 315 B.C. and named after a half sister of Alexander; its population consisted of sailors, longshoremen, and merchant princes, including influential Jews (Acts 17:5). Pella is not mentioned in the New Testament, but only Berea, located to the southwest on the road to Greece (Acts 17:10), which was the capital of the southwestern district of Macedonia. On his second journey, Paul used the Via Egnatia and labored successfully in Philippi, Thessalonica, and Berea (Acts 16:12—17:13). His success in Philippi provoked a counter attack by the Gentiles (Acts 16:19–24). Since the Jews in Rome had been driven out by Claudius around A.D. 50 (see above, p. 205), the Gentile magistrates of Philippi found it opportune to contend that Jews like Paul and Silas were not desirable in a city of Roman citizens (Acts 16:20 f.). On the other hand, in Thessalonica it was the Jews who demonstrated their jealousy against Paul (Acts 17:5–9). It was hardly a mere coincidence that this happened in A.D. 52, the year when Claudius had made his decision, mentioned above, in favor of the Jews in their cultural struggle with the Greeks (see above, p. 205). Thessalonica was later a hotbed of Christian disturbances (I Thess. 4:11); this was related in part to the social structure of the seaport, in part to the eschatological impatience of the newly converted. On his third journey, Paul had amazing success in Macedonia with his collection for Jerusalem (Acts 20:1, 3; II Cor. 8:1–4).

Achaea was Greece proper, including Thessaly and southern Epirus. From 146 to 27 B.C., it belonged to Macedonia; in the latter year, however, Augustus raised it to the status of an independent providence because of the new importance of Corinth. During the years A.D. 15–44, it was again joined to the imperial province of Macedonia, mentioned above; then it became an independent senatorial province once more. On his second journey, Paul visited Athens, the seat of learning, and Corinth, the capital (Acts 17:15—18:18); he was able to remain in the capital more than a year and a half (Acts

18:11) and to found a flourishing congregation there (I Cor.
3:6). In this period, Athens had lost its material importance,
but was famous for its monuments and philosophers. Within
Hellenism, the major subject of philosophical propaganda
was the freedom of the individual; on this point, the Hellenistic and Roman public was fascinated particularly by the
Epicureans and Stoics, two schools based in Athens (Acts
17:18), but also by the Cynics. During the first century, the
Epicureans and Stoics supported aristocratic and republican
ideals, whereas the Cynics preferred to sabotage politics and
culture. The so-called Areopagus was responsible for supervising the Athenian judicial and educational system (Acts
17:19a); it was a Ministry of Public Worship and Education
made up of former *archontes*. In ancient times, it had met on
the Hill of Ares (Greek *ho Áreios págos*) west of the Acrop-
olis; in the time of Paul, however, it probably met in a hall
on the Agora, north of the hill. This body had the authority
to examine the preaching of new doctrines (Acts 17:18b,
19b) and to approve the establishment of religious votive
offerings like those at the altar of the unknown god (Acts
17:23). Corinth was at this time an international metropolis,
famous for commerce, industry, luxury, and immorality.
Beautifully and advantageously situated on the Bay of Corinth and the isthmus, it was the major stopping place on the
land route between Attica and the Peleponnese; its two har-
bors, Lechaeum directly to the north and Cenchreae six
miles to the east, also made it the depot for traffic between
the Adriatic and Aegean seas. Nero planned to build a canal
there, but his plan was carried out only in modern times.
Destroyed in the war with Rome in 146 B.C., so after 44 B.C.,
at Caesar's behest, Corinth became a colony of Italian citizens and made rapid economic progress under the official
name Laus Iulia Corinthus. As in Philippi, the dominant
upper class consisted at first of Italians; but the city gradually experienced an influx of Greeks and especially Orientals, including Jews, who came as workers and entrepreneurs
(according to Acts 18:2, Paul worked for Aquila in Corinth). Religiously, therefore, Corinth was a volatile mixture,

as the Letters to the Corinthians show. In 27 B.C., Augustus chose Corinth to be the capital of the new senatorial province of Achaea. Following the above-mentioned merger with Macedonia from A.D. 15 to 44, Claudius, a capable administrator, reorganized the proconsular regime in Corinth. One of the new proconsuls was an elder brother of the philosopher Seneca, by the name of Gallio; an inscription from Delphi records that he held office in Corinth about A.D. 52.[3] Paul's encounter with Gallio provides a point of reference for Pauline chronology (Acts 18:12–17). It follows that Paul labored in Corinth approximately A.D. 51–53; while he was there, the Jews came to Gallio and accused Paul of preaching contrary to the law. Because the procurator was more concerned than the Jews themselves not to encroach on the autonomy of the synagogue, he refused to intervene in what he declared to be an internal Jewish question. In that very year, 52, Claudius and Pallas had given Agrippa II and the Jews some trump cards in their struggle with Hellenism (see above, p. 205); and Gallio did not want to risk upsetting those who were zealous for the Jewish law. Paul soon found reason to return to Antioch. During his third journey, he had trouble with ultramontanism (see above, pp. 221 f.). After his work in Ephesus, he originally intended to make a brief visit to Macedonia and a more lengthy visit to Achaea (I Cor. 16:5–7; II Cor. 1:15); he changed his plans, however, in order to avoid a painful conflict in Corinth (II Cor. 1:23). Titus was sent to speak for him there (II Cor. 2:13), while Paul himself remained in Macedonia to work for the collection and visited Achaea only briefly (Acts 20:1–3; II Cor. 8:1).

3) *The Pax Romana*

These eastern Roman provinces reached by the Gospel benefited greatly from the new order under Augustus. In particular, the borders had been stabilized; for a long time this enabled the provinces to enjoy the solemnly inaugurated

---

[3] I. Hennequin, "Delphes," in *Dictionnaire de la Bible* Supplementary Vol. 2 (1934), cols. 355–73.

Pax Romana. In two corners of the world the border adjust-
ments undertaken by Augustus and continued by Tiberius
were of crucial importance for the Gospel. (1) The reinforcement of Syria and Galatia lessened the danger from the
Parthians, especially after the measures taken by Vitellius in
the year 36 (see above, pp. 190 ff.). As a result, the kingdom of
God could be proclaimed among Jews, Greeks, and pagans in
Palestine, Syria, and Asia without external disturbances; in
the previous century this would have been impossible. The
renaissance of Orientalism, which had been emanating from
Ctesiphon since A.D. 42 (see above, p. 7), had an immediate
effect on the Jews in Babylonia (Josephus *Ant.* xviii. 310–79);
but it did not affect the Roman Empire until the time of
Nero (pp. 240–44) and did not influence Christianity until
even later. (2) In Macedonia and Greece, Augustus promoted
precisely those cities in which Paul later achieved his greatest
successes: Philippi and Corinth. As the stepson and general
of Augustus, Tiberius was able to extend Roman domination over the barbarian tribes of Illyria, making possible for
Macedonia and Achaea a peaceful and prosperous development; later, this also made it easier for Paul to preach the
gospel and collect money here.

C. The Status Quo under Tiberius

Before his accession, Tiberius (emperor from 14 to 37)
had been a brilliant general; as world ruler, however, he
withdrew from the political arena, although he held the
balance of power in his hands. He was the subject of malicious gossip in fashionable circles and was accused of many
evils, but he always remained supreme in his isolation. The
basic principle of his policy was preservation of the status
quo. He therefore considered it very important to hold
aspiring princes and princesses, senators and magnates, in
check; their intrigues he equally feared and despised. Accordingly, he saw to it that the Praetorian Guard, the powerful military elite of Augustus, were quartered in the northeast part of the city, not far from the Palatine; the site of
their barracks is still discernible at the corner of the Aure-

lian wall near the Porta Nomentana. This heavily-armed, well-disciplined contingent, stationed in the demilitarized capital, provided a new power factor in the Empire. Sejanus, one of Tiberius' prefects of the Praetorian Guard, was allowed to intervene with all the forces at his command whenever the imperial house or the aristocracy were suspected of intrigue. Tiberius let this brutal man go much too far; even the crown prince was slain. Nevertheless, the Emperor's conduct was not based on cruelty and vanity; he was in fact averse to the titles of honor ascribed to him (Suetonius *Tiberius* 26 f.), and thought only of the necessity of continuing the rule of Augustus (Suetonius *Tiberius* 58 shows this indirectly). For this reason, he had his prefect extirpate any real or supposed hybris on the part of the upper class and the Hellenists; for this reason, too, he fought for the ancient Roman discipline and tradition (*ibid.*, 28–35, 71). In the year 19 he also banished from the city the Oriental religions—including Judaism—which had won the adherence of prominent Romans (*ibid.*, 36); the Roman Jews and their numerous proselytes were called to military service (Josephus *Ant.* xviii. 81–85). In order to escape court intrigues and the gossip of the city, Tiberius, like an aged lion, retreated in 26 to Capri. From there he ruled the provinces but let Sejanus continue to look after Rome, until in 31 a conspiracy was discovered and the tyrant of the city was executed.

Because of his interest in the provinces, after the fall of Sejanus Tiberius informed his officials that the special privileges of the Jews must be respected (Philo *De Legatione ad Gaium* 160 f.). This pro-Jewish edict at once aroused the Jews' optimism in their contest with the Greeks, toward whom, despite his Greek education, Tiberius exhibited a notorious skepticism. Even the Pharisees came to think it might pay to advocate loyalty to the Emperor. In 33, they sought to demonstrate this loyalty through their disingenuous question about the imperial tax (Matt. 22:17 and parallels; see above, pp. 183 f.). They likewise collaborated with the high priests to assist in opposing Jesus with the help of

Pilate (Matt. 27:41 and variants; 27:62; John 18:3). In 36 the new self-assurance of the Jewish nationalists, strengthened by the Romans' pro-Jewish diplomacy during the Parthian War, led to the martyrdom of Stephen (see above, pp. 190 ff.). At this time Tiberius was over seventy, a suspicious and careworn autocrat; personally he had nothing to do with the crucifixion of Jesus or the stoning of the protomartyr. He died in 37 without having heard of the Christian movement.

3. CALIGULA, CLAUDIUS, AND NERO A.D. 37–68

A. DISAPPOINTMENT UNDER CALIGULA

Tiberius' immediate heir was a grandson with the same name, but the popularity of the young Caligula (emperor from 37 to 41) led the aging Emperor to allow him to come forward as crown prince. By family law, Caligula was as closely related to the Emperor as was the grandson; for his deceased father was Germanicus, whom Tiberius had adopted, a nephew of the Emperor and immensely popular; his mother was Agrippina I, a descendant of Augustus, a stepdaughter to the Emperor through her mother. Everything went as expected. Hardly had Tiberius died, when the new prefect of the praetorians compelled the senate to acclaim Caligula emperor. The next two emperors, also, Claudius and Nero, were raised to the throne with the help of the Praetorian Guard.

Caligula's official name was Gaius; his nickname, which means "bootee" (a diminutive form of the Latin *caliga,* a soldier's boot), was given him by the legions at Cologne, who had seen him in uniform as a two- or three-year-old boy. Just after his accession to the throne he appeared liberal and aroused general enthusiasm. After a sudden illness, however, he developed an abnormal lust for power, which can be traced in part to the character of his mother and in part to his interest in the Hellenistic system of government. The accession of Caligula marks an important event in Jewish history because he appointed his chariot companion Agrippa I, Herod's grandson, king over northern Palestine (see above, pp. 195, 197). On the other hand, the Emperor's wish that divine honor be paid to his person produced a Greek persecution of the Jews in Alexandria; for the same reason, the Jews in Palestine almost rebelled against the Romans (see above, p. 196). Initially Caligula's Hellenism hastened the spread of the Gospel (see above, p. 194). Soon, however, a group of senators assassinated the Emperor on the Palatine.

B. DEVELOPMENTS UNDER CLAUDIUS

The extreme rightists who killed the tyrant wanted to reestablish the Republic, but were prevented from doing so by the Praetorians who hastily acclaimed his uncle Claudius emperor (he ruled A.D. 41–54). A famous story describes how the imperial bodyguard discovered the terrified man behind a curtain in the palace (Suetonius *Claudius* x. 1 f.).

Claudius was physically handicapped, perhaps by infantile paralysis; he stuttered, and his gait was unsteady. He was ridiculed mercilessly by the imperial house and the aristocracy, deceived by his wives, Messalina and Agrippina II, and mocked by later historians. Nevertheless, he possessed notable intelligence and erudition, and substituted humor for the brilliance that the style-conscious court expected of a prince. His instructions and remarks were frequently over the heads of the Romans; the nobility were unable to comprehend his jokes, a characteristic they share with many modern historians. It was also considered plebeian that he preferred talented freedmen as his associates. Today these aesthetic imperfections do not bother us. After all, this eccentric cripple accomplished much of astonishing importance as a statesman and must be adjudged one of the outstanding rulers of the Empire, even when he is compared with others besides his immediate predecessor and successor. In private life he limped both physically and morally; in the political realm, however, he steered a remarkably firm course with the support of his freedmen and headed his government successfully. Above all, the reign of Claudius is distinguished by the development of the provinces. From the point of view of church history, this period made possible the first and second missionary journeys of Paul.

The new Emperor had to deal with the Jewish question at once. When the throne changed hands in 41, Agrippa I was in Rome; he admonished his former schoolmate Claudius to assert his power against the senate. As a reward, he was made king over all Palestine, a position he kept until his death in 44. In addition, the representatives of the Jews and Greeks in Alexandria hastened to engage in mutual recriminations before the Emperor. Claudius took Agrippa's advice and, in the so-called *Epistula Claudiana* (see above, p. 199), ordered the prefect of Egypt to see that the rights of the Jews were not encroached upon. At the same time, he cautioned the Jews of Alexandria to remain peaceful and forbade them to attract more compatriots into the city for tactical reasons. In addition, Claudius abrogated in Rome the associations that Caligula had again permitted, and, in this connection, cautioned the Jews against holding any mass meetings. Thus he endeavored to preserve the Roman traditions. After the death of Agrippa I, he put all Palestine directly under Roman control, which led to a resurgence of the Jewish Zealot movement (see above, pp. 204 f.). In A.D. 49, probably in connection with this nationalistic reaction, there was unrest among the Jews in Rome and arguments about the Messiah or "Christ"; in 50, the dispute caused Claudius to order the temporary banishment of the Jews from Rome (see above pp. 205, 226). In 52, however, he took the part of the Jews in Alexandria and Palestine (see above, p. 205).

Claudius' foreign policy was characterized by the establishment of new provinces. The example of Britain may illustrate the cultural and historical fruits borne by these extensions of the Roman sphere of administration. The transformation of Palestine into a procuratorship in the year 44, described above, later brought unhappy times upon the Jewish population because of the Zealots. For Christian missionary activity, however, this more intimate incorporation of Palestine into the Roman Empire was in fact advantageous.

For the history of the church's mission, it was also not insignificant that Claudius expanded the system of provincial government in Asia Minor and the eastern Balkans. Thanks to him, the regions visited so successfully by Paul in the course of his first and second journeys were finally able to profit from the *Pax Romana*. For example, the rapid romanization of Thrace and Moesia (the land south of the lower Danube) contributed to the growth of the cities in the province of Asia, along the Hellespont, and in Macedonia, including Philippi and Thessalonica.

During the fifties, Claudius came under the deleterious influence of his flirtatious niece Agrippina II, whom he married. She succeeded in making her son Nero the heir of the throne, and poisoned the Emperor in 54 to guarantee her power.

C. DISINTEGRATION UNDER NERO

1) *Rise and Fall of the Despot*

Thanks to the preparatory measures of Agrippina II and the prefect of the Guard, the sixteen-year-old Nero (emperor from 54 to 68) was acclaimed emperor immediately after the murder of Claudius. Legally, he was Claudius' eldest son by adoption and also married to the Emperor's daughter. He had the real crown prince slain the following year.

Nero was not by nature the wild beast that ancient traditions depicted him to be; nor does the modern talk of tyranomania explain his conduct. It is best to understand him as an aesthete without moral scruples. He had also inherited from Agrippina a strong need for recognition, which was strengthened under the meddlesome guardianship of his mother and her accomplices and could only explode when he was released from the supervision of older authorities in the years from 59 to 62. Throughout his life, Nero remained a timid youth with theatrical ideas of the imperial dignity. Agrippina hired the fashionable Stoic philosopher Seneca to educate the prince, and this mentor convinced the handsome boy soon after his accession that he was destined to become a living revelation of Augustus and Apollo (Seneca *De cle-*

mentia i. 1. 6; also most incautiously in *Apocolocyntosis* iv. 15–35, where Phoebus says of Nero, "like to me in form and grace"). On account of a modest victory in the Parthian War, which had broken out again, the senate in A.D. 55 set up a statue of Nero on divine scale in the Temple of Mars at the Forum Augusti (Tacitus *Annales* xiii. 8. 1), thus introducing the emperor cult into the city of Rome.[4] Portraits on coins show Nero as Apollo, playing the lyre.[5] All this was more than pomp and show: Nero strove with deadly seriousness to play the role of Augustus and Apollo politically, the former role primarily from 54 to 61, the latter from 62 to 68.

During the first half of his reign, Nero served the role of Augustus that had been prepared for him; with the help of Burrus, the prefect of the guard, and Seneca, the court philosopher, he ruled in cooperation with the senate. These were relatively good years, although Nero made too many concessions to the interests of the senators. It was, of course, detestable that he had his mother murdered in 59 so as to have more freedom to govern; he was thus left to the domestic rule of his mistress, Poppaea Sabina.

The second part of Nero's rule, however, turned into a bloody tragedy and ended in a fiasco, because Nero was not fitted for the role he now assumed. After the death of Burrus in 62 and the deposition of Seneca, Nero came forward unhesitatingly as an Apollo dispensing favor and wrath. He assumed this role first politically, as an autocrat beyond good and evil and standing above the legal constitution, then theatrically, as a charioteer and opera singer. The infamous new prefect of the guard, Tigellinus, and obscure Hellenistic collaborators supported him in this hybris, against which the senate and nobility reacted increasingly. Nero sought to suppress uncompromising magnates by sudden murder and star-chamber justice, all the while striving to keep the favor of the populace by means of public festivals and private expeditions. However, aristocrats with constitutional interests and

[4] G. Wissowa, *Religion und Kultus der Römer* (1912), p. 82.
[5] C. H. V. Sutherland, *Coinage in Roman Imperial Policy 31* B.C.—A.D. *68* (cited above, p. 137, n. 11), p. 170; pl. XVI, 6.

praetorians were preparing his fall and considering the fashionable ex-consul Piso as his successor. In the meantime, Nero was dabbling in art and planned a tour of Hellas intended to secure the Empire in the Balkans.

Then, on 19 July 64, a fire broke out near the Circus Maximus in Rome. It burned for six days and then flared up again for three more days, destroying the central areas of the city. The environs of the Circus Maximus and the Palatine were almost completely devastated, as well as the Subura, the old bazaar northeast of this hill, where the Jews were organized into a special synagogue.[6] Only some of the peripheral quarters of the city remained untouched (Tacitus *Annales* xv. 38. 1—44. 1). Nero's stoic attitude gave his enemies the chance to slander him by saying that the Emperor had ordered the fire to be set; we find this rumor later as a defamatory legend in the accounts of the historians Tacitus and Suetonius, both of whom wrote in support of the senatorial party. Nero certainly had no reason to risk the popular Circus Maximus and his new art collection at Domus Transitoria, not far away.[7] In fact, after the fire his great personal sacrifices and wise measures contributed much to the alleviation of the population's misery and the restoration of the city. His senatorial opponents, however, especially the conspirators supporting Piso, spread the rumor of arson and began to incite the mob against Nero.[8] Somehow the government hit on the idea of using the Roman Christians as scapegoats and amused the populace by executing them (Tacitus *Annales* xv. 44. 2–5); we shall discuss this event in more detail below. Those who were conspiring on behalf of Piso, however, continued their intrigues until, in the year 65, they were discovered and slain. In the following summer, an offshoot of the resistance connected with a certain Vinicianus was also suppressed.

The dramatic burning of Rome in fact signalized the disintegration of Nero's power, although magnificent settings

[6] J. B. Frey, *Corpus inscriptionum judaicarum,* Vol. 1 (1936), pp. lxxiii f.
[7] H. Schiller, *Geschichte des römischen Kaiserreichs unter der Regierung des Nero* (1872), pp. 429 f.
[8] *Ibid.,* p. 433.

were provided to maintain the fiction of his splendor. First, the Golden House and magnificent avenues were laid out in Rome (Tacitus *Annales* xv. 42. 1—43. 2) ; this intensified the already serious financial crisis in Italy and the provinces (*ibid.,* 45. 1) . Then, in A.D. 66, the Parthian prince Tiridates and his retinue were invited to Rome; he received the royal diadem of Armenia as he knelt before Nero. Soon afterward, however, Nero ordered the murder of Corbulo, the man who had arranged the Roman successes in the East, and so this act of homage remained a meaningless gesture. Between the fall of 66 and the spring of 68, the Emperor made a triumphant tour of Greece as a charioteer and actor; he also suggested the possibility of political freedom for Greece, while other parts of the Empire were approaching open rebellion. The first revolt broke out in the fall of 66 in Palestine, where the Jewish War was to last for four years, and in some places six. In 67, the governor of Gaul planned an insurrection, which brought Nero back to Rome in the spring of 68; in the meantime, the governors of Spain, Lusitania, and Africa had also revolted. Nero fled from Rome, was condemned to death by the senate, and committed suicide on 9 June 68. Since some did not believe he was dead, later there was lively speculation about his return, which the Greeks awaited expectantly (Tacitus *Hist.* ii. 8; Suetonius *Nero* lvii. 2) , the Jews and Christians with dread (*Sibylline Oracles* v. 137–54; Rev. 13:3; 17:8, 11) .

2) *Nero and the Jews to A.D. 66*

As we have shown above (pp. 206 f.) , immediately after the accession of the Hellenist Nero in 54 the terrorism of the Zealots and *sicarii* began in Palestine. Since Felix, the procurator, no longer had the support of the imperial government, he was barely able to hold the Jewish revolutionaries in check. In addition, there was an uprising of the aristocratic patriots, led by the family of Annas. Felix sent ten Jewish magnates to Rome as hostages. His successor, Festus, also sought to restrain the patriotism of the aristocratic high priests in Jerusalem. After the sudden death of Festus in the year 62, however, one of Annas' sons came forward as high priest, and, claiming to possess unlimited authority, had James, the brother of the Lord, executed. At the same time, Josephus and other emissaries, with the help of the Empress Poppaea, succeeded in gaining the release of the hostages (Josephus *Vit.* 13–16). For the moment, therefore, the patriots belonging to Annas' party were in control both in Palestine and at the imperial court. This was in part due to Poppaea's interest in the Jewish religion and in a Jewish actor, mentioned by Josephus (*Ant.* xx. 195), an interest corroborated by her friendship with several pro-Jewish persons.[9] It was also due in large part to new difficulties with the Parthians. Reports of Parthian military successes compelled the government at this time to exercise diplomatic caution in the Orient. In 64, when the great fire broke out and the regime wanted to place the blame for setting it upon foreigners, the Jews of the Roman Empire were not suitable scapegoats, because their brothers in the Subura had been ruined and especially because they had numerous kin in the Parthian Empire. On the other hand, about the beginning of 65 there seemed to be no danger in proceeding against the Christians, who no longer played an important role in Palestine and were under attack as apostates by Jewish patriots and Zealots. However, the remarkable immunity enjoyed by the Jews in this context turned out to be short-lived. Corbulo warded off the danger from the Parthians, and, because Nero at the time needed much wealth to restore buildings in Rome and to support the army in the Orient, he ruthlessly allowed the two last procurators, Albinus and Florus, to impoverish the Holy Land. The desperate Jews could no longer count on a sympathetic hearing at court, for in 65 Nero had a quarrel with Poppaea, who died in the summer of a premature delivery; and in the following year the Emperor concentrated all his attention on the world of the Greeks. In 66, patriotism, the Zealot movement, hatred toward the Greeks, and social disorder in the Holy Land led to the outbreak of the Jewish-Roman War. The general tendencies

---

[9] R. Hanslik, "Poppaea Sabina," in *PRE,* Vol. 22 (1953), cols. 87 f.

toward disintegration in Nero's regime also made their contribution.

3) *Nero and the Christians*

When an enthusiast for Hellenism like Nero came into power, the relationship between Jews and Christians inevitably became critical, because the Zealot terrorists subjected all their countrymen who had dealings with the Gentile world to severe pressure (see above, pp. 214 f.). For these political reasons, and for traditional theological reasons as well, the Jewish Christians under the leadership of James felt it necessary to concentrate more and more upon Jerusalem and the law, while the Gentile Christian congregations followed Paul in contributing to the westward expansion of the Gospel without the law. We may recall the picture of an ellipse with two foci: one at Zion, the other moving toward Rome.

On the positive side, continued association with Judaism meant that even under Nero the church could still be considered a form of Judaism. The church profited from the religious freedom that had been accorded the Jews since the time of Caesar; it could win new adherents in the Greco-Roman world without legal impediments. Although the official rejection of alien religions found expression in A.D. 58 in a sensational trial before the senate (Tacitus *Annales* xiii. 32. 2), for the time being this had no juristic consequences for the church; the effect was, at most, emotional. There is no trace of Neronian decrees or laws against Christianity, not even in connection with the persecution of the Roman Christians in A.D. 65. New Testament writers like Luke, Paul, and the author of the First Letter of Peter represented the Gospel as something absolutely irreproachable according to Roman law (Luke 23:14; Acts 28:18; Rom. 1:16; 13:3; I Pet. 3:13); failure to mention any decree forbidding the Christians to preach is certainly no misrepresentation. As a prisoner in Caesarea, Paul appealed quite optimistically to Nero and then at Rome associated with his fellow-Christians almost completely without hindrance (Acts 25:11; 28:30). The unexpected persecution in 65 meant legally only that Nero rescinded *ad hoc* the Jewish privileges accorded the Roman Christians. There is no extant evidence of any legislation against the church, and outside of Rome the Christians were not persecuted. Tertullian called the series of later persecutions a "Neronian invention" only in the sense that Nero had initiated the machinations *("institutum neronianum,"* Tertullian *Ad nationes* i. 7. 9) .

On the negative side, however, the traditional association between Judaism and Christianity meant that the provocatory nationalism of Jewish circles affected more and more Christian congregations, exposing them to the suspicion of being asocial. As we have seen, the Jewish Zealot movement put severe pressure on the Christians in Palestine and led to the expansion of an anti-Gentile Judaism and centralism that we can see reflected in Paul's reactions; we can trace their course from Jerusalem through Antioch, Galatia, the vicinity of Ephesus, Macedonia, and Greece to Rome (see above, pp. 214 f., 221 f.) . The proponents of these ideals see the church as a Jewish community based on legal observances and a political entity (Greek *politeuma*) supporting secular goals (Phil. 3:2, 5, 19 f.) . These ideas found especially fertile soil among those Jewish or Gentile Christians who belonged to the lower classes (slaves, freedmen, the poor, non-citizens) , of whom there were not a few (Gal. 3:28; I Cor. 1:28; cf. Acts 6:9, according to which the Jews in Rome were mostly freedmen; this would mean that many of the Christians probably were, too) . In fact, new converts of all classes tended to have a materialistic interpretation of the Gospel and of eschatology, so that they actively sought to bring about the righteousness they hoped for (Luke 12:13, where Jesus is asked to decide a question of inheritance; I Thess. 4:11; II Thess. 3:10 ff., which describes a labor strike; Philemon 11, 15, which mentions a slave's refusal to work and his flight; the later passage Titus 1:10, 14, also describes the asocial conduct of Jewish propagandists) . We may leave the question open whether the Greeks and Romans merely based their attitude on vague ideas of the Jewish temper in the struggle against Hellenism and in arguments about the

Messiah (*"impulsore Chresto assidue tumultantes,"* Sueto-nius *Claudius* xxv. 4), or had actually experienced disturb-ances caused by the fanaticism of the Jewish Zealots and the Christian social reformers. In any event, at the time of the Zealot tension under Nero, ideas about the Jewish Zealots and the expressions of Jewish isolationism were easily ap-plied to the Christians so that the latter were suspected of being asocial.

Paul was aware of this danger, which was especially serious in the capital, when he wrote to the congregation at Rome (Rom. 2:17–29, which is directed against nationalistic Jew-ish arrogance; Rom. 13:1–7, 13, an urgent appeal for loyalty toward Emperor and authorities, rejecting quarreling and zeal [RSV, "jealousy"]; Rom. 16:17–20, a warning against materialism and an admonition to live in peace). During his imprisonment, he was forced to speak out against subversive Christian preachers ("envy, rivalry, partisanship," Phil. 1:15, 17), who were endangering his legal case; some of these men were judaizers (Phil. 3:2). Even without Zealot influ-ence, Christian prophets could proclaim the downfall of Rome on the basis of Jewish traditions, as the cryptic desig-nation "Babylon" shows (used without polemic overtones in I Pet. 5:13, but later ironically in Rev. 18:2). All this evi-dence shows that in the time of Nero the close ties between Judaism and Christianity could easily expose the followers of the Messiah to the charge of anti-social intentions.

In addition, soon after the year 60, the Gospel reached some inhabitants of Rome who had contacts with the author-ities and whose friends were able to call attention to the Christians as a distinct group. Paul wrote that his imprison-ment had made him known throughout the whole Praeto-rian Guard and to many other persons (Phil. 1:13), that it had encouraged the brethren to preach boldly (Phil. 1:14), and had even brought members of the imperial household to the faith (Phil. 4:22). Two of his phrases indicate that he wrote the letter in Rome. First, the word "praetorium" (Greek *praitôrion*) must refer to the Praetorian Guard at Rome (the RSV also renders it thus); for in this context the word cannot refer to any residence of a provincial governor, but only to the soldiers of the escort, since it is followed directly by "and to all the others." Secondly, "those of Caesar's household" can hardly be thought of elsewhere than at Rome. Since they sent greetings to their brethren in the Roman veteran-colony of Philippi, they probably belonged neither to the highest nor to the lowest social class, i.e., they were probably neither members nor slaves of the Julio-Claudian house. However, thinking of them as clients of the imperial household involves no problems. There was in Rome a Jewish *Synagoga Augustensium;* [10] in similar fashion, some freedmen belonging to the imperial household may well have been Christians. As the Gospel spread, many persons connected with the government and the imperial family heard of the difference between the Jews and the Christians and could report on it, although many of them probably did not know what made the Christian preaching of the kingdom unique.

At this time Poppaea was protecting the Jews; in the year 62, she freed the aristocratic patriots who had spent several years in Rome as hostages (see above, pp. 208 f.) . In addition, the Parthian question made it necessary to treat even the Jewish Zealots with consideration.

The few Christians left in Palestine did not have to be considered in this regard. In fact, it did not take much to arouse the populace against the church, which was represented as a subversive and illegitimate sect. Calumnies are mentioned in the First Letter of Peter (I Pet. 2:12; 3:16) , a source which gives no hint of any bloody persecution and can therefore be dated before the Neronian catastrophe, even if the letter was not personally written by Peter.

Because of this disaffection, the fire in the summer of 64 spelled disaster for the Roman Christians. Nero and Tigellinus had to divert the blame for starting the fire and fix it on others, and the Christians seemed well suited for this purpose. Their very numbers, their disregard of the material world, and their apocalyptic theories upset the populace;

[10] Frey (cited above, p. 242, n. 6) , p. lxxi.

maybe some of them exhibited Judaistic zeal for the law and ritual purity or practiced impulsive arguing and prophesying. The persecution therefore came almost automatically. It was not necessary that anyone come forward and denounce the Christians; at least the sources mention nothing of such persons. Instead, the earliest and most important of the available accounts, written in 95 by a Roman presbyter named Clement, ascribes the Neronian persecution to Christian zealotism or fanaticism (I Clement 5:1–7), i.e., Judaistic and anti-social provocation on the part of certain Christian elements (Jewish Zealotism is specifically mentioned in 6:4). Tacitus also gave anti-social tendencies as the cause of the Neronian persecution, although in his typically ambiguous way he accused the Christians of all kinds of criminal acts and general misanthropy (Tacitus *Annales* xv. 44. 4).

After the fire, Nero had barracks set up for the homeless in his park at the Vatican, on the west bank of the Tiber. In this refugee camp a large part of the propertyless population was living. When the senators spread the rumor that Nero had set the fire, the poor refugees proved to be particularly receptive to it. This explains why it was in the Vatican park that Nero and his regime meted out the decreed punishment for the Christians as entertainment for the people. It probably took place around the beginning of 65. The executions followed the two forms that were provided by law for arson committed by members of the lower classes: dismemberment by animals and public burning.[11] We read how Christian women had to play the part of Dirce (a figure in Greek mythology) and be torn apart by two bulls (I Clement 6:2), or how the victims were bitten to death by dogs and set afire as torches (Tacitus *Annales* xv. 44. 4). During these circus games Nero appeared among the people dressed in jockey clothes, on foot or riding in a chariot. But despite his efforts, he did not succeed in making the Christians seem to be enemies of the state; many people began to commiserate with them instead (Tacitus *Annales* xv. 44. 5).

---

[11] For documentation see H. Fuchs, "Tacitus über die Christen," *Vigiliae christianae*, Vol. 4 (1950), p. 68; *idem*, "Tacitus in der Editio Helvetica," *Museum helveticum*, Vol. 20 (1963), pp. 223–28.

Peter and Paul may not have been executed in the course of these particular games; the earliest sources do not describe their deaths. The traditions previously cited, however, make it seem probable that their deaths were somehow connected with the Neronian persecution (see above, p. 218). We may note particularly the account of Clement, who wrote his letter from Rome thirty years after the Neronian persecution. He reminds his readers of martyrs from the recent past, mentioning Peter and Paul as "examples of our generation" (I Clement 5:1), other martyrs as "examples in our midst" (6:1), and adds expressly, "the same battle awaits us" (7:1). One cannot avoid the impression that Clement is thinking of Rome as the site of the martyrdoms of Peter and Paul; and since no other persecution is known from the period in question, the Neronian persecution seems most likely.[12]

Here we have an historical paradox that cannot be overlooked. The two Apostles who appear in the New Testament documents as the most important proponents of an attitude of loyalty toward authority and society (Rom. 13:1–7; I Pet. 2:13–17, regardless of the question of authorship) were apparently persecuted and slain as leading members of a movement accused of anti-social tendencies.

Although the Neronian persecution inflicted heavy losses upon the Christian community in Rome, it remained limited to this particular city and time. Christians were described as *malefici*, not because of laws passed against them, but for propaganda purposes. Even if the example of Rome caused the general calumnies against the church to increase elsewhere, there is no evidence for any other persecution under Nero. There is also no basis for the conjecture that even under Nero the Christians were accused of treason, lese majesty, or sacrilege. Later even Vespasian (A.D. 69–79), who had made his career in the service of Nero and, as regent, guarded the majesty of the imperial house and the state religion with utmost care, left the Christians unmolested

---

[12] O. Cullmann, *Petrus* (1952), pp. 73–169; Eng. trans., *Peter* (2d ed., 1962), pp. 71–157; J. Vogt, "Christenverfolgung, I: historisch," in *Reallexikon für Antike und Christentum*, Vol. 2 (1954), col. 166.

(see below, pp. 291 f.) . Only in one respect did the persecution under Nero affect the one undertaken some thirty years later by Domitian and even later persecutions: following the fire, the authorities were aware of the difference between Jews and Christians, so that Jewish privileges no longer furnished sure protection for the Christian community.

VII

THE ROMAN EMPIRE IN THE
SUBAPOSTOLIC PERIOD

A.D. 67–*ca.* 100

For an historical understanding of the New Testament, the subapostolic period, A.D. 67–*ca.* 100, is also important, because the Pastoral and General Epistles and the Book of Revelation reflect the situation of this period and were probably written during it. We shall leave aside the vexing question whether the literary composition of the Gospels, the Book of Acts, and the letters to the Ephesians and the Colossians can also be set in this period, especially since the content of these documents still refers to the time of Jesus and the Apostles. In all probability, though, the Pastoral Letters, the Letter to the Hebrews, the Catholic Letters (except I Peter), and the Book of Revelation belong to the subapostolic period, not only with respect to their composition or redaction, but also with respect to their content and historical background, which reflects the situation of the church in this period. Of the twenty-seven books of the New Testament, eleven presuppose the political, social, and religious problems of the last third of the first century.

The table below on pages 254 f. shows the rulers and events of the period. Because of the fragmentary nature of the sources, specific events in the history of the church can be dated only for the last few years. Instead, various aspects of the cultural history of the Jewish and Gentile worlds are selected to illuminate the situation of the church indirectly.

The subapostolic age brought changed relationships between the church and Judaism, on the one hand, and between the church and the Empire, on the other. After the

Emperors:	Legates in Syria:	First Jewish War, 66–70:
Nero, 54–9 June 68	Gallus, 63–66	Riots in May 66 in Caesarea and Jerusalem; sacrifices on behalf of the Emperor halted in June; in November, Gallus marches on Jerusalem and then withdraws; Vespasian takes command against the Jews in December.
	Mucianus, 67–69	
	Legates in Palestine (an imperial province since 67):	
	Vespasian, 67–69	1. Galilee conquered by Vespasian between spring and fall, 67. Perea and western Judea occupied spring of 68; a pause after Nero's death on June 9.
Galba, 8 June 68–15 January 69		
Otho, 15 January–16 April 69		
Vitellius, (1 January) 17 April–21 December 69		2. Vicinity of Jerusalem occupied June 69; another pause on account of selection of Emperor on 1 July.
Vespasian, 1 July 69–24 June 79 (Vespasian and his sons Titus and Domitian constitute the Flavian dynasty)	Titus, 70	3. Jerusalem besieged by Titus, April–August 70, and destroyed (triumph in 71, Arch of Titus erected in 81).
	Cerealis, 70	*Other Events:*
	Bassus, 71	Edict against astrologers, 70.
	Silva, 72–*ca.* 80	*Fiscus judaicus,* 71.
		Jewish revolts in Egypt and Cyrene, 72.
		Greece a senatorial province, 73; action taken against philosophers.
		Vespasian honored as *conservator caeremoniarum,* 78.
Titus, 79–81	Salvidemus, *ca.* 80	Musonius, the leading Stoic, recalled from exile, 79.
		Burning of Rome, 80; dedication of the Colosseum; a false Nero appears in the East.
Domitian, 81–96		Arch of Titus, 81
	Longinus, *ca.* 85	Southwest Germany conquered, 83–85; *limes* begun.
		First Dacian War, 86–87.
		Revolt in Mainz, 88; a false Nero appears in the East.
		Second Dacian War, 89; followed by victory celebrations and a persecution of senators and philosophers.

Emperors:	Legates in Palestine (an imperial province since 67):	Other Events
		Third Dacian War, 92
		Persecution of senators and philosophers, 93–94.
		Persecutions of Judaists, including Christians, 94–95.
Nerva, 18 September 96–25 January 98 Trajan, 98–117		Proceedings against senators and Judaists dropped, 96.
		Persecution of Christians in Bithynia, 113; in Syria, 114.
		Second Jewish War, 115–17.

First Jewish War, 66–70, the Christians stood side by side with homeless Jews; after the Roman civil wars of 68–69, both Jews and Christians found themselves under the authority of a strengthened imperial regime, for which Vespasian, the victor in both wars, knew how to gain increased respect and influence. These changes created social and religious problems that are reflected in Jewish apocalyptic, as well as in the latest writings of the New Testament and the earliest writings of the Apostolic Fathers. In the last decade of the century, under Domitian, the growth of imperial self-confidence led to religious persecutions. This set the stage for the next period of church history, the age of martyrdom, which lasted from Trajan to Diocletian.

1. THE JEWISH WAR AND THE CIVIL WARS A.D. 66–70

> Why does your faith drive you
> to revolt against the Romans?
> Josephus, *Bellum Judaicum*
> ii. 364, quoting Agrippa II

Josephus gives a detailed account of the First Jewish War, A.D. 66–70 (Josephus *Bell.* ii. 284—vii. 20), appending a few subsequent events from the years 71–73 (vii. 21–455). His description is an imposing document of Jewish national history and an interesting specimen of Hellenistic historiography. The following pages will mention only the most important events and results of the war, because by this time the church had, for the most part, emigrated from Palestine. We shall also take note of the Roman army revolts that shook the Empire until it was restored once more by the conqueror of the Jews.

A. The First Jewish War a.d. 66–70

It was the cultural policies of the Emperor and the financial measures of the procurator that led to the desperate reaction of the Jews in 66. In 61, Nero had decided the cultural struggle between the Greeks and the Jews in Caesarea by the Sea (see above, p. 207) in favor of the Greek residents (Josephus *Ant.* xx. 184). In the spring of 66, street fighting broke out there; afterward there were pogroms in several Oriental cities. At the request of the Emperor, the procurator Florus demanded seventeen talents from the temple treasury in Jerusalem, and this interference led in May to anti-Roman demonstrations by the multitude; then came a bloody raid by the soldiery, which only strengthened Jewish resistance. Upon the motion of Eleazar Ananiae, the captain of the Temple, it was decided in June that the daily sacrifices on behalf of the Emperor should cease (see above, p. 141). This action officially declared the city of Jerusalem to be in rebellion. Participating in the revolt were Judea together with Idumea, and Galilee together with Perea, but not Samaria. The leaders of the rebellion were (1) the aristocratic patriots in Jerusalem, who had sent the thirty-year-old Josephus to Galilee as commissar; (2) demagogic Zealots in Galilee and elsewhere, who later in Jerusalem split into the various groups to be described below. Despite all their efforts, Agrippa II and other legitimists could not prevent the revolution. Cestius Gallus, the Syrian legate, marched against Jerusalem in November of 66 and occupied the northern part of the city, but had to abandon the siege of the Temple. During their retreat the Roman legions were surprised by Jewish units and scattered; the legate then found it necessary to request the aid of the Emperor, who was on tour in Greece.

Nero was accompanied on his artistic tour by a general

who inspired confidence despite his lack of enthusiasm for vocal artistry, Vespasian, then fifty-seven years old. He came from the class of equestrians, whom Nero favored; his grandfather had been a subaltern officer in the country, his father had become an international financier and eventually ran a bank in Switzerland (Suetonius *Vespasian* i. 3). Vespasian had held commands in Britain and Africa, and was now ordered and authorized to carry out the pacification of Palestine. He started making preparations at the beginning of 67. It may be observed that Vespasian had previously been proconsul of Africa, and now had the rank of legate in Palestine, holding command independent of the legate in Syria. It should also be noted that he made provisions for organizing a Roman administration of the country, and that the governors succeeding him in Palestine were also imperial legates (generals) and therefore superior in rank and power to the procurators (financial agents). It is therefore evident that from the beginning of 67 the Holy Land was no longer treated as a procuratorship, but as a province.

Vespasian first ordered his son Titus to bring a legion from Egypt and then mobilized, in Syria, two legions with numerous auxiliaries and powerful artillery. In the spring of 67, he marched with some sixty thousand men against the rebels, beginning with those in Galilee. Of course, the Jews, sometimes resolute and sometimes uncertain, could never gain a decisive victory against the superior forces of the experienced and disciplined Romans; resistance was possible only at a few fortified places. Josephus proudly describes his defense of the fortress of Jotapata, north of Sepphoris, in which several of his detachment had taken refuge; but the capture of this and other strong points was only a question of time, of which Vespasian had plenty. The only surprise is that Josephus escaped the slaughter and became advisor to Vespasian and Titus; as their freedman he later bore the name Flavius. By the fall of 67, Galilee was in the hands of the Roman general; and, in the spring of 68, Vespasian extended his control over Perea and western Judea.

All that remained in Jewish hands was the region around

Jerusalem and the fortresses in the Dead Sea region. The resistance fighters still holding out were divided, however. (1) Most of the patriots stood behind the high walls of the capital. (2) Some of the Zealots were also in the capital; others were in the strong mountain fortresses of Herod. The patriots and Zealots in Jerusalem, however, were themselves divided by social walls; despite the danger from without, they were locked in bitter class struggle, which later helped the besiegers.

(1) The aristocratic patriots controlled primarily the upper city, the southwest plateau of Jerusalem. They were led by the former high priests Jeshua IV and Ananus II, that son of Annas who in 62 had ordered the execution of James II (see above, pp. 215 f.) . Early in 68 both leaders were slain by rapacious Idumeans who had been let into the city by the Zealots, the party entrenched on the temple plateau. The willingness, then and later, of Idumean volunteers to offer their services in Jerusalem was connected with the isolation at that time of Idumea from other regions: the fortresses to the east were controlled by Zealots, the Nabatean king to the south was supplying Roman auxiliaries, and the coastal plain to the west belonged to the Emperor. Soon, however, the Idumeans in Jerusalem became bored with the left-wing Zealot party and joined themselves to the right-wing patriotic party. The governing consistory of high priests therefore asked one of their number, a priest named Matthias, to summon the most powerful man in Idumea to Jerusalem as protector. This was Simon bar Giora, of Gerasa, a resolute commander who, like David, had come to wield considerable power as captain of guerilla bands. After he had occupied the upper city of Jerusalem with his troops in April of 69, Simon inaugurated a terrible military dictatorship, but was unable to subdue the Zealots on the temple plateau. During this period the bowmen from both camps struck more Jews than Romans. Even during the siege of Jerusalem in the summer of 70, Simon bar Giora ordered the execution of several of the aristocratic patriots who had chosen him as their protector, on the grounds that they were disposed to

surrender the capital. After the destruction of Jerusalem, this headstrong warrior fell into the hands of the Romans. During the triumph at Rome in 71 (see below, p. 285), he was led through the streets and executed. For personal and political reasons Josephus described him as unsympathetically as possible, but the strength and courage of this champion of freedom obviously made an impression on those around him.[1]

(2) The increasingly demagogic Zealots were even more implacable enemies of the Romans. (*a*) They were led primarily by descendants of Judas of Gamala, the co-founder (A.D. 6) of the Zealot party (see above, pp. 136 f.). Two of his sons had been crucified by the procurator Alexander about 46 as Zealot leaders (see above, p. 204). At the beginning of the Jewish War, in 66, a third son, named Menahem, came forward as leader of a warlike band of Zealots and took possession of the fortress of Masada on the Dead Sea together with the prisoners and supplies in it. He fought in Jerusalem against the Romans and made messianic claims by appearing in the Temple in royal garb. There he was slain by the followers of the captain of the Temple, because they were unwilling to see a leader in the struggle for freedom arise from the lower class. Late in 66 a close relative of Menahem, Eleazar Jairi, took over the leadership of his Zealot followers and continued the struggle in Judea from his base at Masada. Only in 72, after superhuman efforts, were the Romans able to penetrate into this fortress. When they finally took it, Eleazar and the others committed suicide. (*b*) After the Roman conquest of Galilee late in 67, another Zealot leader appeared, John of Gischala, who headed a strong resistance movement in Galilee and then fled to Jerusalem, organizing the refugees in military units. He led the Zealot struggle against the aristocrats described above from his base on the temple plateau. Early in 68 John ordered the election of a high priest from among the people; Josephus is quite irritated that the noble families were passed over. The man

---

[1] E. Stein, "Simon" (11), in *PRE*, Vol. 2, 3 (1927), cols. 176–79, presents Josephus' account of the man in compendious outline.

elected, Phineas, became the last Jewish high priest. Then, as described, John turned the Idumeans loose against the wealthy aristocrats. After the spring of 69, however, he was engaged in a desperate battle against Simon bar Giora, Simon's Idumeans, and other military forces on the southwest plateau. Even John's Zealots on the temple plateau engaged in a bitter class struggle, for an aristocratic priest named Eleazar Simonis defected from John early in 70, gathered his own followers in the Temple on the high ground of the Men's Court, and attacked the Galilean upstart. On account of Passover the Zealot followers of Eleazar concluded an armistice with the followers of John, opened the gates so that people could offer their Passover sacrifices, and were thereupon attacked and annihilated by the *sicarii* of John. John of Gischala then fought with energy and cunning against the steadily advancing Romans, even joining forces with Simon bar Giora. After he lost the Temple, he joined Simon in the upper city. But in September of 70 the upper city was also taken by storm; John was discovered in a cave, brought out, and condemned to life imprisonment. This heroic freedom fighter, too, is unsympathetically depicted by the turncoat Josephus, obviously out of personal animosity.

As early as June of 68, after Perea and western Judea had come under Roman control (see above, p. 257), Vespasian and his legions could probably have broken the resistance of those who were still holding out. The expected final assault upon Jerusalem was twice delayed by army revolts in the Roman Empire, once from the summer of 68 to the spring of 69, and again from the summer of 69 to the spring of 70.

B. The Roman Civil Wars a.d. 68–69

> Now the secret of the Empire
> was revealed: that a *princeps*
> could be created elsewhere than
> in Rome.
>
> Tacitus *Historiae* i. 4.2

Vespasian's Galilean successes in 67 freed Nero, who was sojourning in Greece, from his worries about the East, where at the moment even the Parthians seemed to present no danger. In the spring of 68, however, disturbances in the West forced the Emperor to return to Italy. Two of the Roman generals in the West were preparing to revolt: Vindex, in Gaul, with the help of the Celtic nobility; and Galba, in Spain, representing the Roman nobility. Against the forces in Gaul, which Nero hoped to vanquish as effectively as the Jewish forces, the Emperor sent a general who, like Vespasian, was a product of the class of equestrians and therefore beholden to him: Rufus, in command of the legions of the province of Upper Germany (roughly the modern Franche-Comté, northwest Switzerland, Alsace, and its northern extension as far as the Eifel). In June of 68, Rufus defeated Vindex at Besançon. For Nero, however, it was too late: on 8 June the senate had recognized Galba as *princeps* and deposed Nero, who took his life the next day.

1) *Galba and Otho in Rome*

Galba (who reigned from 8 June 68 to 15 January 69), the senate's choice, was seventy-two years old, a rheumatic and pedantic member of the highest nobility. At the time of Nero's death he was still in Spain, but he was expected to march at once to Rome. Vespasian postponed his attack upon Jerusalem and kept his legions ready for other eventualities, since he was in the service of the Emperor and did not belong to the senatorial party. But another general belonging to Nero's party, Otho, the thirty-six-year-old governor of Lusitania (Portugal), well known as Poppaea's former husband and a free-spending dandy, supported his colleague Galba upon his entrance into Rome. Therefore Galba was soon recognized by other commanders in Nero's service, including Mucianus in Syria and Vespasian in Palestine, as well as Alexander in Egypt and Albinus in Mauretania, former procurators of Judea (see above, pp. 204, 210).

Meanwhile the legions in Germany were growing increasingly dissatisfied with the senile and stingy Galba. During the New Year's review in 69 the soldiers in Mainz and Bonn revolted, many of them having fought for Nero, and in Cologne proclaimed as Emperor Vitellius, the new general of Lower Germany (today, Westphalia on the left bank of the Rhine, eastern Belgium, and Holland). He was the son of the elder Vitellius, the legate of Syria at the time of Stephen's martyrdom (see above, pp. 190–93). He had served as Nero's master of ceremonies and was famous for his sumptuous banquets. The Roman praetorians, however, preferred Otho as emperor; he reminded them even more than Vitellius of the happy days under Nero, and was now contributing lavishly to them. Otho was counting on being adopted by Galba. But contrary to all expectations, after the revolt of the Neronians in Germany, Galba adopted the young aristocrat Piso, who was related to the Piso who had been a conspirator against Nero (see above, p. 242), whereupon Otho had the praetorians slay the Emperor.

After 15 January 69, therefore, Otho (who reigned from 15 January to 16 April 69) was in competition with Vitellius for the position of Nero's successor. He assumed Nero's features on his provincial coins and wanted to marry Nero's widow. As soon as possible, Mucianius, in Syria, Vespasian, in Palestine, and the governors of Egypt and Africa swore their allegiance to him. Otho's glory, however, lasted only three months. The legions of Upper Germany had at once pledged their support to Vitellius, and were soon followed by the troops in Belgium, Gaul, Spain, and Raetia. Already in the month of March, two armies under Vitellius marched over the Alps and entered the Po Valley; on 14–16 April 69, they defeated Otho near Cremona. With a gesture worthy of Nero, Otho committed suicide the next day.

2) *Vitellius in the West*

The uprising of Vitellius (who had been elected emperor in Cologne on 1 January 69 and reigned in Rome from 17 April 69 to 21 December 69) was supported by the Roman soldiers in central and western Europe, who were seeking promotion that would take them to Italy, to the south, or to the east. In the capital he was received with enthusiasm by the propertyless classes, who rejoiced in the prospects of support and entertainment; they remained loyal to him to the end. Vitellius at once organized magnificent games and appointed many of his soldiers to the Praetorian Guard.

The Neronians, comprising mostly the *nouveaux riches,* soon reacted against this government with its proletarian orientation; their antagonism was shared by the legionaries stationed in the wealthy South and East and by the Hellenistic world quite generally. Whereas they had approved of Otho, they feared that Vitellius would dismiss them from their positions for the benefit of other classes. It was three Neronian commanders in the East who made preparations for an uprising: Alexander, in Egypt; Vespasian, in Palestine; and Mucianus, in Syria. (1) Of these *triumviri,* Alexander, the nephew of Philo, a Jew belonging to the equestrian, but not senatorial, class, naturally could not be a candidate during the Jewish War. (2) Vespasian, on the other hand, had a strong position. He could point to a career in the senate and military successes: most recently, in May of 69, he resumed his interrupted offensive and conquered Judea and Idumea, which had been incited to revolt by Simon bar Giora, so that now only Jerusalem and the fortresses remained to be taken. Vespasian was the leading candidate from the beginning. (3) Mucianus was ambitious, but effeminate (Suetonius *Vespasian* xiii. 1) and indecisive. His interests ran more to literary than to military achievements; he also had no son, and therefore no plans for a dynasty. The legionaries, furthermore, showed a clear preference for the conqueror of the Jews. Titus came to Mucianus for negotiations; Mucianus took a liking to him and decided not to pick a quarrel with Vespasian, but rather to play the role of a kingmaker and royal protector. Vespasian was able to make an encouraging report to Alexander about the progress of their intrigues.

3) *Vespasian in the East*

At this time Flavius Vespasianus (Emperor 1 July 69–24 June 79) was fifty-nine years old. He was a product of the middle class, but had attained the rank of senator, consul, and general in the service of Caligula, Claudius, and Nero.

An easygoing and realistic commander, he had won the confidence of the Roman military in the East. He had developed slowly and always acted prudently; after Nero's Hellenistic experiments, however, the Empire needed this hardheaded politician with common sense and Roman thrift. He modeled himself politically after Claudius (Suetonius *Vespasian* ix. 1) and delighted in showing a clever wit, but always kept both feet on the ground.

On 1 July 69, in the presence of the troops in Alexandria, the Egyptian prefect, the Jew Alexander, proclaimed the Judean legate Vespasian Emperor; after a few days came the acclamation of the legions in Judea and Syria. In the following months, the whole Oriental and Greek-speaking part of the Roman Empire swore its allegiance to him as Emperor and to his sons Titus and Domitian, twelve years Titus' junior, as "Caesars" or crown princes. The new imperial house of the Flavians was soon represented as a dynastic trinity: Vespasian in the middle, Titus and Domitian on either side. The imperial symbol of these three famous kings later influenced Jewish and Christian apocalyptic (II Esd. 11:29; Barnabas 4:4 f.) .

During the second half of the year 69, which saw four emperors, the unavoidable battle took place between the eastern and western parts of the Roman Empire. It was one of the greatest military undertakings of ancient history, meticulously prepared for by Vespasian, although he himself never had to fight. Vespasian chose blockade as his major strategic resource. Mucianus had a fleet guard the Adriatic and led an army through Asia Minor and the region of the Danube to attack northern Italy; Vespasian stayed in Alexandria to prevent the export of grain and to prepare for an invasion of southern Italy. While Mucianus was still under way the Danube legions marched of their own accord into the Po Valley; in late fall, they defeated Vitellius' followers in a night battle at Cremona, not far from where the forces of Vitellius had vanquished Otho half a year before. When the Danube legions, joined later by the army of Mucianus, approached Rome, the mob rioted, burning the Capitol and murdering the prefect of the city, Vespasian's elder brother Sabinus. Domitian, who was staying with his uncle, as well as his two cousins Flavius Sabinus and Flavius Clemens, barely escaped (Suetonius *Vitellius* xv. 3; *Domitian* i. 2). A few days later, however, Vespasian's followers took Rome by storm and executed Vitellius on 21 December 69.

Thus the East had conquered the West; but the result was not the subordination of the Romanic and Germanic parts of the Empire to Hellas and the Orient. Instead, the unity of the Empire was restored, to the benefit of Roman ideals and Western interests. The political struggle between Vitellius and Vespasian was also a cultural altercation between the two worlds that were later to go their separate ways as Western Rome and Eastern Rome; but with the help of the East and for the good of the West Vespasian had so strengthened the power of the Emperor that it could hold together the Romanic and Hellenistic world until late antiquity.

Vespasian took the capital without leaving Alexandria; he even ruled the Roman Empire from Egypt until the summer of 70, because he wanted to exploit the financial resources of this country. Titus was his assistant there until he marched against Jerusalem in the spring of 70. In the meantime, Rome was governed by Mucianus and Domitian, who laid the groundwork for good relationships between the *princeps* and the senate. External danger began to threaten in the northwest, because the Batavian leader Claudius Civilis was fomenting unrest among the Germanic tribes; but the troops dispatched by Mucianus defeated him. The southeast also remained a focus of military danger as long as the Idumean leader Simon bar Giora and the patriots and Zealots in Jerusalem were not subdued. Vespasian wanted this matter taken care of before his departure for Rome, but he had to leave just after the summer of 70 without waiting for the final capitulation of the stoutly defended city.

C. The Fall of Jerusalem a.d. 70

When his father Vespasian came to power, Titus received the title of "Caesar." He first served in Alexandria as vice-king of the East, until the task of annihilating the Jewish rebels fell to him.

1) *The Siege and Fall of Zion*

After extensive preparations, Titus began the siege of Jerusalem in April of 70. He had at his disposal the Egyptian prefect Alexander as chief-of-staff, four legions with sappers, artillery, and auxiliaries, and Josephus as intermediary. Jewish resistance was hopeless against this force; but John of Gischala and Simon bar Giora fought bravely (see above, pp. 258 ff.), so that the city held out longer than expected. Titus did not suffer as great losses as did the Jews, but several storming parties were turned back. Finally, on 10 August 70, the Temple of Herod, completed just before the war, was taken and burned; a month later, the upper city, and with it John and Simon, fell into the hands of the Romans. Jerusalem may have been only partially destroyed, but much booty was taken for the coming triumph in Rome. Titus celebrated his victory in several Oriental cities and then returned to Vespasian in Rome, where they both held a triumph in the year 71.

2) *Consequences for the Jews of Palestine*

Under the emperors of the Julio-Claudian house, the Holy Land had been a procuratorship and temple territory. After the fall of Jerusalem in 70, its population had been reduced, but the country was by no means dejudaized. It did, however, lose its relative independence and autarchy; it remained the land of the Jews only ethnically, not politically. Palestine was in fact treated as an imperial province and, for the first time during the Roman period, expropriated. Important sites were claimed as Roman colonies for soldiers and veterans, including Caesarea, the newly-founded Flavia Neapolis near Shechem, Emmaus, and the environs of Jerusalem. Caesarea remained the official residence; the governor, however, was no longer a procurator but the general of the Tenth Legion (called *"Fretensis"*), whose soldiers were quartered after the war mostly in the vicinity of Jerusalem, in part at Qumran.

As a political body the Jerusalem High Council vanished

from the stage of history. Johanan ben Zakkai, however, and other Pharisaic scribes were able to reconstitute the High Council at the imperial city of Jamnia as a faculty of law. In the second century, this academy and tribunal moved to Galilee and eventually to Tiberias, where the Mishna came into being (see above, p. 158). In addition, the Jewish War brought to an end the authority of the high priest and the consistory of high priests. The rabbis created a substitute for the high priest in the dean and vice-dean of their law faculty, whom the Mishna calls "prince" and "president of the court" (Mishna *Ḥag.* ii. 2; Hebrew *nāśî'* and *āb bêt-dîn*). The former is probably the figure that Greek and Roman sources of the third through fifth centuries call the "ethnarch" or "patriarch" of the Jews. When the temple service came to an end in the summer of 70, the basic function of the high priest ceased; and so there is no line of succession. Only because the Jews counted on a restoration of the Old Testament sacrificial cult and made certain attempts along these lines (Bar. 1:10) do Josephus and the Mishna speak as though the cult still existed. The ruined priesthood, however, was not able to make much progress after the year 70 before the Second Jewish War (115–17), under Trajan, led to a new defeat and made temple worship impossible.

2. VESPASIAN, TITUS, AND DOMITIAN A.D. 69–96

Vespasian and his two sons are called the Flavian emperors after his family name, Flavius. Under them the position of the emperor and the Roman Empire grew in strength, while the Greeks, Jews, and Christians discovered complications in their relationship to the government.

A. CONSOLIDATION UNDER VESPASIAN

> The task of restoring the Capitol Vespasian assigned to a member of the equestrian class.
>
> Tacitus *Historiae* iv. 53. 1

After being proclaimed emperor in 69, Vespasian gave to each of his sons the title "Caesar" and the rank of co-regent.

The thirty-year-old Titus he kept in Alexandria under his personal control; the eighteen-year-old Domitian he left in Rome with Mucianus as his guardian. In the fall, when Vespasian and then Titus had arrived at Rome, the father appointed his elder son prefect of the Guards and utilized him effectively as co-regent, while his younger son had to take a back seat politically.

This dynastic reorganization led to a change in political emphasis that was not without cultural consequences. Vespasian had conquered Vitellius with the help of the East; he now used the resources of the eastern provincials to restore and enlarge Roman institutions, Italian territories, and western provinces. His first measure was typical of his Rome-centered restoration: he rebuilt the Temple of Jupiter on the Capitol, which had been burned in December of 69, using the Jewish temple taxes for the project. Financially and politically Vespasian sought to strengthen the position of the Roman equestrians, the middle class, of which he was himself a product. This unsophisticated countryman, the son of a merchant and a former supporter of Nero, sought to keep on good terms with the aristocracy and the senate, but ultimate power was put in the hands of the imperial family and the middle class. Vespasian kept the key public offices for himself, Titus, and members of the equestrian class. He appointed several of these financial leaders to the high assembly, and permitted the equestrians to wear a golden ring like the senators and thereby gain the privilege of having an audience with the Emperor [2] (Statius *Silvae* iii. 3. 144 f.; Dio *History* lxv. 10. 4; James 2:2 refers to this mark of senators and businessmen) . The reign of Vespasian thus clearly put the Roman religion, the imperial dynasty, and the Italian capital in a stronger position.

Of course this centralism helped restore the Empire after the previous chaos, but the opposition of the Hellenists and Eastern Romans was unmistakable.[3] This opposition in turn led to increased emphasis on Roman authority. The wags of

---

[2] T. Mommsen, *Römisches Staatsrecht*, Vol. 2, 2 (3rd ed., 1887) , p. 834, n. 4.
[3] H. Bengtson, *Griechische Geschichte* (cited above, p. 38, n. 3) , pp. 521 f.

Alexandria and the philosophers of Greece never tired of appearing as His Majesty's flippant opposition, though without forcing the Emperor to take stricter measures (Suetonius *Vespasian* xiii. 2.; xix. 2; Dio *History* lxv. 8. 2—9. 1; 15. 5). Actually the Greek citizens of the Eastern Roman cities were not opposed to the monarchy, but they hated the Emperor's financial measures, because he favored Italians and Western Romans while imposing special taxes upon wealthy Alexandrians and other Eastern Romans.

In 73, disturbances in Greece led Vespasian to abolish the freedom that had been accorded this land since the time of Nero. For political reasons Vespasian also made Cappadocia a province attached to Galatia and garrisoned it with legionaries; he abolished the clientary status of nearby Commagene and incorporated it into Syria. At the end of the Jewish War in 70, Palestine was organized as a province and partially romanized; after 71, the Jews throughout the Roman Empire had to pay their temple tax to Jupiter Capitolinus. Despite the defeat, the Jewish Zealot movement had not been crippled; it cropped up again during the seventies as a resistance movement parallel to Greek radicalism, as we shall describe below.

Even in Rome opposition was expressed; its leadership was senatorial and its inspiration Greek. In the year 70, the Emperor had banished the Hellenistic and Oriental astrologers from Rome (Dio *History* lxv. 9. 2); about 73, he also attacked the Roman philosophers, who, on the basis of Stoic or Cynic radicalism, were championing the republican ideals of the senate. An historian loyal to the Emperor later said of their dialectical materialism, "It was as though the duty of philosophy were to insult authorities, incite the mob to rebellion, overthrow the existing order, and induce the people to revolt" (Dio *History* lxv. 12. 2). Vespasian ordered the execution of Helvidius, the Stoic leader of the senatorial opposition, on the grounds of sedition, and the banishment of all the other philosophers but one (Suetonius *Vespasian* xv. 1; Dio *History* lxv. 12. 1—13. 3).

Many citizens of the Roman Empire were dissatisfied with

the Flavians, although they shared a new *Pax Romana* under the protection of the stronger legions, three more of which were stationed in the Orient. Awareness of this opposition is important for an understanding of church history during the Flavian period. In 78, however, the Roman authorities honored Vespasian as *conservator caeremoniarum;* in the summer of the following year, with a joke about his own apotheosis on his lips, he joined the gods (Suetonius *Vespasian* xxiii. 4).

B. Relief under Titus

While he was Vespasian's right hand in Rome, Titus (Emperor from 79 to 81) had shared a series of honorary offices with his father; his command of the Praetorian Guard, his loyalty, and his energy were very useful to the Emperor, not least in carrying out proscriptions.

After his own coronation in 79, Titus repressed his younger brother, Domitian, who had also been named crown prince, and the Roman world thought it had gained in him a cruel tyrant. But to everyone's amazement, Titus as emperor exercised great tolerance in both juristic and financial matters, differing from Vespasian in forgoing both treason trials and income from the Empire. Titus behaved like an ideal prince of the Enlightenment when in 79 he restored the leader of the Roman Stoics, Musonius Rufus, who had been exiled to a small island in the Aegean. He likewise sought and received the support of the upper class: he surrounded himself with advisers belonging to the senatorial party (Suetonius *Titus* vii. 2), exempted the senators from trial for lese majesty, ordered, instead, that the informers be flogged and banished (*ibid.,* vii. 2; viii. 5—ix. 2), and during the last year of his life reserved the consulship for the senators. At the same time, he took into account the welfare and gratitude of the Roman lower classes: the soldiers were rewarded generously, the proletariat was sustained and entertained by means of grants, food, and theater—for instance, after the eruption of Vesuvius in 79, after the burning of the Capitol, and at the dedication of the Colosseum in 80. Titus thus showed an inclination toward a diarchic and popular government. When he took sick and died in 81, senate and people sincerely mourned this ostensible darling and glory of mankind (Suetonius *Titus* i. 1; xi. 2) .

It remains questionable, though, whether the middle class and the provincials would have remained enthusiastic about this promotion of the Italian aristocracy and populace if Titus had ruled longer. In any case, the liberality of Titus put his successor Domitian in a difficult position, making him consider it necessary to rule more firmly.

C. TENSION UNDER DOMITIAN

"No useful thing is the rule of a crowd . . ."—Homer, as quoted by the young Domitian

Suetonius *Domitian* xii. 3

The senatorial, Greek, and Christian writers of the second century left to posterity the picture of Domitian (Emperor from 81 to 96) as a tyrant, because he cruelly attacked representatives of the senatorial aristocracy, of Hellenism, and of Christianity, was finally struck down by tools of his political opponents, and was exposed to a disgraceful *damnatio memoriae* on the part of the senate. Modern scholarship is overcoming this ugly propaganda only with difficulty.[4] Historically, it must be recalled that Domitian hit upon intelligent measures for the Empire as a whole and the majority of the people, until he lost control in the nervous final years of his reign. Despite all his vanity, strictness, and pedantry, he was a ruler filled with religious and moral zeal. His personal ideal was Tiberius (Suetonius *Domitian* xx. 1) , but his conduct of politics is more reminiscent of Vespasian, although he lacked his father's popular touch. He was convinced of the necessity for taking a firm stand against the feudal lords and Hellenists, who had prospered under Titus. This decision was due to his experiences in 69, the year of the four emperors, when Rome and the Empire were in an uproar and he himself, trapped on the beleaguered Capitol,

[4] K. Christ, "Zur Herrscherauffassung und Politik Domitians," *Schweizerische Zeitschrift für Geschichte*, Vol. 12 (1962) , pp. 187–213.

almost perished in the fire. Domitian's goals were therefore to secure the borders of the Empire, to improve the administration and communications, and to further romanize religion and morality. Like Vespasian before him, he wanted to promote the interests of the middle class and the Roman people; this could take place only at the expense of the upper class and the eastern provinces, and senatorial and Hellenistic opposition was therefore unavoidable. This opposition was only secondarily directed against the emperor cult, which advanced in a few respects under Domitian but was nothing new to the provincials, and was in theory at least connected with the state, not the particular emperor. If one recalls Domitian's considerable positive contributions to the Roman Empire as a whole and the majority of its people, it is easy to see why Christian writers during the first twelve years of his reign considered the existing form of government and society as offering for the most part positive advantages for missionary work, and only afterward condemned it in apocalyptic terms (see below, pp. 312 ff.) .

Domitian's primary concern was the restoration and adornment of Rome after the burning of the Capitol in 80. He ordered the erection of a whole series of important buildings and monuments, which are still landmarks to modern tourists.[5] (1) First, he finished magnificently the rebuilding of the temple on the Capitol, which Titus had begun. (2) He was especially responsible for some important new structures in the Forum Romanum: to the west, the Temple of Vespasian, three of whose Corinthian columns are still standing; in the center, the new curia for the senate, which was rebuilt in the seventh century as the church of S. Adriano; to the east, the Arch of Titus, built in 81, with artistic carvings depicting the furnishings of the Jerusalem Temple. (3) He also had an enormous palace built on the Palatine,[6] and next to the Forum of Augustus he built a forum that was later

---

[5] S. Gsell, *Essai sur le règne de l'empéreur Domitien* (1894) , pp. 90–130; R. Weynand, "Flavius, 77," in *PRE*, Vol. 6 (1909) , cols. 2553, 2590–92.

[6] Domitian's court poet Statius, invited to the dedication of the new palace along with the senators and equestrians, wrote of the festivities in this vein: ". . . *mediis videor discumbere in astris cum Jove*" (Statius *Silvae*, iv. 2. 10 f.) .

ascribed to the Emperor Nerva. As a builder of Rome, the only man who can be compared to Domitian was Augustus.[7] (4) Finally, roads in Italy and the provinces were built or repaired, and the postal service made great advances.

Domitian took several measures on behalf of those without means, providing festivals and alms and making provision for the support of retired soldiers and needy children of the city.[8] Nerva developed this latter institution into the justly famous "alimentary endowments," which long continued to have social importance. Like his father, though, Domitian did most to advance the middle class, that is, the equestrians who made their living as entrepreneurs and also the freedmen working in government service. Handing out all kinds of distinctions and appointments, he helped these groups rise socially, and used them, under strict supervision, as governmental, administrative, and military officials. For example, Fuscus, the prefect of the Guard, was employed as supreme commander on the Danube, a course that turned out to be overly risky; and a freedman by the name of Etruscus, whose father had been a slave, served as financial minister (Statius *Silvae* iii. 3. contains a bombastic passage in honor of this parvenu). Restraints, however, were placed on the upper class. Domitian used his power as consul and censor (after 85 as *censor perpetuus*) to dominate the senate and control the aristocracy. He opposed the motion to exempt senators from the imperial death sentence, an exemption granted by Titus, attacked with hypocritical zeal the nobles and vestals accused of immorality, and jealously saw to it that Roman magnates in Italy or abroad could not increase their influence. On these points Domitian exhibited remarkable fear, based on his experiences as a youth; the magnates responded with fear and hatred. Nevertheless, only for the upper class and mostly during his last years did Domitian's reign amount to real terrorism.

In foreign affairs it should be noted that Domitian, following in the footsteps of Vespasian, sought a tactical adjust-

[7] Gsell, (cited above, n. 5), p. 119.
[8] Weynand (cited above, n. 5), cols. 2554, 2586.

ment of the borders of the Empire, an adjustment that had a long-lasting effect on the history of European civilization.

(1) Because he considered Agricola's military adventures in Britain too daring, he interrupted the career of this legate, famous as the father-in-law of Tacitus, and withdrew his troops from Scotland. At the beginning of the second century, in agreement with this strategy, the *limes* was built across the north of England, which protected the growth of England's Roman culture.

(2) As soon as possible Domitian directed his attention toward strengthening the Roman positions on the Rhine. Militarily, southwest Germany had long been a source of annoyance. This area, or more precisely, the Celtic and Germanic forest area lying like a great "V" between Coblenz, Basel, and Regensburg, called by Tacitus *agri decumates,* made direct communications between the legions of Upper Germany and Raetia impossible. Vespasian had cut off its southern point by a military road from Strasbourg to Lake Constance. Domitian pursued this course with zeal: between 83 and 85, he subdued the Germans in southern Hessia and was able to occupy all of southwest Germany. He set up a chain of sentry stations, the *limes Germaniae,* later provided with permanent towers by Trajan, Hadrian, and others. This *limes* connected the region below Coblenz on the Rhine with that above Regensburg on the Danube and for almost two hundred years made the Taunus–Black Forest–Swabian Alp triangle a part of the Roman world. Coins bearing the inscription *Germania capta* and honoring the Emperor as *Germanicus* glorified this achievement, which Tacitus and Pliny tried to dismiss as an empty boast; excavations, however, have confirmed Domitian's claims.

(3) After the Rhine border had been secured, the military might of the Empire could be concentrated in the eastern region of the Danube. The pressure exerted by East European barbarians made this concentration necessary for centuries.[9] During the years 86–87, Domitian conducted the

---

[9] E. Gren, *Kleinasien und der Ostbalkan in der wirtschaftlichen Entwicklung der römischen Kaiserzeit* (1941), pp. 95, 113.

First Dacian War. With the help of the Praetorian Guard, he first pushed back the Dacians who had penetrated into Moesia (Serbia and northern Bulgaria) from across the Danube and then let his prefect Fuscus take over the war as supreme commander. In 87, Fuscus advanced northward toward Transylvania, but was defeated in the southern Carpathians. The defeat, not important in itself, had serious consequences. Plots against the government were discovered in the capital; the conspirators wanted to capitalize on the absence of the praetorians (*Acta fratrum arvalium* 22 September 87—"*ob detecta scelera nefariorum*") . In 88, the senatorial general Saturninus instigated a desperate revolt of the legions in Mainz and the Germans along the *limes,* which could have led to a repetition of the war between Vitellius and Vespasian. In both situations, however, Domitian won the day. Before he arrived in Upper Germany, other troops in the province had smashed the revolt. Then the Emperor quickly returned to Moesia, in the vicinity of Belgrade, where the Second Dacian War was fought in 89. He personally marched northward along the Theiss to attack the rebellious Quadi and Marcomanni in Pannonia, though without enough troops and therefore without success. He did, however, send one general with the main force eastward toward Transylvania to conquer the Dacians. Despite some losses, Domitian was thus able to make the Dacian king a vassal. Here, too, on the lower Danube, his military activities laid the basis for a *limes* under Trajan and the later Emperors.[10] Thus Domitian stabilized the Roman colonization of England, southwest Germany, and the Balkans for a considerable period, although the emperors of the second century had much work yet to do. The three *limites* mentioned, of which the *limes Germaniae* fell before the Alemanni in 260, were cultural bulwarks which enabled the Mithras cult, Christianity, and other forms of religion to spread along the border or across it.

After the Second Dacian War in 89, the Emperor held a

[10] C. Patsch, *Der Kampf um den Donauraum unter Domitian und Trajan* (1937) , pp. 3–52.

magnificent victory celebration for the people of Rome, but at the same time began to persecute his senatorial opponents. There is a legend describing the beginning of the proscriptions at a macabre mystery ritual held for the wealthy and the aristocrats in a hall that had been made to resemble a black tomb (Dio *History* lxvii. 9. 1–5). In any case, aristocrats and philosophers were soon executed or banished in great numbers for offending the majesty of the state or appearing to support the ideal of a republic. The money confiscated from those who were proscribed was used to support the army. (1) Among the victims was Flavius Sabinus, the Emperor's elder cousin. (2) One of this man's clients was the banished Stoic-Cynic philosopher Dio Chrysostom, of Prusa, who spread anti-Roman propaganda in the Balkans [11] and was feared by the conservatives as a dangerous anarchist, although he refrained from the crudities of other philosophers [12] (Dio Chrysostom *Discourses* xiii. 1, about his patron; vi. 35; vii. 12, against the tyrant). The bearded Greek philosophers with their radical ideas were quite generally considered enemies of Roman traditions (since 155 B.C., when Carneades, Critolaus, and Diogenes, the leaders of the Academics, Peripatetics, and Stoics, came from Athens to Rome and gained Roman aristocrats as their pupils). Vespasian had banished them, but Titus had brought their most important patron in the senate, Musonius Rufus, back from exile. (3) The educated classes of the Greek world quite generally attacked the Roman government with openness and irony; according to the *Acta Alexandrinorum,* there were Alexandrians of the first and second centuries who treated Roman dignitaries with unbelievable insolence. [13] Domitian added fuel to the flames of this Hellenistic resistance movement by his remarkable zeal on behalf of Roman religion and morality, his one-sided interest in his mother country and the Rhine and Danube borders, and his relative

[11] Patsch (cited in preceding note), pp. 48–51.
[12] R. Höistad, *Cynic Hero and Cynic King* (1948), pp. 150–222.
[13] H. Fuchs, *Der geistige Widerstand gegen Rom in der antiken Welt* (1938), pp. 2–5 (Carneades), 50–53 (Dio Chrysostom *et al.*), 57 f. (the Alexandrian martyrs).

impoverishment of the Eastern Mediterranean world. We read, for example, of a tax revolt on the Syrtis (Dio *History* lxvii. 4. 6) ; there is inscriptional evidence for a special *fiscus Asiaticus;* [14] Domitian's court poet lists abundant contributions from the East (Statius *Silvae* iii. 3. 85–105) ; there is word of unrest in Asia that flared up in 88 on account of a *Nero redivivus* supported by the Parthians; an Asiatic Christian castigates the lucrative Eastern trade of the Roman capitalists (Rev. 18:11–24) ; a forced restriction of Eastern winegrowing is depicted as a gross blunder (Suetonius *Domitian* vii. 2; xiv. 2; a possible allusion in Rev. 6:6). If one keeps in mind this tension between the government and the opposition, the persecution of the senators and philosophers in 89 becomes politically reasonable, even though no more justifiable morally than all state encroachments.

Because the Scythian and Germanic clientary tribes on the borders of Pannonia were still causing trouble, the Emperor waged a Third Dacian War in 92; further attacks were made upon them from Pannonia and Dacia.[15] The Emperor spent the last half of 92 at the front; he was then able to decorate and release certain military units, although the cost of the war led him to forgo a triumph. Domitian had thus pacified the Danube basin in three wars waged up the river, and despite the migrations this sufficed for many years, until in 101 Trajan began a preventive war on a larger scale to stem the tide of Eastern European peoples and preserve Roman hegemony in the East, which later made the Byzantine Empire possible.

After his return in 93 Domitian attacked the senatorial party, beginning with a dramatic trial in the curia.

(1) The senatorial aristocrats and philosophers had accused one of the Emperor's followers, named Massa, of certain kinds of extortion in southern Spain. Massa in turn accused Senecio, the prosecutor appointed by the senate, of lese majesty (Latin *impietas;* Pliny *Epistulae* vii. 33. 4) , on the grounds that he had written a Stoic pamphlet. Domitian

---

[14] M. Rostowzew, "Fiscus," in *PRE*, Vol. 6 (1909) , cols. 2402 f.
[15] Patsch (cited above, p. 275, n. 10) , pp. 32–44.

ordered the Praetorian Guard to keep watch on the curia, intervened personally in the trial, and succeeded in having the senate condemn Senecio, along with several of his compeers and like-minded persons. On this occasion even more Roman aristocrats than in 89 were proscribed and their property confiscated; some were themselves philosophers, others had maintained Greek philosophers and Oriental astrologers or prophets to serve as religious advisers.[16]

(2) Among the Greek philosophers who, like Dio Chrysostom, were banished or forced to keep away from Rome and Italy because of their dangerous associations with Roman magnates, were several celebrities: the Eclectic Platonist Plutarch, who had been allowed to assume the clan name of the senator Mestius Florus; a Stoic named Artemidorus, famous among his contemporaries, who had succeeded in becoming Musonius' son-in-law (see pp. 270, 276); the Stoic Epictetus, held in high estimation by posterity, a Phrygian slave who owed his freedom and scholarly career to the wealthy Secretary of State Epaphroditus (see below, p. 281); and, finally, the clever Pythagorean Apollonius of Tyana (a city in Cappadocia), who was arrested on the basis of his association with the senator Nerva but was treated with respect in the Roman prison by Aelianus, the prefect of the Guard (Philostratus *Apollonius* vii. 8–10, 16–33, gives an anecdotal account, which nevertheless reflects historical details). Attacks upon the Emperor by these Greek philosophers have come down to us only in the case of Apollonius, but Domitian's rage was directed against all freethinkers. On the other hand, he provided support for philosophers who appeared useful to him, like Flavius Archippus, whom he sent to Prusa to neutralize the influence of Dio Chrysostom (Pliny *Epistulae* x. 58–60).

Terror reigned in the curia and the schools, but Domitian was even more fearful of the scope of the reaction. His concern now was to shore up the majesty and security of the Roman Emperor. Although the Germanic and Balkan border tribes, the senatorial opposition, and the Greek free-

[16] Gsell (cited above, p. 272, n. 5), pp. 278–86.

thinkers had been repressed for the time being, Domitian felt called upon by his tutelary deity Minerva to follow Vespasian in continuing the battle on behalf of Roman piety and civic virtue.

(3) Religious persecution of prominent Romans was an unavoidable consequence in his final years, 95–96. Domitian was in fact much more serious about the state religion than his father had been. He enjoyed having flatterers call him "lord" (Greek *kúrios,* Latin *dominus*) and "god" (Suetonius *Domitian* xiii. 1–2). The latter title appeared upon coins in the East. At the Festival of Jupiter he wore a golden crown with the images of Jupiter, Juno, and Minerva, and is said to have ordered the flamen of Jupiter and the college of priests to wear the same images, with the addition of his portrait (*ibid.,* iv. 4). In the center of the Forum Romanum he erected an equestrian statue of himself six times life size (Statius *Silvae* i. 1).[17] The emperor cult had flourished in Asia Minor since the time of Augustus. Now it was augmented in the capital, Ephesus, by a cult of Domitian. The official importance of this cult is illuminated by the remains of a special temple with a gigantic statue of the Emperor.[18] In theory, the Roman magnates were not expected to join in the emperor cult like the provincials; since, however, the *Princeps* claimed the key offices, both political and religious, he believed that he could judge the dependability of the highest dignitaries and his closest officials by their attitude toward the state religion. A mere lack of interest in the ceremonies could bring about the fall of a nobleman or member of the court, especially when there were associations with Judaism, Christianity, or other non-Roman faiths. These religio-political circumstances lay behind the religious persecutions during the last years of Domitian described by Dio Cassius through his epitomator (Dio *History* lxvii. 14. 1–3).

[17] D. Vaglieri, "Scavi nel Foro Romano," *Bulletino della Commissione archeologica communale di Roma,* Vol. 31 (1903), p. 273; G. Gatti, *ibid.,* Vol. 32 (1904), pp. 75–79, 175.
[18] J. Keil, "Vorläufiger Bericht über die Ausgrabungen in Ephesus, 16," *Jahreshefte des Österreichischen Archäologischen Instituts in Wien,* Vol. 27 (1932), Beiblatt, pp. 54–60 and Taf. III.

Following the execution in 89 of Flavius Sabinus because of his association with radical philosophy (see above, p. 276), his brother Flavius Clemens was executed in 95 and his sister-in-law Flavia Domitilla banished. This caused a sensation, because they were the two closest surviving relatives of the Emperor and, after him, the most distinguished citizens of the Empire. Flavius Clemens was the Emperor's cousin and co-consul; his wife was the Emperor's niece. In addition, the *Princeps,* with an eye to the succession, had adopted the couple's two sons. "The accusation against them both was atheism, on account of which many other persons with Jewish inclinations were condemned, some losing their lives, others at least their property" (Dio *History* lxvii. 14. 2). In this context, "atheism" (Greek *atheótēs*) means rejection of the state gods of Rome, an attitude characteristic of Jewish and Christian monotheism. Referring to the same religious trials, in another chapter Dio's epitomator mentions charges of "blasphemy" (Greek *asébeia,* corresponding to the Latin *impietas*), which means disavowal of the Roman majesty, likewise associated with a "Jewish attitude" (*ibid.* lxviii. 1, 2). In theory, Judaism was no more prohibited than philosophy; it was only somewhat suspect because of certain tendencies toward agitation. Domitian, however, was enraged to hear that, after his suppression of anti-Roman philosophy, representatives of the nobility and the equestrians were now inclined to support a type of prophecy critical of this world. The Emperor, with his zeal for Roman piety and solidarity, looked upon the promotion of Greek radicalism as high treason; all the more could this charge be leveled against prominent supporters of biblical monotheism, whose household and clients might easily be dominated by alien political interests.

We shall later (see below, pp. 295–302) discuss whether the nobles slain in the course of these religious trials were adherents of Judaism or of Christianity: namely, Clemens, Domitilla, and Acilius Glabrio, who is mentioned in the same context and who had been consul with Trajan in 91. In any case, personal rejection of the Roman state religion and financial support of Jewish or Christian believers sufficed to stamp such leaders of Roman society as traitors. In itself this did not mean a general persecution of Judaism or Christianity; but circumstances to be mentioned in the following section suggest that there were local persecutions of Christians under Domitian.

For similar religio-political reasons, Domitian had his Secretary of State Epaphroditus first banished and then executed (Suetonius *Domitian* xiv. 4; Dio *History* lxvii. 14. 4). This former freedman, who had become a millionaire and equestrian, represented political liberalism. He had released his slave Epictetus and allowed him to pursue a scholarly career, for which reason he came under suspicion during the campaign against the philosophers in 93. In the same year, Josephus, who likened himself as a Pharisee to the Stoics, dedicated his *Antiquitates* and *Vita* to Epaphroditus (*Ant.* i. 8; *Vit.* 430); he also wrote for Epaphroditus as patron his apology for the Jews, *Contra Apionem* (*Ap.* i. 1; ii. 1. 296). These works were certainly not offensive; the apology must even be considered skillful. But the Secretary of State was sufficiently compromised by his associations with radical philosophy and patriotic Judaism to be punished as described.

As a result of these violent attacks upon members of the court, the family and household of the conqueror of Germany were in mortal terror. The fate of Domitilla made the Empress Domitia, whose passionate nature and business acumen make her resemble a Renaissance princess, tremble for her life (she had, incidentally, patronized Josephus; Josephus *Vit.* 429). Parthenius, a freedman serving as lord high chamberlain, was made uneasy by the fall of his colleague Epaphroditus. He began to make preparations to murder the tyrant (Suetonius *Domitian* xvi. 1; xvii. 3; Dio *History* lxvii. 14. 5—18. 2). After a long search he found a candidate for the succession in Nerva, who was admired in the senate as a follower of Titus and a patron of the philosophers. He then induced one of the praetorian prefects to become a collaborator and persuaded the freedman Stephen to deliver the world from the tyrant. Stephen, a Christian, may have based his action on idealism; as Domitilla's executor he had tried to save what he could of her confiscated property, and this must not have been out of self-interest. He struck down Domitian in his palace on 18 September 96.

The senatorial conspirators had Domitian carried out like a slain gladiator. Nerva was acclaimed *princeps,* and the senate saw to the removal of all monuments that might remind people of the victim: *damnatio memoriae.*

An historical assessment of Domitian demands that one see beyond the *damnatio memoriae* and his tragic end and examine the major part of his life and work. Above all one must keep in mind the years 81–92, during which he vigorously and courageously promoted the interests of the city and the Empire, the administration and the populace. He was stern and sometimes cruel toward the upper class; but he aided the middle class, especially the equestrians and freedmen, and likewise the lower class, at least the soldiers and proletariat. His military leadership, not brilliant but judicious, and his remarkably successful supervision of his officials (Suetonius *Domitian* viii. 2) protected Italians and provincials from external and internal troubles. Loyal spokesman for large classes of the populace could therefore come to terms with the existing order under the Emperor until 93 and in part even later, as was true for Josephus when he wrote *Contra Apionem,* as well as the authors of the Catholic Epistles and the First Letter of Clement.

In the final years, 93–96, however, the religious trials that were intended to contribute to the internal security of the Roman Empire and its emperor finally made Domitian appear a tyrant. This period is probably reflected in the Jewish Apocalypse of Ezra and the Christian Revelation of John. In the second century, Christian writers treated Domitian as a second Nero and a persecutor of Christianity. It is probably true that Domitian ordered local persecutions. The picture was distorted, however, because in his treason trials against the senatorial party he formulated the charges in such a way that they resembled the charges leveled by later emperors in their persecutions of Christians. Whereas under Domitian a supposed threat to the glory of the emperor and the Roman people was considered "blasphemy" (Greek *asébeia,* Latin *impietas*), it was later referred to by the jurists as "lese majesty" (Latin *crimen laesae* or *minutae maiestatis*). And under Domitian, a supposed insult to the religion of the senate, the metropolis, and the Empire was called "atheism" (Greek *atheótēs*), while under Trajan it was stamped more strongly as "superstition" (Latin *superstitio*). These terms drawn from sacral law contributed to the church's *damnatio memoriae* of Domitian during the second century.

D. JEWS AND CHRISTIANS UNDER THE FLAVIANS

Because of the fragmentary nature of the sources, which are often painted in apocalyptic colors, it is impossible to follow the history of Judaism and Christianity in detail under Vespasian, Titus, and Domitian; all we can do is grasp the broad outline. In order to understand the New Testament documents of the subapostolic period we must nevertheless attempt to reconstruct the developments, necessarily relying at times on argument from silence.

1) *Judaism*

After a few remarks about a) the position of the Jews under the Flavians, we shall discuss b) their attitude toward the government.

a) *The Political Situation*

Palestine ceased to be a procuratorship and became a Roman province after the fall of Jerusalem in A.D. 70; consequently it lost its distinctive character as a Jewish temple land, and the Jews living in their mother country were in the same situation as those in the Diaspora. Furthermore, all Jews, with the exception of those families that had acquired Roman citizenship on the basis of special accomplishments, became stateless *peregrini* in the Roman Empire. In principle they could still live in Palestine or visit it, and they looked upon it as their holy land. But they no longer had citizenship of their own there as they were supposed to have had during the procuratorship because of the authority of the High Council. Like Christianity after 65, Judaism after 70 became a religion without a homeland, not according to any theory of the rabbis but in the eyes of the authorities. It remained basically oriented toward life in the dispersion; despite the tradition of nationalism, it was compelled to come to terms on the one hand with the government and on the other with Christianity, which was in a similar position.

Since pre-Christian and apostolic times, the Jewish people was represented in all important regions of the Roman and Parthian empires (Philo *De Legatione ad Gaium* 281 f.; Acts 2:9–11). Including proselytes it numbered several millions and made up between six and nine percent of the total population of the Roman Empire.[19] Thanks to emigration and deportation, the majority of Jews now lived outside of Palestine. In particular they were a characteristic element in the streets of the commercial and industrial cities of Egypt and Cyrene, of Syria, Asia, Hellas, and Italy; sometimes they even had rights of citizenship in Cyrene and Asia, especially in Ephesus,[20] while the Greeks of Alexandria and Antioch sought to deny them equal rights.

Vespasian and Titus did not wage the Jewish War against these numerous and important foreign Jews, but against the Jews of Palestine and particularly the Zealot leaders. After the Jewish defeat, therefore, the rights of the Diaspora Jews were not restricted. It is especially notable that the general prohibition of associations was never employed against the synagogues; the toleration shown since the time of Caesar continued in effect. As before, the Jews enjoyed complete organizational and religious freedom, and this was by no means a matter of course under emperors like Vespasian and Domitian, who displayed great zeal for all things Roman. In fact, the Jews were not compelled to join in the worship of the emperor's image that was usual in the East (Josephus *Ap.* ii. 73, written in the time of Domitian). No general

[19] References to various estimates are found in M. Simon, *Verus Israel* (1947; 2d ed., 1964), p. 53.
[20] Schürer, Vol. 3 (4th ed., 1909), pp. 78–84; J. Juster, *Les juifs dans l'empire romain*, Vol. 2 (1914), pp. 2–5.

persecution of the Jews is mentioned; there were only local altercations.

The subjection of the Jews, however, and their duties toward the emperor were made painfully clear. In 71, Vespasian and Titus, with Domitian at their side, celebrated a magnificent triumph over the Jews in Rome. Simon bar Giora and the other resistance fighters were dragged along in the procession and led away to execution. The golden furnishings of the Holy of Holies were exhibited to the eyes of the mob: the seven-branch candlestick and the table of showbread, along with the festal trumpets; all these things were later displayed in Vespasian's Temple of Peace. Coins with the inscription *Judaea capta* recalled the triumph; after Domitian's accession, the carvings on the Arch of Titus also played their part. To help rebuild the Temple of Jupiter on the Capitol, which had been burned in 69, Vespasian claimed as reparations the Jewish temple tax of two drachmas (see above, p. 168), which every male who called himself a Jew had to pay annually (Josephus *Bell.* vii. 218; Dio *History* lxv. 7. 2). This tax meant an income of several millions for the Emperor. Domitian therefore administered the *fiscus Judaicus* with a heavy hand (Suetonius *Domitian* xii. 2), although he also managed a *fiscus Alexandrinus* and a *fiscus Asiaticus* (see above, p. 277); later Emperors did not treat the Jews so harshly, but the Capitoline tax was not abolished until 361, under Julian. This contribution toward rebuilding the Capitol was a source of religious vexation to the Jews, but certainly not an excessive financial burden, and most of them obviously appreciated the possibility of purchasing religious liberty for roughly a dollar a year ("a taxable freedom," Tertullian *Apology* xviii. 9).

Vespasian, Titus, and Domitian treated Judaism, politically no longer bound to Zion but to Rome, with confidence, or at least with equanimity. Josephus' life and work under the protection of the Flavians is an illuminating example of this. 1. Around 74, under Vespasian, the governor of the province Cyrene-Crete had put down a Zealot revolt and wanted to implicate the whole of Diaspora Judaism. Vespasian and Titus, however, expressed their confidence in the Jewish upper class (Josephus *Bell.* vii. 437–50). 2. Titus had been on friendly terms with Bernice and Agrippa II during the Jewish War, and in 75 they were invited to live in his palace in Rome; he even appointed Agrippa praetor. When well-known Cynics made fun of his supposed infatuation for Bernice, fifteen years his senior, they were executed, and only out of regard for public opinion did Titus send the ambitious couple back home (Suetonius *Titus* vii. 1; Dio *History* lxv. 15. 3b–5). So obvious was his benevolence toward the Jewish upper class that after his accession Bernice made another attempt at rapprochement; this time, however, Titus immediately obeyed the will of the senatorial party and rejected her request (Suetonius *Titus* vii. 1; Dio *History* lxvi. 18. 1). 3. Domitian had no great sympathy toward Judaism; but any suggestion that he might have persecuted the Jews is disproved by his notorious pedantry with regard to the *fiscus Judaicus* (Suetonius *Domitian* xii. 2). It can only be demonstrated that he persecuted those Roman magnates and aristocrats who, in his opinion, exhibited too little interest in the official cult and their obligations to the state and too much interest in biblical monotheism (see above, pp. 279 ff.). The extant sources indicate no attacks upon the continued existence of Judaism, but only efforts to preserve Romanism; to put matters in this light does not render the picture of Domitian's religious trials innocuous, but it does correct the perspective. Judaism, as an ethnically and legally distinct entity, still remained officially inviolate under Domitian, a circumstance of considerable importance for Christianity.

b) *The Social Attitude*

Immediately after the Jewish War, the Jewish upper class was so debilitated that patriotic opposition was out of the question. The surviving aristocrats and scribes took an attitude of solidarity with the Romans, as Agrippa II, Josephus, and others had done even during the war.

We find an explicitly pro-Roman and anti-Zealot attitude

on the part of Jewish aristocrats in the First Book of Baruch, one of the apocryphal books in the Septuagint canon. Rome is alluded to under the name "Babylon" (Bar. 1:1), a familiar cryptogram in Jewish and Christian literature (Sibylline Oracles 5:15:8; I Pet. 5:13; Rev. 17:5). There, in the fifth year after the "Chaldean," i.e., Roman, conquest of Jerusalem (Bar. 1:2) —that is, precisely in 75, while Titus was lodging Agrippa II (son of the Jewish king Agrippa I) in Rome—Baruch the scribe read to the son of the king, the patricians, and the assembly, a letter addressed by him to the priests (Bar. 1:3 f.) ; he took up a collection and sent it to Jerusalem with the letter (1:6 f.). The money was meant to defray the expenses of restoring the temple sacrifices, including prayers for "Nebuchadnezzar," the conqueror of Jerusalem, and his son "Belshazzar" (1:10 f.). The purpose of the sacrifices and prayers was a peaceful life under the protection of this king of "Babylon" and his son (1:12; 2:21). Because father and son are mentioned here as co-regents, their identification with Vespasian and Titus was immediately obvious to contemporaries. In other words, the Roman Jewish community under Vespasian and Titus wanted to see the Jerusalem sacrifices on behalf of the Emperor restored (see above, p. 256) in order to obtain the favor of the two rulers (to "find favor in their sight," Bar. 1:12). Josephus confirms that in the time of Domitian the contributions of the Jews actually made these sacrifices possible once again (Josephus *Ap.* ii. 77).

Pharisaic scribes in Palestine also sought friendly relations with the Flavians, as is confirmed by the restoration of the Jerusalem Sanhedrin as a faculty of law in the imperial city of Jamnia (see above, p. 267). In this regard some characteristic traditions are recorded concerning the first two presidents or chief rabbis of this school, Johanan ben Zakkai and Gamaliel II. Johanan ben Zakkai is said to have negotiated with Vespasian, who prepared the siege of Jerusalem in 69, and to have been assured of permission to continue the work of the scribes in Jamnia, which belonged to the imperial family (*Abot R. Nath.* iv. 6). With respect to his successor in

Jamnia, Gamaliel II, who was active in the time of Domitian, tradition emphasizes his attitude of strict discipline toward the Jews (Mishna *Ber.* ii. 5 f.) but clever diplomacy toward Gentiles (*'Aboda zara* iii. 4). It also recalls a journey to Rome that Gamaliel is said to have undertaken around 90 with three colleagues to negotiate with the authorities and dispute with the philosophers (Midrash *Exod. R.* xxx. 9).[21]

With regard to the Jews in the Roman Empire, however, the scribes in Palestine followed a policy of establishing uniformity along Pharisaic lines. 1. After spirited discussions, Gamaliel II was able to lay down basic norms for defining the canon of Scripture, for recognizing the Halakha of Hillel, and for the compulsory recitation of the Eighteen Benedictions in the synagogue.[22] 2. Furthermore, the dependence of all Jews upon the scribes in Palestine found concrete expression in the introduction of a rabbinic school tax of two drachmas, replacing the priestly temple tax and competing with the Emperor's tax. The suggestion for this tax probably came after the fall of Jerusalem from the rabbis in the Parthian Empire, who, at Nisibis and Nehardea in Mesopotamia, had set up large-scale protected centers for the collection of temple tribute (Philo *De Legatione ad Gaium* 216; Josephus *Ant.* xviii. 311–13); they could immediately send the money under military escort to the Palestinian scholars instead of to the priests. The rabbinic double drachma was only gradually introduced throughout the Roman Empire, and it was said to be a freewill contribution. Agents of the synagogues, called "apostles," had charge of the collection and forwarding of the funds. Until the third and fourth centuries they sent the annual contributions of the Jewish communities to the president or chief rabbi of the Palestinian school, who bore the honorific title of "prince," "ethnarch," or "patriarch."[23] All this contributed to the Pharisaic intensifica-

---

[21] W. Bacher, *Die Agada der Tannaiten,* Vol. 1 (2d ed., 1903), pp. 73–95, esp. p. 79.

[22] J. Bornstein, "Gamaliel II," in *Encyclopaedia judaica,* Vol. 7 (1931), cols. 82–89; R. Gordis, "Gamaliel II," in *The Universal Jewish Encyclopedia,* Vol. 4 (1948), pp. 506–508.

[23] For documentation, see Schürer, Vol. 1, p. 659; Vol. 2, p. 197; Vol. 3, pp. 77, 101.

tion of Judaism, and also distinguished practicing Jews from the outside world. However, the seizure of power by the Pharisaic scribes did not in itself lead to political or social tensions with the Roman Empire.

Of course, the picture is quite different when we take into account the activity of the Zealots, which continued despite the defeat; this movement affected primarily the Jewish lower classes. Their fanatical resistance to the Greeks and Romans did not come to an end with the fall of Jerusalem in 70, but continued on in Palestine for several years and then gradually spread to other lands (Josephus *Bell.* vii. 252–455). It also expressed itself for several decades in apocalyptic propaganda, until at the beginning of the second century, under Trajan, nationalism exploded once more in a second war between Jews and Romans.

1. In the First Jewish War, the Menahem Zealots had been led by Eleazar Jairi after the end of the year 66 (see above, p. 259). After the conquest of Jerusalem in 70 they continued to hold out for a long time in three Herodian fortresses near the Dead Sea, which were besieged by the legionaries ordered to remain in Judea. Masada, the extraordinarily well-protected aerie defended by Eleazar himself, did not fall until April of 72, after furious efforts on the part of the siege troops and the fanatical suicide of the defenders.[24]

2. Since the resistance fighters could do nothing more in Palestine, they sought to continue the revolt in Egypt. There *sicarii* who had fled to the side of the Egyptian Jews fomented unrest; in 72, this constrained the prefect Lupus to close the temple at Leontopolis (see above, p. 60) and his successor to confiscate the temple property and in fact prohibit worship and assembly at the site.

[24] Chronologically it should be noted that Josephus sets the fall of Masada in the month of April in the fourth year of Vespasian (Josephus *Bell.* vii. 219, 409). If one reckons precisely from the official proclamation of Vespasian as Emperor on 1 July 69, one arrives at April 73. But Josephus is referring rather vaguely to the calendar year and therefore means April 72; for later he mentions the consequences in Egypt [see above, §2] under Julius Lupus (*Bell.* vii. 420), who died in 72. See E. Groag, "Julius, 330," in *PRE*, Vol. 10 (1917), cols. 664 f.

3. The revolt of the *sicarii* then moved to Cyrene under the leadership of a weaver named Jonathan, who sought to present messianic signs to a crowd encamped in the desert. The Roman governor of Cyrene-Crete, Catullus Messalinus, dispersed the crowd about 74. He was able to track down Jonathan and arrest him.[25] Jonathan, however, accused Jewish businessmen of supporting the movement, and Catullus went so far as to inform Vespasian that the Jewish upper class in Alexandria and Rome was behind the revolution. Josephus, himself under suspicion, naturally rejected the accusation with indignation (Josephus *Bell.* vii. 447–50). On the recommendation of Titus, who in 75 had Bernice and Agrippa II with him (see above, p. 287), Vespasian acquitted the prominent Jews of the charge. Because of Josephus' restraint, it is not possible to say what circles were actually connected with this Zealot uprising in the province Cyrene-Crete. Yet it was hardly by mere coincidence that at about this time the New Testament Letter to Titus had to warn against anarchistic activity on the part of Jewish propagandists on Crete (Titus 1:10).

In Jewish apocalyptic of the Flavian period a most malicious note was struck against the Roman Empire and the imperial house; these writings must have encouraged the Zealot opposition, although the authors of the apocalypses had in mind passive resistance. 1. The Revelation of Baruch, preserved in Syriac, declared, with an unmistakable reference to Vespasian or Titus, that the destroyer of Jerusalem would perish soon after his Jewish triumph (A.D. 71), whereupon all their enemies would fall before the Jews (II Bar. 67:7; 68:3). 2. The apocalypse called II Esdras (in the Vulgate, IV Esdras) preserved in Latin, looked forward to the rebuilding of Jerusalem (II Esd. 10:44), but also vented its wrath against the Flavians, particularly Domitian, in whom the arrogance of the Roman eagle would reach its height

[25] Catullus had been co-consul with Domitian in 73: Gsell (cited above, p. 272, n. 5), pp. 19 f., so that his governorship of the province Cyrene-Crete can be dated to about 74.

before the Messianic lion should punish the Roman Empire (II Esd. 11:35, 40).

Such disguised propaganda against the Emperor contributed to the continued existence of the Zealot movement. During the Flavian period, the Zealot fire smoldered beneath the surface, but did not go out. In the first third of the second century, the Jewish revolutionaries twice more fanned the flames, once under Trajan and once under Hadrian (see below, pp. 315 f.).

2) Christianity

In this section we shall examine primarily a) the political situation of the church under the Flavians, 69–96; then we shall say a few words about b) their social attitude with respect to the Jews, the Greeks, and the Romans. A study of this attitude should be useful for an historical understanding of the latest writings of the New Testament and the earliest writings of Apostolic Fathers.

a) The Political Situation

Nero's local persecution of Christians in 65 did not leave the Romans hostile to the church, but if anything sympathetic toward the victims (Tacitus *Ann.* xv. 44. 5). During the First Jewish War, 66–70, and the Roman civil war in 69, the attention of the public was distracted from the Christians, so that persecution did not suggest itself.[26]

Contemporary documents do not reveal Vespasian's attitude toward the church, but Christian writers of the second century emphasized his toleration (Hegesippus in Eusebius *Hist.* iii. 17; Melito *ibid.* iv. 26. 9). Tertullian found it remarkable that an ardent opponent of the Jews like Vespasian did not apply any Roman laws against the Christians (Tertullian *Apologeticus* v. 8); the context shows that he was referring to the general prohibition of associations, which later, under Trajan, was turned against the church (see below). In point of fact, after his victory in 70 and his

---

[26] A. Linsenmayer, *Die Bekämpfung des Christentums durch den römischen Staat bis zum Tode des Kaisers Julian* (1905), p. 65.

triumph in 71, Vespasian no longer attacked Judaism. On the contrary: despite the unrest in Cyrene reported to him in 74, he let Titus persuade him to express his confidence in the Jewish upper class (see above, p. 290). If the once-rebellious Jews were treated with toleration, it seems all the more reasonable to assume the same treatment for the peace-loving Christians. Vespasian probably did not equate Jews and Christians; for, so far as we know, the latter did not have to pay the Capitoline tax. He probably looked upon them as two parallel communities of *peregrini,* to whom, by old tradition, the prohibition of associations was not to apply. Only later Christian writers made Vespasian out to be a persecutor,[27] and legendary traditions placed hostility toward Linus of Rome and Apollinaris of Ravenna in his reign.

What can be said of Vespasian with respect to his toleration of the church is also true of Titus. As crown prince, Titus backed Jewish interests and seems for this very reason to have had no occasion to attack Christian interests. At any rate, there is no evidence for any persecution during his reign.

Domitian later put an end to this toleration, though not during the first third of his reign. He wanted to continue the policies of his father, and for this reason apparently left the church inviolate at first. For the first twelve years of his reign, 81–92, there is no evidence for any persecution of Christians. Critical senators and philosophers he attacked mercilessly, but he aided the middle class and *humiliores;* for this reason collective actions against the Christians, most of whom belonged to these groups, were contrary to his interests. Furthermore, the Christian faith was no more illegal than Judaism or the religion of Isis. Domitian's ideological measures were directed exclusively against movements that might impair the primacy of Rome and the Emperor; as long as Jews and Christians were not attempting any political machinations, they did not concern him. Furthermore, he had his hands full with declared enemies until 93: the

---

[27] S. Giet, *L'Apocalypse et l'histoire* (1957), pp. 133 f.

aristocrats and philosophers in Rome, the Germans and Eastern Europeans along the Rhine and the Danube.

In the years 93–96, however, when Domitian had finished his efforts to stabilize the northern borders of the Empire and had turned to the strengthening of his domestic authority and his plans for expansion to the east (Statius *Silvae* iv. i. 39–43), the religious trials mentioned above began. Christians, too, were affected.

In the First Letter of Clement, generally considered to have been written about 95, the Christian community in Rome informed the Christians at Corinth that recently, i.e., about A.D. 94, terrible afflictions had come upon them, and that they were expecting circus martyrdoms like those during the persecution of Peter and Paul (I Clement 1:1a; 7:1b). Although the feared encounters with wild beasts, etc., are not depicted in any sources and were probably not carried out by Domitian, the First Letter of Clement bears witness to official action against the Christians of Rome. This was certainly connected with Domitian's final offensive against the aristocrats and philosophers, which began in 93. Eusebius confirms the chain of events by his statement that in 93 Domitian persecuted Roman *nobiles,* extended the persecution to Christians in 94 (when John was banished to Patmos), and in 95 expelled the philosophers and astrologers from Rome once more (Eusebius *Chron.* 93–95; ed. Helm, pp. 191 f.). That the Christians were suspected of social opposition is shown by the Roman letter, since it warns against anarchistic tendencies at Corinth (I Clement 1:1b, etc.).

Pliny was the governor of the province Bithynia, and there conducted religio-political trials directed against the Christians in 113 under Trajan. In the course of his hearings some individuals were discovered who had publicly renounced their faith twenty years before (Pliny *Epistulae* x. 96. 6). This points to a persecution of Christians in northwest Asia Minor conducted by the government around 94, under Domitian, whether upon orders from the Emperor or on analogy with measures then being taken in Rome. In writing to

Trajan, Pliny described these hearings of Christians *("cognitiones de christianis")* as a practice long familiar to the government, which he had pursued at once upon taking office; his only purpose in writing was to get authoritative instructions about the legal details. In his eyes, the resolute Christians were criminals on two counts: first, their congregational organization was a transgression of the Roman prohibition of associations (Pliny *Epistulae* x. 96. 7) ; second, their faith made them refuse to take part in the official state cult of images and sacrifice *(ibid.,* 5, 6, 10). Pliny probably took over this interpretation from the local authorities who had persecuted the Christians under Domitian. He had to admit, however, that the Christians he interrogated or tortured exhibited little of the anarchistic attitude he had expected from his knowledge of the Greek associations.

The Apocalypse of John presupposes a persecution of the seven churches of Asia (Rev. 1:9; etc.). Although the figurative pronouncements of this book would admit various datings, a dating concurrent with the religious trials in A.D. 94 at Rome and especially with the above-mentioned persecution in 94 in nearby Bithynia provides the most natural historical setting for the afflictions described: John's banishment to Patmos (Rev. 1:9), the execution of Antipas at Pergamum (2:13), and the martyrdom of many Christians quite generally (6:9). Traditions of the second century also connected this Asiatic persecution with the reign of Domitian (Acts of John 5; Irenaeus *Adversus Haereses* v. 30. 3). Jews seem to have come forward as informers (Rev. 6:9), and are said to have directed charges of atheism and anti-social leanings against the Christians (Acts of John 3), perhaps in connection with the *fiscus Judaicus,* which probably offered many occasions to show the officials the difference between Jews and Christians. While the Jews retained their privileges, the Christians in the province of Asia could probably be charged with crimes against the state religion and disobeying the prohibition of associations, as happened in Bithynia under Pliny, so that tools of the Emperor ordered Christians who refused to recant to be punished as atheists and anarchists.

Hegesippus, a second-century Jewish Christian collector of traditions, also heard that in this period leading Christians in Palestine were exposed to the suspicion of insubordination. According to his account, Domitian ordered the arrest of two grandsons of Jude, a brother of Jesus, because of their popularity as descendants of David (Eusebius *Hist*. iii. 19. 1—20. 6). When these simple peasants stood before him, however, he found them politically and financially inoffensive and put an end to the persecution (*ibid*., 20. 5). The origin and details of the account hardly suggest that it is an unhistorical legend; neither is the episode unparalleled, for the Oriental philosopher Apollonius of Tyana was summoned before the Emperor in similar fashion (Philostratus *Apollonius* vii. 9).

The religious trials under Domitian reached their peak toward the end of 95 in the sensational execution of the ex-consuls (1) Acilius Glabrio and (2) Flavius Clemens, as well as the banishment of (3) Flavia Domitilla, the latter's wife (see above, p. 280). We shall now discuss the relationship of these three with Christianity, which is assumed by several scholars and denied by others.

The following biographical data may be considered established (thanks mostly to Suetonius *Domitian* x. 2; xv. 1; Dio *History* lxvii. 14. 13) : 1. Glabrio was a member of the highest nobility. In 91, while still a young man, he had been co-consul with Trajan. During the course of a festival, at the Emperor's command, he had to fight with beasts, was successful (confirmed by Juvenal *Satires* iv. 99 ff.), but was later exiled and in 95 executed by the sword (according to Juvenal *Satires* iv. 95 f.). 2. Clemens was a member of the imperial family. After his brother Flavius Sabinus had been executed by Domitian in 89 for associating with the philosophers, and for other reasons, Clemens was the most prominent citizen of the Empire after Domitian: he was the cousin of the Emperor, husband of Domitian's niece, Domitilla, and father of the two princes Vespasian the Younger and Domitian the Younger whom Domitian had adopted with an eye to the succession. (Smyrna, for example, struck special medals in honor of the elder prince.) [28] There is no evidence that Clemens pursued the usual official career; he is, rather, accused of idleness *("contemptissima inertia,"* Suetonius *Domitian* xv. 1). Nevertheless, the senate was able to appoint Domitian and Clemens consuls for New Year's 95—flattering the Emperor for his willingness to assume the office of consul for the seventeenth time (Statius *Silvae* iv. 1). But in the same year Clemens was suddenly accused and executed. 3. Domitilla, his wife, was the daughter of Domitian's late sister; as a result of the adoption of her sons by Domitian, she acquired extraordinary authority in the eyes of the people. Inscriptions show that she had numerous clients and gave away several parcels of property south of the South Gate of Rome to serve as burial places for deceased members of her household *(Corpus inscriptionum latinarum,* VI. 8942 and 16246); there the Christian catacombs of Domitilla gradually developed.[29] She was not executed, but was banished to one of the Pontine Islands west of Naples, to which ladies of the imperial house had frequently had to withdraw; according to Dio, it was the tiny island Pandatera (Eusebius, *Hist.* iii. 18. 4, simply mentions Pontia, the main island).

With regard to the legal question, the sources point in part to an interest on the part of these three in Judaism or Christianity. Suetonius, assuming merely political motivation on the part of the Emperor, stated that Glabrio was slain as one of the revolutionaries *("molitores rerum novarum,"* Suetonius *Domitian* x. 2) and Clemens on the basis of a very faint suspicion *("ex tenuissima suspicione,"* xvi. 1); Domitilla is mentioned only later, without comment, as the patroness of the tyrannicide (xvii. 1). The extent to which religious factors entered into the proceedings did not interest the worldly Suetonius.

Dio, however, considered religious factors as well as secular. On the one hand, according to his epitomator, he thought that the Emperor was jealous of Glabrio for killing a

[28] H. Cohen, *Description historique des monnaies frappées sous l'empire romain* 2d ed., 1 (1880), p. 539.

[29] H. Leclercq, "Domitien," in *Dictionnaire d'archéologie chrétienne et de liturgie* Vol. 4. 2 (1921), col. 1396; "Domitille, Cimitière de," *ibid.,* col. 1406.

296

great lion in a fight that Domitian himself had commanded (Dio *History* lxvii. 14. 3b) ; this apparent nonsense may be based on mocking comparisons of the lion and the Emperor (a possible allusion in Statius *Silvae* ii. 5) . On the other hand, Dio says concerning Clemens and Domitilla that they, like "many others," were accused of atheism—disavowal of the state gods (Dio *History* lxvii. 14. 2) . He described the "many others" as those "who let themselves be convinced of the Jewish attitude" (*ibid.*) . In the case of Glabrio, in addition to the tale about the lion, Dio also assumed the same charges as in the case of these "many others" (*ibid.,* 14. 3a) . As will be clear from what follows, he had in mind representatives of the Roman upper class who rejected the official worship of the Emperor and Roman gods, sympathizing instead with biblical traditions. Dio states that after the fall of Domitian, Nerva removed the many statues of his hated predecessor, acquitted those accused of lese majesty and of holding Jewish beliefs, and punished those clients who had informed against their patrons (*History* lxviii. 1. 1–2) . Archeological discoveries also confirm that in the last years of Domitian not a few of the senatorial nobility took an interest in biblical piety. As soon as possible Nerva proclaimed upon his coins this happy news for the senatorial party: the arbitrary justice connected with the *fiscus Judaicus* was abolished ("*fisci judaici calumnia sublata*") .[30] In other words, during the collection of the Jewish tax, household slaves and freedmen of the Jewish or Christian faith had divulged that their patrons were also supporters of biblical piety, and so the senate had to accuse several of its members of atheism. Dio therefore rightly emphasized that, toward the end of his reign, Domitian had punished Glabrio, Clemens, Domitilla, and "many others" (by whom Dio meant representatives of the upper class, which was central to his interest) , for a non-Roman faith characterized as sympathetic to Judaism. Politically, this did not mark the beginning of any persecution of ethnic Judaism, which still retained its "taxable freedom," but rather an attempt to deorientalize the Roman

---

[30] M. Rostowzew, "Fiscus," *PRE*, Vol. 6. 2 (1909) , col. 2404.

aristocracy. This project was particularly urgent for the Emperor in the year 95, because a more vigorous romanization of the East was in the works (we may refer once more to Statius *Silvae* iv. 1. 39–43), though Trajan was the first one able to carry out the plans.

If such connections of Roman magnates with a legitimate religion like Judaism were prosecuted by Domitian as criminal atheism, this must have held true all the more for any adherence to Christianity, which did not have legal corporate recognition. Dio mentioned only Judaism; for, to the populace as a whole, in the time of Domitian Christianity was still an offshoot of Judaism, as the writings of the church suggest in various ways (Heb. 8:8; James 1:1; Jude 5; Rev. 7:4; 21:12; I Clement 8:3; Barnabas 4:8). Despite Dio's silence, there is every possibility that Domitian included adherence to Christianity among the criminal inclinations toward Judaism on the part of prominent Romans. More than thirty years before, soldiers of the Praetorian Guard and members of the imperial household had become acquainted with the Gospel (Phil. 1:13; 4:22), which makes it quite probable that by the time of Domitian aristocratic and court circles were influenced by it.

A priori it does not seem unlikely that Glabrio, Clemens, and Domitilla were punished for being Christians. *A posteriori,* however, a distinction is necessary, because the evidence differs in each case.

It is probably more reasonable to connect Glabrio with Judaism than with Christianity, for his fight with the lion hardly suggests the attitude of the Christian martyrs. Fifty or a hundred years later, members of his family are mentioned in the catacomb of Priscilla; but that has no bearing on his own Christianity.[31]

It is highly unlikely, on the other hand, that Domitilla, had she not been interested in Christianity, would have given members of her household the burial grounds mentioned above, for which there is inscriptional evidence and where

[31] For bibliography, see K. Gross, "Domitianus," in *Reallexikon für Antike und Christentum* Vol. 4 (1959), col. 106.

famous Christian catacombs later came into being (see above, p. 296) . Eusebius preserves two snippets from secular authors, a certain Bruttius, well known in his own day, and other historians, according to which during the persecution of the Christians in 95 Domitian banished Domitilla, "the niece of Clemens" (Eusebius *Chron.* 96, ed. Helm, p. 192; *Hist.* iii. 18. 4) . There has been a misunderstanding here, since it should obviously read, "the niece of Domitian and the wife of Clemens." We may nevertheless be dealing here with significant, independent sources; John Malalas bears witness to the interest of antiquity in Bruttius' world history.[32] Taken together, the catacomb inscriptions and these quotations from Eusebius suggest that Domitilla was a patroness of the Roman Christians and was banished for this reason to the Pontine Islands.[33] But she was not necessarily a confessing member of the Roman church, as Eusebius thought. Only the later legend describes her as a virgin and martyr (*Acta SS. Nerei et Achillei* 292. 6. 1; ed. H. Achelis ["Texte und Untersuchungen," 11; Leipzig: Hinrichs, 1894]) , p. 1, ll. 16 f.; etc.) .

Ancient tradition never mentions her husband, Clemens, as a confessing Christian. There were at least two men by his name among the Christians of the apostolic and subapostolic period: about 60, a disciple of Paul at Philippi (Phil. 4:3) ; about 95, a presbyter in Rome, today referred to as Clement of Rome, who in the second century was mentioned as the author of the First Letter of Clement[34] (I Clement 65:2, subscription; Dionysius of Corinth, according to Eusebius *Hist.* iv. 23. 11) and the official correspondent for the Roman congregation (Hermas, *The Shepherd,* Vis. ii. 4. 3 may refer to him) .[35] Finally, in a historical simplification, he was called the third bishop of the Roman community (Irenaeus

[32] H. Peter, *Historicorum romanorum fragmenta* (1883) , pp. 375 ff.; *idem, Historicorum romanorum reliquiae,* Vol. 2 (1906) , pp. ccviii f.

[33] K. Gross (cited above, n. 31) , cols. 104–106, has summarized his cautious discussion as follows: "And so it appears that we must affirm some connection between Domitilla and the catacomb."

[34] A. Stuiber, "Clemens Romanus, I," in *Reallexikon für Antike und Christentum,* Vol. 3 (1957) , cols. 188–97, M. H. Shepherd, Jr., "Clement, Epistles of," in *The Interpreter's Bible,* Vol. 1 (1962) , pp. 648 f.

[35] M. Dibelius, *Der Hirt des Hermas* (1923) , pp. 422 f., 453.

Adversus Haereses iii. 8. 3) . Martyrdom is first mentioned in the case of his fourth successor, Telesphorus. But the name "Clement" was common in Rome, and does not in itself necessarily suggest the consul. Actually, no texts of the first two centuries breathe a hint that a Roman consul and cousin of the Emperor belonged to the church; there should have been some mention of so remarkable a fact. Only in the pseudo-Clementine legend, which began to grow up some time after the year 200, does Clement of Rome appear as both relative of the Emperor and successor to Peter (Pseudo-Clement *Epistle to James,* ii. 2; *Homilies* iv. 7. 2; and *passim*) .[36]

As a result of Constantine's ecclesiastical policies, after about 325 various saints associated with Peter were honored by monuments in Rome. In addition to the new basilica of Peter, the following churches were built at this time: at the catacombs of Domitilla, a church in honor of Peter's daughter, Petronilla, and also one for Domitilla's chamberlains, Nereus and Achilleus; east of the Colosseum, the lower church of San Clemente, located on top of a patrician house of the first or second century and a Mithras chapel of the third century.[37] This multiplication of monuments furthered the growth of the literary corpus attributed to Clement: in the realm of canon law, the Apostolic Constitutions; in the realm of legend, the pseudo-Clementine *Homilies* and *Recognitions*.[38] In the *Acts of Nereus and Achilleus,* written about 500, the legends about Domitilla were assembled; but even here the consul Clemens and Clement of Rome appear as two persons, uncle and nephew (*Acta SS. Nerei et Achillei* 294. b. 2; ed. Achelis, p. 8, ll. 12, 16) . Not until surprisingly late do we find the statement that the consul Clemens died

---

[36] See below note 38.

[37] H. Leclercq, "Clément, Basilique de Saint," in *Dictionnaire d'archéologie chrétienne et de liturgie,* Vol. 3. 2 (1914) , cols. 1873–1902; L. V. Bertarelli, *Roma e dintorni* (1938, reprinted 1947) , pp. 182 f.

[38] F. Nau, "Clémentins, apocryphes," in *Dictionnaire de théologie catholique,* Vol. 3. 1 (1923) , cols. 201–23; H. Rahner, "Apostolische Konstitutionen," in *Lexikon für Theologie und Kirche,* Vol. 1 (2d ed., 1957) , col. 759; B. Rehm, "Clemens Romanus, II," in *Reallexikon für Antike und Christentum,* Vol. 3 (1957) , cols. 197–206.

for Christ (Georgius Syncellus *Chronography* i. 650. 19, written about 800, but based on earlier sources) .[39]

Nevertheless, the facts about his wife Domitilla make it likely that Clemens, too, supported the church, so that he was accused of atheism purportedly on account of Jewish inclinations but in reality on account of Christian sympathies. Certainly during the time of Domitian Judaism and Christianity were still connected in the minds of many people and also in the view of the government. However, it is hard to believe in the case of this married couple, accused of the same crime under the same circumstances, that husband and wife sided with two internally different religions. In addition, Clemens' lack of interest in politics, mentioned by Suetonius (*inertia*—see p. 296) , suggests influence of Christian hope rather than obedience to the Jewish law.[40] It should not be made a question of religious prestige whether Clemens was executed on account of certain contacts with Judaism or with Christianity.[41] It would be more convenient to take Dio's remark about inclination to Jewish attitudes (see above, p. 297) in the more limited sense; but circumstances inevitably make the extended sense of relationship with Christianity seem likely. No more than in the case of Domitilla is it necessary to make Clemens out to be a baptized and confessing Christian. The simplest solution is to consider them both patrons of Christians, a circumstance that, given the situation and the persons involved, may well have struck the government as treason against Rome and the Emperor.

Despite all uncertainties in detail, the pagan and Christian traditions concerning Clemens, Domitilla, and other victims in the year 95–96 appear to suggest that Roman aristocrats were accused of atheistic and Judaistic conduct, but that a few of the most prominent among them had

[39] Peter *Historicorum romanorum fragmenta* (cited above, p. 299, n. 32) , p. 376.

[40] Gross (cited above, p. 298, n. 31) , col. 104: political inaction was "a charge also made in other instances against the secluded life of the Christians (Origen *Contra Celsum* 8. 2; Tertullian *De pallio* 5) ."

[41] H. J. Leon, *The Jews of Ancient Rome* (1960) , pp. 33 ff., assumes that Domitian attacked only Jewish proselytes; he denies that those interested in Christianity were persecuted at all.

shown Christian sympathies.[42] In this context Domitian's purpose was domination of the Roman aristocracy,[43] not an attack upon the Christian faith.

All the same, the political situation of Christianity was difficult under the Flavians, and under Domitian especially so. During the whole Flavian period, dissatisfaction with the autocratic Emperor and contacts with the upper-class opposition were essentially dangerous for the Christians; but not until 93–96 did Domitian defend the ideals of Emperorship and Romanism so vigorously against the aristocracy and the Orient that adherents and patrons of the church were persecuted. In response, the attitude of the church toward the state underwent a change.

b) The Social Attitude

During the subapostolic period, A.D. 67–100, the number of Christians apparently multiplied rapidly. Exact statistics are impossible, but the following considerations may provide a rough picture of the growth.[44]

In the period before A.D. 67, the Jews frequently reacted with violence against the Christians, especially because of Paul's successes; this suggests that the church was no inconsiderable minority in the Jewish world. On psychological grounds we may assume that Christians and those connected with them were outnumbered by Jews and proselytes no more than fifty to one, for a smaller sect would have gone almost unnoticed. If the Jews in the New Testament world numbered about 2,000,000 (higher figures are generally given for the Roman Empire as a whole), then shortly before the year 67 the Christians numbered some 40,000 believers and adherents. Most would be found in Palestine, Transjordan, and Syria, perhaps 25,000 altogether; the struggle for men's souls in Galatia and Ephesus in the time of Paul ap-

---

[42] J. Vogt, "Christenverfolgung, I, historisch," in *Reallexikon für Antike und Christentum* Vol. 2 (1954), col. 1169.

[43] Vogt, *ibid.*

[44] A. Harnack, *Die Mission und Ausbreitung des Christentums in den ersten drei Jahrhunderten*, Vol. 2 (3d ed., 1915), pp. 1–15, assembles quotations from the sources to illustrate this growth and discusses them in detail, but without calculating the actual figures for the first century.

pears to let us assume the presence of at least 5,000 Christians and their associates in Asia Minor; for Hellas and Italy about 2,000 may suffice, and smaller numbers for other lands.

Soon after A.D. 100 a report sent by Pliny to Trajan describing Bithynia in the year 113 illustrates the spread of Christianity (Pliny *Epistulae* x. 96. 9 f.) :

> This contagious superstition has spread not only through the cities, but also throughout villages and rural areas. Its spread may still perhaps be arrested and restricted [Pliny is here thinking of his coercive measures]. It is certain in any case that the almost devastated temples are being frequented once more, and the long-abolished festivals are again being celebrated.

Even if Pliny is exaggerating for strategic reasons, his letter provides a vivid picture of the growth of the church in Bithynia, and, by projection, in western Asia Minor. If the local pagans considered the Christians so ominous a factor, they can hardly have numbered less than a fiftieth of the total population of Asia Minor. But Asia Minor, with its many industrial cities and semitropical orchards in the west, had probably more than 4,000,000 inhabitants (the population of modern Turkey is about 25,000,000, most of whom live in the west). This means that after the year 100 we may reckon with at least 80,000 Christians and their associates in Asia Minor. Perhaps the figure appears surprising, but if anything it is probably too low. With this as a starting point, we may calculate theoretically the total number of Christians. It may be that Asia Minor was the most populous church province in the subapostolic period, as the relevant documents of the New Testament show (e.g., Rev. 1:4— seven congregations in the province of Asia alone). But one glance at the preceding and following periods shows that other lands touched by Christianity shared to some extent in this growth. In addition, Christian communities were already to be found in the prefecture of Egypt, with Alexandria as its center (*Pap. Rylands,* 457, fragments of the Gospel of John dating from 100–120), in the province of Cyrene-Crete (Titus 1:5), and possibly also in the provinces of Africa, with Carthage as its center, and southern Spain, with

Cordoba as its center.[45] At the turn of the century, Asia Minor can scarcely have claimed more than a quarter of the total number of Christians. On the basis of these calculations, each of which gives the probable minimum, for the church as a whole about A.D. 100 we arrive at a total of more than 320,000 believers and adherents. That would be about eight times as many as a third of a century before. A glance at the following forty years appears to justify the assumption of so rapid a growth, for about A.D. 140 a Greek-speaking preacher pointed out to his congregation that, at least in his area, the Christians outnumbered the Jews (II Clement 2:3).[46]

We may now summarize the statistics for the church between the years 67 and 100; they are of necessity hypothetical and approximate, but are hardly exaggerated:

Prior to the year 67:

Jews and proselytes in the New Testament world:	about 2,000,000
Christians and their associates in the Roman Empire (figured on the basis of Paul's conflicts as at least a fiftieth of the number of Jews):	about 40,000

After the year 100:

Population of Asia Minor:	more than 4,000,000
Christians and their associates in Asia Minor (figured on the basis of Pliny's letter as at least a fiftieth of the population of Asia Minor):	more than 80,000
Christians and their associates in the Roman Empire (figuring the church in Asia Minor as a quarter of the whole church):	more than 320,000

If the church increased more than eightfold during the subapostolic period, while at the same time the Flavians were vigorously espousing the sovereignty of the Emperor and of Rome, the question of the social attitude of the Christians toward (1) the Jews, (2) the Greeks, and (3) the Romans became more and more complex. The discussion can be followed concretely through the Christian documents of the Flavian period. We must first compare the Pastoral Epistles (I and II Timothy and Titus), written by some

[45] The later evidence from these lands is cited by B. Kötting, "Christentum, I, Ausbreitung," in *Reallexikon für Antike und Christentum,* Vol. 2 (1954), cols. 1142 ff., 1149 ff.
[46] L. von Hartling, "Die Zahl der Christen zu Beginn des 4. Jahrhunderts," *Zeitschrift für katholische Theologie,* Vol. 68 (1934), pp. 234–52, figures about two million toward the end of the third century.

disciple standing in a personal relation with Paul but without accommodation to his style, and thus probably to be dated to the time of Vespasian (see below) ; next the later Ecclesiastical Epistles (Hebrews, James, II Peter, Jude, I, II, and III John) , which constitute a quite distinctive group and can best be dated in the time of Domitian in view of the problems they discuss (I Peter differs linguistically and in content, and is probably earlier; but II Peter fits beautifully with this group, while to date it later appears unnatural) ; likewise the earlier writings of the Apostolic Fathers (Barnabas, I Clement) , which are closely related to the Ecclesiastical Epistles; and finally the Revelation of John, which both ancient tradition and modern scholarship assign to the last years of Domitian.

1. The Jewish War (66–70) first necessitated a reexamination of the Christian attitude toward the Jews. Immediately after this war, the Jews and Christians in the Roman Empire stood on equal legal footing: both were associations of *peregrini,* given approximately equal treatment and sometimes identified, although the Jews remained more numerous and preserved an identity essentially ethnic, while the Christians were united exclusively by their faith. Jewish apocalyptic circles already considered life in the Diaspora a necessity that would pass away only at the Last Judgment (II Bar. 1:4; II Esd. 10:23) . For leading Christians it was even easier to describe the life of aliens and exiles in the world (already recognized by I Pet. 1:1; 2:11) as divinely appointed destiny (Heb. 11:13–16; James 1:1; I Clement, salutation) . As a result of this parallelism, a new rapprochement took place in the Diaspora between Jews and Christians. Many of the now homeless Jews were converted to Christianity, so that Gamaliel II ordered that there be added to the Eighteen Benedictions (see above, pp. 121, 288) a curse against Jewish Christians (*Shemoneh 'esreh* 12; cf. Justin *Dialogue* 16. 137; Talmud Babli *Ber.* 28b) .

This influx of Jews into the church brought new problems that are reflected in the writings of the subapostolic period.

a.   In the Pastoral Epistles, judaizing tendencies of some Christians in Asia and on Crete are rejected: legalistic impertinence (I Tim. 1:7; Titus 1:14; 3:9), Gnostic disregard of the physical world (I Tim. 6:20; Titus 1:16), and social rebellion (II Tim. 2:22, which is directed against rebellious disposition; [47] Titus 1:10, 16; 2:14, which is directed against insubordination and Zealotism). Instead the author exhorts to political and social solidarity (I Tim. 2:1–6; Titus 3:1–8). The historical background may very well be the Zealot movement that emanated from Cyrene in A.D. 74 (see above, p. 290). Crete formed part of the same province, and from there the movement could spread to Asia (see above, p. 284). Vespasian ordered the proconsul to put down this neo-Zealot movement, but matters never reached the point of a general inquisition, and the danger to the church seems to have passed. It is clear in any case that in the Pastoral Epistles the Pauline circle was concerned to reject a form of Judaism hostile to the world order, which could easily have turned Christianity against pagan authority and the pagan world.

b.   The Epistle to the Hebrews attacks another form of Judaism under Domitian. This letter was addressed to Christians who wanted to be "Hebrews," who believed they could use Judaism as a disguise and thereby rescue Christianity from persecution (Heb. 1:4—the inferiority of the Old Covenant; 2:3—the danger involved in relapse; 2:9—the superiority of Christ's suffering; in the rest of the letter these themes are developed with all possible variations). The Epistle of Barnabas, too, which belongs to the Apostolic Fathers, rejected such inclinations toward Judaism (Barnabas 2:4–10; etc.). It also comforted its readers with a prophecy concerning Domitian's fall, which had been decreed by God (4:4–6; like the three heads in II Esd. 11:30, the three horns mentioned here are an apocalyptic symbol for the three Flavians).

c.   The problem of a rapprochement with Judaism

---

[47] The context suggests that here the Greek *neoterikaì epithumíai* does not mean "youthful," but "revolutionary passions." Cf. *neoterizō* in the sense of "subvert."

cropped up in still different way for John in Revelation. First the prophet felt disturbed by those Jews who were still hostile to the church (Rev. 2:9; 3:9), but then rejoiced all the more over the future sealing of 144,000 Jews from the twelve tribes (Rev. 7:4). Behind this expectation obviously lies the experiences of numerous instances of Jewish conversions in the time of the Flavians. In noncanonical apocalyptic we also find several instances of the borrowing of Jewish elements on the part of Christian tradition, such as those in the Ascension of Isaiah and the Second Book of Enoch.

2. The rapid growth of the church in the Flavian period particularly affected its relationship to the Greeks, for in western Asia Minor and around the Aegean Sea the Greeks undoubtedly provided most of the converts. Features typical of Hellenism were therefore easily taken over by Christianity, giving rise to a series of social and moral problems such as the Pastoral and Catholic Epistles discuss.

a. In the industrial cities of Asia and Greece, the Gospel from the very beginning attracted many of the poor, many domestic slaves, dock workers, factory workers (I Cor. 1:26; Eph. 6:5; I Pet. 2:18). The Pastoral and the Catholic Epistles, in different ways, reflect the worries of the proletariat (I Tim. 6:1; Titus 2:9; James 2:5, 15; II Pet. 2:19; I John 3:17). Quite understandably, a tendency toward materialization of eschatology (*"philía toû kósmou,"* James 4:4) found fertile soil here, because many simple people wanted to hasten the promised righteousness and bliss, to realize it within the church and not leave it to the future. Therefore the later writers of the New Testament had to exhort earnestly to social equanimity and eschatological patience (I Tim. 2:2; II Tim. 3:1–11; Titus 2:12 f.; James 1:3; 3:13—4:10; 5:7; II Pet. 1:6; 3:3).

b. For the church's comprehensive social undertakings, affiliations with the Greek system of associations were practically inevitable and in part advantageous, since these associations were of fundamental importance for Hellenistic society. Such affiliations, however, also had disadvantages, because the Greek societies and associations had from time immemorial inculcated patriotism, fondness for criticism, ambition, and sociability in a way that could make both political and ecclesiastical discipline very difficult. As in other expressions of the Hellenistic way of life, the model was the capital of the East, Alexandria. Philo gave the following description of conditions there (Philo *In Flaccum* 136 f.) :

> There are in the city fraternities [Greek *thiasoi*] with many members. Their unifying principle is nothing salutary, but rather strong drink and intemperance, drunkenness and, consequently, violence. So the citizens popularly call them "encounters" and "banquets." In all, or at least most, of the fraternities the leading role is played by Isidore [the chancellor of the gymnasium], who is termed drinking-master, banquet-master, and municipal agitator. Whenever he wants to create disorder, they all assemble at his signal and shout or do whatever he tells them.

In 55 b.c., Rome had passed the Licinian law, later reinforced by imperial decree, prohibiting the formation of new societies of this sort, because organization of the proletariat and the citizenry was looked upon as a source of unrest. Nevertheless, in the imperial period Asia Minor, with its industrial cities and wage earners,[48] experienced a vigorous growth of the society-system.[49] The Romans were well aware that freethinking and opposition found especially fertile soil there. How suspicious the Asian fraternities appeared to the government can be seen from Trajan's refusal, after a fire in Nicomedia, to allow his Bithynian governor Pliny to organize a volunteer fire department there, because the Greek societies were known to create difficulties (Pliny *Epistulae* x. 33–34). A similar skepticism was harbored toward the Italian fraternities.

It was necessary for the church to avert all the abuses, temptations, or even suspicions that went hand in hand with the society-system.

[48] T. R. Broughton, "Roman Asia Minor," in T. Frank (ed.) , *An Economic Survey of Ancient Rome* Vol. 4 (1938) , pp. 839 f.
[49] F. Poland, *Geschichte des griechischen Vereinswesens* (1909) , p. 528; Broughton (cited in preceding note) , pp. 839–49; M. Rostowzew, *Storia economica e sociale dell' impero romano* (1946) , pp. 210 ff.; idem, *Die hellenistische Welt*, Vol. 2 (1955) , pp. 845 f., 1014; Vol. 3 (1956) , pp. 1372 f.

(1) Private religious societies usually sought rich patrons, preferably representatives of the nobility or the equestrians wearing golden rings, i.e., having political influence (James 2:1-7). Under the anti-aristocratic Emperor Domitian, this was a dangerous strategy. By bribing the *divisores,* functionaries whose job was to divide up the perquisites, these rich magnates could take advantage of the members of a congregation for political purposes,[50] just as Balak used Balaam to disseminate heathen propaganda in Israel (II Pet. 2:15; Jude 11).

(2) Throughout the Hellenistic world, the banquets of the societies often brought dionysian joy to the poor. Because the Christian love meals reminded superficial individuals of these banquets (I Pet. 4:3 f.), they easily became occasions for expressions of bravado and insolence toward all authority (Jude 8-15: during the agape meals, the seducers excelled in reviling and insolence, Greek *asébeia,* "lese majesty").

(3) Within this framework propagandists on behalf of political or social freedom would find adherents among the Greeks and the slaves (I Pet. 2:16), although their activity, aiming at corruption, meant only continued slavery to corruption (II Pet. 2:18-20). How important it was for the church to avoid these excesses or misinterpretations, which came about so easily through contact with the associations and their riotous banquets, can be seen from Pliny's inquisition in Bithynia, soon after the time of Domitian. Taking the Emperor's prohibition of associations as his starting point, Pliny investigated particularly the social conduct and eating customs of the Christians (Pliny *Epistulae* x. 96. 7). Certainly the church's affiliations with the system of societies and banquets popular in the Hellenistic world facilitated evangelization of the masses and greatly promoted charity among the poor. As has been indicated, however, it frequently contributed to a materialistic interpretation of Christian eschatology and the mobilization of Gentile resistance.

Quite apart from the society-system, Christian social work

[50] W. Liebemann, "Divisor," in *PRE,* Vol. 5. 1 (1903), cols. 1237 f.

was a popular object of slander (I Tim. 6:1; Titus 2:9) , thanks to the missionary and charitable successes achieved under the Flavians. That a certain degree of envy was also present can be gathered from a late but illuminating witness provided, unwillingly, by Julian the Apostate: "While the poor were overlooked and disregarded by the [pagan] priests, the godless Galileans understood the situation. . . . By means of their so-called Agape, by hospitality and waiting on table . . . they have seduced innumerable men into godlessness (Julian *Ep.,* ed. Spanheim 305. B-D) .[51]

c. A third characteristic element of Greek society, toward which the subapostolic generation had to define its position, was philosophy. Even the missionary journeys of Paul and his companions had brought about debates between theology and philosophy, for example, on account of the skepticism of the Epicureans and Stoics in Athens (Acts 17:18–32) , or thanks to the success of the Alexandria-trained Apollos and overemphasis on *gnosis* and *sophia* in Corinth (Acts 18:24, 27; I Cor. 1:12, 20; 8:1) , or because of a boastful Jewish-Gnostic asceticism calling itself philosophy in Colossae (Col. 2:8, 16–18) . These were isolated border skirmishes. In the Flavian period it became necessary for the church as a whole to declare its position with respect to the popular philosophical movements, for the positive reason that the Gospel was preached to ever-increasing numbers of people educated in the Hellenistic tradition, and for the negative reason that at the time the Emperor and the philosophers were at swords' points (see above, pp. 269–81) .

On the positive side, it should be noted that all sorts of phrases were borrowed from the everyday language of philosophy; the Greeks could understand these more easily than the biblical terms. The Hellenistic population of the Roman Empire was familiar with all kinds of philosophic speculation and propaganda: offshoots of Oriental mysticism on the one extreme and the schools of Athenian rationalism on the

---

[51] Material on the church's poor relief and the Hellenistic society-system is found in B. Reicke, *Diakonie, Festfreude und Zelos* (cited above, p. 223, n. 55) , pp. 21–164, 308–93.

other. Among the latter, the following schools, developed by Asiatics in the city of Socrates, were especially influential: the Cynics, with their skepticism about civilization (principally represented by Diogenes of Sinope, ca. 400–325 B.C.) ; the Epicureans, intellectual aristocrats (their pioneer was Epicurus of Samos, 341–270 B.C.) ; and above all the cosmopolitan Stoics (a school founded by Zeno of Cyprus, 335–263 B.C.), who also set the style for Hellenistic Judaism (IV Macc. 1:16, the theme of the book, is a Stoic quotation). Representatives of this popular philosophy proclaimed their idea of liberty, equality, and the pursuit of happiness everywhere, in the marketplaces and in symposia; and their idiom gradually permeated everyday language. For this reason, the Pastoral and Ecclesiastical Epistles borrowed a series of philosophic-sounding expressions. God, for instance, is called "the King of the eons, the immortal, invisible, only God" (I Tim. 1:17), "who . . . dwells in unapproachable light" (6:16), "the Father of lights with whom there is no variation" (James 1:17) ; he bestows "knowledge of the truth" (I Tim. 2:4) and allows men to "become partakers of divine nature" (II Pet. 1:4). For the moment, these expressions did not indicate dependence on philosophic dogmas, only the adoption of Greek phraseology. Only in the second century did Greek philosophy put its stamp on Christian theology, as Alexandrian writers gradually drew upon the writings of Plato and Aristotle, Posidonius and Philo.

On the negative side, it is remarkable how the Pastoral and Ecclesiastical Epistles look upon philosophy as a social weapon. (1) The gnosis, "knowledge," rejected by the Pastoral Epistles (I Tim. 6:20) is shot through with Jewish ritual laws and racism (Greek *"mûthoi kaì genealogiai,* I Tim. 1:4, etc.: *"mûthoi kaì entolai,"* Tit. 1:4), which promote controversy in the church but hinder brotherly love and missionary work, particularly among the Greeks and Romans (1 Tim. 1:4–7; 2:4; 6:4, 11, 20; II Tim. 2:14, 23–26; Titus 2:11; 3:4, 9). (2) Among the Catholic Epistles, the Letter of James stresses at the very outset that in worldly afflictions true wisdom could be asked only of God (James

1:5). He goes on to warn the reader against having recourse to men of wealth (1:10 f.; 2:2–7), against expressing social dissatisfaction (1:20, 26; 3:8 f.; 4:2), and against adopting materialistic, aggressive wisdom (3:13–18). The historical background of these motifs becomes clear when the situation of the Flavian period is compared. As we have outlined above, many senators and the philosophers associated with them, particularly under Domitian, stood in opposition to the monarchy and incited the lower classes that wanted to better their position to political unrest, especially in the East. In attacking this opposition, the Epistle of James emphasized that the materialists, despite their claims and promises, oppressed those who were really poor (5:4 ff.). (3) The Second Epistle of Peter also attacked teachers of false doctrine claiming to be philosophers, who based their teaching on myths (II Pet. 1:16) and, at the behest of powerful masters (2:15), agitated on behalf of ostensible freedom (2:19).

The use of philosophy for social agitation condemned by these letters was typical of the Flavian period. We may recall Domitian's repeated measures against the Roman magnates and against the Greek philosophers they patronized. Although the most famous wandering agitators, the Stoic-Cynic Dio Chrysostom and the Pythagorean Apollonius of Tyana (see above, pp. 276, 278), had no connection with the church, they provide a good illustration of the activity of radical philosophers in the class struggle within the Roman Empire and in the cultural struggle between East and West. The authorities writing in the name of James, Peter, and Jude wanted to keep the church above these controversies so as not to promote personal interests and materialistic eschatology.

3. Leading disciples of the Apostles therefore rejected all social agitation, whether connected with Jewish Zealotism, the Hellenistic society-system, Greek philosophy, or the Roman aristocracy. It was therefore natural for the church to take a positive attitude toward the Romans as the legitimate authorities. This was not due to political conservatism or opportunism, but to the desire to consolidate the church's

internal peace, its external mission and its eschatological hope. Jesus and Paul had recommended an attitude of loyalty toward authority (Matt. 22:21 and parallels; Rom. 13:1), as did Paul's companion Silvanus in the name of Peter (I Pet. 2:13–17). (a) The recommendations formulated by Paul were developed in the Pastoral Epistles by the addition of exhortations to intercession and submissiveness (I Tim. 2:1–7; Titus 3:1 f.); such confidence in the legitimate authorities seemed justified under Vespasian (cf. Bar. 1:11). We find a similar optimism, also based on Paul's statements, in the First Epistle of Clement (I Clement 47:1; 60:4—61:2), which was written during the religious trials of the harsh Domitian and nevertheless accorded the Roman magistrates God-given authority, glory, honor, and power (Greek *exousía, dóxa, timé, hēgemonía*). (b) On this point the Catholic Epistles were more cautious, because of the trials already afflicting the church (Heb. 10:34; 11:23; 12:3; James 1:2), and did not mention the Roman authorities in this positive way. They, too, however, were against agitation (Heb. 11:33—kingdoms are conquered only through faith; 13:14—peace with all men; James 1:14—impatience results in trials; 3:8, 14, 16—rebelliousness and intrigue bring misfortune). Malicious disdain of majesty and authorities (Greek *kuriótēs* and *dóxai*) is termed an atrocious sin (II Pet. 2:10; Jude 8). (c) In addition, several of the Ecclesiastical Epistles stress repeatedly and emphatically that piety (Greek *eusébeia*) characterizes the faithful, while the godlessness or lese majesty (Greek *asébeia*, Latin *impietas;* see above, pp. 280, 283) prosecuted by the authorities characterizes men of violence (I Tim. 1:9; II Tim. 2:16; Titus 2:12; II Pet. 2:5 f.; 3:7; Jude 4; 15, repeating the word four times).

For the author of the Book of Revelation, however, the Roman Empire and its Emperor appear as a diabolical power. Exiled to Patmos, the prophet John saw the seven hills and seven Emperors of Rome rise to power in the form of a terrible beast (Rev. 13:1 f.; 17:9). He did not summon the readers to political hostility but, instead, to trust in God's intervention and to stand fast against the emperor cult so highly developed in Asia Minor and against the compulsory measures introduced under Domitian (Rev. 2:2, 7b; etc.). John did not represent another concept of authority, but another attitude toward Roman power than that of Paul and his successors; for he had seen and experienced the tendency of the state to develop totalitarian claims.[52] For the next two centuries, as for later ages, the warnings and exhortations of the prophet turned out to be well founded and necessary.

3) *Nerva, Trajan, and the Beginnings of the Martyr Period*

When the members of the court murdered Domitian in A.D. 96 (see above, pp. 281 f.), they did so in the interests of the senatorial party. The senate appointed the aged Nerva (emperor from 96 to 98) as *princeps* and carried out a *damnatio memoriae* of the murdered man. It also instituted a change in domestic policies. Among the new measures was the abolition, immortalized on coins, of the calumnies against the Jewish proselyte system (see above, p. 297); this relaxation also helped the missionary work of the church, so that both Jews and Christians won a few years of external peace. It is significant that the senatorial party desired this change. Nerva, however, died in 98, and under his successor, Trajan, the situation changed again for both Jews and Christians.

Trajan (emperor from 98 to 117), celebrated by Roman historians, was born in southern Spain in A.D. 53. He served as governor in Upper Germany, and was adopted as crown prince by Nerva in 97 because the soldiers were demanding a worthy military successor to their admired Domitian. After taking power in 98, Trajan played his double role very skillfully, appearing to support the interests of the senators but in fact continuing the policies of Domitian. At great expense and with great profit he fought two more Dacian Wars (A.D. 101–107); he also reactivated Domitian's plans for the Orient and began a war with the Parthians, which, between 114 and 117, led to the conquest of Armenia, Mesopotamia, and Assyria-Babylonia. However, the Second Jewish War (see below) forced him to turn back. He took sick in

52 O. Cullmann, *The State in the New Testament* (1956), pp. 53–84.

Cilicia and died there in 117. Hadrian (emperor from 117 to 138), the protégé of Trajan's widow, at the time governor in Antioch, was acclaimed his successor. For tactical reasons, Hadrian abandoned the new conquests in southern Mesopotamia and Assyria-Babylonia.

Despite his cordial personal relations with senators and nobles, Trajan insisted on his majesty so forcefully among the provincials that outside of Rome his regime was in effect totalitarian, although senatorial historians and panegyrists who were among his intimates have left a flattering picture of the Emperor. After the year 100, he bore the title *optimus*, which linked him with Jupiter. The temples he founded in Pergamum, as well as other institutions, illustrate his vigorous promotion of the emperor cult. Hadrian followed the same course, and also zealously aided the growth of Hellenism in the provinces. Under both emperors, conditions in the Roman Empire were generally splendid; but this did not apply to Jews and Christians, who were exposed in various ways to the demands of absolutism.

In A.D. 115–17, Jewish Zealotism exploded once more in the Second Jewish War, which was fought out of opposition to the powerful Trajan and because there was hope of Parthian support. The war began in Cyrene and Egypt, and the revolt later spread to Mesopotamia. Tens of thousands of Greeks were slain, but the Jews lost even more of their countrymen in battles with the Romans in which they were finally defeated (Dio *History* lxviii. 32. 1–3; Eusebius *Hist.* iv. 2. 1–5). Hadrian supervised the successful counterattack as commandant of Syria.

During Hadrian's reign a local continuation of the revolt took place: the Third Jewish War, fought in Palestine A.D. 132–35. This postscript to Jewish Zealotism was brought about by the Emperor's plan to rebuild Jerusalem as a Hellenistic Roman city. Simeon bar Kosba, called Bar Kochba, led the resistance as "star" and "prince" of Israel. After the Roman victory, Hadrian forbade the Jews to be circumcised (Spartianus *Hadrian* 14) and to stay in Jerusalem, which was rebuilt as a Roman colony (Eusebius *Hist.* iv. 6. 1–4).

He renamed the holy city Aelia Capitolina, because his family name was Aelius, and the Temple was dedicated to the cult of Jupiter. It was not rehabilitated as the biblical city until the time of Constantine.

Personally not comparable to Domitian, Trajan did, however, develop a similar sense of personal supremacy and therefore also began to persecute the Christians. Two famous persecutions took place in provinces close to the scene of Trajan's wars. Hadrian continued the practice of persecutions.

(1)   After the Dacian Wars, Trajan sent Pliny to Bithynia with extraordinary authority. There in 113 he supervised a large-scale persecution of the Christians (see above, pp. 293 f.). His exchange of letters with Trajan shows that his intent was to promote the emperor cult and the official state temples. Compulsory sacrifice before the images of the gods and the Emperor seemed to Pliny an obvious means of obtaining compliance; refusal to participate in the cult was treason, punishable by death. In his rescript, however, Trajan relieved the governor of the obligation of tracking down all the people (*"conquirendi non sunt,"* Pliny *Epistulae* x. 97. 2).

(2)   It was probably Hadrian, appointed governor in Antioch in 114 because of the Parthian War, who undertook the Ignatian persecution in Syria (Ignatius *Ephesians* 1. 2; etc.). During this persecution, Ignatius, the Bishop of Antioch, was arrested and transported through Asia, where he wrote the seven extant letters, to Rome and martyrdom. The cause of the offensive seems to have been the desire to demonstrate Roman mastery of the East before the Parthian campaign.

(3)   Soon afterward, Hadrian ordered his governors to continue the persecutions. About 125, he sent a rescript to the governor of Asia informing him that denunciation and provocation were discreditable weapons and that proper criminal trials must be held (Justin *Apology* i. 68. 2). This demand for proper legal procedures shows that Hadrian considered Christianity criminal in itself.

And so at the end of the New Testament period, as John

prophetically saw, Domitian's state cult formed the background for the church's age of martyrs, which, after the interregnum of Nerva, began under Trajan and Hadrian. It lasted more than two hundred years, reached its climax under Diocletian and his successors, and did not come to an end until the time of Constantine. But all attacks of the state upon the church were mere desperate attempts to snatch Romanism and Hellenism from the victory of the Galilean.

BIBLIOGRAPHY

In order to supplement the sporadic footnotes with a more comprehensive bibliographical picture of modern scholarship, we shall list here general introductory works that have appeared in the last few decades. For particular subject areas, a few older handbooks and recent articles have also been mentioned.

General surveys of the background and environment are listed first. Following this, titles are listed under the chapter that corresponds to their general scope or to the beginning of the period they deal with. For this reason, many titles listed under one chapter will also apply to subsequent chapters.

GENERAL

Abel, Félix Marie. *Géographie de la Palestine*. 2 vols. Paris: Librairie Lecoffre, 1933–38.

Albright, William Foxwell. *The Archaeology of Palestine*. Rev. ed.; Harmondsworth: Penguin, 1960.

Avi-Yonah, Michael (ed.). *Sepher Jeruschalajim*, Vol. I. 1956.

Baly, Denis. *A Geographical Companion to the Bible*. New York: McGraw-Hill, 1963.

———. *The Geography of the Bible: A Study in Historical Geography*. New York: Harper, 1957.

Barloewen, Wolf Dietrich von, *et al. Abriss der Geschichte antiker Randkulturen*. Munich: R. Oldenbourg, 1961.

Baron, Salo Wittmayer. *A Social and Religious History of the Jews*, vols. 1–2. 2d ed.; New York: Columbia University Press, 1952–53.

Barrett, Charles Kingsley. *The New Testament Background: Selected Documents with Introductions*. London: S.P.C.K., 1956.

Beek, Martinus Adrianus. *Geschiedenis van Israël van Abraham tot Bar Kochba*. Antwerpen: N. V. Standard Boekhandel, 1957. English: *A Concise History of Israel: From Abraham to the Bar Cochba Rebellion*. Translated by A. J. Pomerans. New York: Harper, 1963.

Blaiklock, Edward Musgrave. *Out of the Earth: The Witness of Archae-ology to the New Testament*. 2d ed.; London: Paternoster, 1961.

Bright, John. *A History of Israel*. Philadelphia: Westminster, 1959.

Bruce, Frederick Fyvie. *Israel and the Nations, from the Exodus to the Fall of the Second Temple*. Grand Rapids: Eerdmans, 1963.

Bury, John Bagnell, *et al. The Cambridge Ancient History*, vols. 4–11, plates 1–5. Cambridge: Cambridge University Press, 1923–39.

Buttrick, George Arthur (ed.). *The Interpreter's Dictionary of the Bible*. 4 vols. New York: Abingdon, 1962.

Du Buit, Michel. *Géographie de la Terre Sainte*. Paris: Editions du Cerf, 1958.

Ehrlich, Ernst Ludwig. *Geschichte Israels von den Anfängen bis zur Zerstörung des Tempels*. Berlin: W. de Gruyter, 1958. English: *A Concise History of Israel from the Earliest Times to the Destruction of the Temple in A.D. 70*. Translated by J. Barr. London: Darton, Longman & Todd, 1962.

Fiebig, Paul W. J. *Die Umwelt des Neuen Testaments: Religionsgeschichtliche und geschichtliche Texte*. Göttingen: Vandenhoeck & Ruprecht, 1926.

Filson, Floyd Vivian. *A New Testament History*. Philadelphia: Westminster Press, 1964.

Finegan, Jack. *Light from the Ancient Past: The Archaeological Background of the Hebrew-Christian Religion.* 2d ed.; Princeton: University Press, 1959.

———. *Handbook of Biblical Chronology.* Princeton: University Press, 1964.

Grollenberg, Lucas Hendricus, *et al. Atlas van de Bijbel.* Amsterdam: Elsevier, 1955. English: *Atlas of the Bible.* Translated by J. M. H. Reid & H. H. Rowley. London: Nelson, 1956.

Heyden, Antonius Alphonsus Maria van der, *et al. Atlas van de antieke wereld.* Amsterdam: Elsevier, 1958. English: *Atlas of the Classical World.* London: Nelson, 1959.

Land-Nash, Irene. *3000 Jahre Jerusalem.* Zurich: Frets & Wasmuth, 1964.

Meer, Frederick van der, and Christine Mohrmann. *Atlas van de oudchristlijke wereld.* Amsterdam: Elsevier, 1958. English: *Atlas of the Early Christian World.* Translated and edited by M. F. Hedlund & H. H. Rowley. London: Nelson, 1958.

Noth, Martin. *Geschichte Israels.* 4th ed.; Stuttgart: Kohlhammer, 1959. English: *The History of Israel.* Translated by P. R. Ackroyd. 2d ed.; London: Black, 1960.

———. *Die Welt des Alten Testaments.* Berlin: Töpelmann, 1960. English: *The Old Testament World.* Translated by V. I. Gruhn. London: Black, and Philadelphia: Fortress, 1966.

Reicke, Bo Ivar, and Leonard Rost (eds.) . *Biblisch-historisches Handwörterbuch: Landeskunde, Geschichte, Religion, Kultur, Literatur.* 3 vols. Göttingen: Vandenhoeck & Ruprecht, 1962–66.

Ricciotti, Giuseppe. *Storia d'Israele.* 2 vols. Torino, 1932–34. English: *The History of Israel.* Translated by C. D. Penta & R. T. A. Murphy. 2d ed.; Milwaukee: Bruce, 1958.

Riessler, Paul. *Altjüdisches Schrifttum ausserhalb der Bibel.* Augsburg: Filser, 1928.

Ringgren, Helmer. *Israelitische Religion.* Stuttgart: Kohlhammer, 1963. English: *Israelite Religion.* Translated by D. E. Green. Philadelphia: Fortress, 1966.

Robinson, Theodore Henry, and William Oscar Emil Oesterley. *A History of Israel.* 2 vols. 2d ed.; Oxford: Clarendon, 1934.

Roth, Cecil (ed.) . *Jewish Art: An Illustrated History.* New York: McGraw-Hill, 1961.

Smith, George Adam and John George Bartholomew. *Historical Atlas of the Holy Land.* 2d ed.; London: Hodder & Stoughton, 1936.

———. *The Historical Geography of the Holy Land, Especially in Relation to the History of Israel and the Early Church.* 25th ed.; New York: Long & Smith, 1932.

Vincent, Hughes. *Jérusalem de l'Ancien Testament: Recherches d'archéologie et d'histoire.* 3 vols. in 2. Paris: Gabalda, 1954–56.

———, and Félix Marie Abel. *Jérusalem; recherches de topographie, d'archéologie et d'histoire.* 2 vols. in 4. Paris: Gabalda, 1912–26.

Watzinger, Carl. *Denkmäler Palästinas: Eine Einführung in die Archäologie des Heiligen Landes.* 2 vols. Leipzig: Hinrichs, 1933–35.

Wright, George Ernest. *Biblical Archaeology.* Rev. ed.; Philadelphia: Westminster, 1957.

1. JUDAH UNDER PERSIAN RULE, 539–332 B.C.

Alt, Albrecht. "Die Rolle Samariens," *Festschrift Otto Procksch.* Leipzig: Deichert, 1934. Reprinted in his *Kleine Schriften.* Vol. II. Munich: Beck, 1959. Pp. 330–37.

Berghe, Léon van den. *Archéologie de l'Iran ancien.* Leiden: Brill, 1959.

Bickerman, Elias. *From Ezra to the Last of the Maccabees: Foundations of Post-Biblical Judaism.* New York: Schocken, 1962.

Bousset, Wilhelm, and Hugo Gressmann. *Die Religion des Judentums im späthellenistischen Zeitalter.* ("Handbuch zum Neuen Testament," Bd. 21.) Tübingen: Mohr, 1926.

Browne, Laurence Edward. *Early Judaism.* Cambridge: Cambridge University Press, 1920.

Cameron, George Glenn. *History of Early Iran.* Chicago: University of Chicago Press, 1936.

Culican, William. *The Medes and the Persians.* New York: Praeger, 1965.

Christensen, Arthur Emanuel. *Die Iranier.* Munich: Beck, 1933.

Debevoise, Neilson Carel. *A Political History of Parthia.* Chicago: University of Chicago Press, 1938.

Duchesne-Guillemin, Jacques. *La religion de l'Iran ancien.* Paris: Presses Universitaires, 1962.

Ehtécham, Mortera. *L'Iran sous les Achéménides: Contribution à l'étude de l'organisation sociale et politique.* Fribourg: Impr. Saint-Paul, 1946.

Foerster, W. *Neutestamentliche Zeitgeschichte.* 2 vols. Hamburg: Furche, 1956. English of Vol. I: *From the Exile to Christ: A Historical Introduction to Palestinian Judaism.* Translated by G. E. Harris. Philadelphia: Fortress, 1964.

Galling, Kurt. *Studien zur Geschichte Israels im persischen Zeitalter.* Tübingen: Mohr, 1964.

Ghirshman, Roman. *L'Iran des origines à l'Islam.* Paris: Payot, 1951. English: *Iran from the Earliest Times to the Islamic Conquest.* Harmondsworth: Penguin, 1954.

Hinz, Walther. *Iran; Politik und Kultur von Kyros bis Rezâ Schah.* Leipzig: Bibliographisches Institut, 1938.

Janssen, Enno. *Juda in der Exilszeit: Ein Beitrag zur Frage der Entstehung des Judentums.* Göttingen: Vandenhoeck & Ruprecht, 1956.

König, Friedrich Wilhelm. *Älteste Geschichte der Meder und Perser.* Leipzig: Hinrichs, 1934.

Lagrange, Marie Joseph. *Le judaïsme avant Jésus-Christ.* Paris: Gabalda, 1931.

Massé, Henri *et al. La civilisation iranienne.* Paris: Payot, 1952.

Meissner, Bruno. "Die Achämenidenkönige und das Judentum," *Sitzungsberichte der Preussischen Akademie der Wissenschaften,* Phil.-hist. Kl. (1938), 6–32.

Nyberg, Henrik Samuel. *Irans forntida religioner.* 1937. German: *Die Religionen des alten Iran.* Translated by H. H. Schaeder. Leipzig: Hinrichs, 1938.

Olmstead, Albert Ten Eyck. *History of the Persian Empire, Achaemenid Period.* Chicago: University of Chicago Press, 1948.

Osten, Hans Henning von der. *Die Welt der Perser.* Stuttgart: Kilpper, 1956.

Parker, Richard Anthony, and Waldo Herman Dubberstein. *Babylonian Chronology 626 B.C.–A.D. 75.* Providence: Brown University Press, 1956.

Rosen, Georg, *et al. Juden und Phönizier: Das antike Judentum als Missionsreligion und die Entstehung der jüdischen Diaspora.* Tübingen: Mohr, 1929.

Snaith, Norman Henry. *The Jews from Cyrus to Herod.* Wellington: Religious Education Press, 1949.

Welch, Adam Cleghorn. *Post-exilic Judaism.* Edinburgh: Blackwood, 1935.

Widengren, Geo. *Iranisch-semitische Kulturbegegnung in parthischer Zeit.* Cologne: Westdeutscher Verlag, 1960.

Wikander, Stig. *Feuerpriester in Kleinasien und Iran.* Lund: Gleerup, 1946.

2. JUDEA UNDER HELLENISTIC RULE, 332–142 B.C.

Abel, Félix Marie. *Histoire de la Palestine depuis la conquête d'Alexandre jusqu'à l'invasion arabe.* 2 vols. Paris: Gabalda, 1952.

―――, and Jean Starcky. *Les livres des Maccabées.* 3d ed.; Paris: Gabalda, 1961.

Abrahams, Israel. *Campaigns in Palestine from Alexander the Great.* London: Published for the British Academy by H. Milford, Oxford University Press, 1927.

Altheim, Franz. *Alexander und Asien: Geschichte eines geistigen Erbes.* Tübingen: Niemeyer, 1953.

―――. *Weltgeschichte Asiens im griechischen Zeitalter.* 2 vols. Halle: Niemeyer, 1947–48.

Bell, Harold Idris. *Cults and Creeds in Graeco-Roman Egypt.* 2d ed.; New York: Philosophical Library, 1953.

―――. *Egypt from Alexander the Great to the Arab Conquest: A Study in the Diffusion and Decay of Hellenism.* Oxford: Clarendon, 1948.

Bengtson, Hermann. *Griechische Geschichte von den Anfängen bis in die römische Kaiserzeit.* Munich: Beck, 1950.

Bevan, Edwyn Robert. *A History of Egypt under the Ptolemaic Dynasty.* London: Methuen, 1927.

——. *The House of Seleucus.* 2 vols. London: Arnold, 1902.

Bickermann, Elias. *Der Gott der Makkabäer: Untersuchungen über Sinn und Ursprung der makkabäischen Erhebung.* Berlin: Schocken, 1937.

——. *Institutions des Séleucids.* Paris: Guethner, 1938.

——. *Die Makkabäer; eine Darstellung ihrer Geschichte von den Anfängen bis zum Untergang des Hasmonäerhauses.* Berlin: Schocken, 1935. English: *The Maccabees: An Account of their History from the Beginnings to the Fall of the House of the Hasmoneans.* Translated by M. Hadas. New York: Schocken, 1947.

Bouché-Leclercq, Auguste. *Histoire des Lagides.* 4 vols. Paris: Leroux, 1903–7.

——. *Histoire des Séleucides 323–64 avant J.-C.* 2 vols. Paris: Leroux, 1913–14.

Bovier-Lapierre, P., *et al. Précis de l'histoire d'Egypte,* vol. I. Cairo: Institute français d'archéologie, 1932.

Bronkhorst, Alexander Johannes. *De geschiedenis van Israël van Alexander der Grote tot Bar Kochba.* Baarn: Bosch & Keuning, 1964.

Cerfaux, Lucien, and Jules Tondriau. *Un concurrant du christianisme: le culte des souverains dans la civilisation gréco-romaine.* Tournai: Desclée, 1957.

Dancy, John Christopher. *A Commentary on I Maccabees.* Oxford: Blackwell, 1954.

Deissmann, Gustaf Adolf. *Licht vom Osten: Das Neue Testament und die neuentdeckten Texte der hellenistisch-römischen Welt.* 4th ed.; Tübingen: Mohr, 1923. English: *Light from the Ancient East.* Translated by L. R. M. Strachen. New ed.; New York: Doran, 1927.

Eddy, Samuel Kennedy. *The King is Dead: Studies in the Near Eastern Resistance to Hellenism, 334–31 B.C.* Lincoln: University of Nebraska Press, 1961.

Farmer, William Reuben. *Maccabees, Zealots, and Josephus: An Inquiry into Jewish Nationalism in the Greco-Roman Period.* New York: Columbia University Press, 1956.

Festugière, André Marie Jean. *Personal Religion among the Greeks.* Berkeley: University of California Press, 1954.

Frey, Jean Baptiste. *Corpus inscriptionum judaicarum.* 2 vols. Roma: Pontificio istituto di archeologia cristiana, 1936–52.

Goodenough, Erwin Ramsdell. *Jewish Symbols in the Greco-Roman Period.* 11 vols. New York: Pantheon, 1953–64.

Hanhart, Robert. "Zur Zeitrechnung des I und II Makkabäerbuches," in A. Jepsen and R. Hanhart, *Untersuchungen zur israelitisch-jüdischen Chronologie.* ("Beihefte zur Zeitschrift für die alttestamentliche Wissenschaft," 88.) Berlin: Töpelmann, 1964.

Heuss, Alfred. *Stadt und Herrscher des Hellenismus in ihren staats- und völkerrechtlichen Beziehungen.* Leipzig: Dieterich, 1937.

Hopfner, Theodor. *Die Judenfrage bei Griechen und Römern.* Prague: Deutsche Akademie der Wissenschaften, 1943.

Jansen, Herman Ludin. *Die Politik Antiochos' des IV.* Oslo: Dybwad, 1943.

Jones, Arnold Hugh Martin. *The Greek City from Alexander to Justinian.* Oxford: Clarendon, 1940.

Jouguet, Pierre. *L'impérialisme macédonien et l'hellénisation de l'Orient.* 3d ed.; Paris: Michel, 1961.

Kahrstedt, Ulrich. *Geschichte des griechisch-römischen Altertums.* Munich: Münchner Verlag, 1948.

Kornemann, Ernst. *Die Alexandergeschichte des Königs Ptolemaios I. von Ägypten: Versuch einer Rekonstruktion.* Leipzig: Teubner, 1935.

——. *Weltgeschichte des Mittelmeerraumes von Philipp II. von Makedonien bis Muhammed.* 2 vols. Munich: Biederstein, 1948–49.

Larsen, Jakob Aall Ottesen. *Representative Government in Greek and Roman History.* Berkeley: University of California Press, 1955.

Nilsson, Martin Persson. *Geschichte der griechischen Religion.* 2 vols. 2d ed.; Munich: Beck, 1955–61.
————. *History of Greek Religion.* Translated by F. J. Fielden. 2d ed.; Oxford: Clarendon, 1949.

Oesterley, William Oscar Emil. *The Jews and Judaism During the Greek Period: The Background of Christianity.* London: S.P.C.K., 1941.

Pfeiffer, Robert Henry. *History of New Testament Times, with an Introduction to the Apocrypha.* New York: Harper, 1949.

Philippides, Leonidas Joannou. *Historia tēs epochēs tēs Kainēs Diathēkēs.* Athens, 1958.

Préaux, Claire. *L'économie royale des Lagides.* Bruxelles: Edition de la Fondation égyptologique reine Elisabeth, 1939.

Prümm, Karl. *Der christliche Glaube und die altheidnische Welt.* 2 vols. Leipzig: Hegner, 1935.

Reinach, Théodore. *Textes d'auteurs grecs et romains relatifs au judaïsme, réunis, traduits et annotés.* Paris: Leroux, 1895. Reprinted, Hildesheim: Olms, 1963.

Rostovtsev, Michael Ivanovich. *The Social and Economic History of the Hellenistic World.* 3 vols. Oxford: Clarendon, 1941.

Sachs, Abraham Joseph, and Donald John Wisemann. "A Babylonian King List of the Hellenistic Period," *Iraq,* XVI (1954), 202–12.

Schachermeyer, Fritz. *Griechische Geschichte mit besonderer Berücksichtigung der geistes-geschichtlichen und kulturmorphologischen Zusammenhänge.* Stuttgart: Kohlhammer, 1960.

Schaumberger, Johann. "Die neue Seleukiden-Liste BM 35 603 und die makkabäische Chronologie," *Biblica,* XXXVI (1955), 423–35.

Schlatter, Adolf. *Geschichte Israels von Alexander dem Grossen bis Hadrian.* 3d ed.; Stuttgart: Calwer, 1925.

Schneider, Carl. *Einführung in die neutestamentliche Zeitgeschichte, mit Bildern.* Leipzig: Deichert, 1934.

Schubart, Wilhelm. *Verfassung und Verwaltung des Ptolemäerreiches.* Leipzig: Hinrichs, 1937.

Schunck, Klaus Dietrich. *Die Quellen des I. und II. Makkabäerbuches.* Halle (Saale): Niemeyer, 1954.

Schürer, Emil. *Geschichte des jüdischen Volkes im Zeitalter Jesu Christi.* 3 vols. with index. 4th ed.; Leipzig: Hinrichs, 1901–11. English: *A History of the Jewish People in the Time of Jesus Christ.* Translated by John Macpherson et al. 5 vols. Edinburgh: Clark, 1897–98.

Taeger, Fritz. *Charisma: Studien zur Geschichte des antiken Herrscherkultes.* 2 vols. Stuttgart: Kohlhammer, 1957–60.

Tarn, William Woodthorpe. *Hellenistic Civilisation.* 3d ed.; London: Arnold, 1952.

Tcherikover, Victor A. *Hellenistic Civilisation and the Jews.* Translated by S. Applebaum. Philadelphia: Jewish Publication Society, 1959.

————. *The Jews in Egypt in the Hellenistic-Roman Age in the Light of the Papyri.* Jerusalem: Hebrew University, 1945.

————, and Alexander Fuks. *Corpus papyrorum judaicarum.* 3 vols. Cambridge: Harvard University Press, 1957–64.

Tedesche, Sidney Saul, and Solomon Zeitlin. *The First-Second Books of Maccabees.* 2 vols. New York: Harper, 1950–54.

Visser, Cornelia Elizabeth. *Götter und Kulte im ptolemäischen Alexandrien.* Amsterdam: N. V. Noord-Hollandsche Uitgeversmaetschappij, 1938.

Waltz, Pierre. *La question d'Orient dans l'antiquité.* Paris: Payot, 1942.

Wibbing, Sigfried. "Zur Topographie einzelner Schlachten des Judas Makkabäus," *Zeitschrift des deutschen Palästina-Vereins,* LXXVIII (1962), 152–170.

Yoyotte, Jean. "L'Egypte ancienne et les origines de l'antijudaïsme," *Revue de l'histoire religieuse,* CLXIII (1963), 133–43.

Zeitlin, Solomon. *The Rise and Fall of the Judean State: A Political, Social, and Religious History of the Second Commonwealth, 332–37 B.C.E.* Philadelphia: Jewish Publication Society, 1962.

3. THE HASMONEAN KINGDOM, 142–63 B.C.

Most special studies of this period also discuss the Maccabees, and will therefore be found under Chapter 2.

Alt, Albrecht. "Galiläische Probleme," *Palästinajahrbuch,* XXXIII–XXXVI (1937–40) , 52 ff. Reprinted in his *Kleine Schriften.* Vol. II. Munich: Beck, 1953. Pp. 363–435.

Elbogen, Ismar. "Alexander Jannai," *Encyclopaedia judaica,* Berlin: Eschkol, 1928–34. Vol. II, cols. 209–13.

Guttmann, J. "Aristobul II," *Encyclopaedia judaica.* Vol. III. Berlin: Eschkol, 1929. Cols. 326–29.

Neusner, Jacob. *A History of the Jews in Babylonia,* Vol I. Leiden: Brill, 1965.

Obst, Ernst. "Johannes Hyrkan I," *Paulys Realencyclopädie,* Suppl. IV. Stuttgart: Metzler, 1924. Cols. 786–91.

Otto, Walter. "Hasmonäer," *Encyclopaedia judaica.* Vol. VII, Stuttgart: Nerkler, 1912. Cols. 2491–2501.

Plöger, Otto. "Die makkabäischen Burgen," *Zeitschrift des deutschen Palästina-Vereins,* LXXI (1955) , 141–72.

Wasser, Nathan. *Die Stellung der Juden gegenüber den Römern nach der rabbinischen Literatur von der hasmonäischen Zeit ca. 165 v. Chr. bis zum hadrianischen Kriege 132 n. Chr.* Jersey City; New York: Tosy-Shoreson Press, 1933.

4. PALESTINE UNDER ROME AND HEROD, 63–4 B.C.

Adcock, Frank Ezra. *Roman Political Ideas and Practice.* Ann Arbor: University of Michigan Press, 1959.

Alföldi, Andreas. *Der frührömische Reiteradel und seine Ehrenabzeichen.* Baden-Baden: Verlag für Kunst und Wissenschaft, 1952.

Alt, Albrecht. "Stationen der römischen Hauptstrasse von Ägypten nach Syrien," *Zeitschrift des deutschen Palästina-Vereins,* LXX (1954) , 154–66.

Altheim, Franz. *Römische Religionsgeschichte.* 2 vols. Baden-Baden: Verlag für Kunst und Wissenschaft, 1951–53. English: *A History of Roman Religion.* Translated by H. Mattingly. London: Methuen, 1958.

Askowith, Dora. *The Toleration and Persecution of the Jews in the Roman Empire . . . under Julius Caesar and Augustus.* New York: Columbia University, 1915.

Avi-Yonah, Michael. *Map of Roman Palestine.* 2d ed.; London: Oxford University Press, 1940.

———. *Oriental Art in Roman Palestine.* Roma: Centro di Studi Semitici, Istituto di Studi del Vicino Oriente-Università, 1961.

Aymard, André, and Jeannine Auboyer. *Rome et son empire.* Paris: Presses universitaires, 1954.

Bammel, E. "Die Bruderfolge im Hochpriestertum der herodianisch-römischen Zeit," *Zeitschrift des*

deutschen Palästina-Vereins, LXX (1954) , 147–53.

———. "Die Neuordnung des Pompeius und das römisch-jüdische Bündnis," *ibid., Zeitschrift des deutschen Palästina-Vereins,* LXXV (1959) , 76–82.

Bietenhard, Hans. "Die Dekapolis von Pompeius bis Trajan," *Zeitschrift des deutschen Palästina-Vereins,* LXXIX (1963) , 24–58.

Blaiklock, Edward Musgrave. *The Century of the New Testament.* London: Intervarsity Fellowship, 1962.

Buchheim, H. *Die Orientpolitik des Triumvirn M. Antonius.* Heidelberg: Winter, 1960.

Carcopino, Jérôme. *Les étapes de l'impérialisme romain.* Paris: Hachette: 1961.

Donner, Hugo. "Kallirrhoe, das Sanatorium Herodes' des Grossen," *Zeitschrift des deutschen Palästina-Vereins,* LXXIX (1963) , 58–89.

Esser, Alexander A. M. *Cäsar und die julisch-claudischen Kaiser im biologisch-ärtzlichen Blickfeld.* Leiden: Brill, 1958.

Felten, Joseph. *Neutestamentliche Zeitgeschichte oder Judentum und Heidentum zur Zeit Christi und der Apostel.* 3d ed.; Regensburg: Manz, 1925.

Frank, Tenney (ed.) . *An Economic Survey of Ancient Rome.* 6 vols. Baltimore: Johns Hopkins, 1933–40.

Gelzer, Matthias. *Caesar, der Politiker und Staatsmann.* 6th ed.; Wiesbaden: Steiner, 1960.

———. *Pompeius.* München: Bruckmann, 1949.

Grant, Frederick Clifton. *Roman Hellenism and the New Testament.* New York: Scribner, 1962.

Grenade, Pierre. *Essai sur les origines du principat: Investiture et renouvellement des pouvoirs impériaux.* Paris: De Boccard, 1961.

Halliday, William Reginald. *The Pagan Background of Early Christianity.* Liverpool: University Press of Liverpool, 1925.

Harder, Günther. "Herodes-Burgen und Herodes-Städte im Jordangraben," *Zeitschrift des deutschen Palästina-Vereins,* LXXVIII (1962), 49–63.

Heaton, John Wesley. *Mob Violence in the Late Roman Republic, 133–49 B.C.* Urbana: University of Illinois Press, 1939.

Heuss, Alfred. *Römische Geschichte.* Braunschweig: Westermann, 1960.

Hoenig, Sidney Benjamin. *The Great Sanhedrin.* Philadelphia: Dropsie College, 1953.

Jones, Arnold Hugh Martin. *The Herods of Judaea.* Oxford: Clarendon, 1938.

Juster, Jean. *Les Juifs dans l'Empire romain: Leur condition juridique, économique et sociale.* 2 vols. Paris: Geuthner, 1914.

Latte, Kurt. *Römische Religionsgeschichte.* Munich: Beck, 1960.

Lindsay, Jack. *Marc Antony: His World and his Contemporaries.* London: Routledge, 1936.

Mantel, Hugo. *Studies in the History of the Sanhedrin.* Cambridge, Mass.: Harvard University Press, 1965.

Milne, Joseph Grafton. *A History of Egypt under Roman Rule.* 3d ed.; London: Methuen, 1924.

Otto, Walter. "Herodes, 14–25" *Paulys Realencyclopädie.* Suppl. 2, Stuttgart: Metzler, 1913. cols. 1-200.

Pareti, Luigi. *Storia de Roma e del mondo romano.* 6 vols. Torino: Union Lipigrafico editrice 1952–61.

Paribeni, Roberto. *L'Italia imperiale da Ottaviano a Teodosio.* ("Storia d'Italia illustrata," Vol. II.) Milano: Mondadori, 1938.

———, et al. *Storia di Roma.* 6 vols.

(+ 8 vols. on later periods) Bologna: Cappelli, 1938–60 (65).

Perowne, Stewart H. *The Life and Times of Herod the Great.* London: Hodder & Stoughton, 1956.

———. *The Later Herods: The Political Background of the New Testament.* London: Hodder & Stoughton, 1958.

Piganiol, André. *Histoire de Rome.* 3d ed.; Paris: Presses universitaires, 1949.

Rossi, Ruggero F. *Marco Antonio nella lotta politica della tarda republica romana.* Trieste: Università degli studi di Trieste, 1959.

Rostovtsev, Mikhail Ivanovich. *The Social and Economic History of the Roman Empire.* Oxford: Clarendon, 1926.

———, and Elias Bickermann. *Rome.* Translated by J. D. Duff. Oxford: Oxford University Press, 1960.

Sattler, Peter. *Augustus und der Senat. Untersuchungen zur römischen Innenpolitik zwischen 30 und 17 v. Christus.* Göttingen: Vandenhoeck & Ruprecht, 1960.

Schalit, Abraham. "Die frühchristliche Überlieferung über die Herkunft der Familie des Herodes," *Annual of the Swedish Theological Institute in Jerusalem,* I (1962), 109–60.

———. *Hurdus ha-melekh.* Jerusalem, 1960.

Schur, Werner. *Das Zeitalter des Marius und Sulla.* Leipzig: Dieterich, 1942.

Scullard, Howard Hayes. *From the Gracchi to Nero: A History of Rome from 133 B.C. to A.D. 68.* New York: Praeger, 1959.

Stein, Arthur. *Der römische Ritterstand: Ein Beitrag zur Sozial- und Personengeschichte des römischen Reiches.* München: Beck, 1927.

Stier, Hans Erich. *Roms Aufstieg zur Weltmacht und die griechische Welt.* Köln: Westdeutscher Verlag, 1957.

Syme, Ronald. *The Roman Revolution.* Oxford: Clarendon, 1939.

Valgiglio, Ernesto. *Silla e la crisi republicana.* Firenze: La Nuova Italia, 1956.

Vogt, Joseph. *Römischer Glaube und römisches Weltreich.* Padova: Cedam, 1943.

Volkmann, Hans. *Kleopatra, Politik*

und Propaganda. Munich: Oldenbourg, 1953.

Willrich, Hugo. Des Haus des Herodes zwischen Jerusalem und Rom. Heidelberg: Winter, 1929.

Wissowa, Georg. Religion und Kultus der Römer. ("Handbuch der klassischen Altertumswissenschaft," 4.) Munich: Beck, 1912.

5. PALESTINE IN THE TIME OF JESUS AND THE APOSTLES, 4 B.C.—A.D. 66

Adam, Alfred. Antike Berichte über die Essener. Berlin: de Gruyter, 1961.

Alt Albrecht. "Die Stätten des Wirkens Jesu in Galiläa territorialgeschichtlich betrachtet," Zeitschrift des deutschen Palästina-Vereins, LXVIII (1949–51), 51–72. Reprinted in his Kleine Schriften. Vol. II. 1953. Pp. 436–55. English: Where Jesus Worked. Translated by Kenneth Grayston. London: Epworth, 1961.

Bardtke, Hans. Die Handschriftenfunde am Toten Meer. 3 vols. Berlin: Evangelische Verlaganstalt, 1952–62.

Bardy, Gustave. La conversion au christianisme durant les premiers siècles. Paris: Aubier, 1949.

Bell, Harold Idris. Jews and Christians in Egypt. London: Oxford, 1924.

Billerbeck, Paul. Kommentar zum Neuen Testament aus Talmud und Midrasch. 6 vols. Munich: Beck, 1924–61.

Blackman, Philip. Mishnayoth. 6 vols. London: Mishna Press, 1951–56.

Blinzler, Joseph. Der Prozess Jesu; das jüdische und das römische Gerichtsverfahren gegen Jesus Christus auf Grund der ältesten Zeugnisse dargestellt und urteilt. 2d ed.; Regensburg: Pustet, 1955. English: The Trial of Jesus: The Jewish and Roman Proceedings against Jesus Christ. Translated by I. & F. McHugh. Westminster: Newman, 1959.

Bonsirven, Joseph. Le judaïsme palestinien aux temps de Jésus-Christ; sa théologie. 2 vols. Paris: Beauchesne, 1934–35. English: Palestinian Judaism at the Time of Jesus Christ. Translated by William Wolf. New York: Holt, Rinehart, and Winston, 1963.

Calderini, Aristide. "L'inscription de Ponce Pilate à Césarée," Bible et Terre Sainte, LVII (1963), 8–10, 15–19.

Chadwick, Henry. The Circle and the Ellipse: Rival Concepts of Authority in the Early Church. Oxford: Clarendon, 1959. Reprinted in Henry Chadwick and Hans von Campenhausen, Jerusalem and Rome ("Facet Books—Historical Series," 4) Philadelphia: Fortress, 1966.

Cullmann, Oscar. The State in the New Testament. New York: Scribner, 1956.

Dalman, Gustaf Hermann. Orte und Wege Jesu. 3d ed.; Gütersloh: Bertelsmann, 1924.

Davies, William David. The Setting of the Sermon on the Mount. Cambridge: Cambridge University Press, 1964.

Finkel, Asher. The Pharisees and the Teacher of Nazareth. Leiden: Brill, 1964.

Gaechter, Paul. Petrus und seine Zeit. Innsbruck: Tyrolia, 1958.

Gaster, Theodor Herzl. The Dead Sea Scriptures in English Translation. Garden City: Doubleday, 1956.

Goldstein, Morris. Jesus in the Jewish Tradition. New York: Macmillan, 1950.

Goppelt, Leonhard. Die apostolische und nachapostolische Zeit. Göttingen: Vandenhoeck & Ruprecht, 1962.

———. Christentum und Judentum im ersten und zweiten Jahrhundert; ein Aufriss der Urgeschichte der Kirche. Gütersloh: Bertelsmann, 1954. English (of first half of the German work): Jesus, Paul, and Judaism. Translated and edited by Edward Schroeder. New York: Nelson, 1964.

Grant, Frederick Clifton. Ancient Judaism and the New Testament. 2d ed.; New York: Macmillan, 1959, and Edinburgh: Oliver & Boyd, 1960.

———. The Economic Background of the Gospels. London: Oxford University Press, 1926.

Grant, Robert McQueen. A Historical Introduction to the New Testament. New York: Harper, 1963.

Harnack, Adolf von. Die Mission und Ausbreitung des Christentums in den ersten drei Jahrhunderten. 2 vols. 3d ed.; Leipzig: Hinrichs, 1915. English: The Mission and Expansion of Christianity in the First Three Centuries. Edited and translated by J. Moffatt. New York: Harper, 1962.

Hengel, Martin. Die Zeloten. Leiden: Brill, 1961.

Jackson, Frederick John Foakes, and Kirsopp Lake (eds.). The Beginnings of Christianity. 5 vols. London: Macmillan, 1920–33.

Jeremias, Joachim. Golgatha. Leipzig: Pfeiffer, 1926.

―――. Jerusalem zur Zeit Jesu: Kulturgeschichtliche Untersuchung zur neutestamentlichen Zeitgeschichte. 2 vols. 3d ed.; Göttingen: Vandenhoeck & Ruprecht, 1962. English translation forthcoming.

Judge, Edwin Arthur. The Social Patterns of the Christian Groups in the First Century: Some Prolegomena to the Study of the New Testament Ideas of Social Obligation. London: Tyndale, 1960.

Kilpatrick, George Dunbar. The Trial of Jesus. London: Oxford University Press, 1953.

Kopp, Clemens. Die heiligen Stätten der Evangelien. 2d ed.; Regensburg: Pustet, 1959.

Krauss, Salomo. Synagogale Altertümer. Berlin: Harz, 1922.

Kümmel, Werner Georg. Feine-Behms Einleitung in das Neue Testament. 12th ed.; Heidelberg: Quelle & Mayer, 1963. English: Introduction to the New Testament. Translated by A. J. Mattill, Jr. Nashville: Abingdon, 1966.

Lieberman, Saul. Hellenism in Jewish Palestine: Studies in the Literary Transmission, Beliefs and Manners of Palestine in the I Century B.C.E.—IV Century C.E. New York: Jewish Theological Seminary of America, 1950.

Lohse, Eduard. "Die römischen Statthalter in Jerusalem," Zeitschrift des deutschen Palästina-Vereins, LXXIV (1958), 69–78.

―――. Die Texte aus Qumran. 1964.

Maier, Johann. Die Texte vom Toten Meer. 2 vols. Munich: Reinhardt, 1960.

Marie Aline de Sion, Sister. La forteresse Antonia à Jérusalem et la question du prétoire. Jerusalem: Patres Franciscales, 1956.

Menoud, Philippe Henri. L'église naissante et le judaïsme. Neuchâtel: Delachaux Niestlé, 1952.

Meyer, Eduard. Ursprung und Anfänge des Christentums. 3 vols. Stuttgart: Cotta, 1921–23.

Molin, Georg. Die Söhne des Lichtes: Zeit und Stellung der Handschriften vom Toten Meer. Wien: Herold, 1954.

Moore, George Foot. Judaism in the First Centuries of the Christian Era: The Age of the Tannaim. 3 vols. Cambridge: Harvard University Press, 1927–30.

Moule, Charles Francis Digby. The Birth of the New Testament. New York: Harper, 1962.

Musurillo, Herbert A. The Acts of the Pagan Martyrs. Oxford: Clarendon: 1954.

Reicke, Bo. Diakonie, Festfreude und Zelos. ("Upsala Universitets Årsskrift," 51.5.) Uppsala: Lundequist, 1951.

―――. Glaube und Leben der Urgemeinde. ("Abhandlungen zur Theologie des Alten und Neuen Testaments," 32.) Zürich: Zwingli, 1957.

Schoeps, Hans Joachim. Theologie und Geschichte des Judenchristentums. Tübingen: Mohr, 1949.

―――. Urgemeinde, Judenchristentum, Gnosis. Tübingen: Mohr, 1956.

―――. Das Judenchristentum. Berne: Francke, 1964. Translation forthcoming.

Schubert, Kurt. Die Gemeinde vom Totem Meer; ihre Entstehung und ihr Leben. Munich: Reinhardt, 1958. English: The Dead Sea Community: Its Origin and Teachings. Translated by J. W. Doberstein. New York: Harper, 1959.

Simon, Marcel. Les sectes juives au temps de Jésus. Paris: Presses universitaires, 1960. English: Jewish Sects at the Time of Jesus. Translated by J. Farley. Philadelphia: Fortress, 1967.

Smallwood, E. M. "High Priests and Politics in Roman Palestine," Journal of Theological Studies, XIII (1962), 14–34.

Stauffer, Ethelbert. Jerusalem und

Rom im Zeitalter Jesu Christi. Bern: Francke, 1957.

Winter, Paul. *On the Trial of Jesus.* Berlin: de Gruyter, 1961.

6. THE ROMAN EMPIRE IN THE TIME OF JESUS AND THE APOSTLES, 4 B.C.—A.D. 66

Alföldi, Andreas. "Insignien und Tracht der römischen Kaiser," *Mitteilungen des Deutschen archäologischen Instituts,* Römische Abteilung, L (1935), 1–171.

Baker, George Philip. *Tiberius Caesar.* New York: Dodd, Mead & Co., 1928.

Beaujeu, Jean. *L'incendie de Rome en 64 et les chrétiens.* Bruxelles: Latomus, 1960.

Bruce, Frederick Fyvie. "Christianity under Claudius," *Bulletin of the John Rylands Library,* XLIV (1962), 309–26.

Chapot, Victor. *L'Egypte romaine.* Paris: Plon, 1933.

Charles-Picard, Gilbert. *Auguste et Néron: Le secret de l'empire.* Paris: Hachette, 1962.

Charlesworth, Martin Percival. *Documents Illustrating the Reigns of Claudius and Nero.* Cambridge: Cambridge University Press, 1939.

Ciaceri, Emanuele. *Tiberio, successore di Augusto.* Milano: Albrighi, Segati & C., 1934.

Dessau, Hermann. *Geschichte der römischen Kaiserzeit.* 3 vols. Berlin: Weidmann, 1924–30.

DeWaele, Ferdinand Joseph Maria. *Corinthe et Saint Paul.* Paris: Guillot, 1961.

Dibelius, Martin. *Rom und die Christen im ersten Jahrhundert.* 1942.

Dill, Samuel. *Roman Society from Nero to Marcus Aurelius.* London: Macmillan, 1905.

Downey, Glanville, *Ancient Antioch.* Princeton: Princeton University Press, 1963.

Ehrenberg, Victor, and Arnold Hugh Martin Jones. *Documents Illustrating the Reigns of Augustus and Tiberius.* 2d ed.; Oxford: Clarendon, 1955.

Floriani Squarciapino, Maria. "Ebrei a Roma e ad Ostia," *Studi romani,* XI (1963), 129–41.

Gollub, Wilhelm. *Tiberius.* Munich: Callwey, 1959.

Hyde, Walter Woodbarn. *Paganism to Christianity in the Roman Empire.* Philadelphia: University of Pennsylvania Press, 1946.

Johnson, Sherman E. "Early Christianity in Asia Minor," *Journal of Biblical Literature,* LXXVII (1958), 1–17.

Jones, Arnold Hugh Martin. *The Cities of the Eastern Roman Provinces.* Oxford: Clarendon, 1937.

———. *Studies in Roman Government and Law.* Oxford: Blackwell, 1960.

Kahrstedt, Ulrich. *Kulturgeschichte der römischen Kaiserzeit.* 2d ed.; Bern: Francke, 1958.

Kornemann, Ernst. *Tiberius.* Stuttgart: Kohlhammer, 1960.

Leon, Harry Joshua. *The Jews of Ancient Rome.* Philadelphia: Jewish Publication Society, 1960.

Levi, Mario Attilio. *Nerone e i suoi tempi.* Milano: Cesalpino, 1949.

Magie, David. *Roman Rule in Asia Minor to the End of the Third Century After Christ.* 2 vols. Princeton: Princeton University Press, 1950.

Marsh, Frank Burr. *The Reign of Tiberius.* New York: Barnes and Noble, 1931.

Radin, Max. *Legislation of the Greeks and Romans on Corporations.* New York: Tuttle, 1910.

Ramsay, William Mitchell, and John George Clark Anderson. *The Social Basis of Roman Power in Asia Minor.* Aberdeen: Aberdeen University Press, 1941.

Reinmuth, Oscar William. *The Prefect of Egypt from Augustus to Diocletian.* Leipzig: Dietrich, 1935.

Robert, Louis. *Villes d'Asie mineure.* 2d ed.; Paris: de Boccard, 1962.

Rogers, Robert Samuel. *Studies in the Reign of Tiberius: Some Imperial Virtues of Tiberius and Drusus Julius Caesar.* Baltimore: Johns Hopkins, 1943.

Schneider, Carl. *Geistesgeschichte des antiken Christentums.* 2 vols. Munich: Beck, 1954.

Scramuzza, Vincent Mary. *The Emperor Claudius.* Cambridge: Harvard University Press, 1940.

Sherwin-White, Adrian Nicholas. *The Roman Citizenship.* Oxford: Clarendon, 1939.

———. *Roman Society and Roman*

Law in the New Testament. Oxford: Clarendon, 1963.

Sordi, Marta. "Sui primi rapporti dell' autorita romana con il cristianesimo," *Studi romani*, VIII (1960), 393–409.

————. *Il christianesimo e Roma.* Bologna: Cappelli, 1965.

Stein, Arthur. *Die Präfekten von Ägypten in der römischen Kaiserzeit.* Bern: Francke, 1950.

Stevenson, George Hope. *Roman Provincial Administration Till the Age of the Antonines.* Oxford: Blackwell, 1939.

Zucker, Friedrich. *Ägypten im Römischen Reich.* Berlin: Akademie-Verlag, 1958.

7. THE ROMAN EMPIRE IN THE SUBAPOSTOLIC PERIOD, A.D. 67–CA. 100

Arias, Paolo Enrico. *Domitiano: Saggio storico con traduzione e commento della "Vita" di Svetonio.* Catania: Crisafulli, 1945.

Avi-Yonah, Michael. *Geschichte der Juden im Zeitalter des Talmud.* Berlin: de Gruyter, 1962.

Babel, H. *Der Briefwechsel zwischen Plinius und Trajan über die Christen in strafrechtlicher Sicht.* Erlangen: Juristische Fakultät, 1961.

Beaujeau, Jean. *La religion romaine à l'apogée de l'empire.* Paris: Société d'édition Les Belles lettres, 1955.

Bersanetti, Gastone M. *Vespasiano.* Rome: Edizioni Roma, 1941.

Brandon, Samuel George Frederick. *The Fall of Jerusalem and the Christian Church: A Study of the Effects of the Jewish Overthrow of A.D. 70 on Christianity.* London: S.P.C.K., 1951.

Brütsch, Charles. *La clarté de l'Apocalypse.* 5th ed.; Geneva: Labor et Fides, 1966.

Clark, Kenneth Willis "Worship in the Jerusalem Temple after A.D. 70," *New Testament Studies,* VI (1960), 269–80.

Dempf, Alois. *Geistesgeschichte der altchristlichen Kultur.* Stuttgart: Kohlhammer, 1964.

Foakes-Jackson, Frederick John. *Josephus and the Jews: The Religion and History of the Jews as Explained by Flavius Josephus.* New York: R. R. Smith, 1930.

Fuks, Alexander. "Aspects of the Jewish Revolt in A.D. 115–117," *The Journal of Roman Studies,* LI (1961), 98–104.

Grégoire, Henri, *et al. Les persécutions dans l'empire romain.* Bruxelles: Palais des academies, 1951.

Gsell, Stéphane. *Essai sur le règne de l'empéreur Domitien.* Paris: Thorin, 1894.

Henderson, Bernard William. *Five Roman Emperors: Vespasian, Titus, Domitian, Nerva, Trajan, A.D. 69–117.* Cambridge: Cambridge University Press, 1927.

Homo, Léon Pol. *Vespasien, l'empereur du bon sens, 69–79 après J. C.* Paris: Michel, 1949.

Hospers-Jansen, Anna Margaretta Aléda. *Tacitus over de joden, Hist. 5, 2–13.* Groningen: Walks, 1949.

McCrum, Michael and Arthur Geoffrey Woodhead. *Select Documents of the Principates of the Flavian Emperors, Including the Year of Revolution, A.D. 68–96.* Cambridge: University Press, 1961.

Mayer-Maly, Theo. "Der rechtsgeschichtliche Gehalt der Christenbriefe von Plinius und Trajan," *Studia et documenta historiae iuris,* XXII (1956), 311–28.

Moreau, Jacques. *La persécution du christianisme dans l'empire romain.* Paris: Presses universitaires, 1956. German (enlarged ed.): *Die Christenverfolgung im römischen Reich.* Berlin: Töpelmann, 1961.

Munck, Johannes. *Petrus und Paulus in der Offenbarung Johannes.* Copenhagen: Rosenkelde & Bagger, 1950.

Patsch, Carl. *Der Kampf um den Donauraum unter Domitian und Trajan.* Wien: Hölder, 1937.

Pieper, Karl. *Atlas orbis christiani antiqui.* Düsseldorf: Schwann, 1931.

Pleket, Henri Willy. "Domitian, the Senate, and the Provinces," *Mnemosyne,* IV. 14 (1961), 296–315.

Rahner, Hugo. *Abendländische Kirchenfreiheit.* Einsiedeln: Benziger, 1943. Enlarged ed.: *Kirche und Staat im frühen Christentum.* Munich: Kösel, 1961

Ripostelli, Giuseppe. *Triumph of Vespasian . . . 71 A.D.* Rome: Movimento forestieri, 1925.

Rogers, R. S. "A Group of Domitianic Treason-Trials," *Classical Philology*, LV (1960), 19–23.

Schefold, Karl. *Römische Kunst als religiöses Phänomen.* Hamburg: Rowohlt, 1964.

Shutt, Roland James Heath. *Studies in Josephus.* London: S.P.C.K., 1961.

Sordi, Marta. "Le persecuzione di Domiziano," *Rivista di storia della chiesa in Italia,* XIV (1960), 1–26.

Stauffer, Ethelbert. *Christus und die Cäsaren.* 5th ed.; 1960. English: *Christ and the Caesars.* Translated by K. and R. Gregor Smith. London: SCM, 1955.

Strack, Hermann L. *Einleitung in Talmud und Midraš.* 5th ed.; Munich: C. H. Beck, 1921. English: *Introduction to the Talmud and Midrash.* Philadelphia: Jewish Publication Society of America, 1931.

Styger, Paul. *Juden und Christen im alten Rom.* Berlin: Verlag für Kunstwissenschaft, 1934.

Vogt, Joseph. *Zur Religiosität der Christenverfolger im römischen Reich.* Heidelberg: Winter, 1962.

Wlosock, Antona. "Die Rechtsgrundlagen der Christenverfolgungen der ersten zwei Jahrhunderte," *Gymnasium,* LXVI (1959), 14–32.

INDEX OF NAMES AND SUBJECTS

331

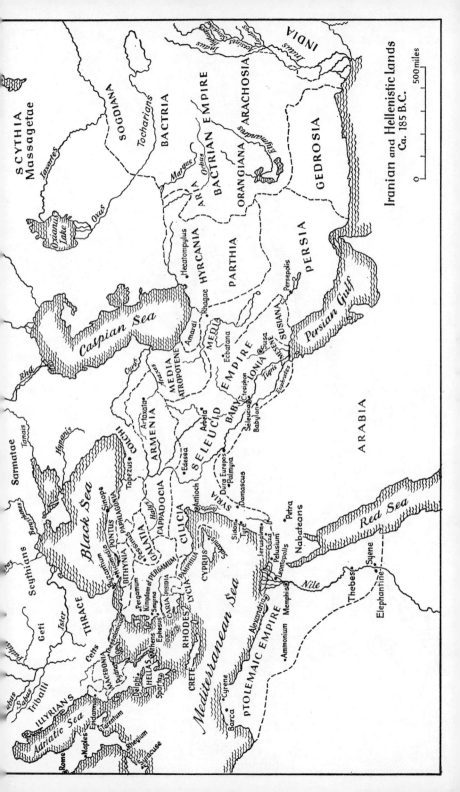

Iranian and Hellenistic lands
Ca. 185 B.C.

0   500 miles

Palestine in the time
of the Maccabees
and Hasmoneans

* * * * under Simon
142 B.C.

- - - - under Janneus
80 B.C.

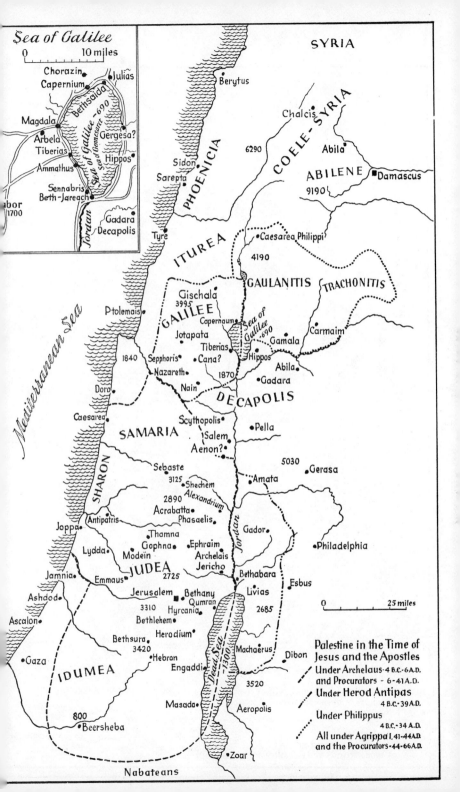

Sea of Galilee

0   10 miles

Chorazin
Capernium
Julias
Bethsaida
Magdala
Sea of Galilee -690
Gergesa?
Arbela
Tiberias
Hippos
Ammathus
Sea of Gennesaret
Sennabris
Beth-Jareach
abor
1700
Jordan
Gadara
Decapolis

SYRIA

Berytus

Chalcis
COELE-SYRIA
6290
Abila
Damascus
ABILENE
9190

Sidon
PHOENICIA
Sarepta
Caesarea Philippi
4190
ITUREA
GAULANITIS
TRACHONITIS
Tyre
Gischala
3995
GALILEE
Capernaum
Sea of Galilee -690
Gamala
Carmaim
Ptolemais
Jotapata
Tiberias
Hippos
Abila
1840
Sepphoris
Cana?
Gadara
Nazareth
1870
Dora
Nain
DECAPOLIS
Caesarea
Scythopolis
Pella
SAMARIA
Salem
Aenon?
5030
Gerasa
Sebaste
Amata
3125
Shechem
Alexandrium
2890
Acrabatta
Phasaelis
SHARON
Antipatris
Gador
Philadelphia
Joppa
Thamna
Lydda
Gophna
Ephraim
Modein
Archelais
Jamnia
Emmaus
JUDEA
Jericho
Bethabara
Ashdod
2725
Jerusalem
Livias
Esbus
Ascalon
3310
Bethany
Qumran
Hyrcania
2685
Bethlehem
Bethsura
Herodium
Machaerus
Dibon
3420
Hebron
Engaddi
IDUMEA
3520
Gaza
Masada
Aeropolis
800
Beersheba
Zoar
Nabateans

Mediterranean Sea
Dead Sea -1300
Jordan

0   25 miles

Palestine in the Time of Jesus and the Apostles

—·— Under Archelaus - 4 B.C.-6 A.D. and Procurators - 6-41 A.D.

—··— Under Herod Antipas 4 B.C.-39 A.D.

········ Under Philippus 4 B.C.-34 A.D.

— — All under Agrippa I, 41-44 A.D. and the Procurators - 44-66 A.D.

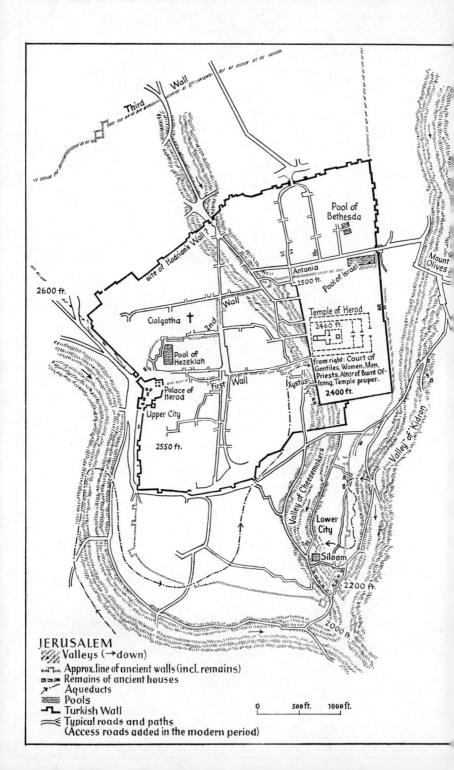

Third Wall

site of Hadrian's Wall?

2600 ft.

Golgotha †

Pool of Hezekiah

Palace of Herod

Upper City

2550 ft.

First Wall

2nd Wall

Pool of Bethesda

Antonia 2500 ft.

Pool of Israel

Mount of Olives

Temple of Herod
2460 ft.

From right: Court of Gentiles, Women, Men, Priests, Altar of Burnt Offering, Temple proper.
2400 ft.

Xystus

Valley of Kidron

Valley of Cheesemakers

Lower City

Siloam

2200 ft.

2000 ft.

JERUSALEM
Valleys (→down)
Approx. line of ancient walls (incl. remains)
Remains of ancient houses
Aqueducts
Pools
Turkish Wall
Typical roads and paths
(Access roads added in the modern period)

0   500 ft.   1000 ft.

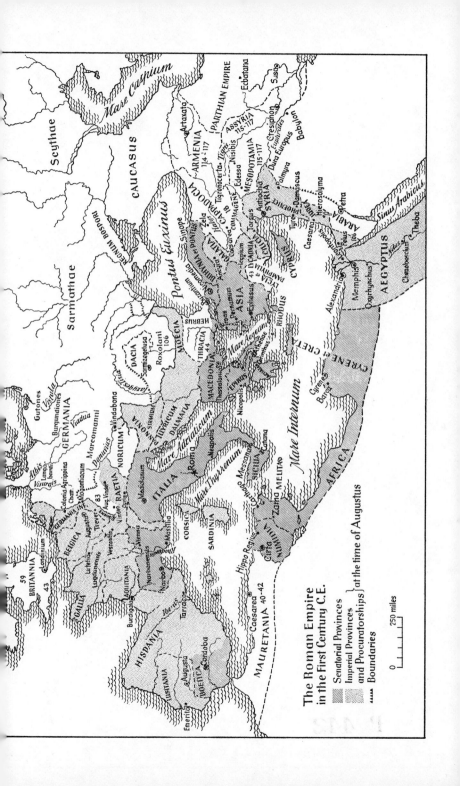

The Roman Empire
in the First Century C.E.

Senatorial Provinces
Imperial Provinces } at the time of Augustus
and Procuratorships
Boundaries

0   250 miles